European Integration and Health Policy

European Integration and Health Policy

The Artful Dance of Economics and History

Panos Minogiannis

Routledge
Taylor & Francis Group

LONDON AND NEW YORK

First published 2003 by Transaction Publishers

Published 2017 by Routledge
2 Park Square, Milton Park, Abingdon, Oxon OX14 4RN
711 Third Avenue, New York, NY 10017

First issued in paperback 2018

Routledge is an imprint of the Taylor and Francis Group, an informa business

Library of Congress Catalog Number: 2002020450

Library of Congress Cataloging-in-Publication Data

Minogiannis, Panos.
    European integration and health policy : the artful dance of economics and history / Panos Minogiannis.
        p. cm.
    Includes bibliographical references and index.
    ISBN 0-7658-0169-8 (cloth : alk. paper)
        1. Medical policy—Europe. 2. Medical policy—Economic aspects—Europe. 3. Medical care—Europe. I Title.

RA483 .M55 2003
362.1'094—dc21

                                                                    2002020450

ISBN 13: 978-1-138-50978-8 (pbk)
ISBN 13: 978-0-7658-0169-2 (hbk)

To Eli Ginzberg, a noble man, who taught me that we may not have all the answers but searching for them is why we are placed in this world.

To my parents Sotos and Chryssa who taught me that each person is different and the time spent understanding them is time well spent.

Contents

Introduction

History and Political Institutions: Setting the Framework for the Analysis

"Man's nature, his passions and anxieties, are a cultural product; as a matter of fact, man himself is the most important creation and achievement of the continuous human effort, the record of what we call history"—Erich Fromm

The 1990s arguably saw unprecedented changes on a global front. From the end of the Cold War to the growth and the globalization of a new economy and from the Internet and other communication technologies to reaching an all time population high, it is quite evident that the world in 2002 is very different from the world in 1990, let alone the world in previous decades. And yet for all these changes, indeed even progress, many of the social ills that have chronically plagued societies have persisted. Hunger and infectious diseases in the developing world, larger stratification between the haves and the have-nots in the developed world present policy makers with tremendous challenges.

Europe is no exception and neither is health care, the two focal points in this book. European states have been consumed with health care reforms and counter-reforms throughout the decade and for an even longer time. The public has come to expect the state to be the agent who will deal with social issues and provide solutions of equality, effectiveness and efficiency. But in today's interdependent world, there are many who question the capacity of the state to act as it did, not so long ago.[1] One has to indeed explore the possibility that the administrative capacity of the state has been eroded and what that might mean for the institutions and social structures we have come to accept as given.

In the European context, the integration process of the European Union presents Europeans with opportunities and challenges that one could not have imagined not too long ago. The main interest and question in this thesis deals with whether the European Union member states are still capable of ensuring equitable and universal access to health care or whether

1

the European integration process is a mechanism that leads to social exclusion. Scharpf argued that economic integration is by nature undermining the capacity for differentiated regimes in welfare provision in the EU and that the existent economic diversity prohibits the creation of a common welfare regime.[2] The way this conundrum gets resolved is of critical importance both for the future of the Union and for the arrangement of welfare provision in general and health care provision in particular. Some analysts have argued that a subversive liberalism is coming. The notion of solidarity and its result of universal coverage is argued to be undermined and eroded in increments.[3] More doom-saying accounts of the future of social cohesion in Europe are given by analysts who consider that, on the one hand, member state capacity to act has indeed been undermined and thus renders it unable to cope with the challenges that the systems face. In fact, the tension between the common market, the euro, the accompanying stability pact on one hand and the social face of Europe on the other is daily being resolved in favor of the former.[4] Ten years of inertia in the high politics of political integration of the European Union, with the sole focus on achieving the Economic and Monetary Union (EMU), was natural to lead to the creation of a number of Eurosceptic groups.[5] They fear that European integration and the paths down which it has progressed will result in societies of two-thirds, where social inclusion and social protection models will emulate those on the other side of the Atlantic.

From a normative perspective, this is actually the question that I take up in the health care field. Simply put, I am asking what the effect of the integration process has been and is likely to be in the near future in terms of health care protection and the enabling of all Europeans to have access to equitable and quality care. This is, of course, a quite general question and throughout this chapter it is broken down and formulated more objectively into two sets of specific ones: First, to what degree does European integration lead to convergence of the individual member states' health care systems, what is the character of such a convergence, and how is it being developed? Second, what is it about the decision mechanisms of the European health care systems—that is the day-to-day decisions about the production and distribution of health care—that, on the one hand, sustains their differences and, on the other hand, presents us to a certain degree with assurances that social cohesion remains high on the agenda of policymakers?

As it is probably evident from the discussion so far, I do not intend to deal with every aspect of health policy. In fact, I intend to deal only with the governing of health consumption or, as mentioned earlier, the role of the principle of social cohesion in the consumption of health care services. There are still three other distinct and important areas of health policy, namely supply of medical personnel, medical technology policy, and public health policy. In fact, the central level of the European Union has appeared more active in these areas[6] than in health care financing and delivery, but for reasons that I have already discussed, I deemed this part of health policy to be the most interesting arena philosophically.

It is indeed commonly accepted that the EU has not played a major role in terms of health care protection at the national level. The right of access to health care in the EU is governed by regulations 1408/71 and 574/72.[7] These regulations are very complex because they have to be applied to fifteen highly differentiated health care systems. They provide only for cross-border health, or the right of access to medical care for a citizen of one member state in the system of another member state. In the end, national provisions are what matter and there is no direct harmonization of benefits or funding schemes. In other areas, such as pharmaceutical prices, medical technology diffusion, movement of medical professionals, educational standards, occupational health and safety, environmental health, and research, all of which relate indirectly to health insurance and health delivery, the EU has appeared to be quite active. Whereas these areas do affect access to care, their politics are sufficiently removed from the politics of health insurance and delivery schemes that they will not be included in the analysis. Topics like pharmaceutical prices, medical technology and occupational health stem from the need to create a common market rather than a common polity, and that is why, whereas I consider them extremely significant and interesting in their own rights, they do not directly speak to the topic of this study and thus I have chosen not to discuss them in the context of this volume.

The EU has not to date taken up the goal—and it remains highly unlikely that it will in the future—of integrating health insurance and delivery schemes. These issues are highly sensitive to the citizenry, require far reaching transfers of authority from the national level to the transnational level, present tremendous technical problems because of variations in the arrangements of each member state and, last but not least, involve high levels of public expenditures. Furthermore, it is not self-evident that a unifying system of health care coverage would be a better arrangement. Perhaps, maintaining the administration of health care services at the member state level, under the subsidiarity rule, would be preferable. In fact, what the history of the EU teaches us is that the integration process is at best a slow one.[8] In this sense, a project trying to link the EU integration process with health policy developments needs to be questioned.

But the main argument of this study is that whereas health care financing and delivery is to date mostly absent from the European integration agenda, it is not the whole story. Through spillover from other policy areas (caused by ECJ decisions and an ideological and social convergence around a managerial and financially disciplined logic of distributing finite resources), health policies are being influenced from the top and are bound to continue to be so.

Specific case studies, however, remind us of the differences in history, politics and culture of the different health systems, the different balances of influence among key players in the several health care systems and the different decision-making mechanisms and explain why these systems will for the foreseeable future remain the responsibility of the member states. Notwithstanding these differences, however, the prominent place of the idea of social cohesion in decision-making mechanisms and of the idea of "the right to health care" at both the central and the member state level all but assures us that social solidarity will remain a primary goal in any reform effort of European health care. Put differently, the EU ought not be viewed as an entity whose goal is to dismantle the welfare state or to eradicate the notion of solidarity. Rather, as it will be shown, other factors (mainly macroeconomic ones and micro-level efficiency considerations) have led all states to consider debates that at times border on such radical departures from the social cohesion for which Europe has been known. In a more optimistic account, the EU can play a role of promoting such an alternative (to an individualistic approach) system of social affairs. And to a great extent it has. To use the metaphor that provides the subtitle for this book, European integration is affecting health care financing and delivery through an artful dance between the historical de-

Figure I.1

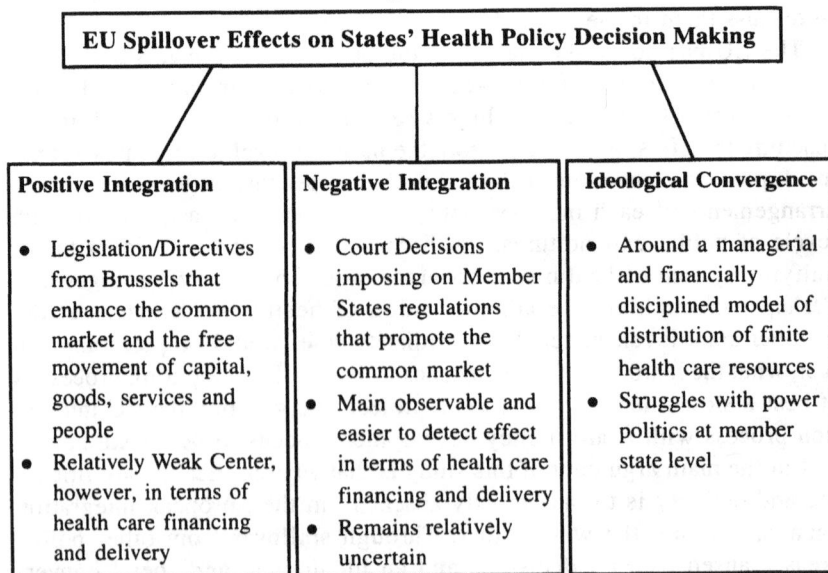

EU Spillover Effects on States' Health Policy Decision Making		
Positive Integration	**Negative Integration**	**Ideological Convergence**
• Legislation/Directives from Brussels that enhance the common market and the free movement of capital, goods, services and people • Relatively Weak Center, however, in terms of health care financing and delivery	• Court Decisions imposing on Member States regulations that promote the common market • Main observable and easier to detect effect in terms of health care financing and delivery • Remains relatively uncertain	• Around a managerial and financially disciplined model of distribution of finite health care resources • Struggles with power politics at member state level

velopment of the health care systems in the member states and the economics of the European integration process. To the degree that the goals of the latter are in line with the goals of the former, and both are in line with social cohesion, no reform would be so dangerous to Europe's social character.

I follow works by Leibfried and Pierson, who examined the connections between European Union involvement in social policy in general, and who have argued that there are indeed linkages between national social policies and the EU.[9] Pierson writes that "the character of social policy is increasingly influenced and constrained by developments 'from above'—that is at the EU level."[10] In economic theory there are two types of economic integration, the positive and the negative ones. Under the latter, barriers to free trade are removed while under the former, economic regulations are reconstructed at the larger unit.[11] Based on these notions, Pierson and Leibfried describe three processes that provide the linkages between the EU and social policy. First, there are "positive" activist reforms taken by the center (Brussels), which are limited. An example would be the social protocol of Maastricht. Second, there are "negative" reforms, which occur through the European Court's imposition of market compatibility requirements that, in turn, restrict and redefine national social policy. An example would be the labor mobility coordination regulations to provide for free movement of people. Finally, there is a third process that indirectly applies pressures on member states to adopt their welfare policies even though they are not legally required to do so. I believe that a large part of the ideological convergence that has occurred falls under this third process and it concerns themes of more efficient allocation of resources, increased accountability and more disciplined financing.

I do not claim that supranational coordination of reform policies has led to a trend of health policy convergence. Maarse and Paulus, in their comparison of the Belgian, Dutch and German health insurance systems, find a convergence towards more market-oriented approaches broadly speaking, but identify the causes of this convergence as the common health policy challenges that these countries face, pointing out that all three acted independently.[12] Similar findings in the cases of Italy, which has a national health system, and again the Netherlands are provided by France and Hermans in their work.[13] It is not, therefore, Brussels pushing for such reforms in a coordinated fashion. Rather, as a result of European integration, which has served in this respect as the vehicle for other factors (economic globalization, for instance), technocratic and political thinking at the national level has converged. This is argued to have had an indirect affect in the health care arena and to have resulted in a trend of convergence on the design and the justification of reforms in all member states that face common health policy challenges.

These common challenges do indeed comprise the reason for the reforms in all member states. Rising public expenditures, increased diffusion of technological advances, changes in demographics, ever-rising expectations, and uneven quality present health care policy makers in Europe with great challenges.[14] The interesting question from a political perspective is why, while there are common problems and a common forum where these problems could have been tackled, we still witness diverging approaches within a similar reform logic in dealing with such issues in the member states?

In this introduction, I begin by presenting the theoretical framework behind this argument through an exploration of historical institutionalism. In order to understand health care protection, one must focus on the history of the institutional developments and the evolution of ideas about Europe and about the proposed health care reforms. To understand policy, the constraints and the ideas that affect policy makers' decisions must be accounted for. And, as it will be shown, both ideas and constraints on policy making are determined by institutions and by the historical development of policy making in the given arena. Having discussed the theoretical assumptions behind the study, I then examine some European integration theories. I do that, not to offer a new theoretical scheme of integration, but rather to try to understand at what level health care protection must be examined. Through this exploration of the integration theories, I follow Pierson who argued that the EU is a multitier government structure and therefore any policy must be examined at both the central level as well as at the member state level.[15] It is true, that some policy areas are affected more from decisions in Brussels than others and, of course, the opposite is also true. Certain policy areas are indeed affected more by decisions at the member state level. But there is no policy arena that is immune from either level and therefore investigating health care protection in the EU requires looking at both levels as well as at the interactions between the two. Finally, I offer within this framework a discussion of the research methods and a roadmap for the remaining chapters.

History and Institutions: Shaping Policy Decision Making

Until recently, it was assumed that decision making in the policy process was achieved through the aggregation of the expressed (which were also the real ones) preferences of all the participants.[16] In recent years, however, there has been a renewal of interest in political institutions, or else "the rules of the game."[17] Institutionalists share a critique of the previous dominant approach of political science, behavioralism. They question the assumption that expressed political behavior reveals true preferences. It is not hard to imagine reasons why a person under one set of circumstances would make a decision different from one that he or she might make under a different set of circumstances. Put differently, the same given actor might interpret his true preferences differently under different conditions. Institutionalist theory analyzes the discrepancy that exists between expressed interests in political behavior and potential interests under different circumstances.

Moreover, even if one were to accept expressed preferences as real does not mean that the ultimate political outcome will be the simple summation of these individual preferences. Behavioralism has always assumed that the political process is perfectly efficient and fair, but one has to question the notion of collective decisions being the simple aggregation of individual interests. Institutions, the mechanisms for aggregating these individual interests, alter and sometimes even shape individual interests.[18] Through the negotiation process and according to the rules at hand (institutions) new ideas are born, interests are redefined, and sometimes even some ideas are assigned priority over others. In short, both individual political behavior (real and expressed) as well as collective decision making are greatly affected by the process of decision making in any given society. This is a critique shared by all strands of institutionalism. The focus here, however, is on historical institutionalism and its specific assumptions.

Historical Institutionalism

What distinguishes historical institutionalism is its use of history in approaching political questions. It is indeed this affinity to history, not only as a methodology but, in fact, as a theory in its own right, that provides us with the theoretical foundation of historical institutionalism.[19] In examining the work of historical institutionalists, Immergut describes three themes that are of great interest to scholars.[20] She calls them historicist because all three emphasize limits and constraints on human rationality that can be understood only through a thick examination of history. The first theme is that of alternative rationalities. Under different conditions, the same rational actor will opt for different things. Furthermore, rationality as observed is itself a historical construct, indeed, one of many possible outcomes and can only be viewed in that way. Institutions act as filters that selectively favor particular interpretations of goals or ways of achieving goals and political actors define their interests and shape their strategies depending on the institutional framework of a given society. The second theme is that causality is contextual. To a historical institutionalist, it is hard, if not impossible, to break down into individual variables the complexity of the different configurations of several factors that are assumed to be causing the political outcome of interest. To historical institutionalists, the generalizability of models across cases is extremely problematic exactly because of this case-specific contextual approach, and therefore generalizability can be achieved only on a higher level of abstraction. And indeed only a historical approach can offer the researcher this thick understanding of the context. The third theme that historical institutionalist analyses share is the theme of the contingencies of history. To a great degree, chance may play a great role in connecting the same variables in different configurations under different settings. Nevertheless, these different configurations will, by virtue of contextual causality, have long-lasting effects and therefore it is only reasonable that a historical analysis is required in order to attempt to reveal contingent developments.

Historical institutionalism has been able to embrace other "variables" of explanatory power to enhance its own theoretical power.[21] Without moving away from the structural and historical contingency way of approaching agency, historical institutionalism has incorporated the ways of some other approaches in political science research, including its arch rival, rational choice institutionalism. It has embraced, for instance, rationality by placing it in its specific settings with the specific environmental constraints on it in order to provide a stronger explanation. Institutional arguments based on historical contingencies and dynamics of a given era's need to be consistent, indeed explain in many cases the rational principles of individual choice making. But it is, indeed, not only the affinity to history and to institutions that matters. It is after all commonplace to write that "history matters." The question is how does it matter?[22] The path dependency literature, involving critical junctures and developmental pathways, is relevant here, since these are some of the assumptions I make about the political development of health care in the member states.

Path Dependency. It is increasingly common for political scientists to describe political processes as path dependent.[23] But, at present, analysts lack a clear definition and an understanding of the theoretical underpinnings of path dependency. Thus, the concept is oftentimes utilized without careful elaboration or a clear definition. A full discussion of path dependency is beyond the scope of this introduction, but for reasons of clarity let me define path dependency.[24] This study conceptualizes path dependent processes as those political processes that are embedded in a dynamic of increasing returns, whereby as Pierson puts it, "the relative benefits of the current activity compared with other possible options increase over time."[25] Another more elaborate definition is provided by Margaret Levi, who writes, "Path dependency has to mean, if it means anything, that once a country or region has started down a track, the costs of reversal are very high. There will be other choice points, but the entrenchments of certain institutional arrangements obstruct an easy reversal of the initial choice. Perhaps the better metaphor is a tree, rather than a path. From the same trunk, there are many different branches and smaller branches. Although it is possible to turn around or to clamber from one to the other—and essential if the chosen branch dies—the branch on which a climber begins is the one she tends to follow."[26]

It becomes quite evident therefore that path-dependent processes are defined by five characteristics. These have been described by many scholars,[27] but they are important enough to be mentioned again here. First, there is an element of unpredictability. Since early events have a significant impact and are to a degree random, a number of outcomes is possible and therefore predicting the end result becomes highly difficult, if not impossible. Second, there is an element of inflexibility in relation to the temporal depth of the sequence. The longer one finds oneself on a given path, the less flexible one becomes to change paths. Third, there is the element of non-ergodicity which means that accidental random events do not constitute noise as they do in many quantitative models of analysis, but are significant in that they feed back in future choices. Fourth, there is the potential for path-inefficiency. The chosen path may not, in the long run, produce the most efficient outcome relative to a foregone alternative. Finally, there is an element of importance related to the sequencing of events. As Pierson notes, "early parts of a sequence matter much more than later parts, an event that happens too 'late' may have no impact, though it might have been of great consequence if the timing had been different." Simply, the order of events makes a difference.

Historical institutionalists were quick to pick up the concept of path dependency in their study of institutions through the model of historical explanation.[28] As we saw earlier, there were two questions that were asked first and foremost. First, how is it that an institution was chosen over possible alternative ones or what was the set of circumstances that led to the genesis of this particular institution? Second, how is it that institutions are able to reproduce themselves, or what are the political processes through which institutions are being reproduced? According to historical institutionalism, the circumstances responsible for the generation of an institution differ from the processes responsible for its reproduction. This is where the terms of critical junctures and developmental pathways were introduced.

Critical junctures are specific time periods when a particular institution, or set of arrangements, was chosen among two or more alternatives. The choice between a national health service or a social insurance-based system can be seen as a critical juncture in the development of health care policy in a given country. Critical junctures works analyze crucial historical moments of institutional formation which result in differentiated institutions in different countries, with different degrees of state autonomy and state capacity and thus ultimately in different policy outcomes. In doing so, they stress that once a choice is made, it becomes increasingly difficult to return to the original point of choice and are therefore informative on how institutions get formed and on why different countries are indeed different. In fact, as Katznelson points out, "this has been the bread and butter of historical institutionalism."[29]

What they do not do sufficiently, however, is explain the replication or the continuation of these institutions over time within a given context or a given country. This void is arguably filled by the developmental pathways literature, whereby the scholars involved basically point out that institutions evolve based on political maneuvers and environmental conditions that constantly are changing themselves. At the same time, this institutional evolution is dependent upon previous settings and past trajectories. The existing institutions try to replicate themselves in the first instance, either by having political actors adapt to the institutional logic of this system or, as already mentioned, favor certain political groups over others to promote their own interest and their own survival.[30] Both changing environmental factors as well as political maneuvering, however, gradually make institutions evolve.

One, of course, has to ask then, whether as of mid-2002, we have reached a critical juncture in the historical development of European health care systems because of European integration or whether integration is only part of the environmental context. This context, that along with political maneuvering, arguably induces institutions to evolve but still on the same developmental pathway, on the same trajectory, on the same branch, to regress to Levi's metaphor, that they have found themselves on through history. Part of the argument of this study is that it is the latter. The EU and the European integration process are indeed influencing the development of health care policy, but not to the extent that one could argue that a critical juncture has been reached, as the case might have been if, for instance, a new federal system of health care financing was decided upon. There is a convergence due to the integration process around a different logic of allocating finite resources in health care, around that is a set of rational cost benefit assessments, a more disciplined policy on the financing side and increased demands for accountability on the delivery side. Power politics, however, within the health care institutional framework at the member state level, remind us that there is resistance to an extent against the full transformation of the systems towards this new framework. The end result is transformations of existing institutions so that they can adapt to the contextual pressures by the integration process. Furthermore, the ideas and values about social cohesion and the right to health care by actors at both the central and the member state levels legitimize the continuation of institutional arrangements in health care that according to strict economic theory may be less efficient than a perfectly utilitarian institutional arrangement, and therefore arguments about Europe losing its strong social traditions are a bit alarmist.

Having offered the theoretical framework behind this study, I will now turn the discussion to how I conceptualize the European structure of governance.

The EU as a Multitier Structure of Governance

European integration, in its current form (based on treaties, not on war), is a process that began after the end of world war II. It has experienced times of intense euroeuphoria as well as times of intense euroscepticism. It remains, to a great degree, an experimental process that has on the aggregate moved forward, even when at any historical juncture this forward movement was very much contested. It has been driven by interests, ideas (or ideals, in some cases), and institutions as member states sought to deal with issues that their context had made too complicated, if not impossible for any one state to deal with. It is a political process affected by multiple factors and actors who interact with one another to generate a multidirectional and often contradictory pattern of governance, juggling authority between the state level and the central level. In fact, the debate between those who prefer an intergovernmental approach to the integration process and those who prefer a federal approach has characterized the development of the Union throughout the past fifty years.

Here, I will examine more closely three theories of European integration, namely functionalism, neofunctionalism, and interdependence theory, and an attempt by the intergovernmental part of the debate to bridge the differences between these theories, namely that made by Moravsik. I will not provide an exhaustive analysis of all theories of European integration, but focus only on those that directly play a role in my inquiry.[31] The basic goal at hand is to find out at what level or levels of governance, health care is best studied. After concluding that none of these theories is satisfactory, I then look at Pierson's formulation of the EU as a multitier structure of governance, which I adopt and therefore argue that any given policy (health care is no exception) is best understood when examined at both the central and the peripheral levels.

In the exercise by political scientists to understand regional integration attempts, especially those like the European one, where the prospect of further integration is always present, there are two questions that are automatically raised.[32] First, the question of timing: Why, at this given historical juncture, did a group of states decide to come closer to one another? Second, the question of the integration dynamics: How is it that integration efforts originally took off and how have they been sustained since then? Based on these two questions, a number of theories have been introduced, especially in the European context, to attempt to describe, explain and predict patterns of European integration. Some of these have focused on the political culture and political ideas of some political elites, others on external pressures on the form of the nation state and on the state's response to such pressures. Others focus on the interests (both strictly economic but also political) of actors in the political arena. Such actors may be political leaders, or representatives of large corporations. Yet another group of theories focuses on the power of the nation-state and in the bargaining that goes on amongst states. One safe generalization that can be made, is that the study of European integration as a sub-area of political science, presents us with a variety of definitions and differentiations that are based on the presuppositions of the experts.[33]

Functionalism

The theory of functionalism was introduced by David Mitrany.[34] According to Mitrany, after the end of the second world war there existed a number of complex civil and technological needs that were not primarily of a political nature but of a technocratic one. Due to this nature, they required, according to his theory, the creation of agencies of experts who would be able to provide solutions. Integration was explained by the need of the different bodies of experts to cooperate in order to meet the challenges at the international level. Furthermore, the necessary cooperation between these bodies of technocrats above the traditional nation-state de facto altered and increased interstate cooperation (leading to integration) by forming the framework within which issues were discussed and understood. Mitrany therefore essentially argued that integration occurred because there was a need and because it served a function. This theory assumed that it would be in the institutions of the states that control over policy would lie. It was rather quiet on the creation of pan-European institutions with transnational powers. According to Mitrany, due to the principle of ramification,[35] the intergovernmental cooperation in certain fields of the policy sphere would automatically be transferred to other areas of that sphere. For example, the creation of the European common market would lead to the formulation of common policies such as a common defense policy or a common social policy. In all these developments, however, it is the state institutions that matter. The theory of functionalism is the first instance in which a framework for understanding European integration is proposed and it is rather evident that the focus is at the state level since at no point is there discussion about the creation of European institutions.

Neofunctionalism

Following in the footsteps of Mitrany and other functionalist theorists, another group of political scientists proposed the theory of neofunctionalism. The major representatives of neofunctionalism are Ernst Haas, Leon Lindberg and Joseph Nye.[36] The main difference between this theory and the theory of functionalism is that neofunctionalism also incorporates the creation of transnational institutions in its propositions and therefore is closer to the actual development of the EU. Whereas functionalism saw a European Union with member states that cooperate and at the same time maintain their national sovereignty and their national institutions, neofunctionalism added to this previous framework by introducing into the debate European supranational institutions.

The central thesis of neofunctionalism is relatively straightforward. In the beginning, the several pieces of "low politics" of the member states in certain policy arenas come together under a common unifying and supranational agency. Through a process of spillover, this supranational agency begins to expand its scope in order to sustain integration in the original policy areas. Facilitated by pressures from interest groups and other actors (who have their personal and primary economic interests in mind), the original embryonic integration begins to grow and is placed in a self-sustaining cycle whereby one policy arena leads to another and the supranational agency ultimately finds itself involved in all policy areas.[37] In fact, neofunctionalism explained relatively well what was going on in Europe in the mid-1950s. Monnet, as the president of the European Coal and Steel Community, viewed the integration of the coal and steel markets as the instrument through which to push the original six members (Germany, France, Belgium, Netherlands, Luxembourg and Italy) to integrate their social security and transportation systems since to him that was essential for the successful continuation of the common market and the eradication of any pricing inconsistencies.

As mentioned earlier, neofunctionalism appeared to be able to describe and explain the process of European integration relatively well. Soon enough, and as the original euroeuphoria slowed down, member states reasserted their power and to date this direct transnational involvement in all policy areas, let alone the federal scheme of governance, remains elusive for the EU. For our purposes, neofunctionalism points to the involvement of both levels of governance, central and state, in policy making and also provides the theoretical underpinning for that involvement.

Theory of Interdependence

The theory of interdependence was developed during the 1970s.[38] All other theories of integration had placed the focus on internal and primarily political considerations that had led to European integration. The interdependence theory takes the focus off the political aspects of integration and places it on the economic aspects.[39] Its two basic assumptions are that (a) besides nation states there are other equally important actors in the international scene, such as multinational companies and international banks, and that (b) there are issues besides security ones that are equally important to the actors in the international scene and therefore one cannot automatically assume that security issues will dominate the agendas in international discussions. According to proponents of this theory, the more free international trade there is, the greater the chances for peace. In a sense, they move from examining internal, that is within the EU, reasons for integration to examining external ones. According to them, through more international trade, states and other actors become interdependent on one another. In fact, the greater the level of trading, the greater the interdependence. And since as interdependence grows, so does the cost of breaking up the relationship of two agents, more economic cooperation can be translated to more security. In that sense, the EU would be built gradually. The first stage would have to do with the micro-level economic cooperation of member states, which was to be followed by macro-level cooperation (as was the creation of the common currency). The demands of international markets, the changing nature of work that demanded specialization, the increasing stability on the international scene, the continuing changes in the structure and operations of multinational companies and the obvious never-ending need for improvements in the cooperation between international actors set the mechanistic way through which European integration would occur.

In the light of the globalization of the economy and of the changes that we have witnessed in the last few years, the theory of interdependence is indeed a powerful one. But in attempting to speak of areas about which the previous theories had largely remained silent, it moved too far away from the politics of the integration process. It does, however, give us one insight for our purposes here and that is that external considerations (and in today's juncture these are primarily economic ones) matter in the formulation of European economic policy. Therefore, to the degree that European economic policy is connected with health care policy (a fair assumption, to my mind), external developments need to come into the discussion when one discusses health care protection in relation to European integration.

More Recent Theoretical Developments

One of the most serious attempts to bridge the insights of previous theories of European integration has been done by Andrew Moravsik.

Building on the insights of Keohane and Hoffman,[40] Moravsik suggests three theoretical propositions about the EU that are clearly intergovernmental but also allow room for supranational action.[41] The first is named supranational institutionalism, the second intergovernmental integration institutionalism and the third, the importance of national sovereignty. In the first, Moravsik focuses on the dynamic and independent nature of international and supranational agents. More specifically, what drives the Union's institutions is the lobbies of large multinational organizations and also some political leaders like Jacques Delors and Lord Arthur Cockfield, a former commissioner for internal market affairs. In the second proposition, Moravsik emphasizes the prominent role of bargaining among states, especially those with greater political and economic power, pointing out that the integration process tends to move as the lowest common denominator of national interests. Finally, in the third prooposition, he points to the importance that states place on protecting their national sovereignty and the fact that they are willing to see it erode only when they perceive that the benefits they acquire are worth the erosion. But for all the insights of Moravsik's theory, it fails to capture the complexities of day-to-day governance of issues of low politics, one of which is health care. Certainly, if the existence of the EU has an effect on health care protection as this study argues it does, then Moravsik's theory fails to include it since it deals primarily with issues of high politics.

As it becomes obvious, there is no single theoretical framework that can include all the complexities of the European integration process. The main argument between European integration theorists is, and has been, whether the EU is destined to become a federation or simply a form of intergovernmental cooperation. This debate is a postwar debate and continues to date with the same level of intensity. The founding treaties of the European Communities never settled the question between intergovernmentalists and federalists. And when the focus is on day-to-day policies that do not directly speak to the future of the Union, or that at least are not subjects of intergovernmental conferences, one also needs to take a distant historical approach to explore more ably the effects of European integration. Paul Pierson and Stephan Leibfried provide us with such a framework for social policy analysis through their formulation of the EU as a multitier structure of governance, a formulation that with only minor adaptations applies equally well for the particular case of health care.

Multitier Governance in the European Union

Even the strongest minded intergovernmentalist admits that in low politics areas, the influence of Brussels over the years has grown, and in certain cases dramatically. In terms of social policy, Pierson and Leibfried view the Union as an emerging multitier structure of governance which, according to them, "is a system of shared political authority over social policy, though one that is far more decentralized than the arrangements of traditional federal states. As the process of economic (and increasingly, political) integration unfolds, however, the EU's presence in social policy continues to expand."[42]

This multitier structure of governance has been created through history, on the one hand, and also exhibits characteristics that affect future policy developments on the other hand. In this sense, this framework is quite consistent with the principles of historical institutionalism and path dependency. More specifically, the EU exhibits strong representation for the individual member states in the decision-making process. Furthermore, the institutional mechanisms of the Union raise political dilemmas in all policy areas and are a cause of changes in the strategic planning of both state and non-state actors at both levels of governance.

Whereas according to intergovernmentalist interpretations of the Union, focus is placed on the sovereignty of the member states, this multitier formulation turns the focus towards the constraints that the integration process places on national sovereignty. Indeed, one of the most unique aspects of the EU is the strong influence that the member states exert on European institutions and in the direction of the Union, in general. Having said this, however, does not refute that very few, if any, policy areas are outside the reach of EU intervention today, even if it is through indirect paths. In the words of Fritz Scharpf, "There will be hardly any field of public policy for which it will not be possible to demonstrate a plausible connection to the guarantee of free movement of goods, persons, services and capital—and thus to the core objectives of the European Union."[43]

It is rather through the strong representation of member states at the European level and the ability of each member state to protect what it perceives its interests to be that common action in many policy areas has been usually one of the lowest common denominator as a result of continuous negotiations. Be that as it may, the majority of decisions taken in Brussels by member states has led to increased European influence in matters where previously the state was the only decision maker. Again Pierson and Leibfried identify four factors/characteristics that point to the distinct European center of governance where states do not firmly control all aspects of decision making. First, there is the autonomy of the activities by European Union institutions such as the Commission, the Court, the Parliament. The second factor is the effect of earlier political agreements by member states at the EU level that locks them into policies they might not have chosen on their own. Third, as already mentioned, over time there has been impressive growth in the scope of issues with which the Union deals as a result of spillover from other areas. This is a process that continues to date and leads, on the one hand, to new initiatives in policy areas previously thought of as areas that only the member states dealt with and, on the other hand, unintended consequences that at times demand common European solutions. Finally, the independent activity of non-state actors at the central level must be taken into account. Employer federations, workers' unions and an array of other organizations lobby directly in Brussels and in this sense circumvent member states. All these characteristics do not appear to their full degree in all policy areas, but they offer a roadmap for how European policy making works and how one can expect a relatively undeveloped policy, like health care, to evolve at the European level. The discussion of Pierson and Leibfried's view of the governing structure of the EU, reveals that there are two analytical levels for any given policy arena in the European context: the central level or the EU level, and the member state level.

The EU level is, in a sense, the broader one since it incorporates all the interacting and interdependent factors of the world system in general and of the EU system in particular. In this sense, external pressures on the EU and on the member states and the ways in which they affect health care solidarity are best analyzed at this level. Moreover, direct decisions and indirect mechanisms of influence that stem from existing European legislation are also best understood at this level of analysis. Furthermore, this level implies a sense of group, of a whole, and thus allows one to focus on the similarities between different approaches to health care protection.

The member-state level constitutes the second level of analysis. Whereas the EU level places the focus on influences from the outside and from the central level and therefore explores similarities in the responses of member states, this second level of analysis focuses on the differences in the health care regimes of the different states. It emphasizes internal politics and policy developments as well as the internal historical development of health care arrangements. Factors like a given state's political legacy, its stage of economic development, its geographical position, its cultural heritage, its historical experiences and its social structure all matter at this level because they probably underlie the differences in the health care arrangements.

In short, health care decision making has two dimensions: the central level and the member-state level. At the first level, one could argue that the behavior of the state is influenced by the integration process, the rules which a state has to respect in order to ensure effective participation in EU institutions. At the second level, the behavior of the state is a function of its internal political economy and its history and therefore can only be explained by internal criteria. Arguably, it is the interaction between these two levels that can give us a complete picture in a given policy area in a multitier structure of governance like the EU. At any historical juncture, decisions may be the responsibility of the central government or of the state government, but the decision-making mechanisms are shaped by the experience of both and, therefore, it is their interactions that produce the institutions through which decisions are made. In this sense, health care finance and delivery must be understood at both levels, and this is what I intend to make clear in this study.

Therefore, in this work I have looked into the political history of health care reforms in Greece, France, Germany and the Netherlands in order to explore any European Union effects on the decision-making mechanisms about health care protection. First, one must ask: why Greece, France, Germany and the Netherlands? The answer is that these countries represent a good and diverse enough sample of the member states. Following the analytical framework from a pilot study by Goldmann,[44] I divided the 15 EU member states into four categories: Europeanized, Pragmatic, Contradictory and Traditional. Always keeping in mind that typologies are nothing more than heuristic devices, the Europeanized and the traditional typologies are of the purest form. The Europeanized countries present a strong affinity to the EU both at the elite and at the mass levels. The elites want to see the EU develop into a stronger supranational entity. In the meantime, a strong sense of European identity is present at the mass level. The Netherlands is a prime example of this group. The traditional countries are more skeptical of the union. They define their national interest in a narrower way. At the mass level, there is no generalized sense of European identity, and the masses are more suspicious of the EU than the elites are. England or Sweden would be good examples in this category. The pragmatic group displays strong opinions in favor of the EU, both at the level of the elite and at the level of the public. However, the sense of European identity present in Europeanized countries is absent here. Greece or Ireland serve as examples. The contradictory group, according to the author of that study, is exactly that. The elites present at times strong, radical positions in favor of supranationalism and at times they oppose it. At the same time, however, mass attitudes are eurosceptic at times as much as public opinion in traditional countries. France or Germany serve as examples of contradictory countries. First, I decided to exclude the traditional group because of its skepticism towards the EU, and so the countries I was choosing all displayed positive views of the EU at the elite level where my research question was focusing. Within each group the countries were chosen based on their size and wealth, the structure of their health care systems, and the type of government they have had over the period that the study covers. In terms of the other variables, I chose countries that differ among themselves. By focusing on these variables, I believe that I have created a sample that is diverse enough so that different effects of European integration may be detected and similar enough so that the project does not become merely a description of the health care arrangements in these countries.

Greece is the poorest member state, a representative of the European south and a relatively small country. There the idea of European integration is received well by the public, and much better by the elites. Moreover, Greece has been governed for the greater part of the last twenty years by a center left government. Finally, it has a national health system, even though as Moran points outs, the character of its governance is an "insecure command and control."[45] Put differently, even though the system is based on Beveridge's notions of the British National Health System (NHS), the system has never managed to display the private sector completely, allowing both private clinics and private physician practices to coexist with the public NHS.

France is one of the largest member states, an architect of the EU, mostly pro-European at the elite level, but not as enthusiastically as Greece. It is also a relatively rich member state and a net contributor to the budget. Moreover, France has experienced center right and center left governments over the last twenty years. Further, it is representative of the social-based insurance system, or the Bismarck model of health insurance. This is a corporatist model where insurance is arranged through a number of public law bodies, broadly known as sickness funds.

Germany is the largest member state, the biggest contributor to the EU budget and has been considered by many (along with France) the locomotive of European integration. It has experienced a center right government for almost twenty years, with a switch to the left more recently. It also has a social based insurance system, but with a much differentiated political decision-making mechanism than France. Moreover, Germany presents an interesting case because Germans have been willing to test a wide range of approaches to achieve their health policy goals and many countries follow their example.

The Netherlands is also one of the richer nations in the Union and a net contributor, but also relatively small. The public has a European identity and the elites are very much in favor of further integration. Moreover, it also has a social-based insurance system. Further, it has also had governments from both the right and the left during the last twenty years, but in a coalition form.

One must also ask: Why only Greece, France, Germany, and the Netherlands? Ideally and in a large-scale operation, the research should be designed to include all fifteen countries. Countries like England, Sweden or Denmark, which are generally considered as opposed to integration in a number of policies, would offer an interesting comparison. Further, the strong command and control displayed by the states in these countries in terms of health policy (different models of an NHS), would also offer an interesting comparison. It has become, however, quite evident that even in countries with eurosceptic approaches, their membership has placed policy constraints on them to follow, albeit less willingly the policies of more europhile countries. Nevertheless, all findings will necessarily be suggestive.

In chapter 1, I begin formulating the argument presented in this introduction by exploring the nature of challenges that health care faces in an era of integration. By examining the philosophical and the political underpinnings of the development of the health care state and its several variations vis à vis the traditional structure of the nation state, I present the ways in which these challenges emerged. The reader is brought up to date with international trends in the several policy areas that formulate the tests for health policy makers today. I argue that the challenges to health care can be divided into two categories: First, those inherent to health care or those that would have been present even without the integration process. Examples here are the demographic trends, the technological advances and the controlling of cost. Second are those related to the integration process itself. Examples here would be cross-border care, competition law as it relates to health insurance, and the boundaries in the roles between Brussels and the member states.

In chapter 2, I turn the discussion to the central level of governance, Brussels, and examine the history of European integration, with a particular focus on its social policy initiatives. I describe the structure and the relations of the different EU institutions, their interactions with member states and examine where health care delivery fits (or where it does not fit) and in which manner. I argue that health care finance and delivery have been mostly left to the member-state level, but not completely. Brussels has itself taken some action mainly through decisions by the European Court of Justice but also through other methods. This highlights my contention that health care finance and delivery are affected by actions or non-actions from above, through the ideological convergence of member-state policy makers around a framework of a more rationalized distribution of health care resources.

In the next four chapters, I develop the case studies—the Dutch, French, German and Greek health reform stories in light of the main argument in this study: that the ideological imperatives and financial constraints imposed by integration have affected national health policy, even while policy decision making largely remains at the country level. I explore the history of the political development of health care institutions with a particular interest in reform proposals in the last fifteen years. Put differently, I examine the reasons and/or the formulations presented to justify such reforms. Throughout, I argue that whereas reforms were justified through means that are associated with this ideological convergence, internal power politics led to the alteration or even total dismissal of certain reforms resulting in an incremental approach that is consistent with the paths that each system has followed over the years.

In the final chapter, I bring together the lessons from the previous chapters and discuss the dynamics of health policy making in the EU. I maintain that without reaching a critical juncture in the development of health care institutions, major changes in the arrangements through which Europeans receive their health care cannot be expected. Moreover, as long as current health care arrangements are not perceived as distorting the market, Brussels will not act. In addition, I discuss briefly the similarities and differences between health care, and education and social security in terms of EU action. I conclude that health insurance will most likely remain for the time being at the member-state level as far as politics are concerned, even though European directives will most likely increasingly have to deal with the issue of cross-border health more comprehensively. Finally, the expressed desire and the inherent value, as well as the historical origins of the idea of social cohesion in decision making mechanisms at both the central and the member-state level, all but assures us that social solidarity will remain a primary goal in any reform effort of European health care.

Notes

1. For an extensive discussion of challenges to the state's sovereignty, capacity and autonomy, see Sassen, S., *Losing Control? Sovereignty in an Age of Globalization.* 1995; Holton, R. J., *Globalization and the Nation-State,* 1998; Braithwaite, J., "Sovereignty and Globalisation of Business Regulation," in *Globalisation versus Sovereignty?,* edited by P. Alston and M. Chiam; Basch L., Schiller, N. G., and Szanton-Blanc, C., *Nations Unbound; The Economist,* January 29, 2000, "Globalisation and Tax."
2. Scharpf, F., "Economic Integration, Democracy and the Welfare State, "*Journal of European Public Policy,* 1997:18-36.
3. Rhodes, M., "Subversive Liberalism: Market Integration, Globalization and the European Welfare State," *Journal of European Public Policy,* 1995: 84-406.
4. Teague, P., "Monetary Union and Social Europe," *Journal of European Social Policy,* 1998:117-37.
5. Eurosceptic groups include groups that are against European integration for a variety of reasons, ranging from loss of national sovereignty to fear of outsiders or the other. The criticism by Eurosceptic groups most relevant here deals with the potential for Europe to abandon its historical tradition of the welfare state.
6. Especially in the areas of pharmaceuticals and other technologies as well as in the area of supply of medical professions, the Commission has issued a number of directives and the ECJ has ruled on a number of cases, protecting the common market and allowing the free movement of people and goods. A good essay on such issues is the one by Theofilatou, M., and Maarse, H., "European

Community Harmonization and Spillovers into Health Regulation," in *Health Care and its Financing in the Single European Market*, edited by R. Leidl, IOS Press, Washington D.C., 1998, 13-37.

7. Altenstetter, C., "Health Policy Regimes and the Single European Market," *Journal of Health Politics, Policy and Law* 27 (4): 813-846, 1992.

8. For two good discussions of the history of European integration, see Wallace and Wallace, *Policy Making in the European Union*, and also Richardson, J., *European Union: Power and Policy Making*.

9. Leibfried, S., and Pierson, P., "Social Policy," in *Policy Making in the European Union*, 3rd ed., edited by Wallace and Wallace, Oxford University Press, New York, 1996, 185-209.

10. Pierson, P., (b)"Social Policy and European Integration," in *Centralization or Fragmentation? Europe Facing the Challenges of Deepening, Diversity and Democracy*, edited by A. Moravcsik, a Council on Foreign Relations Book, New York, 1998, 124-159.

11. For a more analytical understanding of positive and negative economic integration, see Scarpf, F., *Governing in Europe*.

12. Maarse, H., and Paulus, A., "Health Insurance Reforms in the Netherlands, Belgium and Germany: A Comparative Analysis," in *Health Care and Its Financing in the Single European Market*, edited by R. Leidl, IOS Press. Washington D.C., 1998, 230-253.

13. France, G., and Hermans, H., "Choices in Health Care in Italy and the Netherlands, I: Economic and Financial Dimensions," in *Health Care and its Financing in the Single European Market*, edited by R. Leidl, IOS Press. Washington D.C., 1998, 254-264.

14. OECD Occasional Paper: "Health Care Systems in Transition: The Search for Efficiency," OECD Social Policy Studies No. 7, Paris, France, 1990.

15. Pierson, P., *European Social Policy*.

16. For the discussion here, I have largely used notes from an institutionalism seminar at Columbia University led by Ira Katznelson and Charles Cameron.

17. For an introduction, see March, J. G., and Olsen, P., *Rediscovering Institutions: The Organizational Basis of Politics*, Free Press, New York, 1989; also see North, D. C., *Institutions, Institutional Change and Economic Performance*, Cambridge University Press, 1990, and Weaver, R. K., *Do Institutions Matter? Government Capabilities in the United States and Abroad*, The Brooking Institute, Washington, D.C., 1993.

18. Thelen, K., and Steinmo, S., "Historical Institutionalism in Comparative Politics," in *Structuring Politics: Historical Institutionalism in Comparative Politics*, edited by S. Steinmo, K. Thelen, and F. Longstreth, Cambridge University Press, Cambridge, 1994.

19. Ibid .

20. Immergut, E., "The Theoretical Core of the New Institutionalism," *Politics and Society* 26 (1): 5-34, 1998.

21. Hall, P., "The Role of Interests, Institutions and Ideas in the Comparative Political Economy of Industrialized Nations," in *Comparative Politics: Rationality, Culture and Structure*, edited by M. I. Lichbach and A. S. Zuckerman, Princeton University Press, Princeton NJ, 1997, 174-207.

22. For good discussions on this point, read Berman, S., "Path Dependency and Political Action: Reexamining Response to the Depression," *Comparative Politics* 30:379-400, 1998, and Pierson, P., and Skocpol ,T., "Why History Matters," Newsletter of the Comparative Politics Section, APSA.

23. A number of social scientists have pointed to the importance of historical sequences. Examples are Aminzade, R., "Historical Sociology and Time," *Sociological Methods and Research* 20:456-480, 1992; Griffin, L. J., "Temporality, Events, and Explanation in Historical Sociology: An Introduction" *Sociological Methods and Research* 20:403-427, 1992; Isaac, L. W., "Transforming Localities: Reflections on Time, Causality, and Narrative in Contemporary Historical Sociology," *Historical Methods* 30:4-12, 1997; Sewell, W. H. Jr., "Historical Events as Transformations of Structures: Inventing Revolution at the Bastille," *Theory and Society* 25/6:841-881, 1996; Somers, M. R., "We're No Angels: Realism, Rational Choice, and Relationality in Social Science," *American Journal of Sociology* 104:722-784, 1998; Porter, D. H., *The Emergence of the Past: Theory of Historical Explanation*, University of Chicago Press, Chicago, 1981; Tilly, C., "Future History," *Theory and Society* 17:703-712, 1988; Abbott, A., "Sequences of Social Events: Concepts and Methods for the Analysis of Order in Social Processes," *Historical Methods* 16:129-47, 1983; Abbott, A., "Conceptions of Time and Events in Social Science Methods: Causal and Narrative Approaches," *Historical Methods* 23:140-150, 1990; and Krasner, S. D., "Sovereignty: An Institutional Perspective," *Comparative Political Studies* 21: 66-94, 1988.

24. For excellent discussions of path dependency, see Arthur, W.B., *Increasing Returns and Path Dependence in the Economy*, University of Michigan Press, Ann Arbor, 1994, and Mahoney, J., "Path Dependence in Comparative-Historical Research." Paper presented at the 1999 Annual Meeting of the APSA, Atlanta, September 1999. For a strong critical analysis of path dependency, see Liebowitz, S. J., and Margolis, S. E., "Path Dependence, Lock-In, and History," *Journal of Law, Economics and Organization* 11/1:205-226, 1995.

25. Pierson, P., "Path Dependence, Increasing Returns and the Study of Politics," Occasional Paper, Center for European Studies, Harvard University, October 3,1997.

26. Levi, M., "A Model, a Method, and a Map: Rational Choice in Comparative and Historical Analysis," in *Comparative Politics: Rationality, Culture and Structure*, edited by M. I. Lichbach and A. S. Zuckerman, Princeton University Press, Princeton NJ, 1997, 19-41.

27. This part of the discussion relies heavily on Arthur, W. B., *Increasing Returns and Path Dependence in the Economy*, University of Michigan Press, Ann Arbor, 1994, which collects all of Arthur's essays on path dependency. Also see Pierson, P., "Not Just What, But When: Issues of Timing and Sequence in Comparative Politics." Paper presented at the APSA meeting in Boston, 1998.

28. For a good description of the model of historicist explanation, see Stinchcombe, A. L., *Constructing Social Theories*, University of Chicago Press, Chicago, 1968.

29. Katznelson, I., "The Doleful Dance of Politics and Policy: Can Historical Institutionalism Make a Difference?" *American Political Science Review* 92(1): March 1998:191-197.

30. For a relevant analysis, see Thelen, K, "Historical Institutionalism in Comparative Politics," in *The Annual Review of Political Science*, 1999.

31. Besides the functionalism, neofunctionalism and interdependence theoretical frameworks for regional integration there are three other major theoretical strands those of realism (neorealism), federalist (neofederalist) and Marxist (neomarxist). For an extensive treatment of all regional integration theories, see Dougherty, J., and Pfaltzgraff, R. Jr., *Contending Theories of International Rrelations: A Comprehensive Survey*, New York, Harper and Row, 1990.

32 More on the point of how integration theories are formed can be read in Dahrendorf, R., *Essays in the Theory of Society*, Stanford University Press,

Stanford, CA, 1968, and in De Vree, J. K.,*Political Integration: The Formation of Theory and Its Problems*, Mouton, The Hague, 1972.

33. The word integration has been used throughout the literature to indicate either a static final state or a process. One can trace the first group back to works by Hodges, M.(ed.), *European Integration*, Penguin Press, London, 1972; Etzioni, A., *Political Unification*, Holt, Rinehart and Winston Publishers, New York, 1965; Pentland, C., *International Theory and European Integration*, Faber and Faber, London, 1973. The second group can be traced back to works by Jacob, P., and Teune, H., "The Integrative Process: Guidelines for Analysis of the Basis of Political Community," in *The Integration of Political Communities*, edited by P. Jacob and J. Toscano, Lippincot Press, Philadelphia, 1964; Lindberg, L., and Scheingold, S. (eds.), *Regional Integration: Theory and Research*, Harvard University Press, Cambridge, 1971, and Deutsch, K. et al., *Political Community and the North Atlantic Area*, Princeton University Press, Princeton, NJ, 1957.

34. Mitrany, D., *A Working Peace System*, Illinois Quadrangle, Chicago, 1966.

35. More on the ramification principles and in the building of the EU, see Pinder, J., *European Community: The Building of a Union*, Oxford University Press, London, 1991, and Wallace, W. (eds.), *The Dynamics of European Integration*, Pinter Publishing, London, 1990.

36. Haas, B. E., *The Uniting of Europe*, Stanford University Press, Stanford, CA, 1968; Lindberg, L., *The Political Dynamics of European Economic Integration*, Stanford University Press, Stanford, CA, 1963; and Nye, S. J., *Peace in Paris: Integration and Conflict in Regional Organization*, Little Brown Press, Boston, 1971.

37. According to neofunctionalism, the stages that European integration has and will eventually follow are the following: free trade area, customs union, common market, cross-border union, economic and monetary union, political union, and finally European Union.

38. The interdependence theory is closely related to two theories that emerged in the 1980s in international relations. The first was that of international regime's theory, proposed by Stephen Krasner. The second was proposed in 1987 by Joseph Grieco and is coined as "neoliberal institutionalism." For more, see Krasner, S.D., *International Regimes*, Cornell University Press, Ithaca, 1983, and Keohane, R., *International Institutions and State Power*, Westview Press, Boulder, CO, 1989.

39. Keohane, R., and Nye, J., *Power and Interdependence: World Politics in Transition*, Little Brown, Boston, 1977.

40. Keohane, R., and Hoffman, S. (eds.), *The New European Community: Decision-making and Institutional Change*, Westview Press, Boulder, CO, 1991.

41. Moravcsik, A., "Negotiating the Single European Act: National Interests and Conventional Statecraft in the European Community," *International Organization* 45/1:651-688, 1991. For a more recent adaptation of this approach, see *The Politics of European Treaty Reform: The 1996 Intergovernmental Conference and Beyond*, edited by G. Edwards and A. Pijpers, Pinter Publishers, London, 1997.

42. This is probably the best perspective or formulation on the EU that I have come across. With great skill, Pierson and Leibfried not only presented another formulation of the EU but also were quick to compare it with traditional federal states, to assess the degree of its centralization and factors that affect that degree. For the excellent analysis, see Pierson, P., and Leibfried, S., "Multit-

iered Institutions and the Making of Social Policy," in *European Social Policy: Between Fragmentation and Integration*, edited by S. Leibfried and P. Pierson, The Brookings Institute, Washington D.C., 1995,1-41.

43. Scharpf, F., *Governing in Europe: Effective and Democratic?*,Oxford University Press. New York, 1999.

44. Goldmann, K., "Politikens Internationalisering och den Politiska Kulturen. En Pilotstudie," Arbetsrapport, Stasvetenskapliga Institutionen, Stockholms Universitet, 1997.

45. Moran, M., "Death or Transfiguration? The Changing Government of the Health Care State," EUI Working Papers No 99/15, European University Institute, Florence, Italy, 1999.

1

Variations, Commonalities, and Challenges for Health Care

Even a casual observer of social affairs cannot help being struck by the determination and the endurance with which European states have taken to health care reform. The ingenuity and the creation of new ideas, on the one hand, and the rebirth and the institutional resistance of old ones, on the other, converge to provide the framework within which political actors try to persuade one another about the merits and shortcomings of a given policy proposal. Behind all these ideas, old and new alike, are different dimensions of health care policy. One of the most prominent dimensions in the debates for any health care system is its distributive ethic. Another is the level of efficient production and allocation of resources. Still a third one is the level of quality and the comprehensiveness of services offered. In the specific case of the European Union, there is one more dimension that one has to consider. It is the dimension of ensuring the continuity of access between states. The goals can very conveniently be reduced to one statement with which most, if not all, agree: universal access to high quality medical care with a sustainable cost. But that is where agreement ends. What is the most appropriate approach toward reaching these goals? Is health care planning by government what is required or can "the magic of the marketplace" deliver for us? Is it a mixture of the two in a quasi-market and if so what is the appropriate dosage of each? Which level of government ought to be involved? Should it direct and encourage patient choice through the collection and dissemination of information? Should it contract with only a certain number of providers? How many beds, how many physicians, how many nurses and in which combination are needed for optimal delivery of care? Is there to be a private sector in the production of health care and if so to what extent can it be allowed to operate? How much cost sharing is to be accepted? How much, if at all, of an open competitive system can we have in terms of health insurance and between private insurers and sickness funds?

These questions among many others raise the challenges that health care policy making faces in an integration era. In this chapter, I separate these challenges into two categories and in relation to the focus of the study. The first set of challenges constitutes those that are inherent in health care system development and that the societies of the 15 member states would have faced even if the EU did not exist. The second set of challenges is directly linked to the integration process and to the creation of the common market. Since health care systems differ from country to country, in order to understand the ways in which these common challenges emerged, I begin by presenting the considerable variations in health care arrangements in the member states through an examination of relevant trends. I then turn the discussion to exploring the historical and theoretical underpinnings of the health care state and its several variations through an examination of the three main perspectives in terms of the appropriate roles of the government and the market in health care. Having established the parameters and the limits within which different societies move in terms of utilizing government and/or market mechanisms to finance, produce and deliver medical services, I move to similar trends among them and briefly outline through history the emergence of these two sets of challenges. It is argued that it is a multiplicity of factors, including contextual ones like external economic shocks and the integration process, and internal ones like the very success of medicine and the expanding views of what is a medical issue, that has led to some of the redefinitions of the priorities in terms of policy.

Variation among Health Care States

To speak of variations among health care states is a fruitless exercise unless it is done in the context of identifying factors that continue to be different institutional change after institutional change. Such factors, as it is easily understood, directly form constraints to future adaptations of health care states in response to current challenges. In one of the best examples of comparative analysis of differences between European welfare development, Peter Flora identifies two such basic factors that have persisted in their differences over the course of time and thus can be assumed to influence future developments and to explain current institutional differences.[1] Adapting them to health care considerations, the first such factor is the level of the central state's penetration into health care institutions and the available room it allows for other intermediary institutions to meet health care demands by society. The second factor is the degree of fragmentation of health care social protection in terms of class or sector differentiations, which encourages or limits the potential for political conflict.

The degree of penetration by the institutions of the central state into health care arrangements correlates negatively with the degree of penetration into the same arrangements by alternative entities (lower level of government, voluntary organizations, for profit enterprises, etc.). It turns out that the less centralized a state is, the more room there is for alternative, more decentralized "political" entities. If during the formation process of health care arrangements, these alternative entities preemptively assumed the administration mainly of health care financing, there was not much room for the central state to fully wrestle control from them, and thus it assumed different roles in order to achieve its goals. It is indicative that, in many continental states like Germany and the Netherlands which are quite decentralized, the model that has been followed is one of social insurance based on employer and employee contributions and not one of direct public financing as is the case in Great Britain, for instance. The differences between alternative mechanisms not only in financing but in the delivery of services as well, also reflect the degree of social or employment sector differentiation in each state. One may ask whether social transfers are justified based on a notion of citizenship or based on these occupational contributions or on some other characteristic of a group.[2] Furthermore, the differentiations among occupational groups or classes in a society also reflect the different approaches in the creation of health care institutions. The three models that have been proposed by Gosta Esping-Andersen in his seminal book, *The Three Worlds of Welfare Capitalism*, are the social democratic one, the conservative one and the liberal one.[3]

In his construction, the basic factor that differentiated the different welfare regimes was the nature of the political class coalitions. The first and the smallest one reflects the Scandinavian arrangements of rights granted to the entire population independent of income and/or class status. Countries in this regime did not opt for a dualism between middle classes and working classes, and thus social democrats pursued arrangements that would lead to an equality of the highest standards rather than an equality of minimum standards, as was the case elsewhere. The second reflects countries like Germany and France, with strong connections to the class structure of their societies, their religious beliefs and the structure of the family, which converged to create a highly fragmented institutional framework of welfare provision that perpetuated or conserved these status differences. In this model, Esping-Andersen observes that whereas "private insurance...plays a truly marginal role.... On the other hand, the state's emphasis on upholding status differences means that its redistributive impact is negligible." The third model reflects countries like Great Britain and the United States, where welfare policies were based on means tests, minimum universal transfers or modest social insurance. Such systems were based on the notion that a strong work ethic would enable people not to require state assistance. Thus, it minimizes the idea of social rights and accepts "market differentiated welfare among the majorities."

As it becomes quite obvious, the health care arrangements of European states do not fully comply with this framework. For example, the British national health system is an exception to Great Britain's overall welfare system, providing, as mentioned earlier, universal access based on a notion of citizenship. Furthermore, helpful as this framework is for understanding some of the underlying historical factors that have led to institutional variation, it does not very adequately capture institutional arrangements in south European states, where an admixture of the British Beveridge model and the continental Bismarck model appears to be the case. In an attempt to better define the categories of "health care states," Moran proposed a slightly altered version of Esping-Andersen's analysis.[4]

Moran suggests that there are four families of health care states: the entrenched command and control states, the supply states, the corporatist states, and the insecure command and control states. In the first group, Great Britain and Scandinavian states are included. For the purposes of this book that deals with the governing of the production and distribution of health care resources, the distinctive characteristic of these states in that the state is the "absolutely dominant actor." It finances the production through revenues raised through taxation, one of the coercive powers that a state enjoys. It manages the distribution through variant but distinctly public administrative mechanisms. In the words of Saltman and von Otter, "The dominant policy paradigm during this post-war expansion was a relatively rigid command-and-control planning model. Decision making responsibility was vested in elected officials at national level (the U.K.), national and regional (Sweden, Denmark, Norway) or national and municipal (Finland) levels, while day-to-day operating authority was delegated by these politicians to a corps of career administrators and planners."[5]

The second kind of health care state is a supply state. In the countries of the European Union, one does not find such a supply state in health care. The United States serve as the prototype here. Larry Jacobs, in an article in *Health Affairs* summarizes: "the general sequence and form of health policy in the United States diverges from those of all other industrialized nations. The U.S. government's first and most generous involvement in health care focused on expanding the supply of hospital-centered, technologically sophisticated health care.... In contrast to the United States, however, other Western countries have made the expansion of access their first and primary priority."[6] Supply states first decide that they will provide everything to some people based on a market mechanism and then worry about covering up patches of problems with access.

The third type of health care state, the corporatist state, is characterized by strong public law bodies. Germany, the Netherlands and France are examples of this arrangement. The state basically serves as a regulator for such public law bodies and it creates the framework within which negotiations take place between the public law bodies and the social insurance bodies.

Finally, Moran describes a fourth family of health care states, the insecure command and control states, which are the states of southern Europe—Portugal, Greece, Spain and Italy. These states modeled their systems after the systems of the first family of health care states, the strong command and control states. For a variety of reasons, however, the administrative control and the planning process never took off in these cases as they did in those earlier ones. In Greece, for instance, the sickness funds which predated the introduction of the NHS, were maintained as independent entities instead of being united under one financing mechanism. And whereas private provision of services was supposed to be abolished, it never was and today private provision of health services in Greece is one of the fastest growing sectors of the economy.

These variations in the political construction and implementation of health care institutions in the different states have resulted in a number of important and practical differences in terms of the operations of the various health care systems. A few indicative ones are the differences in terms of expenditures, utilization patterns, levels of health care resources, and distribution of such resources between the public and private sector.

Health care spending. Health care expenditures in EU member states differ substantially both in terms of GDP and in terms of per capita health expenditures. The relative investment that each member state makes in the health sector and the relative success of cost control that each member state enjoys ranges greatly. In 1997, one finds the UK, Ireland, and Luxembourg spending the lowest percentage of their GDP (6.8, 6.3 and 7 percent respectively). In the next category, one finds Belgium (7.6), Denmark (8), Finland (7.4), Italy (7.6), Portugal (7.9), and Spain (7.4). They are followed by Austria (8.3), Netherlands (8.5), Greece and Sweden (8.6). Finally, one finds France with 9.6 percent of its GDP going to health care and Germany with 10.7 percent. From the 6.8 percent that Great Britain dedicates to its centrally administered national health system to the 10.7 percent that Germany dedicates to its social insurance based system, European health care systems present uneven levels of expenditures. Since presenting health expenditures masks the absolute differences in these expenditures, it is helpful to examine briefly variations in per capita health expenditures. These variations are indicative of both total health expenditures but also the variations in the relative wealth of the different states. From the Portuguese low of $1148 to the German high of $2364, Europeans pay tremendously different prices for medical care. It is, in fact, not surprising that the wealthier countries like Luxembourg, Germany, Denmark, France and the Netherlands present higher per capita spending, whereas the poorer ones like Greece, Ireland, Spain and Portugal present the lowest per capita spending. It seems to indicate what actually a number of studies have shown that the higher one's income the higher one's expenditures.

Furthermore, the percentage of total health expenditures that comes from the public sector presents a considerable range. From the high end of Luxembourg and Great Britain, where in 2002 almost 92 percent and 89 percent of total health expenditures were public, to Greece and Portugal, that publicly spend less than 60 percent of total national health expenditures, one can make the following observation. The highest public spenders are the strong command and control systems like the British and the Scandinavian ones with a mean of about 85 percent, followed by the social-based insurance systems like the Dutch, the German and the French with a mean of about 75 percent, and then by the mixed loose command and control systems of the South with a mean around the 63 percent range.

Patterns of utilization and health care resources. Substantial variations also exist among patterns of utilization and available health care resources as Table 1.1 shows.

Table 1.1
Variations in Utilization Patterns and Health Care Resources in EU States,
1997 (or most recent year)

	Beds /1 000 pop.	Bed days/capita	Admissions Rate	ALOS(days)
Austria	9.1	2.6	26.6	10
Belgium	7.2	2.1	20	11
Denmark	4.6	2.7	18.4	8
Finland	9.2	3.2	25.7	12
France	8.5	2.5	23	11
Germany	9.4	2.6	22.1	13
Greece	5	1.2	15	8
Ireland	3.7	1	15.2	7
Italy	6.5	1.7	18.5	9
Luxembourg	8.1	2.8	19.4	15
Netherlands	11.5	3.6	11	32
Portugal	4.1	1.1	11.8	9
Spain	1.1	10	11	N/A
Sweden	5.2	1.3	18.1	8
UK	4.5	1.7	23.1	10

Copyright OECD Health Data 99

The total number of beds adjusted for population size indicates once again that the wealthier states have more beds than the poorer ones. Special attention should be paid to the case of the Netherlands which has an average length of stay (ALOS) of 32 days, which dwarfs the next highest one of 15 by Luxembourg, but at the same time also has one of the lowest admissions rates in the Union, resulting in the bed days per capita being much closer to the median of the member states. Overall one can say, however, that with the sole exception of the Netherlands, the more beds a country has the higher its admission rate.

Distribution of health care resources between the public and the private sector. An excellent measure of the variability in terms of the distribution of health care resources among European states is the distribution of beds between the public and the private sector. The percentage of private beds ranges from below 5 percent in the UK, Denmark and Finland to above 50 percent in Germany and Belgium. It is indicative of the degree of state penetration, or the "stateness" of the different health care systems as explained by historical factors and discussed earlier. It is, however, essential to point out that there is much variation on the type of private sector. The voluntary sector (private non-profit) is much more developed in Germany and Belgium, for instance, than it is in France, where total private beds also account for more than a third of total beds. It becomes quickly apparent that these substantive variations among European health care states reflect the historical and philosophical different approaches in terms of the appropriate roles of the government and the market in health care.

The State, the Market and Health Care Policy Making

The ways in which governments and markets do and should relate to oneanother in health care has been and always is one of the most heated debates in health care reform attempts. The topic admittedly is flooded with misunderstanding. On the one hand, most societies take as axiomatic that equitable health care is a right and it follows that government ought to provide it. On the other hand, they also view it as the object of an economic exchange between payers and providers. In this sense, government and market are two competitive mechanisms, two different and distinct approaches aiming for the same goal. Yet, at the same time, they are interdependent in any given setting even while this interdependence differs through time and from place to place, since the same state may approach the pendulum between market and government differently and tilt it more towards one direction or another depending on their preferences, considerations and environment at the given historical juncture. Furthermore, what they mean by the notion of market is oftentimes not the same.

In which specific part of the system and in which manner the invisible hand of the market intervenes is a highly diversified topic. In the words of Larry Brown, there exists "a perpetual dialogue between theoreticians and practitioners of market and government 'approaches'—a dialogue that can range from dogmatic insistence on choosing between the two, to pragmatic efforts to mix and match the best of both worlds. These dialogues differ with place and time, but they seem to display a fairly consistent dialectical character, visible in most places most of the time."[7]

Some clarity about this consistent dialectical character of health policy, can come from examining the three main perspectives on the appropriate balance between market and governmental involvement in health care. A qualification point: These perspectives are not examined in order to order them as better or worse in relation to one another. One needs to always keep in mind that they serve more as a normative guide and as starting points to policy making rather than completely shaping a given health care system. The three different schools of thought are: the market oriented, the neomarxist and the state oriented.

The Market Oriented School of Thought

The market school of thought is characterized by its primary normative position which deals with individual freedom. According to proponents of this position, maximum individual freedom coupled with personal responsibility will result in individual achievement. Therefore, through the aggregation of individual achievements, there is inherent social value in individual freedom.

In this sense, collective decisions should be made through voluntary exchange of information or goods by individuals in the context of a free market. In the opinion of one of the best known theorists of this school of our time, the Nobel Laureate economist Milton Friedman, consumers know their preferences better than anyone and therefore should be free to make individual choices which inevitably will result in the best possible collective result. Therefore, the state's coercive powers must be limited to a minimum. "Every act of government intervention limits the area of individual freedom directly and threatens the preservation of freedom indirectly," writes Milton Friedman in his authoritative essay *The Role of Government in a Free Society*. Ideally, the state should play the role of the referee by designing and enforcing a level playing field for all players. It is viewed as a neutral participant in social affairs with the sole role of mediating among different interests in the context of a free market which is inherently fair. Therefore, supporters of the market are not opposed to government, even though it is a common misconception to think that. In the words of Friedman again, "the organization of economic activity through voluntary exchange presumes that we have provided, through government, for the maintenance of law and order to prevent coercion of one individual by another, the enforcement of contracts voluntarily entered into, the definition of the meaning of property rights, the interpretation and enforcement of such rights, and the provision of a monetary framework."[8]

The ways that members of this school of thought have applied their beliefs in the health care arena have revolved around criticisms of state intervention and health planning. The basis of such criticisms is our ignorance. They worry that planners may simply not get it right. As a result, the health care system may be overfunded or underfunded relevant to the free and true preferences of the citizenry, which, of course, is only the collection of the individual citizens. There is indeed something to this criticism.[9] No effort in financial planning or structural allocation of resources will meet the preferences of all citizens. Even assuming away all political pressures on the decisions in health planning, the most extensive health planning exercise will without fail result in a number of people on either side of the debate arguing for more or less health care. No health planner can know the "right" distribution of health care resources, if such a thing really exists.

Market supporters, therefore, categorically reject planning and look to the market as the solution to the "murky area of societal decision making." This position holds that individuals should be given purchasing power to afford the minimum level of health care judged by themselves as their situation changes. After all, a sovereign consumer is the only one who truly knows his preferences. Assuming for a moment that health care operates like the market for any other good, and based on rational individual decision making and the information provided to him, the patient can judge what type of care he is more willing to purchase. By definition, that level of distribution is an efficient one. We need not revisit hard-to-define terms like societal values, since the aggregation of wise, rational and informed individual decisions will result in the most efficient distribution of health care resources.[10]

In this sense, market supporters offer the free enterprise model of organizing health care. They value voluntary exchange and free market choice and consider health care to be comparable to other products. Again, the main representative of the health care application of the market oriented school of thought is Milton Friedman. In fact, Friedman, in a *Wall Street Journal* editorial amidst the American health care debate of the 1992 presidential election wrote, "The inefficiency, high cost and inequitable character of our [American] medical system can be fundamentally remedied in only one way: by moving in the other direction, toward re-privatizing medical care."[11] Friedman has actually gone further in past writings to attack the system of licensure of physicians since according to him, it only represents the monopoly of the medical profession and results in higher medical fees. Instead he prefers a system where every person would be free to practice "without restriction except for legal and financial responsibility for any harm done to others through fraud and negligence."[12]

There are a number of market supporters who differ with Friedman on this latter point. Whereas they would indeed prefer a system of voluntary exchange between physician and patient without government intervention, they regard the medical profession quite highly. It is obvious that medical associations are in this group and to protect and promote their professionalism they look to the free market model, advocating free selection by the patient of his physician, freedom of prescription for the physicians, fee for service payment and confidentiality between patient and physician.

Differences aside, however, the market string of thought advocates minimum if any governmental intervention, free market choice for consumers, voluntary exchanges between patients (or their representatives) and physicians, and fee for service payment. This puts them in direct opposition to the neomarxist school of thought.

The Neomarxist School of Thought

This school of thought views the modern capitalist state, as it has emerged from the industrial revolution and has been perpetuated through the information revolution as an institution that, at its organizational basis, has the goal of sustaining class relations based on private property, to which neomarxists are vehemently opposed. "The modern bourgeois society that has sprouted from the ruins of feudal society has not done away with clash antagonisms. It has but established new classes, new conditions of oppression, new forms of struggles in place of the old ones," reads the Manifesto of the Communist Party[13] and it is echoed by the theories of neomarxist scholars. Neomarxists, following the writings of Marx and Engels are also opposed to the mechanism of what conservatives called "voluntary exchange." "The bourgeoisie...has left remaining no other nexus between man and man than naked self interest, than callous 'cash payment'. It has drowned the most heavenly ecstasies of religious fervour, of chivalrous enthusiasm, of philistine sentimentalism, in the icy water of egotistical calculation. It has resolved personal worth into exchange value, and in place of the numberless indefeasible chartered freedoms, has set up that single, unconscionable freedom—Free Trade."

The neomarxists put emphasis on the social, instead of the individual, level in terms of freedom and achievement. Freedom is defined as collective self-determination. Achievement and freedom can be realized when social inequalities are reduced, if not eliminated. Neomarxists judge the merits of a policy on its ability to produce equality of results. Whereas the ideal of the market school of thought was the maximization of individual free choice and personal responsibility in order to achieve human development, neomarxists posit as their ideal a classless, cooperative society without private property and therefore without exploitation of one person by another. In this sense and oddly enough neomarxists find themselves like market supporters, against the state and both its planning and its class mediating functions. The reasons behind their opposition, however, are different. As Paul Sweezy comments in his influential essay, *The Radical Theory of the State,*[14] neomarxists reject "the tendency...to interpret the state as an institution established in the interests of society as a whole for the purpose of mediating and reconciling antagonisms to which social existence inevitably gives rise. The class-mediation theory assumes, usually implicitly, that the underlying class structure, ... the system of property relations, is an immutable datum."

Of course, since such a state of social affairs, if indeed forthcoming, lies in the distant future,[15] neomarxists have concentrated their efforts on criticizing the capitalist state and its various functions, including its functions in health care. A general framework of this critique can be found in the work of Claus Offe, where he attributes to the state in modern capitalist societies four main characteristics. First, the state must maintain conditions that allow for capital accumulation and thus arguably cannot be fully supporting of true equitable redistribution. Second, the state is excluded from true control of the production of goods and services, since enterprises are free. Third, the state is dependent on these free enterprises and their workers in terms of funds needed for its own institutional stability. Fourth, and as a response to the three mentioned characteristics, the state attempts to legitimize its existence by conveying an image of an organization that represents the common good and is thus sensitive to justified demands. Part of that attempt is also the state's attempt to plan. Offe, however, contends that the state as an organization in a capitalist society is incapable of planning. "Planning...seems to be inherently impossible in the capitalist state...—impossible not in itself, but because of the acts of retaliation that planning provokes on the part of capital as a whole or individual accumulating units. Such acts of retaliation...tend to make the cure worse than the disease under capitalism, and are thus self-paralyzing in regard to state activity."[16] Therefore, state planning is possible only if the underlying social structure is a communist one.

The neomarxist tradition applies its theory in the health care arena by advocating socialized medicine.[17] To the neomarxists, the goal of medicine ought to be social, health care should be viewed as public (as any other good after all in this tradition), and therefore its portrayal by proponents of either the market or the state as a proper object of economic exchange finds neomarxists opposed. They view all people as part of the social group and since sickness strikes persons because of unfortunate circumstances, a person should not have to bear the costs of treatment alone. To achieve these ends, neomarxists consider it essential that the medical provider (physicians, nurses and other non-physician clinicians) are removed from the sphere of competitive business. Whereas supporters of the market would claim that fee for service payment is enough to safeguard the social protection and the integrity in the physician-patient relationship, neomarxists argue that it distorts this relationship. Medical care cannot be viewed as a commodity and placing physicians in the context of viewing it as such ensures that the public interest can not be adequately safeguarded. A nationalized health system, with free care for all, with salaried medical providers is the ideal. Such a system, however, requires planning by a central authority and therefore in order to be successful requires a different underlying set of relationships between persons in a society.

In short, neomarxists begin with the issue of social equity and reject profit motives, or the assignment of monetary value to different health care procedures. Whereas the market approach considered that such an assignment and individual rationality on the part of the patient/consumer of health care would result in an overall efficient system with inherent social value, neomarxists define social value and health care differently and therefore end up with a completely different set of arrangements for medical provision and for state involvement in those. This places them to the other side of the theoretical spectrum from the market supporters, with the state oriented school of thought somewhere in the middle.

The State Oriented School of Thought

Whereas both the market and the neomarxist schools of thought exhibit a theoretical clarity that is welcomed from a normative perspective, the state oriented school of thought can be viewed as the pragmatic attempt to incorporate the best of both previous models. If the market supporters are unequivocal supporters of the free market and the neomarxists of a state that promotes, indeed ensures, social equality, this last school of thought borrows from both and therefore can, in one sense, be viewed as intellectually confused. On the other hand, however, theirs is the most pragmatic approach asking the question, how can a modern liberal democratic society, which is on its basis capitalist and values personal accumulation of wealth, provide equitable health care?

From these early comments, it becomes apparent that members of this school of thought view both the state and health care quite differently than both supporters of the market and neomarxists. To theorists in this group, the nature of man is hedonistic and individualistic and at the same time noble and socially sensitive. It is rational in the individual and functional sense of the word but at the same time aware of the collective functional difficulties that such rationality embodies.[18] Therefore, they begin their analysis based on the assumption that humans have a very strong materialistic side but also a nobler side that motivates them occasionally.

They also begin with a concern about equity. They support equality of rights,[19] whereas market supporters support equality of opportunity and neomarxists equality of results. In this sense, equity and equality are superimposed on one another under this perspective. If one has a right to appropriate medical care, then it follows that the criterion of access to care is the need for medical services rather than the ability to purchase them. Therefore, redistribution of resources from those who have to those who have not, is justified. Further, the concern with equity justifies, according to this school of thought, state intervention in health care for two reasons. The first has to do with the way that the state is viewed from this perspective. The second has to do with the way that the market is viewed from this perspective.

The class mediation theory of the state that neomarxists oppose is fully supported here. The state is viewed as the mediating force between conflicting interests, as having interests of its own and that through its institutional mechanisms aggregates individual preferences and pursues the public interest. In so doing, it ensures true freedom, which to proponents of this school of thought does not entail state absenteeism from social affairs as supporters of a market approach would have it.[20] In the words of Richad Tawney, "It is still often assumed...that, when the state refrains from intervening, the condition which remains...is liberty. In reality, what not infrequently remains is not liberty, but tyranny."[21] Supporters of governmental involvement do not, however, challenge the basic capitalist structure of the liberal democratic state. In fact, they consider it as one of the two primary foundations of modern society, the other being democracy. According to them, the state and its welfare functions derive their character "precisely through...close relationships with the capitalist market economy and mass democracy. The liberal welfare state is based on the economic surplus produced in the market economy, and its structure must be adapted to the basic laws governing this economic system. At the same time it is also based on the political consensus produced in the democratic mass polity, and its structure must reflect the basic nature of this consensus. Principle limits to the development of the welfare state lie only where it would begin to undermine these foundations." Welfare policies in general and health care policies in particular are the critical elements reconciling capitalism and democracy. Furthermore and because of their belief in the reconciliation of democracy and capitalism, the idea that individuals acting rationally in the context of a free market would automatically result in an efficient and thus inherently socially valuable outcome finds theorists from this school opposed. According to Richard Tawney again, even if a market succeeds in an efficient allocation of resources, such an allocation may not be socially equitable, especially when one is discussing health care, and therefore state intervention is justified. As we saw, supporters of the market hold that the rational behavior of individuals in a free market, pursuing their self-interest, results in substantively rational and thus equitable distribution of resources. Not so, for theorists from this school; according to them even if all individuals act rationally, that does not ensure the achievement (in fact, it may prohibit it) of promoting the notion of the public interest.[22] Since health care is viewed as a right and not as a reward (thus the concept of merit goods in public economics), state intervention is necessary to ensure equitable distribution.

Therefore, supporters of state involvement would have the state intervene in order to correct market failures and/or to redistribute income. They are believers in the ability of the state to achieve any combination of government services and income redistribution that we deem important as a society. It is thus no wonder that they fully support state planning efforts and, in turn, do not seek fundamental changes in the institutional structure of the health care state as we know it today. They focus on pragmatic policies in order to minimize problems as they are perceived in the given historical juncture and in the given place. In so doing, they find themselves in between supporters of the market and neomarxists. As mentioned they view health care as a right, much like the neomarxists. At the same time, they also support models of organizing medical care delivery that resemble very much free enterprise models. They support market incentives for providers and consumers so that a more efficient allocation of resources can be achieved and at the same time like the state to intervene to set institutional mechanisms to hold providers accountable to the notion of the public good. The questions that most often guide them deal with how great the market inability is in terms of satisfying the right to health care of each citizen.

Concepts of quasi-markets, managed care and managed competition and their different applications in different settings are a reminder of the highly differentiated approaches of this school of thought to health care planning specifically and state intervention in the health sector in general. I will discuss these concepts in greater detail later in the chapter. At this point, it is essential, however, to point out that the birth of such concepts is a result of a never-ending dialectical pattern between and within the different schools of thought as it is shaped through history and the context at any given place. As Brown writes, "after the governmental 'thesis' has prevailed for a prolonged period, the eternally unruly problems of the health care system make the market antithesis look fresh and promising. Then trials prove that market forces are as much subject to error as are those of their public sector antagonists, and government regains legitimacy and élan, triggering continuing tensions—never dispelled—that fuel new pragmatic strategic syntheses. However much logic may demand a clear division of labor between markets and government, reality requires eclectic, impure admixtures of both."[23] Therefore, differences among nations notwithstanding, a pattern of swinging back and forth between markets and government, mixing aspects of both, failing and beginning all over again characterize the health care arrangements in all European health care states. In the section that follows, I will examine a general historical evolution of European systems and the factors that have led to this synthesis of ideas over time, pointing out general trends of similarities among nations.

Similar Aspects of Health Policy Development

Having indicated all the variability among health care arrangements in European states does not negate the fact that there are also similar aspects of the development of the different health care states. As with the variations among states, here, too, one must look for underlying factors either internal to the health care systems or external, contextual factors that have led to the similarities in the developments of health care states.

Since 1945, when the second world war ended, most European societies[24] were quick to undergo a number of changes that allowed them to raise themselves from the ashes of the war and recover much faster than anyone could have imagined. This story has been told elsewhere, but it is critical to remember that, not too long ago, most of these societies were lacking both political and economic stability. From that starting point, and through a number of bold policy initiatives, the modernization process of Europe began and indeed accelerated in the process of transforming European states permanently. One of the major policies and one of the most essential parts of this modernization process of that era was the creation of the welfare state. Health care transfer schemes and an expanding role of the state were a large part of that development. The historical origins of such kind of health care arrangements go back into the nineteenth century, but their present institutional structure is very much a product of the afterwar period. There are two main points that need to be made:

- Throughout the second half of the twentieth century, when access to health care became an issue, the state has been the one that in one way or another has taken the lead in ensuring such access.

- At any given historical juncture, the ways a health care system evolved was a function of the contextual macroeconomic and political factors that surrounded the broader political development of Europe and of the specific health care power politics exhibited in each country. In this sense, a number of challenges that health care systems face emerge from the same factors.

The combination of the two previous points has led to the considerable variation that was already examined but also to a number of similarities in the ways European societies approach the challenges of issues such as equity and efficiency in health care.

European Health Policy: A Look Back and the Current Challenges

The end of World War II marked the beginning of a period during which the health care sector has seen tremendous growth both in absolute terms and also relative to other sectors. During this process, the state ended up expanding its role in health care in many ways. Either by directly financing health care, regulating the growth of this sector of the economy, reorganizing the organization of health care institutions or a combination of all these functions, government found itself more and more involved in health care as time passed. The reasons why Europeans looked first to government to deal with such issues are many. First, Europe had just come out of one of the most destructive wars in its history and the private sector was very much nonexistent. Moreover, a strong ethic of social equity had been developed because of the experiences of the war. Furthermore, some of the specific tasks at hand (regulation, for example) could only be executed by government. Finally, once the government began being involved with health care, a certain momentum developed which made it easier for the state institutions to assume more and more responsibility in this sector. As a result, in all European countries health care expenditures skyrocketed (Table 1.2)

In all countries, total health care expenditures as a percentage of GDP displayed impressive growth, especially between 1960 and 1970. In certain cases, such as Spain and Greece, the average rate of growth during the decade was above 6 percent (9.15 and 6.07, respectively). But even in countries with well established health care systems by that time like Sweden, Denmark and the Netherlands, rates of growth were above 4 percent. The growth continued for the larger part of the 1970s. In fact, with very few exceptions, the rates grew for almost all countries, in certain cases substantially (reaching levels above the 4 and 5 percent range).

Soon after, due to among other factors the economic environment, however, the first clouds began to gather over this love affair between the state and the health care sector. Increasingly, voices were heard demanding accountability by providers for the use of limited resources. Increases in the rates of growth over the next seventeen years stabilized and in certain cases partially reversed themselves, if only temporarily. In no country did the rate of growth pass the 2 percent range and in some countries it was a negative one. Nevertheless, health care expenditures were still consuming a large part of national output without proper rational accountable mechanisms of allocation. The second stage of health care development ensued and in the process the role of the state was transformed, acting less as a direct provider and more as an overseer of overall health care provision. People began to look to the market for solutions to the rising health care expenditures. A welfare state backlash was thought to be occurring and the health care systems of most countries had reached a maturity levels that in all actuality did not require the money influxes of earlier decades. At the same time, the EU was creating a new framework of poli-

Table 1.2
Total Health Expenditures in EU States as GDP %
Selected Years (1960-1997)

	1960	1970	1980	1990	1997	Growth Rate			
						1960-1970	1970-1980	1980-1990	1990-1997
Austria	4.3	5.3	7.7	7.2	8.3	2.11	3.79	-0.69	1.96
Belgium	3.4	4.1	6.5	7.5	7.6	1.75	4.83	1.36	0.24
Denmark	3.6	5.9	9.3	8.3	8	5.23	4.64	-1.14	-0.56
Finland	3.9	5.7	6.5	8	7.4	3.8	1.33	2.06	-0.97
France	4.2	5.8	7.6	8.9	9.6	3.22	2.64	1.61	1.17
Germany	4.8	6.3	8.8	8.7	10.7	2.71	3.47	-0.11	2.96
Greece	3.1	5.7	6.6	7.6	8.6	6.07	1.58	1.44	1.71
Ireland	3.8	5.3	8.7	6.7	6.3	3.44	5.05	-2.64	-0.75
Italy	3.6	5.2	7	8.1	7.6	3.61	3.12	1.5	-0.97
Luxembourg		3.7	6.2	6.6	7		5.27	0.57	0.84
Netherlands	3.8	5.9	7.9	8.3	8.5	4.39	2.99	0.5	0.36
Portugal		2.8	5.8	6.4	7.9		7.7	1.02	3.04
Spain	1.5	3.7	5.6	6.9	7.4	9.15	4.22	2.1	0.97
Sweden	4.7	7.1	9.4	8.8	8.6	4.35	2.77	-0.66	-0.24
UK	3.9	4.5	5.6	6	6.8	1.43	2.26	0.65	1.8

Copyright OECD Health Data 99

cies that were spilling over indirectly into considerations about the role of the state as a producer and as a financier. The debate now had shifted to controlling costs, supposedly through the market. The deeply embedded interests from the earlier period of development, as well as the strong beliefs in social solidarity, however, pushed towards a different direction, that of the mixing of state intervention and market solutions. The third and current phase of the development of health policy, that of quasi-markets with both the public and the private sector present had arrived.

Stage 1: A Time to Expand

During the immediate postwar years, the health sector exhibited tremendous growth and in the process propelled government to the central role of European health care states. Three discrete but interacting sets of forces provided the increasing momentum for the sector to grow: advances in curative medicine; the growing public „taste" for medical and hospital care; and the willingness of the government to assume major responsibility for financing facility construction with the subsequent rise to dominance of the hospital. These were originally the ways that governments throughout Europe found themselves increasingly involved in health care.

Advances in curative medicine. It is hard to imagine today that not too long ago medicine had more to do with care than with cure. There was not much that medicine could do for a sick person. With the discovery of penicillin, that era was over. New biomedical knowledge and technological developments were allowing physicians to prolong lives and to add healthy years to previously doomed patients. Equally important was the development of new specialties and the subspecialization of old ones. Immunologists, intensive care unit specialists, pediatric cardiologists are only three of the many examples of specialties that came with this era of development.

Growing public "taste" for medical care. As was natural, the new advances in medicine created a new taste in the public for more medical care. After all, medicine was a good thing and why shouldn't one want more of it? The good economic times of the postwar years also led to increased wealth per capita and that also affected this increased preference for good medicine. Probably, however, the largest precondition was that the average patient was to a great degree sheltered from high costs through either public or social insurance mechanisms, which aligned his incentives to want as much care as possible.

Governmental responsibility for facility construction. Equally important, governments in almost all countries decided either to finance directly or subsidize the building of new facilities, mainly hospitals. Since access to hospital care was something that the public wanted and that physicians demanded, and since medicine was able to deliver good results, both the economic preconditions and the political coalitions for governmental involvement were in place in terms of expansion of the medical facilities. Until the 1940s, the physician who made house calls was the norm. Within thirty years, a new medical complex was created much like the industrial prototype. It centered around the hospital with its focus on high tech acute care, with highly specialized physicians who at times appeared to be able to defy death. Pharmaceuticals companies and a number of biomedical laboratories were surrounding the hospital. In turn, the hospital was transformed from a place where one went to die to a place where one went to get cured, with a growing bureaucratic and professional structure. As increasing flows of monies were injected into the health care sector, its expenditures grew seemingly without an end.

Stage 2: A Time to Mature

During the first three decades after World War II, the macroeconomic environment was quite favorable to this expansion of the health care sector and of the role of the state in it. As a result, health care absorbed a rising share of national outputs. But as the 1970s began, the macroeconomic environment was changing. As a result of the two oil crises and their consequences (higher levels of unemployment, higher public deficits, persistent distortions in the world economy), European states found it extremely difficult to sustain the rates of growth that health care had exhibited during the previous decades and up until 1980. In retrospect, the fact that the rates of growth between the fifties and the mid-seventies could not be repeated was not necessarily a negative development. It was a sign of the systems' maturity. Indeed, the golden age of the relative growth of the health care sector had come to an end and it was time to face the challenges of accountability of how limited resources were being spent. Providers (physicians and hospitals) found themselves under pressure to explain their outlays and it was the first time that different modes of production of medical services (through non-physician clinicians, more primary care, more outpatient services than the expensive inpatient care) were being discussed.

For the first time the goals of the health care system were not only improved quality but also sustainable costs. As the oil crises were hitting the economies of Europe, even in Scandinavian countries, politicians began to use the language of retrenchment.[25] At the time, there was a widespread feeling that the Keynesian consensus of the golden era of growth was no longer in place.[26] What the first and second oil crises of the late seventies started, a wave of neoliberal ideas, coming mainly from England and from the U.S., took over as the 1970s gave place to the

1980s.[27] Discussions about the retrenchment of the welfare state in general and the health care sector in particular were dominating cross-national comparisons of health care.[28] The Organization for Economic Cooperation and Development's (OECD) report in 1981, entitled *The Welfare State in Crisis*, interpreted the slowdown in the rate of increase of welfare expenditures as the result of the low economic growth that countries exhibited after the first oil shock of 1973. It went further in connecting social spending and low economic performance by stating that "some social policies...have negative effects on the economy."[29] A second OECD report in 1985 supported the 1981 findings and seemed to indicate that governments expanded welfare programs in good times and made cuts in bad ones.[30] Retrenchment of the welfare state was supposedly here. In fact, neomarxists, had predicted the end of the welfare state. In their framework of the world and in the words of Gough, "The welfare state is a product of the contradictory development of capitalist society and in turn it has generated new contradictions."[31] And as we saw, neomarxist understandings would have the whole structure of the liberal democratic state rolled back, an admittedly not very practical solution. But the ideals behind the welfare state growth were still very much present and agreed upon by everyone else. What must have been wrong was the mechanisms of production and allocation used, i.e., state planning, or so conservatives argued. Glazer wrote that "any policy has dynamic aspects such that it also expands the problem, changes the problem, generates further problems."[32] In an influential book, even though he only discussed the American case, Murray accused the welfare arrangements of the past two decades for trapping welfare recipients in a vicious cycle of dependency by depressing the incentives to work.[33] What all this meant for health care was that the traditional paradigm, according to which universal access to health services which were produced by either public or private but not for profit voluntary institutions, was financed through either taxation or employer-employee contributions was no longer sustainable. A new paradigm was needed and ,of course, this new paradigm had to look to the market, according to prominent political leaders of the time, for the more efficient allocation of resources. The state had to withdraw as much as possible and as quickly as possible. The private sector would do what government had been unable to do.[34] It was not to be this way.[35]

While, health care policy makers were in the middle of this retrenchment debate, the European Union was growing in influence and in its integration process had switched from a political framework to an economic one. In terms of attempts to control health care costs, two points must be made. First, the EU had a dual effect that can be viewed as contradictory. Second, since the health care debate pointed to the rationalization of resource utilization as the goal, the EU did not lead to such a state.

At most, in certain member states, it served as the catalyst for such reforms. What it did do, however, as we will see in the next chapter, was in the first instance place new demands in terms of cross-border care and, in the second instance, create a common institutional framework where health care challenges were being discussed and, in so doing, led to a convergence in the technocratic thinking of policy makers at the member state level. As the 1980s progressed, the common market was planned and eventually was implemented in 1992, allowing free movement of people, capital, goods and services, which complicated cost control measures. At that time, the decision for the creation of the current currency was taken and strict Maastricht economic convergence criteria were set which continued to apply the pressure that the public sector had felt since the late seventies.

Several factors converged, however, at this period to reject the approach of the market, as that was being proposed throughout the 1980s.[36] They were, as can be expected, political in nature. The first was the protection of the interests of institutions created during the expansion phase. The stage of growth of the health care sector had created vested interests by physicians and hospitals, mainly, who were very much opposed to such market proposals. Moreover, public opinion and its strong sense of solidarity—another product of the health sector expansion—were quite averse to the prospects of privatization of the health care sector and what that might mean for the services they received. Relevant to this point, the distribution of health care under the arrangements of the time was quite popular with the public. The services were for the greater part of high quality and since people could not relate to the actual expenditures, they saw no real reason for reform. Thus, as early as the mid-1980s, proponents of welfare states fought back. Brown wrote that "it is misleading to talk of the unraveling…of the welfare state. Efforts at retrenchment have been more selective and far less successful than many observers apparently believe."[37] If Reaganism and Thatcherism were sweeping across the Anglo-Saxon world, it did not appear to be the case in continental Europe. As Ruggie puts it, "the welfare state in the United States and Britain—where it has always been weak—might be in jeopardy, but the welfare state in general…lives on."[38] The fears for the welfare state's upcoming death were laid to rest, at least in the original dramatic versions.[39]

The changes in the macroeconomic context, however, made quite evident that greater accountability in terms of the ways limited resources get used in the health care sector was a necessity.[40] While the market solution was being proposed, the role of the state was being transformed to a growing regulator which demanded rationalization of the use of health care resources. In practice, therefore, the planning approach did not give much room to the market approach, even though the latter had crept on the agenda. State planners tried through a number of regulations and through setting standards—limiting capital investment in hospitals, evaluating outcomes, controlling provider fees through stricter negotiations and global budgeting, for instance, introducing some cost sharing in the financing of services—to control the rate of increase of health care expenditures. In a sense, what they were doing was to introduce some market elements into planned systems. This brings us to the current stage of development, that of the quasi-markets.

Stage Three: A Time to Reform

The shortcomings of planning the production and distribution of health care, along with the rejection of the pure market approach in health care, left policy makers contemplating what could be done to maintain universal and equitable access to care while not bursting the state budgets. A number of market incentives were introduced, as mentioned earlier, in order to try to halt the increases in the rates of expenditures. To a great degree, these measures were successful in stabilizing health care inflation and the sector's growth. This does not mean, however, that policy makers have found the magic bullet for health care reform. Rather, the marriage of planning and market incentives does hold some pragmatic hope for the future of the health care systems. The exact configuration of the state and private actors and the exact balance between planning and markets, however, remains an illusive concept for all countries.

To better understand this marriage that has been termed broadly by analysts as the quasi-market approach, it would be helpful to revisit its principles through an examination of one of the most prominent forms of a quasi-market. It is the best articulated and also best known form of a quasi-market approach and it was named managed competition by American economist Alain Enthoven.[41] In his construct, quasi-markets in general and managed competition in particular "is defined as a purchasing strategy to obtain maximum value" for patients and payers "by using rules for competition derived from microeconomic principles. A sponsor (either an employer, a governmental entity, or a purchasing cooperative), acting on behalf of a large group of subscribers, structures and adjusts the market to overcome attempts by insurers to avoid price competition." He goes on to state that "managed competition also connotes the ability to use judgment to achieve goals in the face of uncertainty, to be able to negotiate, and to make decisions on the basis of imperfect information. It takes more than mere *passive administration of inflexible rules* to make this market work (emphasis added)."[42] Moreover, managed competition occurs at a level where integrated financing and delivery plans operate, not at the individual provider level. Furthermore, the competition is based on the annual premium of each plan, which makes it easier for a healthy, not stressed lay-person to make a better more informed decision.

The weight of setting the rules of the market falls on the shoulders of the sponsors who are also the payer in this system. Sponsors have five functions in this system. First, a sponsor establishes rules of equity depending on the given market, but in any case ensuring universal and continuous access based on community rates for the same benefit packages. The sponsor also selects participating plans to contract with as the plans are constantly been reevaluated for compliance with the rules of the market and the efficient production and allocation of resources. Third, the sponsor manages the enrollment process through the provision of information and expertise to individual consumers and by serving as the first point of contact of an individual with the system. Fourth, the sponsor strives to create price-elastic demand. The sponsor must set up rules so that the insurers can raise more revenue by reducing their prices and not by raising prices. This means that demand for these plans must be so elastic (the fluidity between jumping from one plan to another) that the added revenue for the insurer exceeds the added cost of serving the new subscribers. Finally, the sponsor manages risk selection. The sponsor eliminates the value from the practice of cream-skimming whereby health plans pick the good apples leaving the rotten ones for the competition. By offering a standardized benefit package of essential services and risk adjusted premiums, a sponsor is theoretically capable of accomplishing this function. The incentives of these plans must be institutionalized in such a fashion so that competition centers around quality of services and consumer satisfaction. In reality, however, this has proven to be the hardest of the functions for the sponsor wherever managed competition or other variations of quasi-market approaches were tried.

Whether or not quasi-markets hold the key for equitable and efficient distribution of health care resources remains to be seen. It is a cliche, but it is also true that markets, and quasi-markets are no exception, are politically constructed. Changes in the physician-patient relationship, technological innovations, tensions in the relationships between providers, managers and insurers, the macroeconomic and political contexts as well as the micro-level political developments (coalitions, changes in positions, etc.) need to be constantly explored to see whether or not the quasi-market approach is working satisfactorily.

Current Challenges for European Health Care Systems

It is at this historical juncture, with quasi-markets proposed in most states as potential solutions to the problems of the health care sector that a number of challenges continue to exist. All of them have emerged from the historical development of the health care arrangements examined in this chapter. In light of the focus of this book on the European integration effects on health care reforms, it may be worthwhile to separate them into two categories, the first being the challenges inherent to the health care sector and the second being the challenges resulting from the European integration process. They are distinct and separate categories of challenges that interact, however, quite dynamically and form the tests for health care policy makers both in Brussels and in state capitals.

Challenges Inherent in Health Care

In this category, as it may be quite easily deduced from the discussion so far, one finds the issue of demographic changes (and especially the aging of the population which transcends all European states), the issue of technological advances and the subsequent costs, the rising expectations about health care as the economies continue to grow, the macroeconomic context within which health care operates, and, of course, as always the double-sword issue of quality care under sustainable cost. I will not go into great detail here about the latter three challenges, since the past effects, and hence the considerations for their future effects, were discussed in the body of the chapter. Suffice it to say, however, that these are the predominant factors in health care reform debates with the integration challenges still not fully on the agenda.

In terms of demographic trends, all European states exhibit aging trends with obvious implications for the financing of their health care systems. Between 1995 and 2025, the European Commission estimates that the number of people over 60 years old will increase by 21.1 percent (from 77 million in 1995 to anywhere between 107 and 122 million in 2025), whereas the number of people between the ages of 20 and 59 years old will increase by only 1.3 percent. The problems get worse when one considers that the number of people between the ages of 0 and 19 will drop by 6.7 percent. As a result, the total number of elderly as a percentage of total population will increase from 21 percent today to almost a third by 2025. This obviously means increased demands not only for acute care on an inpatient basis but also for outpatient procedures, home care services and nursing homes. At the same time the proportion of young people who produce and contribute to GDP growth drops and thus European states will have fewer Euros to finance more services. In this sense, the search for efficiency which began twenty years ago is not likely to stop any time soon. Couple this increased demand with new technologies and European policy makers are faced with a very big issue.

Technology, of course, would never have been on such a list of challenges twenty years ago, or if it were it would have been for the challenge of discovering more, introducing and providing access to more technologies which would be the latest brand of medicine. Since, however, it was suggested as one of the primary factors that lead to increased expenditures, its diffusion may prove to be an attractive place for cuts. In fact, new technologies could lead to a reduction of cost per unit, but have also been so widely disseminated that the absolute number of a test or of a procedure performed dramatically increases and as a result total health care expenditures increase. In fact, since neither population growth nor input prices are controllable, Schwarz argues that the essence of cost containment is exactly the limitation of the introduction of new technology.[43] At the same, time, no single regulatory entity can control the diffusion of technology and the degree of explicit rationing remains a major issue.

Challenges Due to European Integration

At the very least, the EU is a common market where the same currency is being used and the free movement of capital, people, goods and services is guaranteed. For the purposes of this book, the challenges that are raised because of integration are three: cross-border care, boundaries between Brussels and member state governments, and the understanding of the competition law as it relates to health care. All three of these will be discussed in the following chapter where the involvement of Brussels is assessed. There are more issues that European integration has raised, such as the cross-border movement of medical personnel, pharmaceuticals, public health challenges, but as mentioned in the introduction their politics are sufficiently removed from the politics of health care access and governance of consumption that they will not be discussed.

As the twenty-first century begins, all these issues occupy the agendas of health care policy makers in Europe. The differences in the systems between these countries will shape their future steps, on the one hand. On the other hand, as in the past, all countries face similar constraints in terms of macroeconomic constraints. Responses and policy priorities have changed in the past as a response to a multiplicity of factors, including these macro-level contextual ones and those micro-level internal ones that were explored in this chapter. What has not changed are the goals of health care provision and finding ways through the state through the market or through quasi-markets to ensure equitable access and not spending unsustainable amounts will be a large test for policy makers both in Brussels and in the capitals of the member states. Brussels, as will become evident in the next chapter, cannot be viewed as having set out to dismantle social solidarity. If anything, the higher degree of economic stability that membership in the Union ensures all of its members is arguably protecting such notions. Proposed solutions to challenges that health care faces occasionally do appear to threaten such notions, but as shown here the pressures for such solutions are not coming from the EU primarily. To the politics behind proposed solutions, I will now turn my attention by focusing on activities in Brussels.

Notes

1. Flora, P., *Growth to Limits: The Western European Welfare State Since World War II,* Walter de Gruyter, New York and Berlin, 1988.
2. Baldwin, P., *The Politics of Social Solidarity,* Cambridge University Press, 1990.
3. Esping-Andersen, G., *The Three Worlds of Welfare Capitalism,* Princeton University Press, Princeton, NJ, 1990.
4. Moran, M., *Death or Transfiguration? The Changing Government of the Health Care State,* European Union Institute Working Paper EUF No 99/15, Badia Fiesolana, Italy, 1999.
5. Saltman, R., and von Otter, C., *Planned Markets and Public Competition: Strategic Reforms in Northern European Health Systems,* Buckingham, Open University Press, 1994.
6. Jacobs, L., "Politics of America's Supply State: Health Reform and Technology," *Health Affairs* 143-157, Fall 1995.
7. Brown, L., "Government and Market in Three Types of Health Care System: The Practical Dialectic of Accommodation," The Mailman School of Public Health at Columbia University, class notes, fall 1998.
8. Friedman, M., "The Role of Government in a Free Society," in *Capitalism and Freedom*, Chicago University Press, Chicago, 1962.
9. For an excellent analysis on the practical shortcomings of this position, see Reinardt, U., *Accountable Health Care: Is It Compatible with Social Solidarity?* Office of Health Economics, London, 1998.
10. The position is flawed, however, if one examines whether health care operates like other markets. As Kenneth Arrow showed in his classic authoritative 1963 essay, health care does not meet the essential conditions of a true market. The largest problem, however, with this approach is not the weak assumption of market compatibility with the health care sector but rather its stronger and more dangerous, since it is rarely stated explicitly, assumption of the underlying income distribution needed for this idea to operate. If, as we know, in a capitalist society income distribution is not only acceptable but desirable, then it follows that individuals will not be endowed with equitable purchasing power. It follows then that such a society would accept price rationing as the mechanism of distributing finite resources. But assuming that health care is not to be rationed based on price, and if the political process or planning can produce a more equitable distribution of resources, then one has to reconsider the market-oriented position or at least make explicitly clear what it means.
11. Quoted in Reinhardt piece (note 9).
12. Ibid.
13. Marx, K., and Engels, F., "Manifesto of the Communist Party," in *The Marx-Engels Reader*, 2nd edition, edited by R. C. Tucker, W. W. Norton & Company, New York, 1978, 469-500.
14. Sweezey, P., "The Radical Theory of the State," in *Problems in Political Economy: An Urban Perspective*, edited by D. Gordon, Lexington Press, Lexington, KY, 1971.

15. If one agrees with Lukats, who viewed historical materialism as the self-realization of capitalism, then the former "communist" countries of the eastern block were anything but communist.
16. Offe, C.,, "The Theory of Capitalist State" in *Political Power and Social Classes*, edited by N. Poulantzas, New Left Books, London, 1978.
17. Socialized medicine, as it will become obvious, is not what its critics in the U.S. oftentimes claim it is, that is the Canadian or British arrangements of health care production and distribution. Rather, the closest model to the ideal of socialized medicine was the model of the former Soviet Union, which neomarxists would claim failed not because of the theoretical basis of the idea, but rather because of the underlying paradox between historical materialism as that was expressed in the former Soviet Union.
18. Max Weber distinguished two forms of rationality. The first, the substantive rationality, deals to the value of desired goals. In terms of substantive rationality, we observe relative agreement between most theoreticians, who agree that both equity and efficiency, both accountability and liberty, both individual caretaking and social cohesion are goals with inherent social value. The second, formal rationality, deals with the political or technical means used to achieve the substantive rational goals. It is from this level that most of the disagreement stems. Whether individuals acting rational can achieve the collective substantively rational goals is open to interpretation.
19. Marshall, T. H., "Citizenship and Social Class," in his *Class, Citizenship and Social Development*, Greenwood Press, Westport, CT, 1973.
20. The concept of pure markets in health care is highly problematic from a number of different perspectives. They are highly complex mechanisms lacking the simplicity and order of bureaucratic planning. They lack the communitarian distributive ethic of state approaches since they are by definition based on the individual and on competition. Left to their own devices, they result in great differentials between the winners and the losers in the market. In the case of health care, these differentials are, to put it simply, massive inequalities that are hard to accept in a liberal democratic state.
21. Tawney, R., *The Radical Tradition*, cited by A. Donabedian in *Aspects of Medical Care Administration*, Harvard University Press, Cambridge, MA, 1973.
22. Kenneth Arrow's chaos theory and rational choice institutionalism in political science are quite relevant readings on this point.
23. Brown, L., "Government and Market in Three Types of Health Care System: The Practical Dialectic of Accommodation."
24. The focus is on Western states, since these are the ones that at this point comprise the Union. Central and Eastern European states are only now beginning to mold their ways after the prominent liberal democratic model of the West, with all the pros and cons that such a transition entails. A related point: states like Spain and Greece experienced a prolonged period of political instability, which did not end until the mid 1970s. This set them on a different path than other continental countries or Great Britain. Whether or not, southern states need to be considered laggards or simply following a different development is open to interpretation. In fact, they exhibit characteristics of both being laggards and on a different path, as the case of Greece will show.
25. Johansen, L. N., "Welfare State Regression in Scandinavia? The Development of Scandinavian Welfare States from 1970 to 1980," in *Comparing Welfare States and Their Futures*, edited by E. Oyen, Hidershot, England, 1986,129-51.

26. Quadagno, J., "Theories of the Welfare State," *Annual Review of Sociology* 13:109-28, 1987.
27. Day, P., and Klein, R., "Britain's Health Care ," *Health Affairs* 10:35-59, 1991.
28. Hurst, J. W., "Reforming Health Care in Seven European Nations," *Health Affairs* 10:13-17, 1991.
29. OECD, *The Welfare State in Crisis*, OECD, Paris, 1981.
30. OECD, *Social Expenditures 1960-1990: Problems of Growth and Control*, OECD, Paris, 1985.
31. Gough, I., *The Political Economy of the Welfare State*, MacMillan Press, London, 1979.
32. Glazer, N., *The Limits of Social Policy*, Harvard University Press, Cambridge, 1988.
33. Murray, C., *Losing Ground: American Social Policy, 1950-1960*, Basic Books, New York, 1984.
34. Moran, M., "Crises of the Welfare State," *British Journal of Political Science*, 1988:397-414.
35. For a brief review of how the whole retrenchment prediction fell short, see Matsaganis M, "Competition Types in Public Health Care Systems," in *The Competition Challenge in the Health Care Sector* (in Greek), edited by J. Kyriopoulos and D. Niakas, Center for Social Research in Health Care, Athens, 1993, and Matsaganis, M., "Quasi Market reforms in Public Health Care Systems." Paper presented at fifth Conference, entitled *Limits and Relations between Public and Private,* Panteion University, Athens, November 23-26, 1994.
36. Godt, P. J., "Confrontation, Consent, and Corporatism: State Strategies and the Medical Profession in France, Great Britain, and West Germany," *Journal of Health Politics, Policy and Law* 12:459-480.
37. Brown, M. K., "Remaking the Welfare State: A Comparative Perspective," in *Remaking the Welfare State: Retrenchment and Social Policy in America and Europe*, edited by M. K. Brown, Temple University Press, Philadelphia, 1988.
38. Ruggie, M., *Realignments in the Welfare State:Health Policy in the U.S., Britain and Canada*, Columbia University Press, New York, 1996.
39. The debate was more or less settled after P. Pierson's book, *Dismantling the Welfare State? Reagan, Thatcher and the Politics of Retrenchment,* Cambridge University Press, 1994. Also relevant is an article: Pierson, P., "Irresible Forces, Immovable Objects: Post-Industrial Welfare States Confront Permanent Austerity," *Journal of European Public Policy* 1998:539-60.
40. A number of OECD reports from the mid-eighties on were indicating exactly this. Read OECD Occasional Paper: "Measuring Health Care 1960-1983, Expenditure, Costs and Performance," OECD Social Policy Studies, Paris, 1985; OECD Occasional Paper: "Measuring Health Care," Paris, 1988; OECD Occasional Paper: „Health Care Systems in Transition: The Search for Efficiency," OECD, Paris, 1990; and OECD Occasional Paper: "Financing and Delivering Health Care: A Comparative Analysis of OECD Countries," OECD Social Policy Studies No. 4, Paris, 1987; OECD Occasional Paper: "New Directions in Health Policy," OECD Social Policy Studies No 7, Paris, 1995.
41. For more discussion on managed competition, look at Enthoven, A., *Health Plan: The Only Practical Solution to the Soaring Cost of Medical Care*, Addison-Wesley, Reading, MA, 1980; Enthoven, A., The 1987 Professor Dr. F. de Vries Lectures. *Theory and Practice of Managed Competition in Health Care Finance*, North Holland Publishing Company, New York, 1988; and

Enthoven, A., and Kronick, R., "A Consumer-Choice Health Plan for the 1990s: Universal Health Insurance in a System Designed to Promote Quality and Economy," *NEJM*, 320:29-37 and 320:94-101, 1989.

42. Enthoven, A. C., "The History and Principles of Managed Competition," *Health Affairs* Supplement 1993:24-47.

43. Schwarz, W. B., "The Inevitable Failure of Current Cost Containment Strategies," *JAMA* 257 (2):220-24, 1987.

2

The Growing Role of Brussels in Health Care: Subsidiarity, Social Protection, and Economic Growth

A number of studies both by academics and in official documents have looked at the issue of health care in the EU.[1] Most accounts of European Union involvement in social policy in general and specifically in health care present a minimalist version of the role that Brussels plays.[2] The health care state is seen mostly as a national state. The focus of such studies has been on direct activities by Brussels in efforts to harmonize, integrate or converge the systems of the member states. By excluding, however, different mechanisms through which Brussels influences health policy regimes, these minimalist versions miss the complete picture and an important political dynamic. For a great number of Eurocrats, on the other hand, Brussels ought to expand its regulatory and legislative roles in as many policy areas as possible. In fact, grandiose schemes of a federal welfare state, built as the traditional welfare states of European liberal democracies, have been contemplated in certain circles. Such schemes ought to be put to rest, at least for the foreseeable future. Brussels does not exhibit the political capacity or the willingness at this juncture to assume responsibility for such an intimidating task. But that is not the whole of the story either, as the title of this chapter indicates. The center of the European multitier structure of governance is indeed present in health care policy making. And even though this presence is not dominant as is the case in other policy arenas, it is growing and is by no means insignificant.

In this chapter, I ask three interrelated questions: (1) Are European integration in general and Brussels, the center, in particular, pushing towards convergence of the individual member states' health care systems? (2) What is the character of such a convergence? (3) What are the ways through which it is being developed? I argue that whereas Brussels is not actively seeking harmonization of health care regimes across the Union and is quite willing to have member states deal with health care, it nevertheless represents a force for convergence through three mechanisms. First, through actions of positive integration, directly targeting the issue of equitable health care access. Such actions are indeed limited. But Brussels also acts in terms of negative integration (imposition of common market criteria through the European Court of Justice) and also through a third type of integration that centers around an ideological convergence among European elites which calls for rationalization of the use of limited health care resources and the maintenance of universal access and thus social solidarity. Brussels is still approaching the issue of health care financing and delivery from a certain distance. Yet, what has been implemented in other areas, especially in terms of the creation of the common market, the birth of the common currency and the new employment strategy, is greatly affecting health care decisions and quite likely will continue to do so increasingly.

Before the argument develops, it would be helpful to discuss the concept of subsidiarity, which shares the subtitle of this chapter with economic growth and social protection. The three concepts together constitute the three fundamental policy constraints on the European level. And since there will be plenty of analysis of the interaction between economic growth and the changing European discourse on social protection, both of which are relatively self-explanatory terms, let me briefly discuss subsidiarity. As a term, it has come to dominate European political discussions not only about social policy but also about all other affairs. Its origins go back to the Catholic social doctrine and it meant that it was a duty of the higher level of government to enable the smaller units to conduct their affairs in social autonomy. The smaller unit would attempt to solve an issue. If successful, then in a sense it was self-governed. If not, then the higher-level government would have to step in. While the Commission probably had a version of subsidiarity like this in mind, in current political discourse, the term has been reinterpreted to mean a preference for the lowest possible level of government and as much freedom in terms of actions as possible. Wolfgang Streeck writes that the term now means "a general presumption of precedence of lower level over higher level governance, and ultimately a principle of laissez-faire with respect to whatever lower units may do."[3] With this understanding of subsidiarity, I return to the main argument of the chapter.

To understand the role of Brussels in health care, one needs to approach it as a role that places a number of new constraints on the national policy preferences that would not have existed otherwise. I begin with a description of European institutions and their respective places in the policy-making process, as these have evolved over the course of European integration. I then explore the constraints that the EU presents through an overview of the involvement of Brussels in issues that deal with health care. I point to three related tensions that continue to exist to date. First, the principle of subsidiarity, one of the cornerstones of EU policy making which, by definition, as we saw always creates tensions between the center and the periphery; second, the tension between what the creation of the common market and the common currency entail and the sovereignty of the national health care regimes; and, third, the tension between not taking active action (allowing integration to proceed through negative integration) and the issue of sustaining health care regimes in member states.

The Evolution of European Institutions: Why the Social Dimension of the Union Did Not Develop Much [4]

When one looks at the EU in the beginning of the twenty-first century, one sees an uneven development in different policy areas. Economic integration has brought the common market and a common currency, a standardization of national policies in areas as diverse as environmental protection and research and development of new technologies. Even in areas outside the direct competence of European institutions, such as foreign and security policy, policing, and others, there has been progress. The social dimension of the European Union, however, at least as social dimension is traditionally understood, is lagging in terms of integration. The obvious question is why. After all, Europeans are quite proud of the social cohesion their societies exhibit. What was it that made the Union evolve down a path where the social dimension has not developed much? The answer lies in the approaches toward European integration and how these approaches have shaped the policy-making process at the central level, creating what many analysts have called a variable geometry between European institutions. Through a tug of war between federalists and intergovernmentalists, the Union institutions have balanced in different places depending on the policy arena. And in terms of creating a social dimension, they have balanced in a minimal action place. A brief historical review of this tug of war is indicative.

Today, the most powerful institution of the European Union is the European Council, which is held every six months and brings together the president of the Commission and the heads of government from the 15 member states.[5] This is where issues of high politics, like enlargement to the east and institutional reform, are decided. On a day-to-day basis, however, there are five union institutions that constitute the backbone of the central governance in the EU: the Commission, the Council, the European Court of Justice, the European Parliament, and the European Court of Auditors.[6] For our purposes, only the first four are relevant. The Commission is composed of twenty commissioners who make collective decisions. It is the closest to the executive branch of the EU governance structure since it has the right to initiate policy proposals. In other words, if the Commission does not bring up a proposal for discussion in the Council, the Council cannot act. Furthermore, the Commission is charged with ensuring member state compliance with the *acquis communitaire*, the existing union legislation. The council of ministers differs depending on the arena discussed. Thus, it is composed of the fifteen ministers responsible for the given topic of discussion. Depending on the subject, the Council decides either by qualified majority or unanimity. It is an intergovernmental body where member states debate and negotiate community legislation.[7] The Parliament is the democratic expression of the general will of the European people (at least in theory). A large debate about the democratic deficit that exists in the operations of the Union and the powers that the Parliament enjoys are at the center of it. Its basic functions are, in the first instance, to legislate and approve the budget and, in the second instance, to provide checks and balances for the executive branch of government. There are 626 members of Parliament (MEPs) allocated to each member state according to its population size. Finally, the European Court of Justice (ECJ) is charged with interpreting the treaties and the legislation based on them. It is composed of fifteen judges, one from each member state, and has provided much of the momentum for European integration through its decisions, since whereas political calculations may hamper progress in the Council or in different intergovernmental conferences, the ECJ has to act when a case is before it. The ECJ has played an important role in the expansionary role of Brussels in health care as we will see later in the chapter. The institutions of the Union are the historical legacy of the integration process as this has been experienced in the past fifty years and can only be adequately understood in this fashion. In this sense, their interrelationships and their relative powers reflect the tension in terms of how much authority would be given to Brussels. The approach to European integration has shifted often and this is indicative of the current institutional framework.

The idea of a united Europe, in fact a "United States of Europe," has been around for a long time. As early as 1923, during the aftermath of World War I, the Austrian Count Koudenhove-Kalergi founded a movement known as the Pan-Europa movement. Despite the fact that by the end of the 1920s, Pan-Europa contained prominent political figures, academics, journalists, lawyers and others, it had not been successful in winning the support of the European public which remained quite tied to the idea of national sovereignty.[8] The second world war, however, proved to be the catalyst for the idea of a European federation to return. Throughout Europe and as early as 1939 and especially within the resistance circles of all countries, literature was circulated calling for a European federation, which would shelter the continent from another war. Characteristic of such literature is the 1941 Ventonete Manifesto by Italian resistance leader Altiero Spinelli, who, in 1943, founded the Movimento Federalista Europeo. Spinelli was one of the most influential Europeans in winning support for the federal idea after the war.

But his movement was not the only one. By 1946 there was a plethora of organizations that supported the idea of a united Europe. There were the Union of European Federalists, the International Committee for a Socialist United States of Europe, the United Europe movement, the European Parliamentary Union and many more. Each one of these movements had its own version of what a united Europe ought to look like. The lines between federalists and intergovernmentalists were drawn as early as 1948 and today's European Union is very much the evolution of decisions taken during this debate. In May of 1948, 713 delegates from thirteen European nations gathered to discuss the uniting of Europe. In the European Congress in The Hague, as the convention is known, two groups emerged as the most influential ones: the federalist European Union of Federalists and the more moderate confederalist United Europe Movement.[9] In the event an odd compromise was struck in terms of the communiqué that was presented, which was to be indicative of future negotiations about the institutional formation of Europe. It called for the creation of, "a United Europe throughout whose area the free movement of persons, ideas and goods is restored...a Court of Justice, ...and a European Assembly where the live forces of all our nations shall be represented."[10] By October, the European Movement was established and charged with the design and implementation of what the Congress had called for. In this movement, the federalists (Italians, Belgians and French) came once again face to face with the intergovernmentalists (the British and most of the Scandinavians), a scenario that has for the greater part continued to date. The latter group came out on top. The fluidity of the sociopolitical environment in Europe after the war could have allowed for the adoption of a radical departure such as the creation of a European federation. But national sentiment and the strong hold on power that nation-states had developed over the previous two centuries were not easy obstacles to overcome.[11] The Council of Europe, which came out of these negotiations in May of 1949, was an international forum for sovereign national state cooperation in the Committee of Ministers and between the national parliaments in the Consultative Assembly. A last attempt by radical federalists in 1952 to create a supranational form of governance through the creation of a common European Defense Community (EDC) failed after the French National Assembly refused to ratify the Pleven plan, even though the idea of the EDC was a French one.

This marked the turning point in the debate of the future of Europe. In the federalist camp, which was by no means dead, pragmatic federalists like Jean Monnet and Robert Schuman (French Planning Commissariat and Foreign Minister, respectively) took over. In their view, the head-on approach by radical federalists did not work exactly because it was too radical. Small, incremental steps would, in their mind, lead to a federal Europe in the long run. In the words of Jean Monnet, "we believed in starting with limited achievements, establishing a de facto solidarity from which a federation would gradually emerge. I have never believed that one fine day Europe would be created by some great political mutation.... The pragmatic method we had adopted would...lead to a federation validated by the people's vote, but that federation would be the culmination of an existing economic and political reality."[12] Based on this approach, Jean Monnet requested that Robert Schuman come up with a plan for the integration of European sectors of the economy that would be less contentious than the high passion areas of foreign policy or common defense.

Accordingly, Schuman came up in April of 1950 with the Schuman plan, which was presented to the French as a plan to control the growing heavy industries of Germany which, if left unchecked, could lead to another conflict. They proposed that the French and German industries in the production of coal and steel should be united under a common authority of supranational nature, the High Authority (which was to serve as the precursor for the Commission). This authority would oversee the creation of a common market for coal and steel. The French bought it and proposed it themselves to other interested European nations.[13]

In April 1951, in Paris, the European Coal and Steel Community was being formed with six members, France, West Germany, Italy, and the Benelux countries (Belgium, the Netherlands and Luxembourg). Schuman, realizing that there would be a good deal of resistance to a completely federal version of the ECSC, which would likely lead to the defeat of the whole plan, proposed an institutional framework that not only allowed for great member state representation but also for individual state protection through the veto powers allocated to each state. More specifically, five institutions were created, many of which served as the precursors for today's institutions. There was, as mentioned, the High Authority, a seventy-eight member Common Assembly (a prototype for the European Parliament), a Court of Justice (later developed into the ECJ), a Special Council of Ministers (today known as the Council of Ministers), and a Consultative Committee (which today serves as an advisory body known as the Economic and Social Committee).[14] According to the Schuman plan, the High Authority would be a supranational institution so that it could be independent of national interests and serve as the creator of pan-European policies.

To satisfy opposition by smaller states, however, the ECSC treaty also assigned executive power to the Council of Ministers.[15] By 1957, two new treaties were signed with the same signatories, this time in Rome. The first was the EURATOM treaty that pooled European resources in the sector of nuclear energy production, just like the ECSC had done for coal and steel. In fact, in the EURATOM treaty text, it was the first time that there was a special chapter dedicated to health and safety concerns (Articles 30-39). In other words, the legal basis for laying down standards for the protection of health against dangers from ionizing radiation had been established. Despite this chapter and the first mention of health, not much has been done with these articles. The second treaty came out of a proposal by the Benelux countries that had created a customs union as early as 1944. This proposal called for the creation of the European Economic Community and became the EEC treaty and became much more influential, also in terms of health. It differed from the previous two, in the fact that it did not deal with a specific sector of the economy but rather aimed to create a European customs union and a common market. It quickly became the most significant of the three original treaties. Furthermore, its integrative impact is significant in that it expanded the competencies of transnational institutions in areas like agriculture, competition policy and transport, since they were deemed essential in the creation of the economic community. Tremendously important also is that according to the EEC, a social fund (Articles 123-128) and an investment bank (Articles 129-130) were created to facilitate economic development. Their policies were to be financed by a community budget, which was envisioned eventually to have its own income.

A supranational state was in the making, very much like Schuman and Monnet and functionalists scholars had described. In terms of allowing for the creation of a social dimension, the treaty of Rome was silent. It is not difficult to understand why. Political actors in this arena, political elites, unions, employers and others considered the national state as their natural environment for action. It was in this terrain that the different interests would fight and earn equitable patterns of redistribution between them. The EC was viewed as a mechanism that would help such a development, but it was not thought of as a mechanism that could exceed it. It is also important to mention that it is about this time that the national welfare states were being built after the war and they were being tied to national reconstruction. Furthermore, and for a considerable number of years, the state arrangements were able to produce more and better services. In a sense, there was no reason to look elsewhere for a social dimension. It is not therefore that Schuman and Monnet and the other architects of the treaty did not care about the social dimension of the Union, but they thought that such kind of policies ought to be better left at member state level and in the heart of national sovereignty. And as the European Community began to grow so did a number of diverse regimes for social cohesion.

In 1958, the election of General Charles de Gaulle to the presidency of France was to be a turning point in European integration. In the years between 1957 and 1965, an active European Economic Commission, under the leadership of German federalist, Walter Hallstein, was aiming at becoming a true European executive with technocratic capacity that would put the European interest first.[16] In 1965, de Gaulle put a stop to this momentum by not appearing and not sending French representation to community functions between July and December 1965, the famous empty chair crisis. De Gaulle's ideas about European integration were quite different than the federalist notions of the people in charge of the process up to that point. In fact, he had made them public four years earlier when he declared that "there is and can be no Europe other than a Europe of States—except of course a Europe of myths, fictions and pageants."[17] The empty chair crisis came about as a result of French opposition to a number of proposals by Hallstein and his associates, but most critically the ones that would introduce majority voting in the Council of Ministers and grant extensive budgetary powers to the Parliament. De Gaulle viewed both such proposals as undermining French sovereignty and was prepared to pull out of European discussions altogether. The crisis finally came to an end in 1966 in Luxembourg through the Luxembourg compromise, but not before the institutional power was moved from the Commission to the Council of Ministers. The document that came out of Luxembourg did, however, preserve the Commission's right to initiate policy. But in terms of majority voting in the Council, it stated: "[where] issues very important to one or more member countries are at stake, ministers will seek to reach solutions with which all can be comfortable." Any individual state was still able to veto legislation if it did not coincide with its national interest, an intergovernmentalist approach which in the first instance meant that negotiations would always lead at best to the lowest common denominator and, in turn, in the second instance hampered the speed of the integration process. In such a climate, it is no wonder that the creation of a social dimension was not discussed. Furthermore, the national arrangements were still growing and people were quite satisfied with them.

Between the empty chair crisis and the next major development in the high politics of European integration, the signing of the Single European Act in 1986, intergovernmentalism was the norm of how the integration proceeded. Couple that with the oil crisis of the 1970s, the subsequent overall unfavorable economic context, and the enlargement of the Union to include six more states (Great Britain, Ireland and Denmark joined in 1973, Greece in 1981, and Spain with Portugal in 1985), it was commonly thought that the process had moved dramatically away from the federal ideals of Monnet and Schuman. But during this period, a number of developments occurred that set the basis for yet another shift in the momentum of European integration.[18] Without being exhaustive, the following list is indicative:

- The direct elections of the European Parliament that were introduced in 1979 brought the Union closer to the average European citizen. This has not resolved the "democratic deficit" of the Union even to date, but nevertheless sustained a certain degree of momentum for the European integration.
- The creation of the European Political Cooperation (EPC) structure, which brings together foreign ministers to discuss foreign affairs, was an intergovernmentalist approach, but it nevertheless reintroduced the topic of a common foreign defense.
- The introduction of increased budgetary powers for the Parliament in 1970 and 1975 shifted some of the power away from the intergovernmental Council of Ministers and allowed the Parliament to lobby for increased legislative power.
- The gatherings by heads of state every six months was also essential in this process (another intergovernmental development), since it placed leaders in an international forum where issues and challenges were discussed and ideas for tackling problems shared.
- In low politics areas, decisions that had already been taken allowed Brussels to continue more or less unaffected to process policy. Integration was indeed occurring. In fact, the Commission's efficiency (number of proposals sent to the Council) and its effectiveness (rate of success of these proposals) rose steadily during this period as a number of studies have shown.
- Furthermore, the Commission was quietly able to expand the issues in which it had competency. Environment and regional development are only two examples of this increase in issue density which, in fact, is quite consistent with the neofunctionalist notion of spillover.
- The external economic factors (oil crises, etc.) were prohibiting any ideas of federalization, but at the same time were insuring that member states would have to stay closely aligned to face common economic constraints.

During this period, it was becoming increasingly evident that intergovernmentalism was allowing cooperation in areas where national interests converge. And, in fact, a number of initiatives in terms of broader social policy were thought of during this period. But whereas greater ambitions for Europe once again began to emerge, the overall economic context was changing for the worse and once again states decided to maintain their own social protection regimes rather than look at Brussels. Further, the treaty obstacles remained intact, and there was not much room for political maneuvering that might have resulted in a radically different outcome. Still, social concerns were not to be put off indefinitely. Economic stability and economic growth were, however, the only obvious areas of converging national interests. The Monnet method of economic integration, therefore, did not lose its power. In fact, by having been locked in the earlier decisions, European heads of government had little choice than to continue forward. This meant the creation of the common market for removal of trade barriers and the introduction of a common currency for monetary stability.

That is what the Single European Act accomplished. Among other things, it firmly committed the twelve member states to establish a common market (the Single European Market) by January 1993 and also to form an Economic and Monetary Union through the creation of a common currency at a relatively close date. The SEA was the first major review of the Community treaties. It called for closer cooperation in environmental protection and on research and development. It formalized political cooperation through the European Council and the EPC. Perhaps, the most important changes that the SEA made, however, were the changes that dealt with the institutional operations of the Union. The SEA introduced for the first time, qualified majority voting (QMV)[19] in the Council of Ministers and the cooperation procedure in the legislative process between the Parliament and the Council. Under this cooperation procedure, the Parliament is authorized to improve a draft law by amending it. The process requires two readings by the Parliament, which allow members of the Parliament to read and alter both the original Commission proposal and the Council's preliminary position on that proposal. Even though the cooperation procedure is not applicable in all policy areas, it is nevertheless essential because it elevated the Parliament to a higher level in the legislative process and, in turn, balanced the power between the Council and the Parliament.

As mentioned in the introduction, intergovernmentalist theorists explained the SEA through the notions of national interests and a series of bargaining between the member states and especially the larger ones. In sum, what most of these accounts emphasized was the convergence of national economic interests (especially those of Germany, France and England) in the 1980s. And indeed such convergence had occurred. But that is not the whole of the story, because then one would have expected to see agreement on the single market project, but little action on issues of social cohesion (through the regional development fund), even less in terms of environmental protection and none at all in terms of institutional reform. The necessary trade-offs between governments simply fail to capture the totality of this story. And of course, they fail to ask why countries were willing to trade-off preferences to begin with.

Part of this answer lies with the increased international competition as globalization began to accelerate. In this sense, European states saw the SEM project as a form of improved protection from external economic threats. Furthermore, as interdependence theory reminds us, there were non-state actors involved in placing the single market on the political agenda and lobbying hard for it.[20] Multinational businesses and financial groups that stood to gain much from the removal of barriers were strong advocates of European action at this time. In the meantime, the Parliament was lobbying for institutional reform to cover the democratic deficit of the EU and to increase its powers in the process. The Italian MEP and one of the original federalists in Europe, Altiero Spinneli, had formed since 1980 a group called the Crocodile Club that drew up the draft treaty on the European Union which was accepted by Parliament in 1984. It formed the basis of the intergovernmental negotiations that led to the SEA. Furthermore, an active commission under the leadership of Jacques Delors was able to link during the negotiations the single market project with issues like social regulation, institutional reform and economic cohesion.[21] The SEA was a product of both intense intergovernmental negotiations but also of a number of interconnected developments that had begun earlier and that culminated in the passage of the SEA. More relevantly, it signals a change in the strict intergovernmental interpretation of the EU. It places the focus not only at national interest but also at development in Brussels. Finally, it set the path for closer and closer cooperation, if not straight transfer of national sovereignty to Brussels in a number of areas that the leaders in the intergovernmental conference that led to the SEA probably did not think of.

The momentum from the SEA carried over into the next major treaty reform, the 1991 Treaty on European Union, or as it is better known the Maastricht treaty. In the years between the SEA and the Maastricht treaty, European states and Brussels' technocrats were busy integrating in areas of low politics, standardizing regulations, harmonizing approaches, removing trade barriers. In great neofunctionalist tradition, the Commission was also busy pushing for quick steps for what it considered an essential corollary of the single market, the economic and monetary union. By 1988, Delors was able to get Council approval to establish an advisory body that would draw up the proposals for EMU.[22] It was chaired by himself and as members it had the heads of the twelve central banks. In 1989, this committee recommended the adoption of a common currency. A new intergovernmental conference (IGC) was called to discuss EMU. Around the same time, however, the Soviet Union was collapsing, a number of eastern countries (formerly in the communist block) were proclaiming their willingness to join the Western world, and Germany was once again reunified after its defeat in World War II. Uncertainties loomed on the horizon in terms of European security both from within (French concerns about the new Germany) and outside (what did the end of the cold war mean for European security?). All these and many more issues forced yet another IGC at the suggestion of French President Francois Mitterrand and German Chancellor Helmut Kohl, which led to the Maastricht treaty in 1991.

During this same period, the years between the SEA and the Maastricht treaty, the Commission was also busy in terms of its attempt to create this social dimension of Europe. Through the social charter, a number of directives, regulations and non-binding opinions it kept the dialogue alive. The results, of course, were modest because the obstacles to such developments were still present. But realizing that any social dimension for the Union would have to come through demands at the European level and having being enabled by Article 118b of the SEA, which states that "the Commission shall endeavour to develop the dialogue between management and labour at European level," the Delors commission was trying to strengthen ETUC (European Trade Union Confederation), the workers' unions' representative in Brussels.[23] ETUC was a resource-poor organization that was constantly outmaneuvered by the employer's UNICE (Union of Industrial and Employers Confederations of Europe). The Commission enabled ETUC through research and training funding to improve its methods and in the process to be taken more seriously both by UNICE and by national unions. Finally, it allowed privileged access to ETUC which made its voice increasingly heard. Arguably, the subsequent interest of EU in broad matters of social policy starting with the Maastricht treaty (The Social Protocol signed by eleven member states; all except Britain) and increasingly until today (the most prominent example has been the Employment Summit in Lisbon in March 2000) was a result of the Delors Commission's political entrepreneurship. However, there was little taste for discussing the core areas of welfare provision such as health care. Despite the arguments at the time about the retrenchment of the welfare state, the emergence of a neoliberal economic orthodoxy and an actual loss of further welfare expansion at the member-state level, the national welfare states that had preempted these policy areas were surviving. And in the words of George Ross, "there was not much for the EC to fix in the core welfare-state areas, even if it had been possible for Europe to act at all."[24]

The Maastricht treaty created a three-pillar structure by joining the three original treaties in the first pillar, under the title Community Domain, and by creating two more pillars, one for the construction of a common foreign and security policy and one for cooperation in matters of justice and home affairs (immigration, policing, etc.). Whereas the first one fell under the leadership of supranational institutions, the other two were purely intergovernmental mechanisms. In this way, a high degree of integration existed in issues that fell under the first pillar, but issues that were quite sensitive to the idea of national sovereignty remained in the domain of the member states. Within the first pillar, however, QMV was extended to a certain extent but did not become generalized as the Commission had wished. A new legislative procedure, co-decision, was introduced for a number of issues like free movement within the Union and other Single Market ones. This procedure provides for real sharing of decision making between the Parliament and the Council of Ministers. A committee made up of members of the Council, the Parliament and the Commission drafts a joint text that the Parliament and the Council can then adopt. But either one can reject the proposal outright, thus elevating yet again the role of the parliament. Three more points came out of Maastricht. Maastricht established strict fiscal criteria for member states that wished to join the common currency, the euro, by 1999. Moreover, it extended community competency in areas like education, social policy, public health, consumer protection and others, in a neofunctionalist form. On the other hand and in an intergovernmentalist fashion, it affirmed the principle of subsidiarity, restricting community actions to matters where the objectives cannot be sufficiently achieved by the member states. Finally, for the first time an opt out mechanism was devised for the UK and Denmark. According to such a mechanism, these two states could opt out of EMU (the UK out of the social protocol, as well). The significance of this is that it plants seeds for variable development of a more flexible approach to European integration, where a core group of countries could move further than others. Proposals by German foreign minister Joschka Fischer and other European leaders in early 2000 underlied exactly this development. Whereas most accounts of the Treaty on European Union (TEU) approach it as a common denominator agreement, in retrospect the truth lies in the eye of the beholder. Political integration was once again avoided and the word federalism is nowhere to be found in the releases from the IGC or in the treaty itself. Nevertheless, for the first time, states were committed to firm dates for the convergence of their economies and the introduction of the euro. They also committed themselves to at least cooperate in matters that earlier fell completely under the national state umbrella, like foreign policy, policing and social policy. From a 1992 perspective it is not hard to understand why it seemed like the intergovernmmentalist approach (in its stronger French version or its weaker British one) carried the day over the federalist (German, Italian, Beneluxian) one, but in retrospect one has to admit that the integration process moved further forward and it underlined the fact that when states find themselves locked in decisions taken earlier, they could only move forward, albeit with slow steps, that give the impression of intergovernmental victories. From the longer macro-historical perspective, however, the Maastricht treaty brought agreement on the timetable for EMU, partially rebalanced the institutions of the Union towards a more democratic model, further extended the issues that the Community dealt with, introduced a notion of European citizenship, and established an institutional framework for cooperation in a number of additional areas.

The subsequent troubles in terms of ratification of the treaty in a number of states as well as the issue of enlargement to the east brought Europe face to face with some difficult questions. How "European" did people want to be? What did it mean to be "European"? Where are the geographic limits of Europe? In what fashion should integration proceed? In a sense, it was the success of the integration project to that point that was raising such questions. The EU was now touching the lives of Europeans more directly than ever before and that created uncertainty. All these questions had to be answered and had to be answered relatively quickly. A new IGC was called and it resulted in the treaty of Amsterdam. The IGC lasted between March 1996 and June 1997. The Amsterdam treaty admittedly was unable to resolve the major tensions that exist. It pushed resolution of issues like institutional reform and enlargement into the future since no acceptable solution could be found and a new IGC was considered essential for such matters. What little did come out of the Amsterdam treaty was that it extended co-decision in many more areas, thus increasing Parliament's influence and continuing the trend that previous treaties had begun. It also gave more powers to the president of the Commission, who would be able from that point on to choose his commissioners (in consultation with heads of government from the member states). Still, the Commission would have to be approved by Parliament. Interestingly enough, there was some progress made in the two intergovernmental pillars of the Union, since the position of the EU representative for foreign policy was created and a number of agreements ranging from immigration and visa policies to combating drugs and terrorism were made. A development of potentially tremendous importance during the IGC that led to the Amsterdam treaty, however, was that the issue of unemployment came formally on the agenda and has remained there. As may be easily understood, the structure of the labor market is directly linked to core welfare areas and future developments from this string of action will be interesting. Nevertheless, the treaty of Amsterdam brought overall only marginal changes to the framework of the EU integration process. At the same time, however, it did not distort the balance and the trends that had been followed so far. If anything, it progressed integration even if that happened in an extremely slow fashion. The most recent treaty revision, that of Nice in 2000, also did not live up to the expectations observers had beforehand.

Nevertheless, certain key decisions for the future institutional framework of the Union were made. Because of enlargement (the first wave of countries is expected to join by the end of 2003), the representation of the states in the parliament and in the commission was altered. In the large picture, however, the Union did not become more "democratic" and that will likely increase the degree of difficulty of bringing social issues on the agenda.

Where does all this leave the Union institutions and the formulation of policy on a day-to-day basis? As it has become clear, the relationship of the central institutions need to be understood through the tug of war of the future of Europe. Over the past fifty years, different models have been utilized and on the whole the process has moved forward with a remarkable neofunctionalist twist but also with tremendous intergovernmental control. The broader the definition of social dimension one employs, the more involved the EU appears to be. In fact, it appears that through time it is slowly moving closer and closer to core welfare state areas, even though this movement may not be through direct regulation by Brussels. The tug of war between member-state control and Brussels' control of the integration process that was examined also constrains and forms central policy in a number of issues, including our focus, health care access, either directly or indirectly.

Constraints by Central Action in Health Care

As it becomes quite obvious from the earlier discussion, there are a number of obstacles to the active creation of a European social dimension. I contend, however, that Brussels still serves as a force for the convergence of health policy regimes through either a process of negative integration or through an ideological convergence that has occurred. Both these processes as well as the limited actions in terms of positive integration are pushing towards the creation of a common social dimension. In later chapters, we will see the responses to these forces by member states, which remain the dominant actors in these arenas, but it would be invalid not to discuss the expanding role of Brussels in this area as well. Here I examine all three of these processes, positive, negative and ideological integration in turn, in order to show that there are a number of constraints on member-state policies present through actions at central policy making level.

Positive Integration

Any discussion of positive integration in health care policy in the European Union needs as a starting point a brief reminder of how explicit policy initiatives take place in the complicated Brussels environment. Based on the European Treaties, the Commission, which has the sole right for initiating policy, is only allowed to do so in areas that are already covered by these treaties. Furthermore, the Commission is not very likely to propose a policy when it knows beforehand that it will most likely be rejected by the member states. An aggressive agenda, even assuming it were something to wish for, in this area is not likely to be successful. In the area of health care the treaties and the intergovernmental context of decision making make it extremely hard for the Commission, no matter how willing it might be, to bring up any proposals with reasonable chances of success. For starters, the treaties do not allow much action in social policy in general and explicitly prohibit harmonization of health policy regimes. Moreover, the way that EU institutional decision making works, it is much easier to block reforms than to agree on something.

Furthermore, the position of a significant number of member states (Sweden, Denmark, the UK) has been complete refusal to discuss these topics. The conflicts of interests that exist between the different member states more often than not lead to sustaining non-actions rather than positive action. And the one area that states seem to agree upon is that social policy ought to remain in their competency. Welfare regimes serve as a major source of legitimacy of the nation state. To lose authority over these regimes can spell major trouble for the institutions of the member states. As a result, the existing legal base for action by Brussels is quite limited. Whereas the treaty does call for increased cooperation and, as we will see, the Commission has tried to exploit this, the treaty also prohibits explicitly any harmonization of health care systems under Article 129. And as we saw in the earlier section of the chapter, the evolution of the integration process allows very small market-oriented windows of opportunity for the Commission to take action. And even there, notorious struggles exist in terms of how much latitude the Commission has in terms of bringing up proposals under either Article 100a, which covers competition distortions, or under the exception that the SEA made in terms of health and safety. Moreover, the EU budget is an extremely small one and must by law be balanced, which does not leave much room for resources in areas of traditional welfare.[25]

Finally, one observes a change in the social democratic forces or in the parties of the left, to put it more generally. Tony Blair's speech in the World Economic Forum in Switzerland is indicative. He asked, "Does Europe continue with the old social model, that has an attitude to social legislation and welfare often rooted in the 60s and 70s or does it recognize that the new economy demands a re-direction of European economic policy for the future?"[26] And it is not only Britain's liberal ideology that prompts such comments. Whereas the great majority of European states were by 1994 governed by center left parties or coalitions, the policies adopted reminded one very little of the old social democrats.[27] And as of mid-2002, with the center right regaining strength, it seems unlikely that health care will be on the agenda in the near future.

There is one area of legislation, however, that may have considerable effects on health care insurance even though something like this has not occurred to date. Health insurance, especially private one, is considered to be a market just like any other. In this sense, insurance carriers that meet the establishment criteria of a member state can set up shop in all other member states. In principle that should not affect social cohesion since private insurance is supplementary insurance. Assuming, however, for argument's sake that European states were to move to a regulated competition health insurance quasi-market, then an incompatibility between competition and social solidarity exists. Based on the principle of equivalence, insurance carriers have to at least break even in their contracts, which automatically means that they will search for better risks. If insurance were to move to the private sector, then a policy framework to ensure social solidarity would be necessary. A set of risk-adjusted premium subsidies (assuming that the risk adjustment techniques are improved) or certain restrictions on free competition may well be in order. But that would be something for member states to decide. In terms of Brussels, health insurance is considered either private or social. In the former case the regulatory framework that applies is that of the directives on non-life insurance. The latter case is exempt from such directives and subject to regulation 1408/71 which will be discussed shortly. But even if states were to move more towards private insurance carriers, Article 54 of the third directive by the Union on non-life insurance (EC-directive 92-49) creates a possibility that certain restrictions on competition are enforced if private insurance serves as either a partial or a complete substitute for social insurance. The degree of competition that would be allowed in such a scenario would of course depend on the willingness of each member state to allow its system to move to such a direction. It is critical, however, to point out that current legislation by Brussels allows the possibility to bridge insurance competition and social solidarity, always of course considering the needs of each member state.

Notwithstanding all these, however, there is an inherent tension in the building of the common market and state sovereignty in health care and, as we see in the next section, the Commission has been able to exploit it and the Court has been willing to highlight it.

Negative Integration

Arguably much more has been accomplished through the slow and quiet accumulation of case law by the European Court of Justice in terms of convergence of health care systems than through the active policy making of Brussels. Member states have been accustomed to limit the benefits of their systems to their own citizens, an ability called control of beneficiaries. They have also been used to not having to deal with providing services outside their borders, the spatial control based on territoriality. Furthermore, member states have traditionally been able to subsidize certain providers of services, something which may be in contrast with common market rules. These are only but a few issues that the common market integration process has raised for national health services regimes.

To look at them a bit closer, we must first examine the basis of the conflict. Based on the treaties, the Commission has been able to push through legislation that directly influences the issue of health protection in connection with the free movement of persons and workers.[28] Since the beginning of the EEC, the founders realized that if the common market were to work, free movement of workers (both employed and self-employed) had to somehow occur. But to realize such cross-border movement, the social security rights, including health care protection, of these people had to be protected. This was the logic behind Article 51 of the EEC treaty, which states that "The Council shall, acting unanimously on a proposal from the Commission adopt such measures in the field of social security as are necessary to provide freedom of movement of workers; to this end, it shall make arrangements to secure for migrant workers and their dependants:

a. aggregation, for the purpose of acquiring and retaining the right to benefit and of calculating the amount of benefit, of all periods taken into account under the laws of the several countries;
b. payment of benefit to persons resident in the territories of member states."

What Article 51 does is to connect these rights with the person rather than with a given territory.[29] In so doing, it is not altering the systems of provision and financing of the different member states. It rather coordinates them so that the end of protecting the rights of workers can be protected. It is important to stress here that these regulations do not govern private health insurance schemes that are subject to different insurance regulations.

Thus, according to Article 51, the Council has adopted measures in this field in order to protect these rights. The first such measures were EEC regulations 3/58 and 4/58. They were replaced by EC regulations 1408/71 and 574/72 and subsequent amendments to these two.[30] They insure that migrant workers can enjoy their social security rights in general and health security rights in particular. Article 22 of regulation 1408/71 states: "1. A worker who satisfies the conditions of the legislation of the competent state for entitlement to benefits, taking account where appropriate of the provisions of Article 18, and: (a) whose condition necessitates immediate benefits during a stay in the territory of another member state...shall be entitled (I) to benefits in kind provided on behalf of the competent institution by the institution of the place of stay or residence in accordance with the legislation which it administers, as though he were insured with it; the length of the period during which benefits are provided shall be governed however by the legislation of the competent state; (II) to cash benefits provided by the competent institution in accordance with the legislation which it administers. However, by agreement between the competent institution and the institution of the place of residence, such benefits may be provided by the latter institution on behalf of the former, in accordance with the legislation of the competent state."[31] They coordinate member-state legislation concerning parts of social security.[32] The basic principle is that a person shall be subject to the legislation of the member state where he works (even if he resides in a different member state). In the court case *Duphar vs. the Netherlands (case 238/82)*, the Court made clear that the EC treaty does not infringe on the competence of the member states to organize their respective systems.[33] According to regulation 1408/71, these benefits also apply to members of the family. Members of the family are defined as "any person defined or recognized as a member of the family or designated as a member of the household by the legislation under which benefits are provided, or in the cases referred to in Article 22 and Article 39, by the legislation of the member state in whose territory such person resides; where, however, the said legislations regard as a member of the family or a member of the household only a person living under the same roof as the worker, this condition shall be considered satisfied if the person in question is mainly dependent on that worker." Of course all these apply to workers and their families only. Free movement of people theoretically also covers patients.

Member states have, however, been much slower in removing barriers to the movement of people than they have in removing barriers for capital, goods and services. Article 7a of the EC defines the internal market as an area without internal frontiers in which the free movement of goods, persons (not just workers), services and capital is guaranteed. This guarantee is further elaborated by Article 100a which deals with the approximation of laws where the Council (through QMV) and the Parliament decide together. Even though this article refers to Article 7a, it specifically excludes the provisions in the second paragraph of that article that deal with the free movement of persons. Thus, QMV is not the preferred decision mechanism for people movement, even as it is for the free movement of services, capital and goods. Notwithstanding all this, one could use the old Article 100c, which does, however, require unanimity. All this is indicative of the reasons why there has been slow progress in fully abolishing border controls within the EU.[34] Even assuming free movement of persons, it is hard to know what that would mean for the movement of patients. The health care systems will at least in the short and medium term remain the responsibility of member states. But such a situation begs the question of how an administrator can control expenses and quality, redistribution and remuneration mechanisms, when he cannot control the population and the territory to be served. This is something that will have to be dealt with.

And such cross-border care already exists, albeit its numbers and its relative expenditures as percentage of total health expenditures in the EU are relatively small.[35] Regulation 2793/81, which amends Article 22 of regulation 1408/71 provides the legal framework for this kind of care. It lays down that a national social or health insurance authority may not refuse to permit a patient to seek treatment in another member state if, with regard to the current state of health of the patient, the necessary treatment cannot be delivered in time in the patient's own country. However, even in such cases there are conditions. First, the national system must grant permission. Second, the benefit for which payment will be provided must also be in the benefits of the patient's own country. Third, the patient must fill the E 112 form. People who travel and find themselves in need of acute medical care in a different member state are exempt however. But even then, they are supposed to have with them a form (E 111) so that the claim can be processed.

So cross-border care, defined as care rendered in one state, while the patient is insured in a different state or belongs to a different national health service, has three categories: (a) health care for cross-border workers, (b) health care preauthorized by the insurer of the state of origin, and (c) emergency services related to acute treatment for tourists, for example. As it becomes quite obvious, it is based on the notion of free movement of people.

The European Court of Justice in a number of cases over the course of time has actively endorsed cross-border movement and in so doing it has highlighted the tension between national control of health care regimes and free movement of patients.[36] In the *Royer case* (48/75), the Court observed that no discrimination can occur on the basis of nationality. In *Costa vs Enel* (case 6/64) and *Amministratione delle Finanzo delo Stato vs. Simmental* (case 106/67), the Court held that European treaty provisions and legislation that flows from that take precedence over national legislation. In *Levin vs. Staatssecretaris van Justitie* (case 53/81), the Court defined the word worker since that had not been defined by Article 48 of the treaty. The Court declared that the word worker has Community law content, rejecting the Dutch and Danish positions that national criteria ought to apply. Such criteria had to do with number of hours worked, minimum wage, etc. The importance of this last ruling is that it suggests minimum standards of protection for Europeans. It opens the door for future legislation and it also precludes divergent interpretations for the right to health care of different workers. The Court, considered by many an activist institution that always looks to expand its role, went even further by ruling in *Kempf vs. Staatssecretaris von Justitie* (case 139/85), that the status of the worker cannot be denied because payment is below the minimum national subsistence levels. In so doing, it includes not only workers in the traditional sense of the word but all people, allowing for cross-border care by tourists and marking a decisive step towards free movement of patients. To have true free movement of patients, however, all bureaucratic red tape should be abolished. The Court again took the lead and by ruling in two cases that national preauthorization rules were out of order in those two cases, it has set legal precedent for seeking care without prior authorization. That is one interpretation of the court's rulings. The two cases, *Decker N. vs Caisse de Maladie des employes prives* (case C120/95) and *Kohll R. vs. Union des Caisses de Maladie* (case 158/96), deserve a separate analysis since the rulings that came back on April 29, 1998 caused a stir in health policy circles in Brussels and member-state capitals.[37] *The Kohll and Decker Rulings.*[38] The two rulings that the Court handed down in 1998 are arguably two of the most important rulings in this area. A complete legal analysis of the two cases is beyond the scope of this study. What is offered here, however, is a discussion of the implications of the two rulings in terms of the sovereignty of the member state health care systems, their ability to organize, finance and administer care and especially their ability to preauthorize cross-border care. Some observers were surprised by the two rulings but with the advantage of retrospect, what is surprising is that it took this long before such cases dealing with the incompatibility of preauthorization with free movement of people were brought before of the Court. In the words of an EU civil servant, "the Kohll and Decker cases caused the sudden realization by national health care administrators that internal market law and other community law can have an impact on health systems came a bit as an unpleasant shock."[39] The degree of surprise caused by the rulings depends on where one views them from.

In the Kohll and Decker rulings, the Court concluded that national rules which require preauthorization in order to determine the eligibility of claims for cross-border care are in principle incompatible with the provisions of the EC treaty's articles on the free movement of goods (Article 30) and services (Article 59). Beyond this general point of agreement, however, opinions diverge on what exactly the implications of these two rulings might be. On the one hand, one can expect increased patient mobility and decreased state capacity (both de facto and now also de jure) to control the affairs of its health care system. On the other hand, the relatively small number of cases seems to encourage member states that the rulings are not going to bring down their arrangements. Furthermore, this latter view holds on to the point that the Court did not conclude that all national preauthorization mechanisms are out of order, but simply the ones used in these two cases. To the degree, that rules can be proven to be necessary for the public health and the survival of the population, they may be upheld. More specifically, the Court upheld the need to secure the financial stability of the different health care systems but in its view preauthorization rules in terms of the reimbursement of the cost of foreign medical goods or services do not have a significant detrimental effect on this stability and thus could not be applied. But even then, it allowed that the reimbursement of services must be in accordance with rules prevailing in the country of residence.

From the perspective of health care provision, one has to admit that the implications of the two rulings have at least the potential for a quiet revolution. From a European case law perspective, however, the rulings should not have been such a surprise. As discussed earlier, the Court had returned a number of decisions that pointed out that at least the potentiality for this development was present. Furthermore, in other policy areas where the issue of prior authorization had come up, the Court had ruled that such rules are hard to reconcile with the free movement of people, services and goods.

The two articles of the EC treaty (Articles 30 and 59) in question do in principle forbid all national rules which may impede the free cross-state lines movement. This does not only apply to rules that directly forbid movement but also to rules that may indirectly or potentially burden this interstate movement. In previous cases, the Court had concluded that medical products such as pharmaceuticals or medical technology are to be regarded as goods and therefore Article 30 applied to them. Similar rulings came down in terms of medical care which was judged to be a service and therefore fell under Article 60. And as already mentioned, the Court had expanded the free movement of workers to non-workers in terms of obtaining medical care. In this sense, the Kohll and Decker rulings were not that surprising but rather were to be expected. After all, preauthorization rules do indeed inhibit the free movement of goods and services.

Or don't they? The treaty does indeed provide for national rules that would not be inconsistent with the principles of the common market. According to Articles 36 and 56, this kind, or rules that can be justified if in "the public interest," is to be protected. Such a public interest may be the protection of public health from a hazardous product. A second way that national rules may be justified is through the rule of reason. This is a similar rule which also allows member states to create rules that, assuming reasonable judgment, are necessary to protect the public interest. This was the predicament in these two cases. Did the rules by Luxembourg fall under these two exceptions or didn't they?

The argument went as follows: Preauthorization rules were necessary in order to protect the financial stability of the Luxembourgian health care system and of the different insurance schemes.[40] Since the price of medical acts, pharmaceuticals, examinations, etc. differ substantially among member states, if one member state is coerced to reimburse according to tariffs of another state, this can lead to increased health care expenditures (a problem already), and in the process jeopardize the financial stability of the different schemes and ultimately pose problems for social cohesion in health care. Thus, the protection of the public good demanded that national preauthorization rules are needed. Not so, concluded the Court. In previous cases, it had already settled the issue that Articles 36 and 56 of the treaty do not justify rules based on economic reasons. Furthermore, the rule of reason had to be applied in a nondiscriminatory fashion in terms of origin of the good and/or the service. That is to say, that if the rule of reason applies, then the rules must apply equally to "national" and "foreign" goods and services. And since it is hard to make the case that preauthorization rules applied equally to both national and foreign goods and services, the argument could not stand. Moreover, and depending on the member state in question, there may be economic benefits from seeking care abroad where goods and services may be cheaper.

A similar argument was made in the Kohll case only. According to this argument the national rules were necessary in order to ensure "a balanced medical and hospital service to all." If free movement was allowed, health care planning of personnel supply, distribution of hospital beds and of other facilities would be impossible. Without a given territory or, better put, a given population to plan for, undercapacity or overcapacity were more than certain. This argument's chances were not great either for the same reasons as the argument based on protecting the financial stability of the system. The rules again did not fall under the exceptions to the free movement of services. Furthermore, the capacity argument as protecting the public good (plausible as it sounds) is silent about the discriminatory nature of the rules which automatically exclude it from the rule of reason. The only argument that appears to have reasonable chances of success is an argument that would link preauthorization rules with the protection of public health under Article 56. In fact, the Court went out of its way to state this, moving in a sense a bit back from an earlier ruling. In prior case law (the Duphar case), the Court had rejected such a line of argument as it pertained to Article 36. Therefore, preauthorization rules of such nature are difficult to justify in court. Nevertheless, the Court did point out in these rulings that if the argument were made well, it could stand.

What do such rulings mean for the future of health care in the EU? This is indeed hard to tell. They will certainly not prima facie change everything within a short amount of time. But by making health care goods and services subject to free movement, the Court has introduced a transnational aspect to health planning.[41] Pharmaceuticals and other technologies may now be purchased from lower-priced countries and in the process ease the tension in terms of health care expenditures for some member states where these products are relatively expensive. For pharmaceuticals, for example, the price differentials between countries like England or Germany and countries like Portugal, Greece, Spain or Italy are substantial so payers in the former group can benefit significantly from this kind of trade. Payers can take advantage of such an arrangement independent of the nature of the system, whether it is a national health service or a social insurance system, since either staying under a centrally allocated budget or reducing the rate of increase in insurance premiums are both strong enough incentives. In either case, however, national policies for the pricing of goods seem to be in trouble. Hospitals can also take advantage of such an arrangement since a significant portion of their expenditures as providers are pharmaceuticals and technological devices. They will now be able to ask for bids from a larger range of suppliers and in so doing reduce their costs. Furthermore, increased patient mobility can be expected. To the degree that the rulings simplify the bureaucratic process, to the degree that perceptions of differences in the quality of medical care in different states are real, and to the degree that waiting lists pose a problem for the individual patient, increased numbers of patients can be expected to seek care "abroad." For both national payers and national providers this has the potential for trouble as they tried to argue in the two cases. Increased health care expenditures for the payers may be an immediate effect. At the same time, care rendered abroad is care not rendered at home, and thus providers can expect a significant loss of income. Such pressures can be expected in the long run to lead to a convergence in prices of goods and services, and similar waiting periods as well as an overall convergence in the administration of health care, assuming certain other developments. Health care will be available with wider choice within the common market and with the advent of the euro, comparison of prices will be much easier in this area as well, pushing for transparency in the ways health care is financed. Furthermore, the systems which deliver services deemed "substandard," will have to catch up if they do not want to see large numbers of people seeking care abroad.

There is an inherent tension in this free movement and social solidarity. The Kohll and Decker rulings may force Europeans to sit and discuss their options and maybe try to collectively institutionalize certain rules. There are certain principles that the Community is committed to. First, there is a principle of high health care protection as an objective of the Community. There is also the principle of free movement of goods, services, capital and people. And, third, there is the principle of subsidiarity (dealing with policy topics at the lowest government level possible). The challenge before European governments today is how to best reconcile these principles, which as these two cases showed, are at times at odds with one another. The issue is how to combine them and produce results that are consistent with all of them rather than making one subordinate to the other through a coherent community political response rather than leaving it to the judicial process. This needs to be based on a very thorough process of consultation between the member states. "The potential of these judgments is anywhere between trivial and apocalyptic," said an EU health policy expert, and he went on to state that leaving the process up to the court, convenient as it may be in terms of political cost since the issue is quite sensitive, may not be the wisest solution.[42] The Court interprets community law but there is not a set of regulations about health care that the Court can follow since member states have not been very willing to discuss them. In this sense, the Court is left interpreting common market principles and thus the inherent tensions remain and ultimately it may not result in fair health care arrangements.

One thing is certain, however. Either through a political consultation process or through the judicial venue, negative integration (compatibility with the common market principles) is already affecting national health care from above and therefore national administrators must take it into account.

The national reactions to the Kohll and Decker rulings were characterized by an original negative surprise and then a cautious concern about them. The German Presidency at the time held a preparatory meeting in Bonn on November 23 and 24, 1998 to discuss the implications of the rulings.[43] The tensions discussed earlier became clear. Still, the states (at least a number of them) did not appear very willing to begin a process of common solutions. They preferred rather to continue to discuss these issues. Two things became clear, however. First, the states all realized that the common market and EU law does indeed influence national health systems, a marked change from the period before the rulings. Second, they all presented the need to avoid the health care sector being fashioned by the judicial sector only without the political will of the member states being reflected. Indicative is the Danish viewpoint, which did not see the rulings in and off themselves as too problematic for their systems since they do not apply to benefits in kind. Yet their fear was further decisions by the ECJ in greater areas of application. If this were to occur, then it would jeopardize the right of the member states to decide on their social security systems. As a solution they saw a more flexible organization of the EC regulation 1408/71. The Germans held that the rulings concerned the Luxembourg health system and were not transferable to systems that did not operate with the principle of reimbursement. The Dutch, in a pragmatic approach to the rulings, viewed them as inevitable and at the same as non-threatening to the core of their system. Their ability to maintain the benefits-in-kind principle is not substantially challenged as they see it. In a sense, they do not see any reason why Dutch insurers cannot contract with foreign providers. The Dutch were quite open to the notion of at least discussing these issues on a European level. The French view was that after these rulings minimum standards and norms ought to be established and that subsidiarity ought to be maintained in terms of the organization of the systems. Furthermore, they were the biggest proponents of establishing legislative regulation instead of letting the ECJ regulate the health care sector. The British viewed the judgments as inconsequential for the NHS. They do not view the system as an enterprise and thus do not see that it can fall under competition law. The other states that were present in the meeting positioned themselves along similar lines.

The inability of member states to face up to the new realities that the Kohll and Decker rulings presented them with is not surprising given the slow speed of political reforms in Brussels in general and the sensitive nature of social protection. That, however, by no means meant that the Court would sit and wait for the member states to decide to act. In the most recent case that it dealt with and that had direct effect on health insurance systems, it further clarified its points in two critical rulings.

In the joined Smits and Peerbooms case (C-157/99) that dealt with the definition and application of health services, the Court gave a further push towards convergence of national health systems by ruling, in a sense, that each member state has to clarify its benefit package. Mrs. Smits, a Dutch national who suffered from Parkinson's, went to Germany where she received a multidisciplinary treatment that dealt with all of her symptoms. Upon her return home, she sought reimbursement through her insurer based on the 1998 rulings of the Court. She was refused, since the treatment she received in Germany was not considered "normal" in the Netherlands. Similarly, Mr. Peerbooms, also a Dutch national who had fallen into a coma, was taken to Austria where he received a special neurological treatment that actually was successful. He also was denied reimbursement by his Dutch insurer since the treatment was considered in the Netherlands to be experimental. The Court returned with a decision that clearly shows that whereas member states are still in charge of their health care systems, this does not mean in any sense that the rules of free movement of services, goods and people do not apply here. The question was whether hospital treatment was a service or not. The Court went further than its previous rulings by stating that hospital treatment is a service and therefore the free movement rules apply to it. The Court, however did not go as far as to say that all hospital/medical treatment offered in one state is automatically transferred to all Europeans. That is to say, that it specifically recognized the right of each member state to explicate the benefits it would cover under its health care system. In their own words:

> It follows that Community law cannot in principle have the effect of requiring a Member state to extend the list of medical services paid for by its social insurance system: the fact that a particular type of medical treatment is covered or is not covered by the sickness insurance scheme of other Member States is irrelevant in this regards." (Paragraph 87 of the ruling)

Therefore, the Court did not strip away the administration or the capability to successfully administer a health care system from the member states but it did demand that the states make clear what they cover and what they do not cover under public funds. If one were to assume that it would be increasingly difficult from a political point of view to exclude a treatment that is offered in other parts of the Union, one can conclude that the recent rulings bring the European health care systems closer to one another than they have ever been before. What the end of this process might be is still unclear, but one thing is certain. Member states would be better off to start talking to one another to clearly make rules to govern health care administration in the EU.

Ideological Convergence

Such thorough political consultation process among member states has not gone ahead full steam for obvious political interests on the side of the member states. However, and especially after the recent rulings there is a discernible ideological convergence in terms of how health care policy is viewed. The EU has played a role in this convergence. But the EU has also led to a different kind of ideological convergence that does not deal with regulations and directives but rather with how member states perceive the challenges and the potential solutions in terms of their health care systems. European integration has effects which are indirect and therefore difficult to quantify. Nevertheless, they are present and perhaps much more consequential than all the other EU effects on health policy and they certainly add to the growing role of Brussels and the supranational constraints that it places on member-state health policy makers. Especially because of economic and labor policies by the EU, there is this technocratic convergence about how social protection systems ought to be modernized in order to respond to the challenges of the twenty-first century.

The EU has achieved this ideological convergence of health policy makers in the member states largely because of a number of interrelated mechanisms. The EU serves as a forum for the exchange of ideas and a discussion around them whereby the participants are already locked in through earlier decisions and therefore this forum offers itself as the basis for further cooperation in future affairs. One of the cornerstones of the "ideology" of the EU is the promotion of economic growth through open markets, and based on their earlier decisions, member states view success in terms of the measures taken to achieve economic growth as a one-way street. Following that, it is not surprising that the EU leaders' views also appear to have converged in terms of flexibility in labor relations in the EU since this is seen as a way to curb high unemployment figures. At the same time, the creation of the economic and monetary union (EMU), demands strict fiscal discipline and efficiency in the services of the public health sector. Through these ideas, the challenges that the health care systems face today in all member states are being subjected to a common analysis, and because the constraints on the financing of the systems are directly related to the aforementioned ideas, one can conclude that similar tools will be proposed in the different member states. Of course, since there are substantial organizational differences, these tools will be applied differently in different settings. Nevertheless, by constraining policy making at the member-state level, the EU is increasingly playing a role in health policy decision making.

Originally the fear had been that economic integration would spill over into social policy as social dumping. Member states, in order to attract businesses, would lower indirect labor costs time after time in direct competition with one another. Not much evidence of such a trend, however, has been offered. The European approach has been one that, depending on one's point of view, is either optimistic, pragmatic or plain naïve. The approach is based on certain ideological principles. This convergence of ideology among mainly European elites that calls for rationalization of the use of limited health care resources and the maintenance of universal access and thus social solidarity, centers around the following four principles. First, and based on the principle of subsidiarity, member states ought to remain the administrators of health care. Second, EU member states ought to cooperate with one another, improve common information systems and exchange views to try to find the best solutions in terms of providing high quality care with sustainable cost. Third, social protection in general and health protection schemes in particular must be consistent with economic policy, as that is conceptualized by the EU, in order to achieve economic growth. Relevant to this third principle is the fourth one, which does not see any inconsistencies between more flexible labor relations and health care protection since higher employment will lead to stronger finances for the health care systems of the member states. Let's look at how these principles came about.

From the brief historical overview of the integration process in the beginning of the chapter, it becomes quickly obvious that the member states have viewed the EU as a way to safeguard what their societies have achieved up to this point and as a "guarantee" for future economic growth. Of course, this guarantee assumes certain moves on their part, which they have ultimately come to accept when the alternative of non-action is no longer a viable option. Therefore, we see the slow transformation of the EU from a free trade area to a customs union to an economic community to a common market and finally to a quasi-state with a common currency. Every time that future economic growth was in question, the member states found ways to agree. During all this time, the assumption that social issues could stay off the agenda was in a sense implicitly made. This is, however, a dubious assumption, and this is something that the Union has come to realize in the last decade or so.

As pressures to reach the Maastricht criteria for EMU grew, and the common market rules were demanding the liberalization of trade, systems of social protection in general and health care systems in particular quickly came under the microscope in terms of how they operate and how they produce and allocate resources. Social issues were on the agenda and along with them they brought this technocratic convergence on how to modernize them. The high unemployment figures that the whole of the Union and each member state were experiencing served as a catalyst for this discussion since labor relations were the most directly related social issue to the already agreed affairs of the Union, primarily the common market.

The link between EU employment strategies and the future of social protection was, in fact, made by the Commission itself in its 1995 communication entitled *The Future of Social Protection: A Framework for a European Debate*.[44] There it states, "The developments in Community policy since 1992, notably the Community-wide framework for employment presented by the Commission in 1993 and the White Paper on Growth, Competitiveness and Employment presented to the European Council in Brussels in December 1993, call for more extensive joint reflection on this matter. In particular, some of the means for improving the employment situation in the Community, defined at the Brussels, Corfu, Essen and Cannes European Councils refer to social protection and its funding, whether by reducing indirect labor costs or through the combined effects of tax schemes and aid schemes on readiness to offer and to take up jobs." It would therefore be worthwhile—critical in fact—before examining the debate that the Commission began in 1995 through this communication, to closely examine the employment strategy of the EU.

Three recent articles have characterized unemployment within EU Member States as a "specter" haunting the Union.[45] In fact, by the early

1990s and as unemployment appeared indeed to be a ghost haunting Europe, one could begin to see a consensus that the EU was experiencing an employment crisis. The Commission, but also the Council to a lesser degree, considered such a crisis extremely serious since it would threaten both the competitiveness of European economies in the global market and the social cohesion that had been part of Europe since the end of the second world war.[46] In fact the Commission called high and continuous unemployment the EU's "major deficiency."[47]

And certainly the employment data is quite worrisome even to date, when unemployment has begun to drop throughout the Union. The seasonally adjusted unemployment rate for the 15 member states was 9.1 percent in October 1999. A year earlier it stood at 9.7 percent.[48] Until very recently, the *overall* employment figures and the ability of European economies to create new jobs did not look very good at all. It was not until the end of 1998 that unemployment levels fell below the 10 percent point for the first time since 1992.[49]

As unemployment has come on the agenda and has gained political importance during the 1990s, it is not surprising that policy makers searched for solutions. The obvious comparison with the U.S. unemployment figures (the U.S. has enjoyed close to perfect employment for the greater part of the 1990s) led many to search for reasons and therefore solutions for the crisis across the Atlantic and in American patterns of labor relations. As a result the debate began by highlighting the presumably drastic difference between the U.S. and continental European countries in labor market performance.[50] More and more voices began to be heard pointing out that the reason that the U.S. is better at creating jobs or turning population growth into employment is that it has a more flexible labor market. Most academic analyses seemed to agree with the following assessment in an op ed piece: "more flexible wages, employment practices, and laws in the U.S. better conduce toward job generation than do the more rigid practices and laws in Europe."[51] Policy makers in the EU were quick to grab the flexibility bit and try to envision how to apply it in the EU economy.

The EU's claim to develop a strategy for the Union as a whole, which would be consistent with economic growth and competitiveness, was first established in the Commission's White Paper of 1993.[52] The 1993 white paper was followed by what has been known as the "Essen process." During the 1994 European Council meeting in Essen,[53] the EU started an "integrated employment strategy." It was the first time that Brussels was planning (even though informally) medium-term policy on employment. This decision enabled the Commission to monitor and present annually the employment policies of the member states, so that a collective strategy could be debated in Amsterdam. Furthermore, five priority areas of action were also identified. They served as beacons in the design of employment policy at member-state level. Henceforth, alongside economic competitiveness and economic growth, the Union had committed itself to promote employment growth.

Based on the process that began in Essen, the Commission proposed in 1996 the Confidence Pact for Employment Commission.[54] The European Council in Florence that June endorsed the Commission's proposal. Member states were urged to adopt a number of initiatives to create new jobs. These were not binding in the legal sense of the word but they nevertheless placed informal pressure on member states to follow them and in doing so converge their policies. In the next European Council in Dublin at the end of 1996, the Council further urged all the social and economic partners to play their part in employment matters. All these were preparations for the IGC of Amsterdam, where as we already mentioned the member states formalized this ongoing process by placing it in the treaty. For the first time in the history of the Union, employment growth had become an objective for the Union (Article 2 of the EC). More specifically, the objective is to achieve a high level of employment without weakening the competitiveness of the EU. In the tradition of EU operations, the treaty enabled Brussels, above the powers of the member states acting individually, to come up with a coordinated strategy for employment, a set of common guidelines that would not be legally binding but that would nevertheless place pressure on state capitals.

The Amsterdam treaty introduced a new Title on Employment (Title VIII) into the EC treaty, along with the Title on Economic and Monetary Policy (Title VII). The combination of the two is a step-by-step process spelled out in the treaty and based on the coordination of member state employment policies and structural reforms of their economies in terms of removing labor rigidities. The new strategy, set out in Articles 125 to 130 EC, is a new power vested in the Union, *supplementary* to that of the member states to create a set of annual common guidelines following the example of the Essen process. The process begins with the European Council adopting conclusions on the employment situation in the Union, based on a joint annual report by the Commission and the Council (Article 128). Based on this endorsement, the Commission then proposes the guidelines, which must be consistent with the economic guidelines established under Article 99(2) for monetary union. Monetary union success and employment growth go hand in hand. I will return to this point later. These guidelines are then adopted by the Council through qualified majority voting and after consultation with the European Parliament, the Economic and Social Committee, the Committee of the Regions and other interested agents that participate in the Employment Committee (Article 128(2)). Member states then take these guidelines and take measures in order to implement them. They report back to Brussels annually (Article 128[3]).

A key point must be made here. Even if one were to assume that Brussels would eventually assume competency in the field of social protection, this most likely will not lead to a harmonization of health policy regimes. As the employment guidelines process shows, it is closely modeled after the EMU process, but has two distinct differences. First, the common employment guidelines do not push for the harmonization of national policies. Second, there are no distinct criteria through which success or failure can be measured as was the case with EMU.[55]

The first set of Guidelines in December 1997[56] centered around four "pillars"—improving employability, developing entrepreneurship, encouraging adaptability in businesses and their employees, and strengthening the policies for equal opportunities. These pillars are expanded through nineteen guidelines. Of the four pillars, that of "adaptability," a different word for flexibility, is the most relevant for our purposes. The Guidelines define adaptability as "encouraging adaptability of businesses and their employees to enable the labor market to react to economic changes." In a sense, by introducing flexibility into the European labor markets, they open up the issue of social protection including health care policy. In a sense and quite consistent with the history of European integration, member states saw flexibility or adaptability of the labor force as the only way out of the employment crisis that was jeopardizing the success of EMU. So, adaptability became a guideline.

To underlie this point is the following. During the Amsterdam IGC, it was also the first time that the Union formally accepted that high employment and the success of EMU were causally related. High employment levels were not to be achieved solely because they are good in and of themselves, but also because they are a requirement for the success of EMU. In the words of a Commission document:

> The European employment strategy is of fundamental importance in tackling the employment problem, and will be even more important when Economic and Monetary Union is implemented. While high employment and well functioning labor markets are priority objectives in their own rights, high employment is the best way to make EMU successful.[57]

Once this connection was made, it was not too difficult to see that matters of social protection including health care would soon follow since the only model that achieves the EU's dual objective of monetary union success and high employment levels is the U.S. one. There was about to be a change in ideological discourse in the EU which would perceive social protection somewhat differently. Social protection would have to become "employment friendly." What exactly that meant for health care would be revealed in a number of communications by the Commission. Sure enough, as early as 1992, the Council had adopted two Commission recommendations,[58] one on the convergence of social protection objectives and policies and the second on common criteria concerning sufficient resources and social assistance. Based on these recommendations, the states, while maintaining their diverse systems, set common objectives and set out individually to achieve them. In the meantime, they were exchanging information. The Commission, starting in 1993, would issue an annual report[59] on Social Protection in Europe, which would analyze common challenges in the different traditional welfare areas and different member-state responses to them. Furthermore, the publication of a green paper in 1993 on the future of European social policy, whose aim was to "raise a large number of issues linked to the future of social policy," indicated that social protection would be in the forefront of political issues in the following years.[60] Furthermore, the issues raised in that green paper for discussion all revolved around the theme of social inclusion and integration in the labor force. Arguably, one could say that nothing would stand in the way of the Union achieving its dual objective of EMU success and high employment rates. In 1994, the green paper was followed by a white paper on European Social policy where this link was made even more explicit.[61]

Nevertheless, this approach was judged not to be enough in order to achieve the new EU objectives as these had been developed through the employment policy debate and the necessity for EMU success. Thus, in 1995, the Commission, as mentioned earlier, had published its framework for a European debate on matters of social protection.

Two points must be made about the starting point of this debate. First, the need to modernize social protection systems (a term that would soon be adopted in Brussels jargon) "in response to the need to adapt to rapidly changing social and economic conditions, to contain costs, and to replace the old rigidities with more flexibility while at the same time maintaining this objective of solidarity," was the obvious aim of the framework for discussion publication. The interesting and optimistic aspect of this modernization process was that the Commission explicitly realized that social protection systems are essential for social solidarity. In fact, the document defines social protection as "all the collective transfer systems designed to protect people against social risks." It goes on to state that "social protection...is an essential component of solidarity between the peoples of the Member States of the European Union resulting both from its aim to provide universal coverage and the absence of a proportional link between contributions levied to finance the system and the individual vulnerability of the persons covered." Nevertheless, the link between the employment policy and the need to make social protection employment friendly was the overarching theme of the document.

Second, the Commission also realized that the political context within which it had to move dictated that member states would have to remain the main actors in the design and implementation of any reforms. At the same time, it also wanted to increase its degrees of freedom in this area so that it could better coordinate state policies and place them along the same evolutionary path. Thus, in the beginning of the document it also explicitly put to rest any fears of a pan-European welfare state: "It is clear that each Member State remains responsible for the organization and the financing of its own particular social protection system. However, given the common challenges facing Member States in this area, there is considerable value in launching a debate on these issues at European level." At this historical juncture, the Commission viewed that the best way of applying the principle of subsidiarity is to maintain control at member state level and still coordinate more from a central level.

Within this context, the Commission went out of its way to explain the need to reform social protection systems. On one hand, it listed the negative aspects of social protection systems. Besides the fact that they were designed a long time ago for differently structured societies (low unemployment, for instance), they also pose an increasing economic burden on those who work since they have to subsidize those who do not. Furthermore, the rigid structures of current social protection measures increase labor costs to a degree that makes it hard for employers to create new jobs, for the economy to be competitive and, in the final analysis, jeopardizes the economic growth that Europeans have already achieved. On the other hand, social protection has, of course, positive aspects. It is, as the Commission put it, "crucial to the very working of our societies." It has combated poverty to a large degree, especially when compared with the other side of the Atlantic. It has led to a healthier and a more educated, therefore a more qualified labor force. The Commission went on to show that it realized that the vast majority of Europeans recognizes the value of social protection systems, and wants them maintained and improved since they represent an "essential vector of social cohesion." But faced with the unemployment crisis, something had to be done.

The Commission did not hesitate to openly state that social protection systems had to follow the employment policy path. "In order to help increase job opportunities,....it has proved necessary to put in place an active employment policy.... How can social protection be made more conducive to this active employment policy? How can it be integrated in employment promotion...? How can it be ensured that social protection promotes integration into the labour market?"[62] Besides this general approach, the Commission did not push too far for specific policy objectives. Again, its aim was to get member states discussing these issues. If cooperation were deemed necessary or essential to a certain degree, then things would follow that road. In such fashion, the Commission was content to raise questions about the financing of social protection, about the demographic challenges that the EU faced and about changes in health care systems. The framework also covered issues of cross-border movement and how states could best tackle those, an issue that refers us back to negative integration attempts.

The challenges of financing and of demography were discussed in the first chapter and therefore not much must be said here. One point is critical, however. In both sections in the communication, the Commission connected debate at European level with better, more viable solutions, by rhetorically asking time after time, "is there a need for closer Community cooperation on these matters [financing of social protection] between the Member States?" or "Is there a need to discuss the impact of such changes [demography], for example, on economic growth and job creation and the objective of maintaining solidarity between generations?"

In terms of health care, a similar push was made by the Commission for member states to begin discussing how they approach specific health care challenges at a European level. The 1992 Council recommendation had already explicitly stated the policy objectives in health care. First, "a high quality health care system geared to the evolving needs of the population, to the development of pathologies and therapies and the need to set up prevention" and, second, "to ensure for all persons legally resident access to necessary health care as well as to facilities seeking to prevent illness." Of course, on first sight both these goals are noble, but a third objective is also to keep public health care expenditures under control. The way to bring together in one policy a means to meet these objectives is obviously difficult. The Commission did not pretend to have any answers here either but, as mentioned before, it saw the solution coming through closer discussions: "Given the complexity of these problems, exchanges of experience in this area would therefore be particularly useful. Moreover, closer cooperation between all concerned would now appear useful to identify the best solutions to the evolving needs of the population."[63] The only suggestion the Commission had was that it would be well worth it for interested parties to discuss whether contractual arrangements between payers and providers from different member states could lead to efficiency gains? In the typical questioning fashion of the document, it states, "could agreements be envisaged between the paying bodies to allow access where appropriate to the health-care system of another Member State?"

The framework for a European debate was set, and at the very least it would get Europeans on the same page to discuss these issues and in this sense it represents a force for the convergence of the different health care systems. When one looks at it from a distance, it appears as a typical neofunctionalist approach. EMU is decided upon and states want to see it succeed and therefore higher employment levels are needed. But in order to achieve such higher levels, social protection systems must be modernized. Each and every time, there are politics between member states, but when one clears all the smoke and all the rhetoric what remains is a more or less neofunctional progression from one policy area to another. Member states find themselves and their policy design mechanisms increasingly constrained from above in policy area after policy area in order to safeguard what prior agreements have achieved. One could venture to say that such is the case in health care as well.

The 1995 communication led to a series of discussions as it had intended which lasted for the following two years. Written exchanges, conferences, meetings between scientific experts and policy makers were indicative that the Union was thinking of social protection. In 1997, another communication by the Commission, entitled *Modernizing and Improving Social Protection in the EU*, was circulated.[64] In this communication, the Commission argued that after two years of debates and the contributions of a number of interested parties, there was much agreement between the different reactions. More specifically, it writes that:

- The European social model is valued and should be consolidated. This model is based both on common values and the understanding that social policy and economic performance are not contradictory but mutually reinforcing...
- To preserve social protection implies adapting European systems in their various forms, since the context in which they were established has changed...
- ...Each Member State has to find solutions that are adapted to its own particular system. Member states should continue to pursue the convergence strategy as outlined in the 1992 Council Recommendation.
- The means of adapting social protection systems have to be in line with the process of European integration, and in particular the internal market, moves towards EMU...
- The ability to learn from each other and adapt quickly is a key factor for success. The European Union should act as a catalyst to enable Member States to learn from one another...

Therefore, the principles that this communication was based on were similar to those in the framework for debate communication. The marked difference this time was that the Commission, taking stock as it oftentimes does of what had been debated, set out in this 1997 communication to "map out some avenues for improving European social protection."[65]

Specifically for health care systems and in terms of improving the services offered, the Commission proposed as an objective the following: "Improve the efficiency, cost effectiveness and quality of health systems so that they can meet the growing demands arising from the ageing of the population and other factors.[66]" The key actions that it suggested were three. First, an assessment of the potential impact of prevention in terms of reducing health care costs ought to be carried out. Second, an analysis of the role of market forces in health care ought to be performed. At the same time, a number of states were thinking of market forces as a mechanism for reducing costs and improving services and as the Commission put it "competition between service providers is thus encouraged.[67]" The Commission wanted to know to what degree market forces could be expected to lower costs and foster better quality. Finally, the Commission offered to undertake to bring together analyses of member states' health care systems in terms of relative efficiency and effectiveness. Policy makers could thus assess what initiatives could be taken at Community level in order to assist states to achieve the dual goal of better quality with lower costs. It becomes quite clear therefore that the ongoing reform proposals coming out of Brussels envisage the adaptation of health systems to the new realities by making better use of the resources available, not by lowering social protection or social solidarity.

Two points must be made about the Commission's ideas. First, and as it is relatively obvious, its third suggestion (the undertaking of the collection of common statistics for all member states) obviously speaks to the heart of the issue of whether Brussels is more and more involved in health care affairs. Undertaking the comparative study and trying to identify community level actions may be translated into offering more guidelines that would further push for convergence. The second point is that introducing market forces, even in their quasi-market approach, is something that Brussels appears to favor, since it is quite consistent with the internal market. At the same time, however, the Commission wants it done right, avoiding traps of risk selection and social exclusion in terms of health care access. As the document states, "subject to proper conditions to avoid distorting effects, each insurer should be able to contract with those service providers which will provide them with the best services at affordable prices." And it goes on to add, "it is crucial that the freedom to provide health services and place relevant products on the internal market is underpinned by such a framework so as to benefit the health systems and result in continuity and affordability of health care across the Community."[68] The Commission's assessment achieved broad support. All EU presidencies from 1997 to 2002 have organized conferences on different aspects of these ideas. Furthermore, the discussions within the European Parliament and the Economic and Social Committee were quite positive for the positions of the Commission. Moreover, at the European Social Policy Forum, which was held in Brussels in June 1998, civil society organizations also endorsed the proposals by the Commission.

At this time, the Commission also published a communication on the development of Public Health Policy.[69] Therein, among a number of other topics relevant to public health, it also covered some of the same issues that the earlier social protection communications had discussed. It elaborated on the need to change the health care systems and the challenges that high health care costs, demographic trends, technology and perceived expectations place on the systems of the member states. Finally, it also called for the need to better collect and exchange information in all areas of health policy.

In 1999, the Commission took yet another step in this process of reflection. It published its most recent communication entitled, *A Concerted Strategy for Modernizing Social Protection*.[70] This communication had the aim of establishing an "agenda of deepened co-operation," which would be supported by improved mechanisms of collecting, monitoring, and exchanging information. This cooperation would be based on four key points related to the modernization process. One of these four was to ensure high quality and sustainable health care. This time around, the Commission explicitly wrote what it thought the proper directions of health care policy ought to be. It outlined four steps. The first had to deal with placing the focus on prevention. The second was a response to a growing need for better long-term care arrangements. The other two, which are closer to the aspects of health policy examined here, stated that European states need to "ensure access for all to high quality health services and reduce health inequalities," and that they also must "contribute to improve the efficiency and effectiveness of health systems so that they achieve their objectives within available resources. To this end, ensure that medical knowledge and technology is used in the most effective way possible and strengthen co-operation between Member States on evaluation of policies and techniques."

Hence, one sees a progression from setting the issue, asking about it, coming up with broad ideas and then with more specific ones and all along creating a convergence around an ideological framework based on the rationalization of available resources in health care. Equally important is that all along, the Commission was going out of its way to assure member states that it is they who would remain in charge of social protection and that harmonization of policies or uniform policies across Europe directed by Brussels is not the goal. Therefore, one sees only broad general ideas coming from above with strong incentives if they are followed, even though they are not legally binding. It is, however, a dominant influence on member states' policy, perhaps much more at this historical juncture than either positive or negative integration attempts, since the challenges and the constraints, because of what the integration process has achieved so far, are real. Member states have found themselves walking or being pulled, depending on the state, the time, or the issue, down a convergence path of their social protection schemes in general and their health care systems in particular, which, if one were to take it to the theoretical extreme, would lead very closely to resembling health care arrangements. There is, however at the same time a different path that health policy walks on, and that is the domestic political path that has been able to maintain the significant variations among the different systems and also to influence this convergence path through the principle of subsidiarity. I will now turn my attention to the politics of four health care systems, the systems of Greece, France, Germany and the Netherlands.

Notes

1. In fact, studies began as early as 1975. A few indicative ones are Maynard, A., *Health Care in the European Community*, Beckenham, Kent, 1975; Leidl, R., "How Will the Single European Market Affect Health Care?" *British Medical Journal* 303:1081-82, 1991; Hermans, H. E. G. M., Casparie, A. E., Paelinck, J. H. P. (eds.), *Health Care in Europe after 1992*, Aldershot, Dartmouth, 1992; Svensson, P. G., Stephenson, P., "Health Care Consequences of the European Economic Community in 1993 and Beyond," *Social Science and Medicine* 35(4):525-29, 1992 ; L' Association Internationale de la Mutualite (AIM). *The Cross Border Health Cares within the European Community*, Study for the Commission of the European Communities, Directorate V, Brussels, April 1991; Mossialos, E., and Le Grand, J. (eds.), *Health Care and Cost Containment in the European Union*, Ashgate Company, Brookfield, VT, 1999; Leidl, R. (ed.), *Health Care and Its Financing in the Single European Market*, IOS Press, Washington, D.C., 1998. Gouvras, G., "Public Health Policy in the European Community," *Gesundheitswesen* 59 (12): 657-8, December 1997.
2. Examples of such "minimalist" approaches are De Swaan, A., *Social Policy Beyond Borders: The Social Question in International Perspective*, Amsterdam University Press, 1994; Altenstetter, C., "Health Policy Regimes and the Single European Market," *Journal of Health Politics, Policy and Law* 27 (4): 813-846, 1992; Lange, P., "The Politics of the Social Dimension," in A. M. Sbragia (ed.), *Euro-politics: Institutions and Policymaking in the "New" European Community*," The Brookings Institute, Washington, D.C., 1992.
3. Streeck, W., "From Market Making to State Building? Reflections on the Politcal Economy of European Social Policy," in S. Leibfried and P. Pierson (eds.), *European Social Policy: Between Fragmentation and Integration*, The Bookings Institute, Washington D.C., 1995.
4. As of late 2000, institutional reforms have been proposed by the French presidency to prepare the EU for enlargement to the east so that it can accept the countries of central Europe, Malta, and Cyprus. Nevertheless, the discussion here is offered as a guide for the next section of the chapter so that the reader who is not well versed with the EU can follow it.
5. The brief description of the institutions of the Union is largely expanded in a booklet by the Commission, European Commission: "Europe...Questions and Answers, How Does the European Union Work?" 2nd ed., DG for Information, Communication, Culture and Audiovisual Media, Brussels, 1997.

6. The composition and the decision-making mechanisms were the topic of negotiations in the most recent intergovernmental conference in December 2000, where decisions were made to ensure a workable institutional framework for the expanded Union of 27 members. Twelve countries are expected to join by 2010.

7. In actuality, the negotiations take place beforehand through a complex mechanism of committees where member state civil servants hammer out details and present the Council with a more or less complete draft.

8. Lipgens, W., *A History of European Integration, 1945-1947: The Formation of the European Unity Movement*, Clarendon Press, Oxford, 1982.

9. Among the delegates present were West Germany's Chancellor from 1949 to 1963 Konrad Adenauer, Winston Churchill, and about twenty more former prime ministers, and leading academic scholars. For detailed information on the Congress see Vaughan, R.,*Twentieth-Century Europe*, Croom Helm Publishers, London, 1979.

10. European Congress Communique of May 1948 meeting, The Hague, The Netherlands, 1948.

11. Peters G., "Agenda Setting in the European Community," *Journal of European Public Policy* 1 (1):9-26, 1994.

12. Monnet, J., *Memoirs*, Doubleday Press, New York, 1978.

13. Willis, F. R., *France, Germany and the New Europe 1945-1967*, Stanford University Press, Stanford, CA, 1968.

14. From this point, and for reasons of clarity, I will refer to all these institutions by their current names.

15. Urwin, D., *"Western Europe since 1945: a Political History,"* 4th ed., Longman Press, London, 1989.

16. Featherstone, K., "Jean Monnet and the "Democratic Deficit" in the European Union," *Journal of Common Market Studies* 32 (2):149-170, 1994.

17. Pinder, J.,*European Community: The Building of a Union*, Oxford University Press, 1995.

18. Caporaso, J., and Keeler, J., "The EU and Regional Integration Theory," in C. Rhodes and S. Mazey (eds.), *The State of the European Union, vol 3.* Lynne, Reine and Golman Press, Boulder, CO, 1995, 29-62.

19. QMV works as follows: Each member state is allocated a certain number of votes by the treaties depending on its size, for example, Germany, France, the UK, and Italy all have 10 votes, whereas Luxembourg has only two. For a decision to be made, it requires sixty-two votes.

20. For the lobbying role that large multinationals played, see Green, Cowles M., "Setting the Agenda for a New Europe: The ERT and EC 1992," *Journal of Common Market Studies* 33 (4): 501-526, 1995; Majone, G., "Regulatory Federalism in the European Community," *Government and Policy* 10: 299-316, 1992; Mazey, S., and Richardson, J., *Lobbying in the European Community*, Oxford University Press, 1993; Sandholtz, W., "Choosing Union: Monetary Politics and Maastricht," *International Organization* 47:1-39, 1993; and Van Schendelen, R. (ed), *National, Public and Private Lobbying*, Dartmouth Press, Dartmouth, NH, 1992.

21. The Delors Commission wrote a White Paper on completing the internal market. Through this paper it placed a specific time limit to the creation of the common market by coming up with the slogan "1992," and, in turn, rejuvenated the integration process. It catered to the needs of key member states and in doing so made the IGC happen. During that IGC, the Commission linked the

common market with a change in decision-making mechanisms so that the stalemate of Luxembourg would finally be over. QMV for all the major areas covered by the White Paper was introduced. And whereas the areas relating to the free movement of persons and those relating to the rights of employed persons were excluded from QMV, it is certain that the setting had changed from strict intergovernmentalism. The assumption that social issues could be left off the agenda while economic integration progressed was at best dubious, at worst naive.

22. Mazey, S., "The Development of the European Idea: From Sectoral Integration to Political Union," in J. Richardson (ed.), *European Union: Power and Policy-Making,* Routledge Press, New York, 1996.

23. Ross, G., "Assessing the Delors Era and Social Policy," in S. Leibfried and P. Pierson (eds.), *European Social Policy: Between Fragmentation and Integration,* The Bookings Institute, Washington, D.C., 1995.

24. Ibid.

25. There is a good deal of cross subsidization between wealthier and poorer regions of the Union through the EU budget (European Regional Development Fund, European Social Fund, etc.). Such cross subsidization, however, aims at elevating the standard of living of the poorer regions, but does not affect traditional areas of welfare, including health care directly.

26. "Europe's New Left," *The Economist,* pp. 19-22, February 12, 2000.

27. To be sure, even here there is great variation among the ways European Social Democrats define their purpose. Lionel Jospin's "market economy yes, market society no" is rather illuminating. Nevertheless, there is this turn towards policies more compatible with the market, largely attributable, as we will see, in the following sections, to EU integration.

28. The Commission has been able to pass through legislation in many related health areas such as pharmaceutical regulation, the education of health professionals, free movement of goods, occupational and public health, the environment, and others. In connection, however, with social solidarity in health care, it has been only in terms of cross-border care that positive integration appears to be occurring.

29. Dommers, J., "An Introduction to European Union Health Law," *European Journal of Health Law* 4:19-41, 1997.

30. Hermans, H., and Berman, P., "Access to Health Care and Health Services in the European Union: Regulation 1408/71 and the E111 Process," in R. Leidl (ed.), *Health Care and Its Financing in the Single European Market,* IOS Press, Amsterdam, ND, 1998.

31. Official Journal EC No C323, 1992.

32. Regulations 1408/71 and 574/72 cover cash benefits and benefit in-kind which are paid out for the following benefits: sickness and maternity benefits, disability benefits, survivor's benefits, old-age benefits, benefits related to occupational accidents and diseases, death grants, family benefits and unemployment benefits.

33. Case 238/82, Duphar vs. the Netherlands, Jur. 1984.

34. Some member states have moved forward on their own through the Schengen agreement, but still not all member states have joined this agreement.

35. Hermans, H., and Berman, P., "Access to Health Care and Health Services in the European Union: Regulation 1408/71 and the E111 Process.

36. The cases are briefly discussed here. For more information look at European Court Reports: Royer case 48/75. 1976:497; Costa vs. Enel Case 6/64, CMLR

425, 1964:585; Amministratione delle Finanze dello Stato v Simmental Case 196/77, CMLR263, 1978:629; Levin v. Staatssecretaris van Justitie Case 53/81, CMLR 1137. 1982:1035; Kempf v. Staatssecretaris van Justitie Case 139/85, CMLR 764. 1986:1741.

37. The Decker and Kohll Cases [Case C120/95- Nicolas Decker v. Caisse de Maladie des Employes Prives; and Case C-158/96, Raymond Kohll v. Union des Caisses de Maladie] are surrounded by much uncertainty which, in and of itself however, is a constraint on national policy preferences.

38. For much of the analysis here, especially the legal aspects of it, I am in debted to my respondents in Brussels both in the Commission and in the Parliament. Also see van der Mei, A. P., "Cross Border Access to Medical Care within the European Union—Some Reflections on the Judgments in Decker and Kohll, *Maastricht Journal of European and Comparative Law* 5(3):277-97, 1998.

39. Interview with Commission's civil servant, Brussels, March 8, 2000.

40. The implication is similar for all member state systems.

41. Kanavos, P., "Health as a Tradable Service: A Prospective View of the European Union," *Eurohealth* 5 (1):18-20, Spring 1999.

42. Interview with a Commission Civil Servant, Brussels, March 9, 2000.

43. Gobrecht, J., "National Reactions to Kohll and Decker," *Eurohealth* 5 (1):18-20, Spring 1999.

44. Commission of the European Communities: *The Future of Social Protection: A Framework for a European Debate*, Communication from the Commission, Brussels, COM (95)466 final, 31.10.1995.

45. Buchele, Robert, and Christiansen, Jens, "Do Employment and Income Security Cause Unemployment? A Comparative Study of the US and the E-4," *Cambridge Journal of Economics* 22, 117-136, 1998; Friedman, Sheldon, and Weller, Christian, "One More Time: Labor Market Flexibility, Aggregate Demand, and Comparative Employment Growth in the US and Europe," *Comparative Labor Law and Policy Journal*,19, 307-319, 1998; Siebert, Horst, "Labor Market Rigidities: At the Root of Unemployment in Europe," *Journal of Economic Perspectives* 11: 3, 37-54, 1997.

46. Competitiveness and social cohesion are, as Article 2 of the Treaty states, guiding principles of the Union. See also Commission of the European Communities (CEC) *Employment Rates Report 1998: Employment Performance in the Member States,* Luxembourg, Office for Official Publications of the EC (OOPEC), COM (98) 572 final, p. 5.

47. CEC, *The EU Economy at the Arrival of the Euro: Promoting Growth, Employment and Stability*, Luxembourg, OOPEC, COM (1999) 7 final, p. 6.

48. Eurostat: Statistical Office of the European Communities in Luxembourg, *Press Release No 120/99*, December 6, 1999.

49. CEC, *The 1999 Annual Employment Report*, Luxembourg, OOPEC, Introduction.

50. CEC, *Growth and Employment in the Stability-Oriented Framework of EMU: Economic Policy Reflections in View of the Forthcoming 1998 Broad Guidelines*, Luxembourg, OOPEC, II/33/98-EN, 1998, pp. 5-6.

51. Editorial Comment, "The US 'Employment Miracle': Employment Protection and Job Generation," *Comparative Labor Law and Policy Journal* 19, 278, 1998; see also Siebert, Horst, op cit., 1997.

52. CEC, *Growth, Competitiveness, Employment: The Challenges and Ways Forward into the 21st Century*, Luxembourg, OOPEC, COM (93) 700 final, 1993. This White Paper was the result of the consultative procedure engendered by the Green Paper on European social policy (COM(93) 551 final).

53. European Council, Meeting of December 9-10, 1994, SN 300/64.

54. CEC, *Action for Employment in Europe: A Confidence Pact*, Luxembourg, OOPEC, CSE (96) 1 final, 1996.

55. CEC, *The Amsterdam Treaty: A Comprehensive Guide*, Luxembourg, OOPEC, 1998.

56. The 1998 Employment Guidelines, Council Resolution, 15.12.1997; at http:// europa.eu.int/comm/dg05/-empl&esf/docs/guideen.htm.

57. CEC, *An Employment Agenda for the Year 2000: Executive Summary*, Luxembourg, OOPEC, COM (97) 479 final, 1997.

58. Council Recommendation 92/442/EEC of July 27, 1992 on the convergence of social protection objectives and policies, OJ L245 of August 26, 1992 and Council Recommendation 92/441/EEC of June 24, 1992 on common criteria concerning sufficient resources and social assistance in social protection systems, OJ 1 245 of 26 August 1992.

59. CEC, "Social Protection in Europe-1993," COM(93)531, 1993. Two more reports have come out in 1995 and 1997 with one more due out in 2000.

60. Green Paper on European Social Policy: Options for the Union available at http://europa.eu.int/scadplus/leg/en/cha/c10111.htm.

61. White Paper on European Social Policy: A Way Forward for the Union available at http://europa.eu.int/scadplus/leg/en/cha/c10112.htm.

62. CEC Communication: *Modernising and Improving Social Protection in the European Union* available at http://europa.eu.int/comm/dg05/soc-prot/social/ commu/commuen.htm

63. Ibid.

64. CEC Communication: *Modernising and Improving Social Protection in the European Union* available at http://europa.eu.int/comm/dg05/soc-prot/social/ commu/commuen.htm

65. Ibid.

66. Ibid.

67. Ibid.

68. Whether this is a workable assumption remains to be seen and depends on one's perspective. Certainly, however, any government must take into consideration external realities like globalization, technological developments, and internal ones like demography.

69. CEC Communication on the Development of Public Health Policy available at http://europa.eu.int/comm/dg05/phealth/general/phpolicy2.htm.

70. CEC Communication: *A Concerted Strategy for Modernising Social Protection*, (COM 99-347), July 14, 1999.

3

Dutch Health Care Reforms: Here Comes the Market, There It Goes!

A founding member of the European Union, the Dutch have always had an international perspective.[1] In fact within the Union, the Netherlands is one of the strongest proponents of a balanced supranational authority. It was one of the first countries to embrace the new economy and, despite recent turbulence in the economy of Europe, the Dutch have enjoyed low unemployment, high productivity, growth and high quality social services.[2] Everything is not great, however. Social protection systems here as well as in other countries, partly because of integration and partly because of financing and quality pressures within these systems, need to be reformed. What is, however, unique in the Netherlands is that the discussion about such reforms occurs within the corporatist tradition of the Dutch and results through political constraints to technocratic solutions that are continuously evaluated.

In this chapter, I examine the reform experience of the health care system in the Netherlands. It presents great interest since it has often been cited as an example of a common trend, a common move towards an internal market model.[3] As of 2001, however, a more accurate description of health care reform in the Netherlands seems to be what the title of the chapter indicates and that is the yearning of certain policy makers for such policy developments and the political obstacles that they faced in their implementation. In the overall framework of the study, however, the Dutch, too, moved towards the modernization of their health care system with similar objectives as the other two case studies here. In fact, the different arrangements and the idea that the health care system (and social protection systems, in general) needs to be reformed so that financial burdens on employers can be eased, an idea that transcends the Union today, began here. As we saw earlier, the first priority for European governments today is sustainable economic growth that will in the medium and long run achieve higher levels of protection for the entire European population. In the meantime, to achieve such economic growth, more flexible labor markets are required which, in turn, leads to the moderniza-tion of social protection systems. Here too, however, domestic politics moved the evolution of health policy down the path of its former develop-ments. In short, health policy in the Netherlands exhibits broad similari-ties with developments on this front in other countries, but upon closer examination the differences that give substance to each system remind us that convergence of health care systems in the EU has its limits.

I begin by exploring the overall Dutch political culture within which the health policy debates take place. I go on to describe the main charac-teristics of the Dutch health care system and of Dutch health care politics. Then, through a discussion of the historical evolution of the Dutch health care system, I turn the focus to my central argument. Whereas by the late 1980s, the Dutch government came to propose a bold plan that would move the Dutch system towards an internal market after the Enthovian model of quasi-markets, the lack of subsequent proof that such radical reform was in fact required, interest group pressures and a change of gov-ernment from a center right coalition to a center left one turned the debate towards more incremental reforms and less risky policy steps. The role of the state was by no means diminished. Whether or not the Netherlands are still moving down the path of creating managed competition depends on one's perspective. One thing is certain. The traditional corporatist spirit of Dutch policy making, which has become an institution in its own right,[4] once again prevailed, albeit changed as we will see. It has in the first instance led to above average care taking and to a continuous search for greater efficiency in the second instance. As mentioned earlier, here, too, one sees a move toward the rationalization of health care resources alloca-tion with an eye on controlling cost and improving quality. Dutch think-ing has arguably greatly influenced how other European Union member states think about reforming their social systems today.

Dutch Political Culture

The politics in this country, for a large part of the twentieth century, were dominated by religious parties. In the last quarter of the twentieth century, however, the influence of religion on politics was substantially reduced. Today, only one party, the Christian Democratic Alliance (CDA) has based its ideology on religious principles. All the other parties' ide-ologies are based on differences of opinion between the role of govern-mental intervention in social affairs, best means of achieving economic growth, social cohesion and so on. What is mostly remarkable about the Netherlands is that no matter what parties have found themselves in power, the country does present an overall consistent direction. The Dutch, as mentioned, are realistic optimists. They believe that based on rationality, a fair balance between personal and social responsibility, an open market and the spirit of corporatism, the state of social affairs in their land can always improve. Whereas analysts have looked at countries like England, France, Germany or the United States for a pragmatic approach to the challenges that modern liberal democratic societies face through theoretical schemes such as the third way, the new center, new democrats and so on, the Netherlands has quietly proven itself to be the paradigm for such an approach. Either because of the institutional mechanisms of elections or because of an apparent balanced split of the population among the different political parties, the Netherlands has been governed for the greatest part of this past century by coalition governments. This, however, has not led to political stalemate but to incremental and consensual political steps in many policy areas. This is not to say that there is an ideological consensus in the Netherlands. Quite the contrary, there are many parties, with four major ones covering the entire ideological spectrum.

The social democratic party, the PvdA, is occupying the left. The party was formed in the immediate postwar period, aiming to put an end to the denominational domination of prewar Dutch politics. It was a collection of people of many different ideologies, ranging from radicals to Catholics and Protestants, who wanted to see their churches out of the political process. But whereas PvdA was able to beat the denominational parties in many elections, it was not able until recently to break from old way Dutch politics. As one observer notes, "although Labour did not put itself forward as a class party it failed to make the hope for breakthrough to new groups of supporters: the country's post war political structure proved still to be largely dominated by traditional denominational and ideological divisions."[5] But PvdA found itself in opposition from 1958 until 1973, with only a small break of eighteen months in 1965-66, after having been part of coalition governments throughout the late forties and the fifties. Then the party underwent internal changes with the introduction of many "New Left" elements. Today, the party can be viewed as the traditional social democratic party found in European countries, with its main concerns focusing on social fairness and social equality.

Its main opposition is the CDA, the Christian Democratic party, which occupies the center of the political spectrum. The CDA was the result of three denominational parties coming together in 1977 to compete in that election in order to try to maintain the denominational character of political life. To a large extent, they were successful, even though as of 2001, this characteristic has been greatly reduced in political discourse. CDA, however, has remained consistent with denominational beliefs, and especially in health policy it has pushed in the first instance for increased participation of interest groups in the political process and, in the second instance, for safeguarding the private character of many of the voluntary institutions that churches have set up.

There is also the VVD, a social conservative and economic laissez-faire party that occupies the right of the spectrum. It was formed a few years after the PvdA, by a group of liberals (in the laissez-faire sense of the word) that broke away from the Labor party. Whereas they agreed that the denominational division of Dutch politics had to stop, their disagreements on economic and social policies finally led to their breaking away. Still, the evolution of the PvdA and the introduction of the VVD were part of the trend away from denominational lines of difference. This process was also assisted by the introduction of the fourth main party in Dutch politics, Democrats '66.

Democrats '66, the conservative party, is a progressive laissez-faire party, which has actually seen its power increase over the 1990s. The Democrats '66 group was first and foremost a dynamic expression of the spirit of the 1960s (when the party was formed). The party was formed by a group of progressive liberals who wanted to see an end to both the denominational but also the ideological divisions of Dutch politics. After an impressive welcome by the voters in its first national election, the D'66 party has been on an electoral roller coaster ever since. In 2001, it seems to have positioned itself well among the other three major parties, representing the Dutch answer to bridging social progress and economic conservatism.

No party has traditionally been able to achieve unified government and therefore the norm in the Netherlands has been coalition governments. Traditionally, CDA had been one of the partners in government even though the last two electoral returns have kept it out of the coalition governments. The current government is a coalition of Democrats '66, PvdA and VVD, but over the years a number of combinations have found themselves in government. The only constant about Dutch political discourse seems to be that the Dutch strongly believe that the future of their country depends on the maintenance of Dutch competitiveness on the international front. This requires a strong economy and the Dutch population has not been willing to sacrifice the strength of their economy for any ideology. Starting in 1981, electoral results indicated exactly this. The Dutch believe that social progress can be achieved without jeopardizing economic progress. In fact, the two have to go together in order for both of them to occur. Achieving economic growth for the Dutch has always meant open and free trade. And achieving social progress has always meant strong solidarity and constant reexamination of social affairs. Any party that may move more to the left or to the right of this consensus will have to pay the political cost as they have historically. This may be why no party has ever been able to win a majority and why the Dutch are quite independent in their voting, often shifting among the different parties. And this is the type of thinking that dominates the design of health policy and thus demonstrates itself in today's system, to which we now turn our attention.

The Health Care System and Its Participants in the Netherlands

As with most continental European health care systems, the underlying principle of social solidarity and the broad elements of funding and contracting are also evident in the Dutch case. Here too, however, there are also distinct characteristics that make the system unique. As Okma comments, "there are three important characteristics which set the Dutch system apart: (1) the mix of public and private funding; (2) the predominantly private provision of care; and (3) the typical Dutch neo-corporatist policy arena."[6] Each one of these characteristics corresponds respectively with the demand side, the supply side and the political side of Dutch health care. The main contours of the system have been in place since the 1970s but in the case of the Netherlands a barrage of reform plans in subsequent decades makes it hard to pinpoint exactly the point of origin of the current system. Nevertheless, there is a distinct split in the Netherlands between health care financing and health care delivery and, therefore, the generic split between the demand side and the supply side is quite applicable.

The Demand Side

The demand side of the Dutch health care system exhibits great private initiative and equally impressive and detailed governmental regulation. The latter spans from price setting, to risk adjustment planning to cost containment in both the private insurance and the social insurance sectors. As a result, the Netherlands spends about 9 percent of GDP on health care. Financing of health care is primarily the responsibility of health insurers. The term includes both private health insurers and social funds called sickness funds. There is also a central fund where public money and employer/employee contributions go that is distributed among public insurers (the sickness funds), in an attempt to equalize the risk undertaken by these insurers.

The government in 1994 distinguished between three different funding categories for health care. The first was insurance provided by either the sickness funds or private health insurers, the second was the universal AWBZ coverage and the third was supplemental private insurance.[7] As Table 3.1 indicates, one can also differentiate between the basic private and the sickness fund insurances. The degree of governmental intervention differs in these three categories. An important point is that what services are covered under which scheme has been an issue of debate in Dutch reforms, as we will see in the historical section later on.

As Table 3.1 indicates, the Netherlands also has universal coverage[8] even though health coverage is not mandatory and no national plan has ever been introduced. Under current rules, about 40 percent of the population need not be insured even though almost everyone chooses to carry private insurance. The remaining 60 percent of the population, which includes the people below the given income threshold of 64,000 guilders (about 31,000 euros) and their dependents, are compulsorily insured under the compulsory sickness fund scheme (ZFW) as the Sickness Fund Act of 1964 prescribed, by a sickness fund of their choice.[9] There are about thirty of these sickness funds. Their average membership was 300,000 people, but this number hides great variation. The largest funds have a membership of over a million whereas there are small funds with a membership of around 1,000.[10] Since 1991 they have operated nationwide, whereas prior to that year they operated regionally.

The main goal of the Act was to maintain relatively stable the percentage of the population covered by ZWF. This goal has indeed been achieved with the percentage in the last fifteen years, from 1985 to 2000, ranging from a low of 61.4 percent in 1990 to a high of 66.4 in 1985, and currently standing at 63.2 percent.[12] Despite this stability, there have been major changes in the sickness fund market in the Netherlands, especially during the last decade. A number of funds have merged in their attempts to cover geographically the entire nation, develop new products and to capture a larger market share. Some of them have even affiliated themselves with private insurers since by law they cannot merge without altering the legal status of either the private insurer or the sickness fund. In the beginning of

Table 3.1
Health Insurance Schemes in the Netherlands

Sickness Fund Insurance, ZFW	Private Insurance (including civil servant scheme)	Long-Term Care Insurance, AWBZ
60 percent of the population covered for acute medical risks such as GP care, dental care under 18, specialized medical care, obstetrics and midwifery, short-term hospital stays, transportation, medical aids and appliances and prescription drugs.	40 percent of the population covered for similar benefits with the ZWF or even more luxurious conditions of care.	100 percent of the population covered for exceptional medical risks, including long-term care and stays in hospitals and nursing homes; psychiatric care; home and community care; preventive care; and public health services.

Adapted from Laetz and Okma[11]

1999, three sickness funds, ANOVA, ZAO and ANOZ decided to merge and in doing so they became the six largest insurers in the country. Their membership reaches 1.7 million people. Achmea is larger by about a million and VGZ and CZ both have about the same number of enrollees as the new conglomerate. Following these four are Amicon with 1.1 million enrollees and Nuts Ohra with about a million. Between these six, the vast majority of the 60 percent of the population that is covered by sickness funds is insured. The other smaller sickness funds do not have a membership of more than 1,000, as mentioned earlier.[13]

The sickness funds are not allowed by law to employ physicians or other providers or to own and manage other health care institutions like hospitals and nursing homes. In other words, the split between supply and demand of care is protected by law. The sickness funds negotiate with providers and the terms of agreement are then examined by a central body, the Sickness Fund Council which by statute supervises the management of the sickness funds. The benefits that the sickness funds offer are comprehensive, but they do not cover catastrophic health risks which, as we will see, are covered under a different plan. The benefits provided are in kind and cover up to a year hospitalization, physician services, prescription drugs and some basic dental care. The contributions to the funds are determined each year by the government as a percentage of gross income and are split between the employers and the employees. In other words they are income related. In 2000, the rate of contribution for the first taxable income bracket (25,000 euros) was 8.05 percent. The employer share was 6.4 percent and the employee share the remaining 1.75 percent. They are also subsidized by a 10 percent on average flat rate premium per adult that is paid directly to the fund. In 2000, the flat rate was 180 euros per person per year. All these contributions are collected in a general fund that is administered by the Sickness Fund Council.[14] The ZFW's character was traditionally related to employment, but after recent reforms, the ZFW now also accepts elderly people (above 65) who had previously taken private insurance but now have an income of below 36,000 guilders. Therefore, it is more of an income-related social insurance scheme rather than an employment social insurance scheme as it used to be.

As mentioned earlier, around 40 percent of the Dutch population is not required by law to be insured. To be more precise, a small group of civil servants (around 6 percent of the population) have their own scheme. The other 34 percent is not required to carry insurance. Nevertheless, most of them opt to take out private insurance policies, making the Dutch system one of the most privatized in Europe. All higher income employee groups, the state government officials, and the self-employed are privately insured. The percentage of the uninsured in the Netherlands in 1999 was a meager 0.8 percent of the total population. There are about fifty competing plans in the Netherlands.[15] Private insurers reimburse their enrollees after care is provided since they do not contract with health care providers, even though there is a trade association that is supposed to. As a result, fees for the Dutch population are rather uniform. Private insurance companies set their own premiums and benefit packages. Private insurance premiums are risk rated per individual. On average, privately insured individuals pay about 2,000 guilders per person (approximately 1,000 euros) annually.[16] The benefits offered are usually the same as the ones offered by the sickness funds. They are also able to determine their underwriting standards, with the exception of pensioners and members of high risk groups, who are entitled under the Private Health Insurance Access Act of 1986 (WTZ) to a standardized package that is subsidized by a private risk pool that all privately insured individuals contribute to which was set up at the time. The premiums under these arrangements are the maximum ones and can reach 50 percent of expenditures. In 2000 the rate for the beneficiaries was 250 guilders per month or 115 euros and the rate for the other privately insured patients who subsidize the WTZ was 190 euros or 420 guilders per year on top of their regular premiums.[17] A better term here instead of insurer would have been administrator since the private companies bear no financial risk for these two high risk groups since they get reimbursed fully for their expenditures. Interestingly enough, a large portion of the private insurance business is this latter one, reaching 35 percent of their annual turnover.

The third type of coverage in the Netherlands is the universal system AWBZ. This system, which was created in 1967 under the Exceptional Medical Expenses Act, serves exactly this purpose. It insures against exceptional medical expenses like nursing home care, hospital stays that are more than one year or home care. The services covered under AWBZ were expanded in the 1980s and in the 1990s as part of a reform effort to create a single national health insurance plan. The administration of AWBZ, however, is still primarily a responsibility of health insurers (both sickness funds and private ones). The AWBZ premium is income related up to a certain income level. Following the principle of social solidarity, the Dutch finance the AWBZ through income-related contributions. Therefore, in 2000, the first taxable income bracket paid 10.25 percent of their income.[18] Because of the income-related nature of the contribution, it follows that people without income pay no contribution. The insurers carry no financial risk for administering the AWBZ since they get fully reimbursed for their expenditures. Finally, there is also voluntary supplemental insurance, which can be purchased by all insurers (both social and private ones). The premium in this case is risk rated per individual and it usually covers services not covered by AWBZ or by the usual benefit packages of either sickness funds or private insurers.

This mosaic of coverage practices adds up to the following expenditures for the Netherlands. Direct government contributions out of general taxation are less than 6 percent of national health expenditures. Direct patient payments (out of pocket, deductibles, co-payments, etc.) add another 7 percent. The remaining 85 percent of national health expenditures comes from the arrangements just discussed (social insurance, private insurance and tax subsidies).[19]

The Supply Side

Provision of services is largely in private hands; either in the hands of physicians in terms of physician services, or religious orders, charities and non-profit foundations in terms of hospitals. This is a tradition that dates back a long time. Private provision of the broadly acknowledged collective good of health care by voluntary organizations started with the medieval guilds that offered financial protection to their members in case of illness. Local communities and church organizations also contributed to this tradition by setting up voluntary hospitals and mental institutions for the homeless and the elderly.

There is a pointed distinction between general practitioners and specialists. General practitioners serve as gatekeepers to the system and each person registers with a general practitioner in their area. In principle, individuals have to go through their generalist before accessing specialized services, but health insurers, especially private ones, have been rather relaxed about this rule.[20] Still, most Dutch people register and go through their generalist. Generalists usually work in group practices. The vast majority of generalists belong to the National Association of General Practitioners, which is charged to negotiate on their behalf with the Association of Sickness Funds for their uniform capitation payments. There are 7,400 general practitioners in the Netherlands.[21] Traditionally, the capitation payment is set so that a generalist with an average practice (around 2,350 patients) can earn an income comparable to highly ranked governmental officials. Private insurers usually also use the negotiated rates between the sickness funds and the generalist physicians.

There is also an adequate number of specialists who numbered 10,000 in 1999.[22] Specialists practice for the most part within hospitals. The majority of specialists set up private group practices of around six or seven physicians and cooperate with the hospitals where they have admitting privileges, in terms of utilizing their beds and other services. The remaining specialists are employed at academic medical centers under contract. The specialists also have a collective trade association, the National Association of Specialists as well as two smaller associations that split from the main one because their members thought that their interests were not been adequately represented. The National Association of Specialists is, however, the officially recognized body in both fee negotiations and policy consultations. Health insurers reimburse specialists on a fee for service basis. Sickness funds had reached agreement with specialists on the process of determining the fees as early as 1949. By 1969, so did the private insurers. Traditionally, fees paid by private insurance have been significantly higher than those paid by the sickness funds.[23] After the 1994 Biesheuvel report,[24] there has been a turn towards providing lump sum payments to hospitals and letting hospital management work out the details with the specialists either through contract agreements or through passing on the payments. Moreover, also according to the recommendations of this committee, specialists and physicians in general have increased their involvement in the management of the hospital. As it becomes relatively obvious, the Dutch have a liberal, if not completely free, choice of provider. It is true that individuals insured by the ZWF are limited to the sickness fund network of physicians, but in actuality the sickness funds have contracted with all providers, or at least most of them, and therefore there is no real restriction on choice of provider.

Hospitals are independent not-for-profit organizations but are still highly regulated by government. There are 143 hospitals that have 55,400 beds, a staff of 197,600 people and about 8,000 self-employed specialists. From these hospitals, 102 are general hospitals (44,300 beds), 33 are specialized ones (4,000 beds) and 8 are academic centers (7,100 beds).[25] The capacity of all hospitals is controlled by the Hospital Facilities Act and therefore building new hospitals, adding beds to already existing hospitals or introducing new technologies are all dependent on governmental approval. Payments to hospitals are regulated by the Health Care Prices Act. The per diem charge is calculated based on capital and operational costs and it must be negotiated with health insurers under rules and under the supervision of the governmental central office on health prices (COTG). There are also a number of other provider institutions such as home care organizations and retirement homes. In 1999, there were 123 home care organizations with a personnel of 156,000, around 1,200 retirement homes with 110,000 beds and a staff of 104,000, 327 nursing homes with 50,000 and staff of 84,000, 154 institutions for handicapped people with 36,200 beds and a staff of 99,900 and 148 mental care institutions with 28,100 beds and a staff of 56,300.[26] These institutions are regulated very much in the same fashion that hospitals are.

During the last decade, governmental reforms, new technologies and changing market dynamics led to a series of integration attempts both horizontal (same service providers) and vertical (different service providers). The government had for a long time aimed to reduce inpatient care in favor of ambulatory care services. As new technologies allowed a number of procedures to be performed on an outpatient basis with substantially lower costs and less trouble for the patients, hospitals realized that the move towards outpatient care and other "medical products" would be essential for their institutional survival.[27] Moreover, as managed care seemed to become the norm, the hospitals and other providers realized that sooner or later they would have to have bigger leverage in negotiations with insurers. Larger size could do this for them. Furthermore, as they would have to provide evidence of the quality of their services, the introduction of computers and new measurements was also essential. As a result of all these trends the number of inpatient beds decreased in the 1990s. Hospitals created networks through affiliations or mergers with primary care providers like nursing homes and home care organizations and therefore a number of institutions are now offering a full set of services from primary to tertiary care under the same institutional roof. New computer technology is allowing faster and more efficient management techniques for health care institutions which have enabled these integration attempts to be viable. The government has encouraged them in this sense since it provides subsidies for the introduction of information technology.

Physician and medical personnel supply in general is closely watched, as all capacity is watched, by the government. The primary responsibility for undergraduate medical education lies in the Ministry of Education and the Ministry of Health. The number of university openings is capped based on estimations of future needs. Students can study undergraduate medicine in one of the eight medical schools of the land. In order to specialize they must be accepted in the programs of one of the eight academic medical centers. This part of their education is controlled by the profession itself even though governmental plans in 1998 provided for the creation of an institute to regulate the supply of specialists in cooperation with the profession.[28] During the 1990s, a number of reports pointed to labor shortages, but as of 2001, the topic is still being debated.[29] Despite the issue of waiting lists that seems to be the number one concern of the Dutch public with the system, it has been extremely problematic to link these lists with a shortage in the numbers of personnel. As of 1999, there were, as mentioned earlier, 7,400 GPs and 10,000 specialists. Moreover there were 7,300 dentists, 43,800 physiotherapists, 13,400 pharmacies and 380,000 nurses.[30] Therefore, both the mix and the ratios of personnel per population are quite satisfactory and this is probably why the shortage warnings have not been taken too seriously. Furthermore, the geographic distribution of personnel is adequate. As in other countries, physicians and nurses tend to concentrate in large urban centers, but access to primary and emergency care has not been a problem for the Dutch.

In terms of financial resources allocation, hospital care and physician services consume 40 percent of total expenditures, around 29 billion guilders or 13 billion euros, with nursing homes and chronic care in general a distant second at 22 percent, 16 billion guilders or 7 billion euros Pharmaceuticals consumed 11 percent of health care funding (7.5 billion guilders or 3.5 billion euros). No other category was above 10 percent. Table 3.2 shows the complete breakdown of the allocation of funding.

The Political Side

As Schut writes, "traditionally, Dutch government policy has been affected by two important principles: subsidiarity...and social solidarity."[31] This tradition still holds today. Politics in general and health care politics in particular in the Netherlands are characterized by these two principles. Social solidarity indicates the commitment and understanding of the Dutch society that the rich ought to assist the poor, and the healthy ought to assist the sick. Subsidiarity indicates the understanding of the Dutch that decision-making power for policy ought to lie at the lowest governmental level, if, in fact, it lies in the governmental arena at all. In other words, whereas government is understood to represent the public interest, interest groups are expected to have the power to represent their constituencies. Van Schouwenburg points out that this principle transcends the different religious traditions in the Netherlands.[32] The only difference is in the name of it; the Roman Catholics call it subsidiarity whereas the Protestants call it sovereignty for their own interests. These two prin-

Table 3.2
Allocation of Health Care Funding, 1999
(Millions of Guilders, Euros, and Percentages)

	Guilders	Euros	%
Hospitals, general practitioners, other acute medical care	28,419	12,892	40
Nursing homes, retirement homes, home care	15,736	7,141	22
Pharmaceuticals and medical aids	7,668	3,480	11
Care for handicapped	6,303	2,860	9
Mental health care	5,198	2,359	7
Public health and prevention	1,219	553	2
Administration	6,567	2,980	9
Total	71,126	32,276	100

Source: Ministry of Health, 1999

ciples of policy making, on the one hand, call for strong governmental intervention so that social solidarity can be insured and, on the other hand, constrain governmental power through the empowerment of several interest groups which are actually officially recognized as participants in the political process. In return for this official participation in the policy-making process, these corporatist institutions are expected to promote the public interest as well as their constituency interest. The threat of bigger governmental involvement is always present. As a result, Dutch policy-making exhibits relative stability and rather incremental reforms whereby changes are easier to block since many different groups have a chance to influence proposals. This theory of policy making can also be applied (in fact, quite strongly) to health care.

The health policy arena exhibits all these characteristics of Dutch policy making. In other words, it has evolved based on a pattern of corporatist arrangements between government and interest groups.[33] After World War II, the two aforementioned principles brought both the government and a number of advisory bodies that represented formally almost all health care interest groups into the policy arena. In the beginning, physician associations were given dominance, but as other concerns (cost containment, for instance) came onto the agenda, more groups saw their influence increase. Within such an open access political system, ample opportunity was offered to the different interests to shape the design, implementation and therefore ultimate outcome of health policies.[34] And because of their large numbers, it is easily understood why incremental reform became the norm in Dutch health policy. This corporatist spirit of policy making is as strong today as ever, even though there have been changes in recent years. After a number of expert committees suggested that these corporatist structures be downsized in importance, a number of coalition governments reduced the number of such bodies in decision making. Despite this, as Okma reminds us, as of 1998, government explicitly provided institutional access "to major interest groups in the newly organized consultations on multi-year budget allocations for health care, the *meerjarenafspraken*."[35] Perhaps, it would be helpful to look a bit closer at some of the political players and their roles in health policy.

The party spectrum in Dutch politics is covered by four major parties, as we saw earlier. And also, as mentioned in the beginning, the norm has been for the Dutch to have coalition governments in order to avoid the threat of ideological polarization. The critical point here for our purposes is that no single party ever had enough power to push a policy based solely on ideology. Rather political compromises had to begin within government. At the same time, policy proposals, as mentioned, are closely influenced and scrutinized by a number of interest groups. Because of their official status the representative bodies of these interest groups have come to be known as the "middle field."[36] What this middle field consists of are actually the federations and the peak associations of the consumers, the providers and the insurers. Following the decentralized nature of the health care system, interest groups from the local level form these peak associations at the central level for more political leverage. For instance there are more than two hundred consumer and patients' groups in the country. They are represented by one central federation that they have formed. In terms of insurers there were traditionally two peak associations, one of the sickness funds (VNZ-Netherlands Health Insurance Association) and one for the private insurers (KLOZ-Peak association of Private Insurers). In 1995, however, and due to recent governmental reforms that were opening up the insurance market, the two associations merged into one known as the Health Care Insurers Netherlands (ZVN). Even the lower levels of governments use this model of representation in policy debates at the central level. The Municipalities have formed a peak association called VNG and the regional authorities have also formed a peak association known as IPO. At any moment in any of the more than thirty advisory bodies[37] that the government has for health care, one can find representatives of these and many more associations representing labor, employers, physicians, hospitals, insurers and so on. Couple this plethora of corporate interests with the number of governmental ministries involved (finance, health, education, development, etc.), and the broader macroeconomic goals that they bring on the agenda, and one can easily understand why long negotiations in the Netherlands have been the norm. In fact, it is rather interesting how the Dutch are able to enact policy at all. The answer goes back to that spirit of cooperation and the fact that the players all exhibit a rationality unmatched in politics anywhere else. Nevertheless, Dutch health politics are characterized by a continuous evaluation of the state of affairs, continuous reports that call for changes and continuous incremental mingling with the system. As Frederick Shut writes, "Within the complex structure of checks and balances that has emerged in the postwar period, neither government nor any of the major interest groups have had sufficient power to make fundamental changes independently. However, each had sufficient influence to obstruct the other's initiatives. Therefore, Dutch health policy is marked by many disregarded advisory reports and defeated bills. Unilateral government intervention can only succeed if self-regulation clearly fails to support public interests."[38]

And amidst all this mingling with the design of the system, a number of studies from the Ministry of Health and academics reveal that the health of the Dutch population is good. Life expectancy is high and expected to rise. Still, a sense of perpetual uneasiness is felt when one speaks to Dutch policy makers about their system. This sense of uneasiness that dictates that public systems must change as the world that we live in is changing is quite evident in the rationale behind recent reforms. But to understand these recent debates, we must trace the institutional evolution of the Dutch health care system through history.

The Evolution of Dutch Health Care Politics

As mentioned earlier, there are three characteristics of Dutch health care that have been produced through the historical evolution of the system: the unique public/private mix, the private provision, and the neocorporatist arrangements of political negotiations. There are still three more characteristics that mark Dutch health politics and that come through history. First, the shifting of power from the consumers to physicians and then to government, or the introduction of new players in the health care arena that demanded a saying in health politics. Second, Dutch health policy seems to follow patterns that are consistent with the macroeconomic conditions and that will not inhibit the macroeconomic goals of the country. The final characteristic of Dutch health politics is that the Dutch are not fearful to try system designs that have not been proven successful elsewhere and to confront difficult questions that policymakers in other nations seem to avoid. In this sense, the Netherlands oftentimes offer new ideas and new evidence of new policies for other countries. In the sections that follow, I trace how these characteristics have developed during the course of the last one hundred years.

1900-1945: Subsidiarity, Volunteerism, and the Origins of Corporatism

As was the case in other Western European countries during the Middle ages, guilds had set up forms of collective arrangements for the provision of care, not only for illness but also for inability to work or death of a spouse. Since at the time medicine was not advanced, churches and local charities would set up institutions (an early form of today's hospital) for the poor, the mentally challenged and the dying.[39] With the advent of industrialization, the first sickness funds were set up by labor unions, churches and other philanthropies in the eighteenth and nineteenth centuries. During the early years of the twentieth century, the proven willingness of these voluntary organizations to financially protect their members as well as poor people led to a familiar debate about the appropriate role of the state in this arena. In the meantime and as medicine was progressing and could do more for patients, the profession of medicine began to gain political influence as well and demanded control of the health care system. Numerous proposals and even more regulations were debated over the first forty or so years of the century, essentially around these terrain issues, but very few actually were successfully passed and implemented.

The first attempt to create some legal framework around the health insurance arena was done in 1904 by a Protestant politician named Abraham Kuyper.[40] His original aim was to legislate compulsory health coverage for low income people that would offer a number of services ranging from medical care to income support during illnesses. Because of political problems, he finally opted to propose the legislation only for low income workers.[41] According to the Kuyper proposal, regional governments would set up sickness funds (social insurance). Private companies would be allowed into the market if and only if they were willing to accept similar regulations as the sickness funds. So from the planting of the seeds of the current health insurance system in the Netherlands, there was always a will to bring social insurers and private insurers closer to one another so as to ensure social solidarity and social fairness. This type of thinking is as present today as it was in 1904 and, in fact, has been strengthened by a number of governmental reforms.

By providing for the establishment of the sickness funds and the introduction of private insurance into the mix, Kuyper opened a debate about health care that was immediately entered and influenced by a number of corporatist interest groups. Both employers and employees through their respective associations wanted themselves to have control over the administration of the sickness funds since they were the major contributors. Physicians on the other hand were vehemently opposed to such an idea. A few years after the Kuyper proposals and the pressures from labor unions and employers to take control over the sickness funds, KMBG, the Royal Society for the Advancement of Medicine, published in 1908 an 800-page report to make its case for administrative control of the funds. At the very least it demanded that sickness funds enter into contractual agreements with all physicians. Moreover, the Society demanded that even if it did not have direct control over the sickness funds it would be able to control their incomes through these mandatory contractual provision.

By 1910, a new government was in office and opposition by practically every interested group led the new minister to revise Kuyper's proposals. The fundamental difference was that coverage would not be mandatory for any income group. It also divided the original legislation into two pieces. The first was a proposal for income support in case of illness or death, the Ziektewet. The second was a proposal for the reimbursement of medical expenditures, the Radenwet or Act on Social Security Councils. The latter, which gave more power to the social partners, as the employers' associations and the labor unions were and still are known, passed three years later. The former legislation had to wait thirty years until its goals were realized. By all accounts the social partners were the original winners of the battle over turf. But the medical associations were gaining power and soon there would be a shift in power. Throughout this period, the profession was gaining power, its association was increasing its membership and therefore was also increasing its political power. KMBG was able to organize a strike against the limited contracting practices of certain funds and, as early as 1912, it had prohibited its members from doing business with such funds. Nevertheless, membership in sickness funds increased significantly and quickly. By 1914 almost 50 percent of the population had joined a fund while the mutual funds had set up a federation. There were, however, too many different types of funds and in order to counteract the position of the social partners, the profession sponsored some funds itself.

By 1940 there were over 600 funds in the Netherlands.[42] It seemed as if every interested party was setting up a fund. There were non-profit "mutual funds," where the insured formed the board. There were funds called the "doctors' funds" that were established by physicians in rural areas in order to provide a better payment mechanism for poor patients that were recipients of charity care up to that point. There were funds launched by the Society for the Advance of Medicine that were created to offer an alternative type of fund that would be provider sponsored. In this sense they very much resembled the doctors' funds. There were also funds set up by large employers for their workforce. There were funds set up by the Catholic church since it feared that otherwise there would be no religious differentiation in the proposed funds and for a society like the Dutch one in the beginning of the century that would have been unheard of. Only Catholics could be members of these funds. Since some funds did not cover hospitalizations (the hospital was only then becoming the central institution in health care), a number of hospitals created associations of hospital nursing that were basically collective arrangements for the financing of hospital care. These at the time were distinct from the funds. For low-income people who could not afford membership a number of charities as well as churches provided care.

After the end of the first world war, the issue of health insurance re-emerged on the political agenda. And even though the difficult financial times that the government was facing did not allow for great governmental intervention, a proposal for voluntary insurance administered by the sickness funds surfaced in 1920. In this respect, it did not bring any changes to the existing system, but the proposal also called for sickness funds to include physicians on their boards. The medical association also lobbied towards the end of limited contracting whereas the funds opposed such a move. The debates resulted in a stalemate and the proposal never made it into law. In retrospect, one observes the beginning of a power shift from the sickness funds boards, controlled mainly by the social partners, toward the profession that was demanding more and more autonomy. It is indicative of the reasons why a proposal the following year, which would maintain the social partners as the only represented bodies in the sickness funds boards, never gained enough support. That is not to say that the social partners were losing their power. They were still able to stop initiatives by physicians and other providers if they thought that they were against their interests. This was the case in 1922, when a report called the "unification report" would have elevated the Association of Medicine to the same political level as the Federation of Mutual Funds. By 1924, a new government had reverted back to the 1910 proposals by the then minister Talma.[43]

As the 1920s gave way to the 1930s, three more mandatory health insurance proposals were made by the coalition governments that were in power. All three failed.[44] The first one was withdrawn in 1935 amidst criticism by the medical association and the Federation of Associations of Hospital Nursing, the FVZ. That proposal included hospital care in the benefits that insurance would cover and therefore placed the hospital funds in direct competition with traditional funds. The other two were made in 1936 and 1939 and both generated similar reactions and results as the first one. Yet a new actor had joined the debate, the Society for the Advancement of Pharmacy. It was also opposing the power that the funds had accumulated and was demanding a seat on their boards just like the medical profession was. The pharmacists were also opposed to direct ownership of pharmacies by funds.

When the Germans took over during the Nazi occupation of World War II, mandatory health insurance finally passed since there could not be much political opposition at the time by any interest groups.[45] By a decree known as the *Ziekenfondsenbesluil*, in 1941, the Germans mandated that wage earners below a certain income level would have to be insured in one of the sickness funds. The decree further introduced income-related premiums and employer contributions, a comprehensive benefit package including hospitalization as well as state control and unifying rules for all funds independent of their sponsorship. Through this latter measure, the number of funds quickly decreased even after the occupation was over. While in 1940 there were over 600 funds, in 2000 there were about 30.

It was the first time that the role of the state was introduced in such a fashion. Until that time, government had tried to accommodate the different political interests rather than direct them. Private organizations, churches, and philanthropies were the key players of that period. During this time the long tradition of private provision of health care services that lasts until this date, as was examined earlier, began. Furthermore, the corporatist style of politics that characterizes Dutch politics took strong hold of health politics at this period and has never really eased its grip. The main advantage that the state had, however, was that it was the one that would decide to whom to offer access to decision making and/or which group to treat preferentially. It decided in a sense to use this advantage by introducing a number of advisory bodies, some of which have been granted formal authority in the decision-making process and others serve as advisory bodies where different interests can raise their concerns.

System Expansion: 1945-1970

The years after the war are characterized by conscientious attempts by the government to create a framework where private enterprise could produce economic growth so that the overall standards of living in the Netherlands could improve. No policy area was excluded from these attempts. For the first few years of reconstruction, government dominated the decision-making process with the goal of developing a strong economy. As soon as this goal was achieved, however, Dutch health politics reverted to the familiar patterns of corporatism and the system exhibited tremendous growth in the 1960s and 1970s.

When it started to become clear that the allies would win the war, the self-exiled Dutch government in London established a committee of experts to advise it on postwar social security, including health care. Clearly influenced by the Beveridge report in England,[46] and under the leadership of Aart van Rhijn, the committee presented its report in three volumes in 1945 and 1946.[47] The first two dealt with social security issues and the Dutch government adopted them to a large extent. The third volume was on health care and it would push the Dutch system down a path similar to that of the British NHS. Instead the government, fearing major political opposition to such a development, opted to maintain the system of sickness funds as the basis of the health care system in the period after the war. It thus opted for a regulatory role for itself rather than a role of owning the sickness funds, or a unified fund. During the following period the government would expand this regulatory role as the funds would obtain more authority and the system would grow more complex.

In its attempts to revive the damaged economy, among many other measures, the first government after the war aimed to minimize labor costs so that the economy could become more competitive internationally. The coalition between the Social Democrats and the Christian Democrats strictly controlled hospital and physician charges. The premiums of the sickness funds were constantly set as low as possible so that the Dutch employers would not face too high of a labor cost. To achieve agreement by interested parties, the government established the Sickness Fund Council (ZFR) in 1949 in order to carry out health policies that would be consistent with macroeconomic growth. The ZFR would advise the government on all matters concerning the social insurance market in the country. Eventually its role expanded to include administrative responsibilities for the central fund of the ZWF and the AWBZ. In retrospect, it appears as an uncalculated position but it really was not. Exemplifying the corporatist spirit of politics in the Netherlands, the government created thirty-seven seats in the ZFR. The government, the providers, the sickness funds, and the associations of the social partners all have seven representatives; while patients' groups have two. Two outcomes were possible. Either the members of the ZFR would find themselves in a deadlock of negotiations among the different interests represented or they would be able to muster enough support to issue advice to the cabinet. If the former occurred, the government would be free to pursue its economic plan without much debate with the partners in terms of health care. If the latter occurred, and since the advice would most likely be in the favor of the different interests (i.e., higher premiums and therefore increased labor costs), the government had made sure to establish another advisory board, the Social Economic Council (SER), which advised lower premium rates in order to hold down labor costs. As it turned out the latter situation occurred and the cabinet followed the SER advice. But such a state of affairs could only be tolerated because of the reconstruction period after the war. Soon enough, pressures even from within the coalition government (especially from the Christian Democratic side) were pushing for a less direct governmental involvement whereby private initiative could maintain lower costs.

Whereas the government would adversely interfere, according to corporate interests, in health affairs during the early postwar years, it also made new funding available, especially in terms of capacity building. As we saw in chapter 1, health care systems throughout the industrialized world underwent major transformation in the postwar period. New technologies made new cures available and access to care was subsidized in terms of hospital construction throughout Europe. This was the case in the Netherlands and the government assisted this expansion of the system through new funds. More specialists were produced, the hospital came to the center of medical care delivery, more of them were built and existing hospitals expanded. The coverage of hospitalization in the meantime (based on the 1941 German decree) was leading to increased demand and higher health expenditures. In fact, the expansion of the capacity of the system was rather in line with the governmental focus on economic recovery. Construction of hospitals and all the subsequent effects were affecting positively national GDP growth.

At the same time, however, and as the years progressed, increases in national health care expenditures began to threaten economic growth by taking limited resources from other sectors, or at least so was the thinking. Financial planning, however, was not an easy thing to accomplish after five years of growth in the sector. When, in 1949, the minister of health from the social democratic party proposed a hospital planning bill, he faced strong opposition from the religious parties that were closely connected with the private providers. Economic reconstruction had been achieved to a considerable degree and the Dutch were looking to return to their familiar politics of negotiations. In 1956, the Health Insurance Act (ZFW) replaced the German occupation decree, but for all intents and purposes it maintained the situation that was created after 1941. Also in 1956 the Central Health Council (CRV) was set up in another attempt to shake the health care sector. The expected by now corporatist character of this body was strongly supported by the Christian Democrats and almost without fail its advice was followed. It did not try to bring any changes to the health care sector.

In December 1958, the postwar coalition was broken and the Christian Democrats found themselves as the majority partner in another coalition government, this time with the liberal party. It is not hard to understand that the Christian Democrats, with their close ties to the private providers and the laissez-faire ideology of the liberals, would leave little room for governmental cost control. Leaving the responsibility for the allocation of resources and, in turn, for cost control, to corporatist organizations in an era when health care was expanding in the entire Western world, would not lead to disciplined fiscal policy. So the hospital expansion continued, more specialists were produced and expenditures increased. In turn, sickness funds had to increase their premiums in order to break even. And, in turn labor costs were increasing.

The same situation continued throughout the 1960s despite a few attempts by the government to arrest the growth of national health expenditures. In 1965, the Hospital Tariffs Act (WZT) was enacted which established the COZ, a body that determined prices in health care and its members represented government, hospitals and sickness funds. The COZ did not provide any measurable results in cost control. National health expenditures actually increased from below 4 percent of national GDP in 1960 to more than 7 percent in the beginning of the 1970s.

By 1967, costs for medical care that exceeded one year in the hospital or long-term care were becoming such a large issue that the government had to pass the AWBZ, the Exceptional Medical Expenses Act, for the entire population. By shifting the costs around, however, nothing was really being accomplished. And while the economy was doing well in the 1950s and in the 1960s, the problem was not acute. With the oil crises in the early seventies, however, health care expenditures became a prime target for governmental intervention. Would corporatism be replaced by strong governmental involvement?

A Political Pendulum between Government and Interests: 1970-1986

It was quickly becoming evident that the model of corporatist bargaining that had been followed in the postwar years was unable to control the increase in the rates of growth of national health expenditures. Despite private interest differences between providers and insurers, they all had a common interest in more money going to health care. Absent a strong force countervailing their power, it would be very difficult to see any changes in the trends. Overlaying this situation and its realization by the Dutch government were the achievements of the Keynesian model of macroeconomic stabilization that was producing a number of success stories in England and in other European countries. This led to a changing attitude toward state intervention in social policy in general and health policy more particularly. A new consensus was arrived at in the Netherlands that the state had to become more central in health policy so that macroeconomic stabilization and continuous economic growth (through lower labor costs) could be achieved.[48]

As early as 1971, a new act, the Hospital Facilities Act (WZV) had made its way through the legislation pipeline. Government was charged, based on this act, with the planning responsibility of hospital and nursing home facilities. The act was not and has not to this date been very effective.[49] Even though it provided for a central decision on regional construction plans, that central decision could be vetoed in turn by any one of the middle field organizations that were also by law required to take part in the process. The act established a new advisory body called the Council of Hospital Facilities (CVZ), where representatives from all interested parties (physician federations, hospital associations, fund federations, etc.) were appointed. Equally important is that more than half of the members of the CVZ were provider representatives (either physicians or hospitals). It is not difficult to see why the requests would most likely be viewed positively by the CVZ. And to be sure, most of the requests were approved, but not before a considerable time lag. This latter fact was perhaps the only evident result of the act. The decision for expansion of the facilities took longer under this act. It may have conserved some resources, but only at the margin. Corporatism was still strong enough to reject quasi-interventionist measures. Either the state would have to step in heavily or intra-interest bargaining would perpetuate the situation.

The change, however, in the ideology of the time and the realization that costs needed to be controlled (not only in health care but in general) revealed itself in the next general election in 1973, when the PvdA (the Social Democrats or Labor Party) won after fifteen years of center right coalition governments. Even though the new government was still a coalition one, its focus had shifted to the left, with the Social Democrats becoming the dominant partner. Since governmental planning was viewed at the time as the appropriate way to run an economy, the left was strategically located on the political spectrum to deliver. Within months of the election, the Social and Economic Council recommended that a national health insurance program (that implies full state control over the health sector) similar to the British NHS be implemented.[50]

Within a year, the Ministry of Public Health and Environment issued a memorandum "On the Structure of Health Care."[51] In that memorandum, the Ministry presented the broad outlines of its extensive planning ambitions in the health care sector. The Ministry was explicitly stating that government had to become the main decision maker in health policy. "The central government has the general responsibility for a well-structured, democratic and effective system of health services which must be anchored in legislation.... Policy should not be left to other agencies, the central government being only able to act repressively...the central government should establish an overall long term plan defining the objectives and instruments of policy," read the memorandum. The implications were obvious. The state had decided to bring fundamental changes to the health care sector without much consideration about the middle field organizations or the concerns of the social partners. The allocation of health care resources and the control of costs needed to be improved by central and regional planning. The Ministry in that memorandum outlined three basic goals for its reform plan. First, it also embraced the idea of a national health plan that would provide uniform coverage to all Dutch by integrating all existing insurance schemes into a single social insurance. It also aimed at the improvement of the Hospital Facilities Act so that its original planning goals could be achieved. Finally, it was imperative that a new health care prices act that would expand the jurisdiction of the Hospital Tariffs Act over all provider prices be passed. Indeed, the reform outlined in the memorandum aimed at instituting a different type of health politicking in the country. It was to be expected that the middle field organizations would not let such a challenge go unanswered. In fact, they were able in effect to block the realization of all the major goals of the government even though they had to change themselves in the process by becoming more sensitive to public good concerns.

A few months after the memorandum surfaced, the government leaked its specific plan for the creation of the Dutch NHS. According to that plan, twenty-six regional organizations would administer the new system. Comprehensive coverage would be offered and cross-subsidization would be significant. The imposed eradication of private insurance as well as the significant new redistributions of resources raised opposition in many quarters. Opposition in fact came even from within the governmental circles. The Finance Ministry wanted to see cost control measures in place so that public expenditures would not skyrocket. The introduction of the bill to the parliament was postponed indefinitely. But in 1976, the government introduced two other plans dealing with price setting and facility planning, respectively.

The bills did not have a chance to pass before the 1977 election. That election reversed the coalition government composition. The Social Democrats were succeeded as the dominant partner in the new government by the Conservative Liberal Party, the VVD. The liberal ideology of the VVD led all plans for a Dutch NHS to be abandoned. But, the new government was not prima facie against greater governmental control over health care expenditures. The international faith in Keynesian macroeconomic policy at the time transcended political ideology. Therefore, the planning attempts in terms of facilities and prices were to continue. But the new government reopened the door for the middle field organizations. Whereas the original 1976 bill provided for a considerable shift in price setting from the corporatist organizations to governmental agencies, the new modified version strengthened the role of the middle field by allowing them to negotiate prices in the new price setting body. This body, the Central Organization for Health Tariffs (COTG) that absorbed and, in the process, extended the 1956 Central Organization for Hospital Tariffs (COZ), would set prices based on governmental guidelines. There were eighteen members in the COTG. The membership represented all interested parties, but was heavily weighed towards the providers. The modifications and subsequent political negotiations did not allow the Health Care Prices Act (WTG) to pass until 1982. This act replaced the 1965 Hospital Tariffs Act, the WZT. By allowing, however, providers to negotiate prices with insurers, the final version of the Act had little chance of being effective. Neither the sickness funds that were retrospectively reimbursed fully, nor private insurers that preferred higher expenditures that meant higher premium incomes for them, could or would provide any serious resistance to the inflationary tendencies of providers. And as it turned out, it was the government that had to negotiate with providers.

By 1984, costs that had continued to rise made it imperative that a new system be introduced. So the price setting system was discontinued and a comprehensive budget system took its place.[52] These budgets are, however, also decided by COTG. In this sense, the influence of the providers and the insurers has remained largely intact. Admittedly, the middle field organizations have become more sensitive to cost control and one could argue that this is part of the reason that they have been able to maintain their political influence.

The fate of the facilities planning act was similar. The change in government in 1977 led to renewed negotiations and the final act, the Health Services Act (WVG) as it is known, did not occur until 1982. It provided for a three-level control of facilities planning. The central government would be responsible for interregional facilities of high specialization. The provinces would have authority for inpatient care and the supply of specialists. Finally, municipalities would be responsible for outpatient facilities and GP practices. The Central Health Council was replaced by the National Health Council. Consistent with the corporatist tradition, social partners and middle field organizations were well represented in the forty-five appointed members of the council. To ensure that the implementation of the WVG would go smoothly, a three-region demonstration project was designed. Because of growing administrative difficulties and turf control between the different levels of government, however, the project was continuously delayed. By 1988, the demonstration project was officially abandoned and the full implementation of the WVG suspended. As it turned out, in practice the WVG ended up regulating only the setting up of new GP private practices. Its ineffectiveness as an institution led to its demise in 1992.

In short, between the poor design of the reform of 1974 and its subsequent versions, the institutional opposition by the middle field, and the squabbling between the different governmental levels, the first real attempt at the restructuring of the Dutch health care system was doomed to fail. In the meantime, a neo-liberal wave was traveling from the U.S. and England across to the Netherlands. The recession of the late 1970s that led to large public deficits and to higher unemployment rates, created firm opposition to the ideas that had led Dutch macroeconomic planning for the better half of the 1960s and 1970s. It was increasingly being argued that extensive government planning could not produce efficient results and what was required were free markets absent any destructive governmental interference. The 1982 coalition government between the Christian Democrats (CDA) and the Conservative Liberals (VVD) pushed an aggressive agenda for the liberalization of all economic sectors. Reducing public spending and government regulation became the new article of faith in Dutch politics. The goal was still to have an internationally competitive economy. The tools to achieve it, however, were perceived remarkably different in the 1980s than they were in the 1970s. In 1984 and 1985, two expert committees recommended radical revisions in the governmental planning process and even complete withdrawal was discussed. The stark difference from the 1973 report of Social and Economic Council that had recommended the creation of a national health system is the only evidence one needs to comprehend the change in Dutch technocratic mentality within ten years.

Within this context, in 1986, the government commissioned yet another expert committee under the leadership of the former head of Phillips, Dr. Wisse Dekker, to advise it on health policy. Its recommendations were to send the Dutch health system into a policy experiment unlike any other elsewhere.

Here Comes the Market, There it Goes: 1986-

This last period presents the greatest interest since the concept of reform has been present in Dutch health politics from the mid- 1980s and until today. Moreover, the current system has been shaped by these developments substantially and, in this sense, a closer look at the politics behind health care reform attempts in the past fifteen or so years is well worth it. As happened throughout the world, escalating health care costs, became a major worry for all governments. And since Dutch policy makers believed that employer contributions were decreasing international competition for the Dutch economy something had to be done to attack the problem at its root. So strong was the feeling that labor costs to employers had to be lowered somehow that it was universally accepted. In the words of Joe White, "In Holland (as in Germany, France, and other related systems) the "burden on employers" from their required contributions plays the same role, providing an argument that in order to increase employment and growth, some of the financing of an entitlement (if not the entitlement itself!) must be reduced. I was extremely struck, at the conference and outside of it, by the unanimity with which Dutch policymakers insisted that required employer contributions burdened Dutch employers in a competitive market. This evidently has become an article of faith."[53]

The government commissioned the Committee on the Structure and Financing of Health Care, better known as the Dekker committee, to come up with a major redesign of the Dutch health care system. The Dekker committee reported one year later.[54] The title of its report is indicative of how much agreement it would require for a successful implementation of that or any other reform plan. "Willingness to Change" was presented in March 1987 and it aimed to bring fundamental changes to the Dutch system. In the words of Schut, "the Dekker Committee recommended that the government completely reverse its attitude towards health care. Instead of accumulating enough power to control the behavior of providers and health insurers directly, the government was urged to follow a 'divide and rule' strategy by sharing the responsibility for cost containment with the health insurers."[55] In other words, the solution to Dutch health care problems lay in the incentives structure of the system.[56] Change the incentives and the market would produce both efficient and desirable results. Structure the market in a way that equity is not hurt and all would be well. This seems to have been the logic of the report. Its main elements were not new. In previous reform proposals, both within the Netherlands and abroad,[57] the broad outlines of such a regulated market were designed.

The Dekker committee recommended among other things the placing of almost all benefits in a basic insurance that would cover 85 percent of the total costs. Supplemental coverage would be provided for the benefits that would be excluded from the basic package through voluntary private insurance. This way the different insurance schemes would cease to exist and the system would be easier to administer and would be more consumer friendly. The funding of the new system would be based on two kind of contributions. The first, an income-related one, would collect the money in a central fund to administer the basic package. The second would have been a flat rate premium that would go towards supplementary insurance directly to the insurer. Both sickness funds and private insurers would be allowed to offer the supplemental insurance and they would compete against one another over the flat rate premium. To avoid adverse selection effects, the committee recommended that a capitated fund be set that would be distributed to the several insurers based on risk adjustment techniques. Finally, the committee was recommending that the government pull back from most of its regulatory functions. If the divide and rule attitude was to prevail, more competition among providers and insurers would be needed. Thus, selective contracting between insurers and providers and reduced regulations over facility planning and price setting were recommended. Selective contracting, instead of the mandatory contracting that had prevailed in the Netherlands to that point, would force real negotiations between insurers and providers over prices and volumes of the services provided. In the long run, efficiency was guaranteed by economic theories. The government would also play an important role in ensuring that the quality level of services was not compromised. Therefore, regulation would still be present, only this time it would be rule setting regulation that would level the playing field for the different market players to compete. The Committee proposed that the new system should be in place within five years.

The belief that something had to change radically in the health care system transcended political ideologies. Around the same time, all four political parties published reform proposals of their own. The interesting aspect of these proposals was their similarity with the Dekker reform plan but, more importantly, the similarity between them. While in the 1970s conservatives and social democrats alike believed in central planning, the 1980s had seen a turn toward a devolution of responsibility from the central government to the actual market players, insurers, providers and the public. It is indicative of how international trends in "proper macroeconomic management" sometimes overpower ideological preferences. There are of course differences at the margin that are important as the 1977 change in government reminds us of, but in broader terms the constraints set on governmental policy by these trends are formidable.

The question, however, that needs to be asked, at least in retrospect, is why such fundamental reforms and why so much agreement on their direction? Obviously, cost control would continue to be an unpleasant political exercise, but that hardly seems to be enough of a reason to justify the fundamental shifts of control that in the first instance were barely acceptable anywhere (with the exception of some academic circles) and, in the second instance, had never been successfully implemented by any country. Explanations are many. Lack of faith in governmental macroeconomic planning had become the norm and not only with right wing advocates. International theories of macoeconomic planning were moving away from Keynesianism and towards monetarism and more liberal market-oriented solutions to public policy issues. There was even an obvious lack of self-confidence by governmental civil servants that they could continuously maintain health care costs at acceptable levels. Einte Elsinga, who was staff director of the ministerial task force that was charged to respond to the Dekker report, commented in an interview that, "we always said government regulation would fail in the end."[58] One of the reasons why governmental planning was viewed as difficult to sustain was the frustration that was caused by the never-ending bickering both by other ministries and private interests. As Okma writes, regulations "resulted in more or less permanent fights between the health ministry and the central organizations of the professionals and health care institutions."[59] At the same time, since the Ministry of Finance would never be satisfied with the level of labor costs, there would always be internal governmental arguing. Therefore, either way health ministry officials would find themselves in the middle of a corporatist system of negotiations with actors who would never be completely satisfied. Thus, a simple devolution of responsibility to the "market" allows the ministry to demand results from these same actors.

A similar argument was the political version of the economic argument about moral hazards. In the words of Hugo Hurts, "Consumers of health care have few real incentives to make careful decisions on whether or not to satisfy their in principle unlimited demands for health care services. The cost of extra health care is not weighed against other consumer preferences. Therefore, there is constant public pressure for expanding health care expenditure. At the same time, it is not really clear whether consumers are prepared to pay for that. This places government in the permanent unsympathetic role of having to say no."[60] Therefore, unless some sense of who is really paying for health care was instilled to the Dutch public, the Ministry could expect to find itself in never ending conflict with providers and patients.

Another part of the reason was that the Dekker plan had something for everyone. It provided for a flexible system wherein patients could be moved from a hospital to a nursing home to home depending on their needs. Providers enjoyed the removal of strict governmental regulations that made their practices much more difficult. With regulation, providers were categorized and therefore it was difficult to see such shifting. In the words of a 1993 Ministry of Health publication, "the present funding and insurance system presents barriers to substitutions of this sort," and "regulations tend to block developments which would render the medical services more efficient and flexible."[61] At the same time, sickness funds were happy with the idea of increased responsibility and larger geographic expansion. And private insurers could for certain expect their markets to grow.

Similarly, the Dekker report had something for every political party. It was the ultimate political compromise or the product of ingenious political thinking. The CDA was happy with a plan that offered cost containment without jeopardizing the two fundamental principles of subsidiarity and solidarity. The PvdA was happy because of the removal of the split between social and private insurance and, in turn, its class connotations. The VVD was happy with the use of market forces. And the D'66 were also happy because of the bridging of governmental regulation and market competition in a seemingly flawless fashion. In this sense, it becomes quite obvious that there were a number of advantages not only for the government but also for the opposition at the time to endorse the Dekker report and its version of managed competition. Besides the chance that the reforms could actually work (after all they had never been put to the test), there were all these political advantages that one could think of and that increased the attractiveness of the proposed plan.

Despite all these reasons and the initial positive response by the government, the opposition and the middle field, the consensus that something had to change did not mean that the Dekker plan was the plan to follow. Soon a number of selective criticisms of the plan started to air. The fundamental reforms it suggested were threatening interests in the health care sector and they were not ready to sit there and take it. There were two main criticisms of the report. The first was a generic one and came from many different quarters, even from proponents of managed competition. This first criticism had to do with the time horizon for the implementation of the reform. Five years for such a fundamental metamorphosis of one of the most sensitive areas of social policy, was charged, were not enough. The second criticism had more to do with the degree of willingness of the several actors to actually change their practices. In 1987, in the Netherlands it appeared that everyone agreed that health care reform was needed just as long as their interests were protected. As Bjorkman and Okma write, "Many organizations also qualified their general appreciation of the Report by criticizing selective aspects so that the 'willingness to change' was not quite as widespread as the Committee had implied (or perhaps only hoped)."[62] Patient advocate groups criticized the split between basic and supplemental insurance which, according to them, would lead to adverse selection with the bad risks left either uncovered for the supplemental services or left paying too high of premiums. Furthermore, the flat rate premium for the supplemental coverage was attacked by advocates of poor people who would disproportionately be paying for the same services. Essentially the criticism was the same, since for most cases the worst risks were the poorer people and the elderly. Finally, the merit of competition itself in health care was questioned both by insurers and providers. The argument went that competition would lead to unnecessary duplication of services within close geographical proximity and that that would increase rather than reduce costs.

The center right coalition government at the time, however, was determined to see the proposal implemented. But it was a delicate political balance that it was trying to uphold. Thus, it decided to follow the safe approach of the social dialogue, giving interested parties the chance to raise their objections. While the ultimate goal of structuring the market based on appropriate incentives was not up for discussion, and the government was very much in favor of the structural distinction between fundamental and supplemental insurance, it also realized that a full-blown war with practically everyone within a context of uncertainty that the untested theory was creating was not a very good idea. Thus, it opted for incremental implementation of the proposal.

A year after the Dekker report was made public and after intense discussions within and outside of the cabinet, the government essentially adopted the Dekker proposal and developed a four-year implementation plan that was presented in its report, entitled "Change Assured."[63] The report aimed at the creation of a health care system that combined rationalized allocation of resources based on effective market mechanisms and the quintessential social cohesiveness of social insurance. In a letter to parliament, the government reiterated the reasons why the reform was needed. The uncoordinated financing of health care and long-term care, as well as other social programs like social work and family assistance, did not allow for substitutability between services and therefore led to inefficiencies. The lack of incentives for efficiency in the structure of the financing system was also leading to the indifference of many providers to cost control. Furthermore, the detailed regulation of facility planning and prices had led to a chimera that was no longer workable. Finally, the many different types of insurance were complicating the system unnecessarily and thus inefficiently. For those reasons, the government was proposing a set of criteria that the new system would have to meet in order for the underlying forces of cost increases to be tackled. The criteria were: (1) more service substitution through the integration of health and social care; (2) maintaining or improving quality of services; (3) assuring access to health care; (4) equity; (5) efficiency in health care; (6) less regulation; (7) sustainable cost control in the health care sector; (8) alleviation of negative effects on personal incomes; (9) limits on cost shifting; and (10) limited budgetary consequences on public financial deficit and collective funding of social charges.

As it can be expected, the coalition government of CDA and VVD was adapting with minor modifications the Dekker proposals. The fundamental reform, of course, had to do with the role of the state which was moving to the periphery as the committee had suggested. To share the responsibilities, however, with the other actors, the government also proposed a number of other reforms in this four-year plan. The AWBZ was chosen to serve as the carrier of the new basic insurance package by slowly transferring benefits into it from the other types of insurance. Under the First Health Reform Act that came into effect on January 1, 1989, medical aids, ambulatory psychiatric care and other services were moved from the ZWF and private coverage into the AWBZ in 1989. Also in 1989, part of the income related contributions to the sickness funds were substituted by flat rate premiums so that the duality of contributions (income related for basic, flat rate for supplemental) could begin. Selective contracting of providers by health insurers was introduced, thus ending a fifty- year-old practice of mandatory contracting. This was definitely a strong blow against provider control of the system. Price setting by the COTG continued, but the prices set were now assumed to be maximum tariffs rather than fixed ones, therefore allowing contracting to take place at rates below the COTG ones. In terms of facility planning, GPS could now set up practice anywhere without needing municipal authority, and the process for obtaining license to build was also simplified.

In June 1989, the center right coalition government resigned. The new government (yet another coalition) was of center left orientation. The two parties were the CDA and the PvdA. But even though the new Cabinet announced slight modifications on the health care reform process through their report, entitled "Working on Health Care Innovation,"[64] they still embraced the fundamental guidelines of the Dekker report. The new Health Minister Hans Simons, a social democrat, announced that the government would slow down the implementation of the reform. But that was done as much as a political escape to ease tensions with the middle field as it was done for the reasons actually stated (expand coverage of basic insurance so that substitutability could work better). The reform plans were more or less similar. In the words of Van de Ven,

> Although the main lines of the 1988-government reform proposal were the same as the 1990 proposal, the vocabulary was different, reflecting Simons' social democratic background. Key words in the 1988-proposal of the then center-right coalition cabinet are competition, market and incentives. In the 1990 proposal of the center-left coalition cabinet these key words are replaced by terms like shared responsibility between parties, consumer choice and decentralization. Nevertheless, the main lines of 'Plan Simons' (1990) were the same as those of 'Plan Dekker' (1987)."[65]

Simons' plan was put in policy form as the Second Health Reform Act that started to be debated in Parliament. In June 1991, the act passed and it went on to the Senate floor in November. There strong opposition expected it. CDA leader Kaland, even though his party was part of the coalition government, attacked the plan and specifically the provision that would allow the Deputy Health Minister to expand the AWBZ coverage as he saw fit through the use of ministerial decrees rather than through legislation. The point was won by the Senate and the reform plan had to be altered. It passed, however, and was enacted as of the beginning of 1992. More services were added to the AWBZ coverage. Prescription drugs, rehabilitation and other services moved into the basic AWBZ coverage. The second reform act also provided for the elimination of geographic limits in terms of the operations of the sickness funds and the introduction of a new budgeting system for these funds. There was not going to be a third health care reform act, even though one was planned in 1992. It never reached the floor of the Parliament and it was eventually withdrawn all together, marking, according to many, the official end of the Simons-Dekker plan.

In the middle of the debate of the second reform act in both the upper and lower houses, opposition to the direction, the substance and the administrators of the reform started to resurface and to be stronger than ever before. Fueled by ideological preferences or by reports commissioned either by the government itself or by other bodies, newspaper criticisms, criticisms from almost all parties and arguments from even within the cabinet were installing huge roadblocks for the successful continuation of the reform attempt. And even though the arguments raised against the reform oftentimes contradicted one another, the government found itself fighting everyone rather than having the different critics fight the points academically among themselves. So, the reform attempt lost momentum and was eventually abandoned.

In 1991, Marck Chavannes, the senior editor of the daily newspaper, *NRC Handelsblad*, published a number of editorials[66] on the health care reform plans by the government. He criticized them intensely, leading to the notorious effect, in Dutch health politics, known as the "Chavannes-effect." He labeled the reform crazy, cost-increasing, socialist, Unitarian health insurance and attacked the government every chance he got. In another Dutch weekly, *Elsevier*, columnist Van Rossum labeled the reform plan "Simons' Satan's Plan."[67] placing the focus on the person of the Minister. And as if that was not enough for the Health Minister, he was also defeated according to analysts[68] in a debate on October 3, 1991, by Alexander Rinnoy Kan, chairman of the largest employer's association, the VNO. Kan argued that the Ministry had underestimated the significant negative income effects that Simons's plan would cause, especially for privately insured people. The debate was somewhat ironic with Kan, the employer representative, supporting a stronger role for government, and Simons, a social democratic minister, advocating increased market competition.

A few months later, however, the split between basic and supplemental coverage was supported by two commissioned reports. The reform was not dead just yet. The first report, entitled "Choices in Health Care," was produced by the Government Committee on Choices in Health Care, or, as it is better known, the Dunning Committee.[69] The Committee was charged by the Ministry "to examine how to put limits on new medical technologies and how to deal with problems caused by scarcity of care, rationing of care, and the necessity of selection of patients for care."[70] It was made explicitly clear that rationing in health care services would have to occur. The question was how to best do it so that solidarity would not be compromised. In its report, the Dunning Committee noted that "solidarity can be restricted." And whereas "the Committee...considered the possibility of developing such restrictions based on age, life-style, personal choices, and reciprocity," it presented "arguments against each of these potential methods of restricting solidarity. On the other hand, the Committee saw no objection to restricting care on the basis of costs and benefits." Thus, it proposed a funnel system that services had to go through and pass four different sets of criteria in order to be included in the basic package of services. In the words of the Committee: "The Committee feels that services in the basic package must satisfy four criteria: the care must be necessary, effective, efficient and cannot be left to individual responsibility." The second report, entitled "Medical Practice at Crossroads," was produced by the Health Council.[71] In that report, medical practice was presented as highly inefficient with large and hard to explain variation in practice patterns. The two reports seemed to lend a helping hand to the governmental reform efforts and allowed the reform to go on for a while. But at the same time, they galvanized support for the opposition as well.

Whereas, the Dekker report seemed to offer something for everyone, five years after its publication almost everyone seemed to be against it. In 1992, more reports were made public by advisory bodies, middle field organizations and the two coalition partners, criticizing the proposed reform. The health insurers seemed confused at the time but also critical of the government. In a joint commissioned report, the federation of the sickness funds and the peak association of health insurers argued for further privatization and decentralization on the one hand and a stricter, lasting governmental role in cost control and the allocation of capital funds.[72] At the same time, they claimed that the problem was not so much in the reform itself but in its slow implementation. A crucial point here is that the two organizations were speaking together, a process that was formalized in 1995 with the merging of the federation and the peak association. The National Health Council also joined in the governmental criticism but from a different angle. In its 1991 report,[73] the NRV chairman Van London argued against what he called "a blue print ideology." According to this report, more freedom was necessary so that market actors could produce efficiency results. Hanging on to governmental control was only impeding this process. In the meantime, the PvdA report, entitled "Towards a New Health Care System,"[74] argued for stronger governmental control and regional collaboration whereas the CDA report, entitled "Better Care Based on Solidarity and Individual Responsibility,"[75] supported the health insurers' convergence, but also wanted fewer benefits included in the basic package. It wanted to use the methods described in the Dunning Committee report a few months earlier. The CDA further argued for mandatory deductibles and the establishment of measures for public spending. It seemed that the two partners were becoming uncertain about the reform and were not prepared to see it all the way through or at least were not willing to swallow the political cost for doing so.

The Cabinet was at a crossroads. Either it would move forward with the reform plans or it would have to reconsider. It opted for the latter, and through a letter to Parliament, it set out its positions under the title "Modernizing Health Care: Carefully Ahead."[76] It suspended further implementation until the effects were examined. It wanted to see whether changed structure of incentives in the health care market could lead to more efficient production and distribution of services. And, whereas it was still advocating universal health insurance with the eradication of the distinctions between social and private insurers, it would wait for the reports of the advisory bodies to proceed. The Sickness Fund Council, after a request by the Ministry, produced a study about the effects of the health reform so far. Oddly enough, no major disturbances were found in terms of the administration of the system. Politically, however, the report argued that the reforms had led the system, as Okma puts it, in "a semi-permanent state of transition."[77] The report argued that more time should be allotted for discussions among the interested parties. Amidst this climate, the third stage of the reforms was suspended indefinitely as of 1994.

To understand what had gone wrong in the reform effort, Parliament commissioned yet another report by the Willems Committee. After thoroughly studying the politics behind the reform and its implementation the committee concluded that there never really was as strong a consensus as had been thought.[78] While general agreement existed that reform was necessary and the broad outlines of that reform were somewhat accepted, interested parties, including the political ones, never moved past their own narrow interests. In this fashion, every group was able to criticize aspects of the reform it deemed as challenging to its interest while not appearing to be completely against the idea of the reform. No group said that things ought to be kept as they are; they only argued that the reform ought to be somewhat different. The government found itself caught between the rock of having to implement a reform that was supposedly accepted and the hard place of having to convince every group, including at times its own members, of the value of the reforms. And balancing between the different demands was extremely hard, if not impossible. The employers were against the expansion of compulsory insurance since it would de facto lead to higher public spending, which, in turn, would mean higher labor costs. Higher income groups opposed the compulsory insurance, since now they would have to pay more as a premium (income-related contribution) to subsidize the care of the poorer part of the population. On the other hand, labor unions were supportive of the universal insurance scheme, but opposed the flat rate premiums since they would disproportionately affect negatively lower-income workers and would hurt social solidarity. And whereas providers welcomed the increased flexibility that the new system would afford them, they starkly opposed the ending of mandatory contracting. Insurers, on the other hand, supported the elimination of mandatory contracting, but private insurers wanted the system of incentives and competition for the private market. Within such a climate and with contradictory interests, the government had failed to provide the necessary clarity about its proposals or the required strength for the reforms to be seen through to the end. Corporate interests were able to chip away support of the reform and the situation came to an impasse in 1994.

On May 3 of that year, national elections were held. Both the CDA and the PvdA, the two partners of the governing coalition, experienced significant losses. The two opposition parties the VVD and the D'66 both exhibited significant gains. For the first time in postwar Dutch politics, the CDA was left out of government while the three other parties coalesced to assume the responsibility of governing. The "purple coalition," as it came to be known, took office in September and during its programmatic declarations, it stated that the health reforms of the previous two cabinets would be abandoned in favor of incremental reforms. The large ideological differences of the three governing parties, as well as their ties with different interests in the health care field, did not allow for a comprehensive handling of the health system. And after all, the system was working fairly well by international standards. The country, as well as the rest of Europe, was, however, facing an unemployment problem. Economic thinking at the time dictated that public spending had to be streamlined and be made more efficient if unemployment was to be successfully tackled. For the Dutch, this was not a new idea. In this sense, they were the ones that had influenced European technocratic thinking in this direction. The question, however, remained in health care. How does one compromise traditional health policy with the need for modernization of the system? After all, even though the system was performing relatively well, both its internal (demography, technology, increased demand, service production inefficiency) and external (lower public spending, EMU convergence criteria, lower unemployment, lower inflation) challenges were still present. Faced with this predicament the new cabinet embarked on a "no-regret course," meaning that the three parties would take measures to have the health care system consistent with the overall direction of the country, even if they still disagreed about the ultimate shape that the system should have.

The interesting and ironic aspect of the 1994 governmental proposals for health care was that the principles upon which the proposals were based were the same as they were for the Dekker and Simons' plans. In this sense, the comments of van de Ven that "the point-of-no-return towards regulated competition on both the insurance and the provider market for *non - catastrophic* risks has been passed in the early 1990s" and that "for political reasons, government referred to its proposals as 'incremental changes' rather than a continuation of the reforms."[79] The 1994 government aimed for an equilibrium between societal and individual responsibility, increased participation for providers, consumers and insurers in the cost containment attempts, convergence between the sickness funds and the private insurers. But the measures proposed were not necessarily the logical continuation of earlier reforms. On the one hand, there were stricter supply controls by the government and, on the other hand, there were greater financial incentives to both producers and insurers for more efficient allocation of resources. As Okma states, "The mix of supply-oriented measures and demand-oriented measures showed the mix of 'old' and 'new' health policies."[80]

The new government preferred voluntary convergence of the sickness funds and the private insurers. But it was going to make certain that their interests were towards this wanted convergence. So even though it announced that within the compulsory insurance system, there would be two regulatory mechanisms and not one as would have been the case under the Dekker or the Simons plan, it made sickness funds assume more financial risk for non-catastrophic risks as we will see, therefore prompting them towards more "private" models of administration.

The method that the 1994 purple coalition decided to use has been called the "Double-Dekker" model. The regulatory regime that was proposed under the Dekker-Simons plans would continue, but only for the non-catastrophic risks (like hospital care and physician services). For the catastrophic risks (nursing home care, hospitalization over a year, etc.) the strict governmental regulation regime would apply. In this sense, we see that the road to managed competition continues in the non-catastrophic risks area but not so in the catastrophic ones. In these latter cases, no competition would occur between insurers that bear risk. Instead, costs would be covered by a central fund and insurers (both private and social) would only administer the services. In the cases of non-catastrophic risks, competition among risk-bearing insurers as well as among providers would continue. And as it can be expected, since catastrophic risks have a different regulatory regime, all non-catastrophic risks that had been transferred into the AWBZ, now had to be transferred back to social and private coverage.

Thus, whereas government still regulates facility planning, it is scheduled to deregulate it soon. Furthermore, hospital budgeting is set to be removed so that insurers can better negotiate with providers. Sickness funds and private insurers are now more exposed to financial risk and allowed to do business throughout the Netherlands. For instance, while in 1995 sickness funds ended up being responsible for only about 2.5 percent of the difference between the actual expenses and the expenses estimated based on a number of risk variables, the government proposed to increase that percentage to about 65 percent by 1998. Even though this percentage stood at 36 percent in 2000, it still is a significant increase in the financial risk that sickness funds assume. In the private insurance market, the government announced open enrollment, mandatory insurance for all citizens that are not insured by the sickness funds and premium regulation. These measures would have increased the financial risk of these insurers as well, if they had taken place. But, as of 2000, they remained inactive. Nevertheless, perhaps because of anticipatory behavior, there has been much cooperation between the two, and voluntary convergence seems to be occurring. At the same time, in order to introduce more flexibility on the providers' side, the government aimed to follow many of the recommendations of the Biesheuvel committee. As mentioned earlier, this committee recommended that specialists become more involved in the management of hospitals, that fee-for-service payments ought to be replaced by capitation or through combined payments to both hospitals and specialists, and that GPs should be paid based on a system of bonuses in relation to their performance indicators.

In 1998, the elections returned the purple coalition to government and therefore significant changes to health policy direction did not occur. The government announced that it would follow the path of the previous government.[81] In the non-catastrophic risk area, the government is expected to attempt to create an "appropriate health plan," which is very reminiscent of the Dunning funnel approach. After a 1997 report by the Netherlands Scientific Council for Government Policy, entitled "Public Health Care, Priorities and a Sound Financial Basis for Health Care in the 21st Century,"[82] that argued that there are limits to collective responsibility, the government will once again try to figure which services are necessary. The government will continue to increase the financial risk of the sickness funds, and will further deregulate the hospital sector. Furthermore, in each of the thirty regions of the country, a "regional care office" will be appointed (expected to be the dominant sickness fund), which will have the responsibility and authority to selectively contract with providers, thus boosting competition. Having said all this, however, as of 2002, one cannot claim that the market has settled in Dutch health politics. It is more appropriate to say that the longing and experimentation for more efficient production and allocation of resources has led the Dutch to experiment with market mechanisms. But it would be very difficult to find much support for the argument that internal markets improve significantly any aspect of health care delivery. The case of the Netherlands does offer ample support for the case that quasi-markets, managed competition or relevant concepts is politically very attractive in an era in which public spending must be curtailed, overall inflation must be kept low and governments cannot run huge debts. Therefore, it is far-fetched to imagine that the Dutch experiment might not be attempted by others.

The move towards the internal market in the Netherlands cannot be explained solely on the merit of the idea (an idea that still has to prove itself), but rather on the institutional alignments and interactions between the different actors that set the Dutch health care system upon its particular trajectory. The unique public/private mix of insurance, the provision of services largely dominated by the private sector, the corporatist character of Dutch health politics, the introduction of new actors in the course of time in the health care arena, Dutch discipline and simultaneous obsession to create a health policy that would be consistent with macroeconomic stability and development goals and, finally, the willingness of policy makers in the Netherlands to experiment with unproven theories of public management, set the theater of Dutch health politics. From private interests to government and to the market, the Dutch have continuously searched for adaptations in their system. Today, just as at any other point in the past century, they continue this search. One thing is certain and that is that the Dutch have, primarily through the EU, tremendously influenced technocratic thinking and macroeconomic planning approaches in many European countries. They now approach social policy with the mindset that the economy must grow based on open markets and that social policy must accommodate this growth without leaving people behind. This mindset is quite evident in the cases of Germany, Greece, and France that follow.

Notes

1.   Daalder, H., "The Role of a Small State in the European Community: The Case of the Netherlands," Working Paper 1991/21, Centro de Estudios Avanzados en Ciencias Sociales, June 1991.

2. Visser, J., and Hemereijk, A., *A Dutch Miracle—Job Growth, Welfare Reform and Corporatism in the Netherlands*, Amsterdam University Press, Amsterdam, 1997.
3. For relevant articles, see Hurst, J. W., "Reforming Health Care Seven European Nations," *Health Affairs* 10:7-21, 1991; Schut, F. T, "Workable Competition in Health Care: Prospects for the Dutch Design," *Social Science and Medicine* 35(12):1445-55, 1992; Von der Schulenburg, J.-M., "Forming and Reforming the Market for Third-Party Purchasing of Health Care: A German Perspective,"*Social Science and Medicine* 39(10):1473-81, 1992; Van de Ven, W. P. M. M., "Perestroika in the Dutch Health Care System," *European Economic Review* 35:430-40, 1991.
4. Look at Lijphart, A., *The Politics of Accommodation: Pluralism and Democracy in the Netherlands*, University of California Press, Berkeley, 1975, and Schmitter, P. C. "Interest Intermediation and Regime Governability in Contemporary Western Europe and North America," in *Organizing Interests in Western Europe*, S. Berger (ed.), Cambridge University Press, Cambridge, 1981.
5. Interview with Dutch journalist, March 11, 2000.
6. Okma, K., "Health Care, Health Policies and Health Care reform in the Netherlands," Ministry of Health, The Hague, the Netherlands, March 2000.
7. Ministry of Health, Welfare and Sport: *Health Insurance in the Netherlands*, 4th ed., The Hague, Netherlands, 1998.
8. *Financiel Overzicht Zorg 1999*. Kamerstukken II, 1998-1999, 230456, nrs1 en 2, The Hague, The Netherlands, 1998.
9. Netherlands Scientific Council for Government Policy: "Public Health Care" Report # 52, The Hague, the Netherlands, 1997.
10. Netherlands Central Bureau of Statistics–2000 Costs and Health Care Insurance 1995-1999.
11. Laetz, T. J., and Okma, K. G., "Rise and Demise of Health Reforms in the Netherlands, 1988-1998," Ministry of Health, Welfare and Sport, The Hague, The Netherlands, 1998.
12. Ministry of Health figures.
13. Interview with Professor van de Ven at Erasmus University, March 12, 2000.
14. Ministry of Health, Welfare and Sport: *Health Insurance in the Netherlands*, 4th ed. The Hague, Netherlands, 1998.
15. Van den Broek, P., "Wie Met Wie 1995," *Zorgverzekeraars Magazine* 3:17-39, 1995.
16. Interview with Louise Gunning, Amsterdam Medical Center, March 11, 2000.
17. Ministry of Health Statistics.
18. Ministry of Health Statistics.
19. Ministry of Health, Welfare and Sport: *Jaaroverzicht Zorg 1999*. Kamerstukken II 1998-1999, #1-3, The Hague, The Netherlands, 1998.
20. Interview with Nik Klazinga, Amsterdam Medical Center, March 11, 2000.
21. Nivel/NZI: *Branche Rapport Curatieve Somatische Zorg (Branch Report Acute Care)*, Utrecht, The Netherlands, 1998.
22. Ministry of Health.
23. Schut, F., "Competition in Dutch Health Care Sector," Ph.D. diss., Erasmus University, Rotterdam, The Netherlands, 1995.
24. Summary in English (Sharing Care, Better Care) of the Report by Commissie Biesheuvel: *Gedeelde Zorg:betere zorg*. Rapport van de Commissie Modernisering Curatieve Zorg. Ministry of Health, Welfare and Sport, The Hague, The Netherlands, 1994.
25. Ministry of Health Statistics.

26. Ibid.
27. Interview with Niek Klazinga, Amsterdam Medical Center, March 11, 2000.
28. Okma, K., "Health Care, Health Policies and Health Care Reform in the Netherlands," Ministry of Health, The Hague, the Netherlands, March 2000.
29. Vermeulen, H. J. J. M. et al., "Prognoses van knelpunten op de arbeidsmarkt van de zorgsector," IVA, Tilburg, 1998.
30. Ministry of Health Statistics.
31. Schut, F., "Health Care Reform in the Netherlands: Balancing Corporatism, Etatism, and Market Mechanisms," *Journal of Health Politics, Policy and Law* 20(3): 615-646, Fall 1995.
32. Van Schouwenburg, M. L. G., "Hevorming der sociale verzekering,"*Sociaal Maanblad Arbeid* 12: 269-282, 1947.
33. Rutten, F. F. H., "Market Strategies for Publicly Financed Health Care Systems," *Health Policy* 7:135-48, 1987.
34. Elsinga, E., "Political Decision-making in Health Care: The Dutch Case," *Health Policy* 11:243-55, 1989.
35. Okma, K., "Health Care, Health Policies and Health Care Reform in the Netherlands," Ministry of Health, The Hague, The Netherlands, March 2000.
36. Okma, K. G. H., "Studies in Dutch Health Politics, Policies and Law," Ph.D. diss., University of Utrecht, The Netherlands, 1997.
37. Examples of such advisory bodies include the COTG, which is responsible for health care prices, the Sickness Fund Council, which supervises the administration of the sickness funds, and the National Council for Public Health, which is the main advisory body for health policy.
38. Schut, F.,"Health Care Reform in the Netherlands: Balancing Corporatism, Etatism, and Market Mechanisms," *Journal of Health Politics, Policy and Law* 20 (3): 615-646, Fall 1995.
39. De Swaan, A., *In Care of the State. Health Care, Education and Welafre in Europe and the USA in the Modern Era*, Polity Press, Oxford, 1988.
40. Bjorkman, J. W., and Okma, K., "The Institutional Heritage of Dutch Health policy Reforms," *Health Policy, National Schemes and Globalization*, in J. W. Bjorkman and C. Altenstetter (eds.), MacMillan Press, London, 1998.
41. For details on the early history of Dutch health insurance, see Van der Hoeven, H. C., *Voor Elkaar. De Ziekenfondsen te Midden van Sociale Veranderingen*, Centrale Bond van Onderling Beheerde Ziekenfondsen, Utrecht, 1963.
42. Zeven, P. A., *De ziektekostenverzekering*, De Bussy, Amsterdam, 1963.
43. Van der Hoeven, H. C., *Voor Elkaar. De Ziekenfondsen te Midden van Sociale Veranderingen*, Centrale Bond van Onderling Beheerde Ziekenfondsen, Utrecht, 1963.
44. Okma, K. G. H., "Studies in Dutch Health Politics, Policies and Law," Ph.D. diss., University of Utrecht, The Netherlands, 1997.
45. Van de Ven, W. P., "Choices in Health Care: A Contribution from the Netherlands" *British Medical Journal* 51: 781-790, 1995.
46. The Beveridge report that came out in England around this time called for an extensive and publicly financed welfare state that would provide the battered (by the war) British people with significant coverage in terms of social security and health care.
47. Commissie Van Rhijn, *Sociale Zekerheid*, Rapport van de Commissie ingesteld door de Minister voor Sociale Zaken op 26 Maart 1943 (3 delen), 1945.
48. Simons, H. J., and Okma, K., "Mniselsel in de gezondheidszorg?" *De Toekomst van de Welvaarsstaat. Preadviezen voor de Koninklijke Vereniging voor de Staathuishoudkunde*, Stenfert Kroese Uitgevers, Leiden/Antwerpen, 1992.

49. Read a report by Van Schouwenburg, N. G. J., Ministry of Welfare, Health and Cultural Affairs: "Provincie en gezondheidszorg in beeld," The Hague, The Netherlands, 1992.

50. Social and Economic Council, *Advies inzake de structuur van de verzekeringen tegen de kosten van geneeskundige verzorging* [Recommendation concerning the structure of insurances against the costs of medical treatment], Social and Economic Council, The Hague, 1973.

51. Ministry of Public Health and Environment, *Memorandum on the Structure qf' Health Car*, Ministry of Public Health and Environment, Lcidschendam, 1974.

52. The prospective budget system does not cover the services of specialists and thus cannot achieve total control of in-patient health care costs

53. Memorandum by Joe White to colleagues entitled, "Joe White trying to figure out Holland," 1995.

54. Commissie Dekker, *Bereidheid tot Verandering Rapport van de Commissie Structuur en Financiering Gezondheidszorg, Ministerie van Wezign, Volksgezondheid en Cultuur*, 1987.

55. Schut, F., "Health Care Reform in the Netherlands: Balancing Corporatism, Etatism, and Market Mechanisms," *Journal of Health Politics, Policy and Law* 20(3): 615-646, Fall 1995.

56. Lapre, R. M. "A Change of Direction in the Dutch Health Care System?" *Health Policy*, 10:21-32, 1988.

57. Reports by Godefroi in 1963, Zeven in 1973, and Van de Ven in 1983, as well as Enthoven's managed competition theory that started in 1978, all played around the theme of a regulated market in health care services. For more details, see Enthoven, A. C., "Consumer Choice Health Plan," *New England Journal of Medicine* 298:650-8, 709-20, 1978, and Godefroi, L. S. *Het ziekenj6ndswezen in Nederland: ontwikkeling en perspectieven* I Sickness Fund Insurance in the Netherlands: Development and Perspectives], Martinus Nijhoff, The Hague, 1963.

58. Interview with Joe White in 1995.

59. Memorandum by Joe White to Colleagues, entitled "Joe White trying to figure out Holland," 1995.

60. Interview with Joe White. Also see Hurst, J. W., "Reforming Health Care in Seven European Nations," *Health Affairs,* Special Issue, pp. 7-21, Fall 1991.

61. The language is from Ministry of Welfare, Health and Cultural Affairs, "Fact Sheet: Health Care Reform in the Netherlands," 1993.

62. Bjorkman, J. W., and Okma, K., "The Institutional Heritage of Dutch Health Policy Reforms," in *Health Policy, National Schemes and Globalization*, J. W. Bjorkman and C. Altenstetter (eds.), MacMillan Press, London, 1998.

63. Ministry of Welfare, Health and Cultural Affairs, "Change Assured: Changing Health Care in the Netherlands." The Hague, The Netherlands, 1988.

64. Ministry of Welfare, Health and Cultural Affairs, "Werken aan zorgvernieuwing (Working on health care innovation)," Tweede Kamer, 1989-1990, 21545 (2), The Hague, The Netherlands, May 1990.

65. Van de Ven, W. P. M. M., "A Decade of Health Care Reforms in the Netherlands" Institute of Health Care Policy and Management, Erasmus University, Rotterdam, The Netherlands, October 1999.

66. See Chavannes, M. articles in *Handelsblad*, September 18, 21, 25, and 28, 1991.

67. See Van Rossum articles in *Elsevier*, numbers 32, 33, 34, and 35 of 1991.

68. See related articles on October 4, 1991, in *De Volkskrant*: "Debat van scepticus met gelovige ongelijke strijd"; in Handelsblad: "Beschaafd welles-nietes over

plan-imons"; in *Het Binnenhof*: "VNO-voorzitter: Kabinet moet verplicht eigen risico invoeren"; and in *Het Financieele Dagblad*: "VNO cijfers Simons veroordeeld."

69. Committee Dunning: *Choices in Health Care*, A Report by the Government Committee on Choices in Health Care, Ministry of Welfare, Health and Cultural Affairs, The Hague The Netherlands, 1992.

70. Letter from State Secretary for Welfare, Health and Cultural Affairs Simons to Professor J. Dunning, August 30, 1990.

71. Gezondheidsraad Rapport: "Medisch handelen op een tweesprong," The Hague, The Netherlands, 1991.

72. Bjorkman, J. W., and Okma, K., "The Institutional Heritage of Dutch Health Policy Reforms," in J. W. Bjorkman and C. Altenstetter (eds.), *Health Policy, national Schemes and Globalization*, MacMillan Press, London, 1998.

73. NRV 1991 Annual Report, Zoeterme, The Hague, The Netherlands, 1992.

74. PvdA: "Naar een nieuwe gezonheidszorg," Discussion of the PvdA working group, Amsterdam, The Netherlands, 1992.

75. CDA: "Betere zorg op basis van solidatiteit en eigen verantwoordelijkheid," Discussion of the CDA working group, The Hague, The Netherlands, 1992.

76. Ministry of Welfare, Health and Cultural Affairs, "Modernisering Zorgsector. Weloverwogen Verder" Kamerstukken II, 1991-1992, TweedeKamer, 22393, nr 20, 1992.

77. Okma, K. G. H., "Studies in Dutch Health Politics, Policies and Law," Ph.D. diss., University of Utrecht, The Netherlands, 1997.

78. Commissie Willems, "Onderzoek Besluitvorming Volksgezondheid," Kamerstukken II, 1993-1994, 23666, nrs 1 en 2, The Hague, The Netherlands, 1994.

79. Van de Ven, W. P. M. M., "A Decade of Health Care Reforms in the Netherlands," Institute of Health Care Policy and Management, Erasmus University, Rotterdam, The Netherlands, October 1999.

80. Okma, K. G. H. "Studies in Dutch Health Politics, Policies and Law."

81. "Kabinetsformatie 1998," brief van de informateurs, Tweede Kamer, 1997-1998m 26024, nr 9, 1998.

82. Netherlands Scientific Council for Government Policy: "Public Health Care" 52nd Report of the Council, The Hague, The Netherlands, 1997.

4

Healing the Greek National Health System Requires Political Surgery

*"Healing is a matter of time, but it is
sometimes also
a matter of opportunity."*

—*Hippocrates*

Political Environment in the 1990s

To understand, health policy reform attempts in Greece in 2001, or any other policy for that matter, one must first be aware of the surrounding political environment and the changes that the last decade has brought. Admittedly, what follows is a cursory look at the many complexities of Greek politics in the 1990s. Yet it is necessary as an introduction to the changing economic and political environment. If there were only one country that had to change its ways because of European Union membership, it would be Greece. With one of the most remarkable turnaround economic stories of the decade, Greece was able to join EMU as the twelfth member in January 2001. The challenges for Greece, its government and its citizens are now concentrated on how the country can sustain economic growth within the EMU zone, while truly converging its economy in terms of social protection levels and in terms of creating a flexible labor environment. For a state that until quite recently was characterized by a mixed capitalist economy and an enlarged public sector, joining the EMU had been elevated to a national goal. The public sector, which had always been large in Greece, experienced during the 1980s a tremendous growth, jumping from 55 percent of GDP in 1981 to a little below 62 percent in 1989. Since then and especially since 1993, years of austerity policies coupled with a hard drachma policy and increased privatization have led to a downward trend in inflation[1] which stands at the lowest level in twenty-five years and has allowed the country to meet the Maastricht criteria for EMU membership. The next goal for the current

143

government and for the country as a whole, as the recent election results indicated,[2] is how to bring about the structural reforms necessary for economic growth without hurting and indeed improving social protection systems. During the 2000 summer, the freshly re-elected PASOK (socialist) government took on a number of issues on the social front (education system, health care, labor relations) and then during the fall also opened the issue of social security and its modernization. After seven years of trying to reach the stated Maastricht criteria, the government has turned its attention to continuous economic growth, which would allow Greece to have a standard of living similar to the more economically advanced states of the North. It is estimated that within ten years, this will have occurred, assuming an economic growth of 5 percent annually, an assumption that the finance ministry appears to believe is quite workable.[3]

Greece, however, due largely to its turbulent political history, has not been accustomed to long- or even medium-term planning. Furthermore, the technocratic terminology of current government officials and the Eurocratic style of governance is also something that Greeks have not been used to, and skillful politicians oftentimes take advantage of this distrust towards government.

Since the inception of modern Greece in 1829, the country has experienced national divisions, which have led to a civil war and numerous military dictatorship or to a number of farcical pseudodemocratic governments.[4] A historical review of Greek politics is beyond the scope of this essay and has been told elsewhere sufficiently. For our purposes suffice it to say that it was not until 1974, and arguably 1981, that Greece became a stable democracy.[5] It was at that time that the first transfer of power from one side of the political spectrum (the right) to the other side (the left) was completed, based on the will of the people without interference from either foreign states or domestic actors like the army. Interestingly enough, the period coincides with the time that Greece became the tenth member of the European Economic Community (1981). In this sense, the first relatively stable political times of modern Greece have also been associated with European membership.

From 1981 and until 1986, the socialist government pushed for increased state *dirigisme* in the economy and continued the policies of the late seventies whereby the state bought private sector companies. In the latter part of the 1980s, the government, on the one hand, had realized that the policy was not producing economic growth and, on the other hand, it was trapped because of the political cost it would have to accept for an economic U-turn similar to the French one of 1983.

When the conservatives came to power in 1990, their attempts to reform the economy, coupled with unpopular welfare reform proposals that would have placed social cohesion at jeopardy, and an extremely important foreign affairs issue, forced the government to call elections a full year before its term was over. The socialists returned to power, and this time around they not only performed the economic U-turn that the country required but they had also changed their attitudes towards Greek membership in the EU. Whereas the socialists had traditionally been opposed to Brussels and any transfer of authority to the center, after 1993 they came to see a number of benefits for Greece through its European Union membership. Furthermore, being a net recipient of the Union's budget has also brought economic benefits and therefore it is small wonder that EU membership is valued highly by the Greek population. This attitude is what has started to change the country. Joining the EMU and striving for sustainable economic growth is part of this attitude.

As of 2002, this requires strict fiscal policies according to the confidence pact that members have signed, which, in turn, must lead to a more disciplined, leaner, more efficient and more effective public sector. As part of a complete policy package to reach this goal, a number of public companies have been privatized and a number of them are scheduled for privatization in the upcoming months. A second part of this strategy has to do with modernizing systems of social protection. In this chapter, I examine the reform attempts in one such system, that of health care, arguing that there are two driving forces behind the proposed reforms: first, the admittedly much needed face-lift of the health services in Greece in terms of quality and cost control; second, and equally important, the adaptation of social protection as a whole, and of health care as a part of it, to the new economic realities being created by Greek membership in EMU. In other words, it is both the internal need for reform that the system itself dictates and the external need for adaptation of the national economy to European norms that has led to reforms on the health care front. The Greek case is especially interesting because the health care reform process is ongoing at the time of the writing, and in light of the changes that Greece had to bring in other sectors of its economy, it is also indicative how certain ideas travel through the Union usually from the more economically developed states toward the less economically developed states. In so doing, it also offers us some insight on how the integration process proceeds. As is the theme in the other two country chapters, here, too, domestic politics and health care politics more specifically take over. Whereas there is an overall current towards one direction, specific interests either slow it down or adapt it to domestic realities depending on one's point of view. Improving health care services in Greece, however, or healing the national health system requires radical political surgery and the decision to adapt the national economy to European norms can and most likely will provide the catalyst and the political rationale for the needed reforms.

All of the observers of the National Health System(NHS) of Greece agree that it is in trouble. And one would think that in a country like Greece, where the parliamentary system gives absolute power to the government, radical reform would not be hard to achieve. But Greek health care policy is characterized by the paradox of the simultaneous coexistence of universal dissatisfaction with the system and endless calls for reform with the equally universal resistance to this much needed reform. Here, I first sketch out the main contours of the system. Then I turn the discussion to my central argument that, whereas the overall directions of reform for the health sector are more or less agreed upon, strong political interests, the way Greeks have historically perceived government, and the relationship between individual rights and community responsibility have successfully resisted major reform attempts. Whereas everyone is tired of the inefficiency and ineffectiveness of the system as a whole, an individualistic mentality, characteristic of Greek political culture, has allowed each player to manipulate the system to his benefit. In the process, such "rights" have become institutionalized, therefore constraining further reform attempts and the rationalization of the system. It is indicative that whereas a number of pieces of legislation have made it through Parliament, very few have actually been implemented fully, leading to a continuous circle of dissatisfaction and more calls for reform. Within this context, the health care system has been slowly evolving to its current stage.

Placing the Players on the Health Map

The main elements of the current health system were put into place with the enactment of the NHS in 1983. Legislation 1397/83 instituted for the first time a comprehensive national health system. This legislation was one of the most important works of the first socialist government of PASOK and an ambitious attempt in reorganizing the significantly fragmented health care delivery system that existed up to that date.

Going through the civil war, the tumultuous fifties, and the military dictatorship had not allowed for any comprehensive handling of the health sector. Successive governments had opted to place their political interests in other areas that were either more pressing or more intriguing. The futile attempt in the closing year of the seventies to pass the Measures for the Protection of Health, by the then Minister of Health Doxiades (New Democracy), brought health care to the forefront. The political impulse for the creation of the NHS, however, was deeper than just a political reaction to the Doxiades attempt. The widespread feeling that the Greek record of social services was indeed a depressing one compared to Greece's European partners in the EU, coupled with the overriding socialist principles of the new government (elected in 1981) that dictated that it was the nation's obligation to provide quality health care for all, converged to create the window of opportunity for the passage of legislation. Even the main opposition party of New Democracy at the right of the political spectrum supported action in the health care sector, albeit in a different form from what was actually passed. Their support was rooted mostly in the fact that if Greece ever wanted to develop its economy, an improvement of its social services was imperative. But they also realized that if they were to ever recapture power they needed to win the swing voters who were mandating action. So, either out of feelings of national duty or of political attractiveness, the entire political world supported legislation at the time and has maintained its support for the idea of the NHS since then.

What underlined most of the political decisions of that period and of subsequent years was the strong societal consensus that health care is a right. It followed that it would have to be provided by the state. The state as the authorized personification of a society was responsible for the provision of other goods, which by nature could not be adequately or equitably provided by the private sector. The creation of the NHS was another attempt to create a feeling of national solidarity. In an otherwise highly divided society, still healing from its historic wounds (civil war, military dictatorship), social protection in general and health care in particular could serve as one of the focal point of social cohesiveness.

Some key decisions that were made during this period would affect the functioning or the dysfunctioning, depending on one's point of view, of the system for the years to come. These decisions set the Greek health care system upon its particular trajectory: The socialist government paradoxically chose to base the system on the preexisting obligatory employer-employee contributory insurance, rather than adopting a Beveridge model all tax financed system. And unlike the British, who nationalized the entire medical corps, Greece left private practitioners in place, albeit with restrictions. Most importantly, however, Greece chose not to establish a strict referral system between general practitioners who could deliver ambulatory care and hospital based specialists. It rather opted, partly because of the lack of general practitioners, for a peculiar overlap between generalists and specialists in ambulatory care, which would no doubt lead to uncoordinated links between ambulatory and hospital sectors.

The medical system is thought of as a mix of socialized access to health care, which fulfills the vital goal of national solidarity, and a mosaic of public and private practice of medicine, which preserves both physician autonomy and the mystique of the doctor-patient relationship.[6] Much like the French *La Médecine liberale*,[7] the practice of medicine in Greece has in practice been founded on the same four principles: (1) free choice of physician by the patient; (2) freedom of prescription by the physician; (3) fee for service payment system; and (4) direct payment by the patient to the physician. This paternalistic view of medicine is as strong today as it has ever been. In light of the challenges that health care faces and that have been discussed in earlier chapters, one can easily see the future conflicts that are forthcoming. These four principles apply to the entire ambulatory care sector, even after the enactment of the NHS. Interestingly enough, even though the physicians who are contracted by the NHS are forbidden to enter private practice, most of them do anyway. As far as ambulatory care is concerned, patients in Greece choose their physician freely, seek care directly by specialists, and physicians may give out prescriptions without any of the administrative hassle observed in other Western nations, or at least not much of it. There is a catch, however. The reimbursement rates are not what the patients would like them to be, and this results partly in Greece leading all OECD countries in out-of-pocket payments (42 percent of total health expenditures).[8] The creation of 190 Health Centers and 1,311 ambulatory care centers in rural areas has improved access to primary care even though most of them operate without adequate personnel. It has been estimated that 30 to 40 percent of the necessary positions are vacant.[9] In urban centers where urban ambulatory sites never came into existence (even though they were supposed to, according to the NHS legislation), primary care is still provided by the primary care centers of the different sickness funds, the ambulatory sites of major hospitals, private offices of physicians and diagnostic laboratories. In the decade between 1981 and 1991, the total number of visits in the ambulatory sites of hospitals more than doubled, reaching nine million in 1991. Today, it is closer to 10 million.[10]

This relatively uncontrolled ambulatory system coexists in an oddly comfortable way alongside the hospital system, which by contrast is at least centrally directed by the Ministry of Health in Athens. Based on the 1983 legislation, all hospitals were supposed to become public, but this never occurred and, as of 2001, the private hospital sector still has a significant presence. In 1980, there were 608 hospitals (both public and private) with 59,327 beds. Most of these were rather small units that were absorbed into the NHS after the passage of the legislation in 1983. As a result, in 1993 there were 368 hospitals with 52,144 beds and in 1995, 358 hospitals with 52,227 beds. Public beds increased between 1981 and 1995 from 34,614 to 36,717 whereas private beds decreased during that same period by 7,500 beds. Whereas in 1981 before the NHS passed, 41 percent of total beds were private, today 30 percent of the beds are private. Overall, there was a drop of 7,000 beds, which means that there are 5.1 beds per 1,000 people. This number places Greece next to last in the EU, leading only Portugal.[11] Another major issue in terms of the number of hospital beds is their unequal distribution on a geographical basis. So whereas there are 5.1 beds per 1,000 people on average for the entire country, in the Athens area there are 7.8 beds per 1,000 people, in the Salonika area (second largest area) 5.1, in Crete there are 5.3, whereas in other areas like the island of Evia there are only 1.5 beds per 1,000 people or in Thrace where the number is 2.6 beds per 1,000 citizens. A similar situation in terms of geographic maldistribution of resources exists in terms of physician supply for hospitals. Not surprisingly, since doctors go where the hospitals are, Athens, Salonika and Crete have 3.3, 1.8 and 1.7 physicians per 1,000 people whereas Evia and Thrace have 0.4 and 1.1 physicians per 1,000 people. The average for the entire country is 1.9.[12]

In 1992, the creation of private clinics was once again allowed by the government and this led to the increase of the private sector throughout the decade of the 1990s. This occurred mostly through the creation of private laboratories where physicians send their patients for tests. Oftentimes, there are kickbacks from these centers to the physicians, or the physicians are part owners, which offers them the economic incentive to ask for more tests than would have otherwise been necessary. In 1996, there were 403 such centers. Sixty-seven percent of them were in the Athens metropolitan area. There were 12.5 cat scanners and 1.2 MRI units per million population. For comparative purposes, the EU average is 5 and 0.8 respectively. Furthermore, there is an aggressive expansion in the market for private insurance and for private hospitals. In the latter, a number of businessmen (previously unrelated to the health care sector), but also physicians with an entrepreneurial spirit, have started private clinics that have expanded in the last few years through horizontal integration (acquisition of smaller clinics) but also through vertical integration (creation or plans for creating primary care centers, etc.). In the insurance market, a number of insurance companies have begun to offer packages, but more relevantly have begun to coordinate their actions and cooperate with clinics and large hospitals so that they can forcefully enter this market. Despite all the rhetoric against or for the private sector involvement, one thing is certain. As we will see, it has served as the catalyst for reforms in the public NHS so that the quality of services can be improved.

Physicians that work for the public NHS are considered professional civil servants. The salary that is paid to them is small by comparison to private practice earnings, but many physicians choose to stay within the system where they can shop for customers for their "illegal" private practice. More specifically, in 1996 full-time salaried physicians in the NHS earned an annual salary ranging between $12,000 and $21,000. IKA (the major sickness fund) physicians, who officially work five and a half hours a day for the institute(often less), earned an average salary of $5,500 in 1996. The major portion of their income, however, comes from their private practice and from a uniquely Mediterranean side economy illegal payments to salaried physicians, termed *fakelaki* (little envelope), essentially a bribe to facilitate services covered by insurance. This income—private fees and illegal payments—was estimated to be close to $31,000 annually per physician in 1992.[13] For comparative purposes, a mid-level civil servant had an income of just below $16,000 in 1996. These figures emphasize the significance of the salaried positions for most physicians. They provide them with a moderate source of income, but more importantly, they serve as a source of patients and therefore income for their private practices. Another significant aspect in terms of the profession is its numbers. Greece has proportionately more physicians than any other country in the EU with 1 per 250 people whereas the UK has 1 per 562 people and France 1 per 336.[14] And despite this large supply of physicians, most of whom are specialists, there is an issue of access since more than 50 percent of them choose to practice in the Athens area. When one adds the Salonika area, the second largest metropolitan area, then the percentage jumps close to 85 percent. Greece also has one of the lowest numbers of nursing staff in the Union. Their numbers stood at 24.47 per 100,000 population in 1980, 34.31 in 1990, and 43 per 100,000 in 1995. This number places Greece once again second to last (Portugal has the smallest) in the EU. There is an issue of geographic maldistribution with nursing staff as well. In Athens, there are 5.6 nurses per 1,000 people and in Crete 4 nurses per 1,000 people, whereas in Evia and in Thrace the respective numbers are 1 and 2.6.[15]

Furthermore, the lack of trained management in hospitals has resulted in their overspending and posting of deficits, which the government then has to cover. In short, in the ambulatory care sector there are no incentives to economize, since there are no controls either on the demand or on the supply side of care. Also, in the hospital care sector, the lack of management and questionable practice patterns by physicians are two of the main reasons that have led to increased cost. And whereas, according to 2001 OECD figures, public health expenditures in Greece had not exceeded 5.5 percent of GDP (and there had been a steady increase of public expenditures from 3.7 percent of GDP in 1980 to 4.8 percent of GDP in 1990 to 5.3 percent in 1998), total health expenditures are closer to 9 percent (8.6 percent).[16] This places Greece in the same category with richer nations like the Netherlands, Germany, and France, and is indicative of the shortcomings of the public sector in the first instance, and of the large side economy that coexists alongside the NHS in the second instance.

The administrative work in the Greek health care system is being performed by the different sickness funds. There are seven main ones, accounting for insuring almost 95 percent of the population.[17] These seven are IKA (Social Insurance Institute), OGA (Agricultural Insurance Organization), TEBE (Professionals Fund), the fund for public employees, the OTE fund (for employees of the telecommunications organization), the DEI fund (for employees of the electric company), and TYPET (the fund for bank employees). Some of these funds are non-profit self-controlling bodies whereas others are public ones. Between all the sickness funds, virtually the entire population of the country is insured. The sickness funds are responsible for overseeing the enrollment of those covered, for collecting the contributions by employers, employees and the central government as well as for reimbursing claims. The sickness funds provide both ambulatory and hospital care, but there is no standardization of benefits. Finally, at the direction of the government the sickness funds negotiate levels of reimbursement.

A not very effective administrative system, the sickness funds have often become the target of series of complaints by patients, who oftentimes choose not to deal with them until they have first consulted a private physician. Then they proceed through the system either for a second opinion or just for the prescription, so that they will have to pay only 25 percent of the cost. In a recent survey, four out of ten patients consulted with a physician in private practice at least once a year. The funds, under the direction of the central government, are also responsible for the economic sustainability of the system. To date, however, not many cost containment measures have been designed, or when designed effectively implemented.

The sickness funds' problems become more complicated by the fact that the decision-making point lies within the central government and its centralized bureaucracy in Athens, despite the provision in the law for the creation of regional bureaus of health. These bureaus never came into being and decentralization remains a major issue in the health care debate. The government acts mainly through the Ministry of Health and the Ministry of Labor, but also through a number of other ministries depending on the issue at hand. Whereas the Ministry of Health is the main actor in formulating overall health policy, the Ministry of Labor plays an important role, for instance, in negotiations with the unions. The Ministry of Education is responsible for undergraduate medical education, and any limits on the number of students allowed to enter medical school have to be channeled through this ministry. Furthermore, the Ministry of Development plays a significant role in setting prices for pharmaceutical products. The lack of coordination between these ministries is also partially responsible for the highly fragmented picture that health care presents today in Greece. In short, the health sector appears to be a mix of private practice and public service, centrally regulated with few provisions for cost containment. Its vast bureaucracy and the sub-optimal ways of delivering care have led it to receive the worst ratings of public satisfaction compared to any other health care system in the European Union.

A few words about the political treatment of the NHS by the different parties since its enactment: it is commonly accepted by informed observers today that the NHS was established late compared to other Western nation's systems and that by the time it started operating it was already outdated. The two main political parties, PASOK and New Democracy, have both been in favor of the NHS notion. But as in other issues, there has never been a political consensus about what the NHS should be expected to accomplish. On the contrary, political rhetoric and political games have not allowed the two main parties to reach agreement on how to modernize the NHS. In short, the NHS has mostly been used as another weapon by the party of opposition (whichever it might be at the time), without ever really aiming at the actual improvement of the system. A striking example, but by no means the only one, are the successive amendments to the NHS in 1992 and 1994 by the governments of New Democracy and PASOK, respectively. New Democracy's government changed the contracting agreement between the NHS and physicians, allowing physicians to choose between part-time NHS employment and the right for private practice vs. full-time NHS employment and no right for private practice. The PASOK reforms of 1994 eliminated the measure even though only 400 physicians had opted for the part-time option.

As with any other policy arena, the state and its institutions have to interact dynamically with interests groups from society, which press their demands on the government. Here I focus on organized medicine and the Greek public. The Panhellenic Medical Society (PIS) represents all physicians of the country, and membership in it is mandatory. It is composed of fifty-eight official local societies. Its functions are spelled out in the law. Its most important functions are the coordination of all local societies, the regulation of compliance with the code of ethics, the advisement of the Ministry of Health, Welfare and Social Insurance on matters like medical education and research and the representation of Greece's physicians in the world's medical association. There are some other associations of physicians. The main one is the Union of Hospital Physicians in Athens-Piraeus (EINAP). It was formed, as were others, like the Society of Professional Health Personnel of IKA (SEIPIKA), the Society of Hospital Physicians, and the Society of Generalists, because their constituents felt that their interests were not represented satisfactorily by PIS. In general, Greek physicians feel under-appreciated and underpaid in a society, which nevertheless regards them as privileged. By international standards Greek physicians earn less than their counterparts in other countries but, be that as it may, they still earn three times more than the average citizen. The interesting phenomenon is that physicians have chosen to exploit the current system, rather than try to improve it through political influence. The truth of the matter is that being controlled by the state, as a public institution, has not made it any easier for organized medicine to enjoy any significant political influence. Moreover, the most significant characteristic of organized medicine in Greece is the political party penetration within all organizations that Colombotos and Fakiolas described.[18] Candidates for leadership positions identify themselves with a political party and oftentimes the party, which controls the organization, passes its political line. In this fashion, different parties sometimes control different societies and therefore organized medicine fails in presenting a unifying front. This is not to say that organized medicine does not affect politics. For instance, after the 1983 passage of the NHS by PASOK, the PASOK candidates lost the 1984 PIS election, in a professional protest over the passage of the legislation. The net effect of this political penetration into organized medicine, however, remains the fragmentation of the latter along party lines and therefore the compromise of professional interests.

Interestingly enough, despite the creation of the unofficial medical societies, organized medicine in Greece does not appear to be divided along professional lines. In other Western countries, balancing between the collective interest of the profession and the specific interests of its several segments is a hard task. In Greece, either because of the increased political penetration's role as a confounder of such divisions or because of the overlap between salaried and private physicians or both, the profession is still relatively free from divisions originating within it. Absent also are divisions along demographic lines: male vs. female physicians, young vs. old physicians, etc. Whereas it is true that establishing a practice is extremely difficult in Greece, young struggling doctors have not turned against older and more established physicians. They have rather chosen to exploit the system by working both within it and outside of it. The poor quality of care provided by the sickness funds and by the NHS and the prosperous underground economy, as explained earlier, feed on each other and form an immoral circle, which cries out for intervention. Physicians, however, have been very slow to mobilize politically for reform of the system. They do after all have a vested interest in maintaining the current system.

One would think that public outrage with this system would by now have reached gigantic proportions. Long waiting lines, exploitation by physicians, a side economy, lack of preventive care, delays in the low reimbursements would, in any other country, lead to a 'rebellion' of the citizenry. Not in Greece! Whereas the public is quick to condemn the system and all its faults, it has also learned to live with it. The overarching theme is that the use of personal connections in pursuing individual goals overrides the use of collective means in pursuing collective goals. And as far as personal connections are able to provide what "the organized official system" fails to provide, the public is content to criticize it without realizing that its own behavior weakens the very idea of a national health system. The public has never been unified in demanding specific changes. It is by and large apathetic to political organizing. This does not mean that it does not have distinct political opinions, but, more often than not, these opinions are likely to be heard in the realm of a debate, whereby two people blame each other's political party for the pathetic state of the NHS. A striking example of the public's willingness to play along with the immorality of the system is that 42 percent of total national health expenditures are private. From that 42 percent, only 0.86 percent goes to private insurance and the rest is either for personal expenses or for illegal payments. Nevertheless, a recent survey performed in the Athens area indicates that 70 percent of the population is willing to pay more even out of pocket or in the form of increased taxes or premiums if that were to be translated into better services. Interestingly enough, the result was consistent across socioeconomic categories with the middle class exhibiting the highest level of 72.3 percent.[19]

I shall now summarize some of the most important problems of the system. I realize that simply their mention does not improve the situation, but their collective presentation serves as a good point of departure for exploring Greek health policy history. First, the irrational ways of allocating resources: whereas almost 9 percent of the Greek GDP is consumed in the health care sector, a significant portion of it (close to 40 percent) are payments in the private sector or in the side economy. Furthermore, as can be expected when such a large part of total health expenditures is not public, there are tremendous differences in terms of access between the wealthier and the poorer strata of society. The second problem is the unethical and sometimes even illegal behavior of medical professionals. It is a common secret that the following occur, but by nature it is very hard to estimate either the rate by which they occur or the true financial burden that they cause. The fakelaki to hospital-based physicians and others to expedite a specific service is not only given by the public but also oftentimes even demanded by the professionals themselves. A recent survey estimated, based on anecdotes, the additional income for physicians to be an average of $1,000 a month. Specific cases have been rumored to demand up to $4,000 as a fakelaki.[20] Pharmaceutical companies have traditionally been willing to give cash to physicians or fly them to medical conferences abroad in order for them to prescribe their products. Moreover, physicians add to their income by sending patients to specific diagnostic centers, of which sometimes they might even be part owners. NHS and IKA physicians are also known to direct patients for treatment to their private practice, where the fees are significantly higher than their salaries in the system. Finally, it is rumored that most physicians avoid maintaining extensive files for tax evasion purposes. The third problem is that the public is highly dissatisfied with the system, but at the same time it is willing to play along with these practices that infuriate it in the first instance. It is, however, encouraging that two-thirds of the population are willing to see an increase in their taxes if that increase were to be followed by visible improvements of the system. Finally, a plethora of problems relating to the organization of the system add to its sub-optimality. Geographic differences in the distributions of beds, physicians and public financing of the system have left rural areas severely underserved. The lack of a standardized benefit package between the several sickness funds superimposes more inequalities in terms of health insurance. The major centralization and the vast bureaucracy in Athens does not allow for much improvement since it is impossible for the central officers to be aware of daily problems and community needs at the local level. Moreover, the lack of incentives for these bureaucrats, coupled by their constitutionally protected permanence of position, lead to an indifferent attitude on their behalf. The lack of quality standards and of a data collecting system which would allow for monitoring quality have resulted in a series of complaints and also a lack of the much needed empirical data which could be then be used to improve faults of the system through an informed debate. Finally, the large presence of the private sector de facto demands a better framework of coordination between the NHS and the private sector, which has, however, eluded Greece.

Where does all this leave the NHS? Whereas it is true that the system has not satisfied, one needs to acknowledge the importance of its existence if only to underlie the official commitment of Greek society, as all European societies, to health care for all. In the same context, one also needs to mention that in terms of life expectancy, Greeks post better numbers compared to most Europeans and to Americans. Furthermore, the NHS has, despite its problems, improved access to health care services to a significant degree. It is customary and useful at times to compare today's situation with an imaginary perfect system, but it would be equally useful to think at times where the health care services sector, the access of the average citizen and the issue of social cohesion would have been without the existence of the NHS. Finally, whereas some of the NHS problems stem from the legislative process, most of them are born by the political constraints on health policy choices that are created through history and that is where one should look first for answers. With that in mind, I shall explore the health policy path to examine the birth of these political constraints.

The Health Policy Path in Greece: The Creation of the Constraints to the Rationalization of the Distribution of Health Care

Any attentive observer of the Greek health care policy scene would readily recognize that whereas significant tensions and justified reasons for reform seem to dominate the system, overall inertia appears to be the overwriting characteristic of policy making, at least in all practicality. Because one might very well argue that four pieces of legislation in the past seventeen years and yet another set of reforms that are being debated as of 2002 prove exactly the opposite; that the policy mechanism is working and working rather hard indeed. But the truth of the matter is that either because of political games or true ideological differences, the two major parties that have been exchanged in power in this period have found it difficult to formulate and implement a strategic plan that could lead to overall system improvement. Changing a political system, which is based on entrenched institutional powers, is obviously easier said than done. What can a government do? What type of policies does it create?

In order to answer these questions, the first thing one should do is examine the policy path that brought the system to where it is today. To disregard history is the surest way to err in the future formulation of policy and for that reason alone a journey through time is imperative. As a result, one should be able to evaluate different policy options as they appear.

1922-1980: Fragmented Policies and the Problems They Cause

By 1917, the Ministry of Care was instituted. By 1922, its name had changed to Ministry of Health and Social Care and it was responsible for all health services in the land. One could not say much for the Greek health care system, however. A minute segment of the population had health insurance and neither the hospital infrastructure nor the medical personnel supplies were sufficient. But even at that time the government was dedicating considerable amounts of money for medical education, which was free in Greece. After the 1922 Minor Asia catastrophe[21] and the great inflow of one and a half million refugees, this lack of infrastructure became a pressing problem. The international commission for the refugees also created, among a number of measures, rural health centers in the north of Greece where a great number of refugees went. Health services were being provided by voluntary institutions and local government without systematic planning. The government then decided to subsidize the creation of temporary hospitals; a policy, which resulted in 2,630, beds being created.[22] Most hospitals, however, were in urban areas. By 1929, half of all available beds were in the cities and 40 percent of available physicians were in the Athens area, while only one-sixth of the population lived there.[23] In fact, more than 55 percent of available beds were in the two largest metro areas (Athens and Salonika), where only a quarter of the population resided.

In 1928, an epidemic struck 1.3 million Greeks and forced the progressive government of Venizelos to consider seriously a national policy for health. The physicians, however, were quick to oppose any such governmental intervention, arguing that physicians would end up becoming employees.[24] Furthermore, they argued that political compromises based on calculated benefits for the different parties would lead to an inefficient and expensive system. And the frequent changes in government (for reasons unrelated to health care, but critical to the political instability of the land) did not allow for a stable political framework.[25] Nevertheless, the government asked for assistance in 1928 from the League of Nations, following the suggestion of Minister Doxiades. A year later, an international team of experts led by Dr. Rajchman went to Greece where it performed a number of studies.[26] It wrote 148 separate conclusions. The most striking comment in all of the Commission's work was one that characterized the land as a "dangerous country in terms of health conditions." Among the conclusions reached by the Commission were that the quality of services was extremely low, hospital care was almost nonexistent, and health care organization was embryonic. The Commission was the first ever to recommend the creation of a National Health Service, which would serve as the coordinating venue for all health services.[27] A team of experts who would plan the health map of the land would advise it. Health centers were to be created in accordance with local needs. The commission suggested five-year implementation funds, involvement of the local authorities and political support for the plan. In retrospect, it sounds very much like a number of other proposals that have come afterwards, as we will see. As a proposed plan, it looked great on paper but it got stuck in the political arena. The first step that the government took was to create the Health Center of Athens, the Nursing School, and the Public Health School, which was fought from the beginning by the Athens Medical School and other professional organizations. The plan did not move forward since organized interests and political calculations condemned it from the beginning, a story that was to be repeated many times afterward.

In the meantime, approximately 90 percent of the population had no health insurance. In the beginning of the thirties, as the world fiscal crisis was dominating, workers went on strike, with one of their main demands being insurance coverage (mainly pensions but also health insurance). In 1932, the progressive Venizelos government passed legislation 5733/1932 that provided for health care coverage for the urban populations. All medical professional organizations pledged to fight the legislation.[28] The declared war by the medical organized interests and the change in government from the progressives to the conservatives did not allow the plan to materialize. In 1934, IKA was created under Act 6298/34, but it did not start operating until 1940[29] because of successive changes in government and political turmoil, which ended with the Metaxas dictatorship. Metaxas, in his attempt to gain popularity, implemented the Act. The financing mechanism of IKA is based on obligatory employer-employee contributions. According to the 1934 legislation, the administration of the system was the responsibility of PIS, which is of the profession. In this fashion, the fee for service payment mechanism as well as the free choice of physician and the right to freely prescribe were de facto established.

Finally, in 1937, under mandatory Act 965/37, the financing of public hospitals was spelled out. The government devoted large grants of money to increasing the capacity of hospitals. It was, and still is, the major financial source for hospitals, and in that sense subsidizes the inflow of medical technology. Biomedical research is not very extensive in Greece, and reliance is placed on medical innovations invented in other countries. The political climate was a favorable one for these policies. With the creation of the Ministry of Health, Welfare, and Social Insurance in 1922, policy makers debated and realized that if Greece were to create any type of medical care system, sizable portions of money needed to be dedicated to health care. The lack of infrastructure, coupled with the Minor Asia catastrophe and the world economic crisis, pushed social protection problems to the forefront. People were concerned about social inequalities and lack of care and a probable statement posed to the governments of the time could have looked something like this: if the government doesn't build the hospitals needed and provide health coverage, then we will find one that will. The profession was not opposed to the building of hospitals since they would provide physicians with a place to work. Since the administration of the system was in their hands, governmental funding was not feared. Proponents for the different Acts built their argument on two basic premises: First, these programs would provide solutions to imperative issues of national importance such as access to medical care and, second, the entire population stood to win something. It was a win-win situation that presented politicians with at least short-term popularity gains, which, in those politically turbulent times, was more than they could have hoped for. Policy makers at the time rationalized their decisions based on the analytic formulation that the only thing wrong with the Greek health care system was that there was just not enough money in it. The dominant theme of those days was to build capacity. Increase capacity and the health care problems would go away. And capacity was indeed increased, albeit not programmatically or equitably.

The crowding of cities caused by internal emigration related to industrialization, as well as the coming of the refugees led to the building of hospitals mostly in the major urban centers. IKA was also responsible for covering salaried workers, who, by definition of their jobs, were most likely to be concentrated in the large centers. This meant that a sizable segment of the population, the rural population composed of farmers and their dependents, had neither access to the new hospitals nor health insurance coverage. And because physicians go where the hospitals are, there were not that many physicians serving that population either.

World War II turned the interest of both the public and policy makers to other issues. At the end of the war, however, yet another attempt was made to organize comprehensively health services in the country. Under the leadership of Professor Louros, one of the most ambitious plans to date was suggested. The basic premise of his proposals was that universal coverage was a right of the citizenry. Clearly influenced by British thinking at the time (it was just a few years before the Beveridge report in Great Britain), Louros suggested the merger of all sickness funds. He also suggested that all physicians should work for the government even though the right to freely choose a physician would be maintained. Urban and rural health centers were to be created. Pathologists who would serve as the first point of contact with the system would staff them. Physician incomes would increase since they were viewed as the pillars of the proposed system. They would be paid either through a monthly per capita scheme or through the traditional fee for service scheme. Louros' proposal never became a reality for a variety of reasons. For starters, Greece was about to enter a bloody civil war and the political uncertainty that was created by this development did not leave many degrees of freedom for action. The social division that would come between communists and anti-communists left little room for ideas of social cohesion necessary to establish the proposed plan. Furthermore, sizable portions of the population could not afford to contribute to the new system and occupational groups already covered wanted to protect such coverage. Finally, physicians were not willing to give up private practice. Louros' proposals, admirable as they may have been be, could not have been implemented in civil war Greece and teach policy makers a lesson about the importability of foreign systems without adaptation to social and political realities.

The end of the civil war, however, provided the state with an opportunity to regroup. In 1951, Minister of Social Care Zaimis sent a memorandum to the office of the Prime Minister regarding the situation of the health care sector in the country.[30] In that memorandum, Zaimis spelled out his proposals about the rationalization of the use of health care resources and a way to provide universal and equitable coverage to both urban and rural populations. The specific proposal did not move forward largely because the political climate even after the civil war was still one of national division. Nevertheless, it had placed the issue on the political agenda and in September 1953 under the government of Papagos, under Act 2592/53, the country was divided into thirteen health regions with clear hierarchical relations between the central, region, and local governments. The legislation aimed at providing access for the entire population to both primary and secondary care. New terms like Regional Health Stations and Agricultural Health Center entered the vocabulary of the policy debate of the time. Furthermore, this legislation established hospitals as non-profit institutions and set rates for hospitalization. The norm of the prewar era of building capacity was still held rather strongly. The lack of managerial knowledge, problems in the operational connection of these regional stations with hospitals and the concentration of services in Athens and Salonika, however, increased social inequalities. It was becoming abundantly clear that by building capacity alone, the problem was not going to get solved.

All along it was thought that simply by injecting more money into the system, by building hospitals and insuring part of the population, the net benefits would leak down to the entire population, and that the inequalities based on social class and geographic location would disappear. This leakage approach did not work and the end of the civil war found the Greek medical infrastructure severely depleted by the ongoing warfare and therefore inadequate at best and tragic at work.

In 1955, the Karamanlis government had tried to finesse the issue of lack of coverage of rural populations through the creation of a network of rural clinics, which actually had some net benefits. It was not enough, however, and it was definitely not sustainable. In 1961, under Act 4169, OGA was created to cover all farmers and their dependents, whose percentage at the time stood at 57 percent of the population. The main source of financing for OGA was designated to be the central government through tax revenues. This stood directly in direct contrast to the obligatory contribution on which other sickness funds were based. It has since given birth to a lively debate about the need to standardize financing mechanisms and benefits between the different sickness funds. Under the OGA legislation, rural populations gained access for the first time to medical care. Residents and nurses who would refer patients to hospitals in urban centers when it was deemed medically necessary would provide primary care in the rural clinics. The lack of medical personnel was partially solved in 1968 when all generalists were required to serve in a rural area for at least a year.

The OGA creation signifies the loss of faith that most politicians and policy makers had experienced with the leakage approach. It was painfully—both ideologically but perhaps more importantly politically—evident that the agricultural segment of the population was lacking access to the medical care that their urban counterparts enjoyed. Ethics and economics were at the heart of the matter. The moral foundation that health care is a fundamental right associated with citizenship was always strong, and having 57 percent of the population uninsured was just wrong. The question was where the money would come from, and since there was no employer the state decided to pick up the tab. Another reason, however, is that by directly financing OGA, politicians aspired to maintain control of local groups in the periphery of the land trying to propel themselves into a higher office. In Greece, a prominent strategy of party competition has traditionally been to strengthen local allegiances and electoral relationships by gaining credit and control for the performance of esteemed local organizations, placing emphasis on the virtue of solidarity. And after all, political clientelism was the surest way of practicing politics at the time.

This was a favorable time to do this, at least in economic terms. The 1950s and 1960s were decades in which most countries presented considerable economic growth. Greece, albeit with a five-year lag in joining this company of fiscal growth, posted an average economic growth rate of 7 percent between 1960 and 1975, compared to the average OECD figure, which was 5 percent. As the seventies' world oil crisis entered the scene, however, Greece took a hit much like all other Western nations did. This fiscal crisis resulted in a social one whereby health care delivery was inadequate both in quantity and quality.

But even after the creation of OGA, the issue of inequity continued to dominate health policy debates. In 1970, amidst a disastrous military dictatorship, the government in an attempt to improve its popularity, asked Professor of health policy Patras for a new plan for national health policy. As it turned out, the move was made, based simply on political calculations since the military government never really intended to fight the medical status quo. In his proposals, Patras suggested the creation of a National Health Service, which would be based on the coordination of the different sickness funds. He further suggested the reorganization of primary care, which would be provided by family physicians in urban centers and the much-improved rural clinics in rural areas. Furthermore, eight large hospitals would be built so that the issue of inequity of access could be tackled. Hospital physicians would fully work for the hospital but would be allowed to practice privately on the premises of the hospital twice a week. There were also measures for the improvement of medical education, public health promotion and the control of pharmaceutical consumption. Much care was shown to provide better access to those who did not have it, generally to the reduction of inequities and to the more efficient use of health care resources. But whereas on the one hand, the Patras' proposals appeared to want to tackle inequities, on the other they were weak-willed in terms of standing opposite certain interests.[31] The private sector expanded during this period. The merging of the financing mechanisms is something that the dictatorship never really went after. In short, whereas the reform was proposing one thing, the actions of the government indicated that maintenance of the status quo was all right. By the time the military junta was ousted in 1974, the health care landscape did not exhibit major structural differences from previous decades, and the population wanted changes.

1980- :Reorganization, Regulation and the Search for a Solution

This most recent period of health policy is a most interesting one as well for two reasons: first, because the players on the political scene are the same as today and, second, as I mentioned earlier, because the basic contours of the system today were put into place in 1983. This is why a more in-depth look is worthwhile in this period.

Overture to the NHS. The Greek health care system had emerged by the late 1970s with a significant degree of resemblance, at least in its broad essentials, to the health care systems of other European nations. Through the gradual absorption of the different occupational groups into different sickness funds, virtually the entire population was offered health care coverage. Most of these sickness funds, with the notable exception of OGA, were financed by obligatory employer-employee contributions. Greece, much like Italy, however, had a distinct difference. The benefit packages and funding mechanisms between the different funds varied significantly. Whereas the fund for bank employees, for instance, covered extensive benefits in both inpatient and outpatient care and the quality of services is unquestionably high, TEBE does not have its own ambulatory care centers and therefore its enrollees are limited to the services provided by the physicians associated with TEBE. Contributions also varied among occupational groups even within the same sickness fund.

The regional inequities, despite the efforts to counteract them, proved rather resistant and applied mostly to lower social groups: the wealthier urban centers of Athens and Salonika were better equipped with hospitals, medical personnel, and several medical technologies than were the poorer rural towns and villages. In 1980, there were 59,327 beds available. Out of these, 25,905 (44 percent) belonged to the public sector, 8,347 (14 percent) belonged to the non-profit sector, and the remaining 25,705 (42 percent) belonged to the private sector. Athens and Salonika were better endowed in terms of these beds, especially the non-for-profit and private ones. The system as a whole seemed to most observers uncoordinated and unfair. Most pointed to the needless segmentation of the system and called for the reorganization of services. Furthermore, and as the 1976 report by KEPE (the National Center for Economic Studies) indicated, there was a large issue with the development of the side economy as well as with supply induced demand on the part of the physicians who had found ways to maximize their incomes in the organizational deficit of the system. The 1976 report once again suggested that all sickness funds ought to merge.[32] In 1977, Minister of Health Doxiades charged a working group with preparing a comprehensive reform proposal. Two years later the plan was on his desk.

The crucial juncture came in 1980, when Minister Doxiades of the conservative New Democracy party introduced the Measures for the Protection of Health. His plan provided for a central and a regional health planning council that would be representing both providers and consumers, the decentralization of services in order for them to become more accessible to the rural population, the restriction of entry into graduate medical education based on competitive examinations, and a system of full-time employed hospital-based physicians prohibited from entering private practice. The plan was not met with much enthusiasm by organized professional and political interests. Even though PIS at the time was controlled by the conservative party, it was able to muster enough support to fight the plan. And the main opposition party of the socialists also fought the proposals, even though they were rather close to their ideology, choosing the issue rather than a policy. The bill went to Parliament only four months before the national election of 1981 with practically no chances of ever passing. Its lasting legacy was, however, that it had brought health care to the forefront of the policy agenda for all political parties.

Not many doubted that reform was necessary by that time. It is indicative that even while PIS was fighting the Doxiades plan, it did not offer an alternative solution to the health care problems of the country. There were two profound ideological currents on the Greek political scene at the time that converged powerfully in the health care arena, even though they were quite different from one another. First, students of the continental welfare states had warned adamantly that a centrally controlled system would sooner or later require decentralization measures and citizen participation. This belief, which was present in other countries, found fertile soil in Greece and grew, since the central government had never enjoyed the widespread respect of the electorate. These critics of the centrally controlled welfare state were quick to add that the public health system needed to be publicly controlled. Their concern was whether or not it would be controlled at the local/regional level or in Athens. The creation of the thirteen regions in 1953 gave them enough practical leverage in pushing for their position. They argued that these regions could assume the whole administrative responsibility in the new order of things.

Second, the gloomy prospects for successful incremental reform building on the base of the existing institutions united with the traditional left (including socialists, who were for the first time in power, having won a political landslide in 1981), which had very much set its sights on minimizing the reach of the market and on overcoming social and regional inequalities through governmental planning. To them social equality and social solidarity could only be achieved through the uniformity of benefits, the creation of one sickness fund. A reorganized sickness fund system, even with heavy regulation imposed on it, was still a reminder of the different economic status of the different strata of society. Furthermore, the "minor" adjustments, as they saw them, to the existing system would, even in the unlikely event that they would work, at best insure against disease and not try to work for wellness. Preventive medicine, a must in the mind of the left, required a public health system that would give overall control to the government. It required, by definition and nature, extensive central planning and central financing.

The two ideologies, despite certain disagreements on the logistics of the system, did indeed agree on a generic form for the new system. Their basis for agreement was the rationalization that central budgeting, since Athens knew how to raise the money, would be well complemented by a decentralized network of decision making, whereby the public's needs would be taken more into consideration, and whereby the decision makers would be directly accountable to both the patients and to the central government.

Overlaying this ideological consensus were the political motives of the governing party. In 1983, reforming the medical care system served the electoral ends of PASOK, which was preparing for the national elections of 1985. Whereas a reorganized sickness fund system, assuming that it was successful and that the public credited the government, would create only a one- time political gain, a decentralized public system would serve as the mill of never-ending political opportunities for building relations with the local organizations, relations that were much needed to ensure political success. The conservative New Democracy, having been in power until 1981, enjoyed strong ties with the sickness funds and the management of the hospitals, and was opposed to the "socialization" of medical services. New Democracy preferred preservation and renovation of the existing system, which would ensure it of the maintenance of those ties. Those very ties were the reason why PASOK would not entertain the thought of maintaining the current system. In light of public pressures for "change"—the political slogan of the 1981 election—the Socialist leader Andreas Papandreou hoped that a brand new system would allow him to extend his power at the local level and assure him of another four years in power.

One more development proved critical for the passage of the 1983 legislation. That was the change in the leadership of organized medicine. Whereas up to the futile Doxiades attempt, PIS was opposed to the creation of an NHS, the change of guard from the older conservative physicians to younger more liberal ones provided the catalyst for the reform.[33]

Act I: A Law written in Heaven and the problems of implementing it on earth. After an aggressive debate between the two main parties, the National Health Service was passed into law in September 1983 under Act 1397/83, designed by Minister Avgerinos and passed by Minister Gennimatas. The legislation aimed at universal coverage of the population and the efficient allocation of health resources. The state would be responsible for the delivery of services, the financing of services would be directed through a single source, and the different sickness funds were to be absorbed into a unified fund, which, in turn, would decentralize decision making to the different localities. The cornerstones of the new system were the PESIs, local public health councils whose role was both advisory to the central health council but also managerial for their specific localities. The PESIs embodied the political ideology of the times. They honored patient participation, and local control, while they reported to the central health council and ultimately to the central government in Athens. These measures were never effectively implemented. The law also provided for the prohibition of the creation of any new private hospitals. Some of the already existent private and non-profit hospitals were bought out and incorporated into the NHS. Like the New Democracy-sponsored Measures for the Protection of Health in 1980, this law prohibited NHS doctors from entering private practice.

The 1983 law was a radical surgery performed on the medical care system. It captured indeed the political longing for change that had propelled the Socialists into power two years before, and was an extremely well-prepared mix of the different expert views of the time. An ingenious but superficial, as the future showed, venture into a complicated world of political economy of health, the NHS stressed the importance of social equality, national solidarity, and uniformity of benefits, which satisfied the left while maintaining that the decentralization of decision making would complement central planning, which satisfied the right. And, most importantly, it provided for primary, secondary and tertiary care services for the entire population. More specifically, in the first article of the 1983 legislation, the basic philosophy of the NHS is stated:

> The state has the responsibility for the delivery of services to the whole of the population. Health care services are being offered equitably to all citizens independent of economic, social or professional situation, through a comprehensive and decentralized national health system.

Health care is recognized as a public good, which should not obey the orders of profit making. The basic goals of the legislation were the decentralization of health services, a unifying planning, development and operational strategy for the system, the equitable distribution of health care resources, the development of primary care, the reform of the hospital sector and the distinct separation of the public and private sector. To achieve these goals, legislation 1397/83 provided for the creation of a central health board (KESY) and ten regional health boards (PESY).[34] According to the plan, all health services in the land would eventually be provided through the NHS. In the first stage all hospitals, except for the academic medical centers and the military hospitals, would belong to the Ministry of Health. Eventually the academic and military hospitals would also join the NHS. The ambulatory care sites of hospitals, and sickness funds would eventually merge into a public system of health centers of urban and rural character. Four hundred new primary care sites were to be created (180 rural ones and 220 urban ones). Another provision was that all the financial resources of the sickness funds would be pooled into a common entity, which was thought would eventually lead to the merging of all the sickness funds. Furthermore, the legislation provided for an increase in hospital beds from 32,247 in 1982 to 42,215 in 1988 and for their more equitable geographic distribution. A number of departments in the hospitals, which were outdated, would be eliminated, new ones would be created and all would be modernized. All new hospitals would be public and belong to the NHS. Through the NHS, hospitals would be divided into general and specialized. All hospital positions were to be publicized again and filled in accordance with the needs of the overall reform. The newly hired physicians were to work only for the NHS and give up private practice. Finally, the legislation aimed at the complete separation of the public and private sectors in health care, which would eventually lead to the demise of the latter as the public NHS developed and was modernized. To that end, the legislation prohibited the creation of new private hospitals or other centers and the expansion of old ones. The law seemed to have been written in heaven, and it is small wonder that implementation problems brought everyone back to earth very, very quickly.

The implementation of the NHS presented problems from day one, problems that have never been really overcome. Most derived from the central government's inability or unwillingness, depending on one's point of view, to honor decentralization of decision making and at the same time manage to maintain overall control of the system. The 1983 legislation was very much a document of wishful thinking, which did not really provide for administrative ways of implementing what was wished for. The legislator had very conveniently avoided any mention of the difficult and complicated trade-offs that the legislation would cause. The plan, for instance, called for the organization of ambulatory care under public auspices. No one, however, knew how to monitor what the physicians were doing. Likewise, almost everyone involved with the system agreed that there were too many hospital beds in Athens and Salonika, but none was willing to implement a policy aimed towards the reduction of beds, which would conceivably mean the closing of some hospitals in the wealthier parts of the land. Finally, whereas most people were satisfied with the plan's provision for the eventual absorption of the different sickness funds under one unified fund, few were willing to try to harmonize the immense bureaucratic systems of the sickness funds.

In short, the government had supplied no systematic method of linking central planning with local decision making. Any central planning attempt tthat tried to protect social equality was in direct contrast with local interests, and if local decision making was to be the pillar of the new system, none of these attempts could be enforced. These implementation controversies irritated both sides. Local representatives pointed out that the stubbornness of Athens to allow them to make the decisions was strengthening the regional disparities and did not allow for the full implementation of the NHS. They charged that the central government's failure to provide direct guidelines that would equitably treat all localities was representative of the old political world. Government officials, on the other hand, countercharged that the localities were not able or willing to take responsibility for such a huge system, and blamed local interests as wanting to exploit the system.

As if the governing controversies were not enough, physicians and sickness funds also fought the implementation of the plan. While organized medicine had either supported the NHS plan or remained silent about it during the 1983 election (its leadership was controlled by PASOK), the 1984 PIS elections gave control to the New Democracy candidates and the association then turned against the PASOK-backed NHS. Physician strikes are a common phenomenon in Greece, and when these strikes are directed against the new and seemingly disordered system, physicians have a major tool through the media of faulting government, which cannot deliver on its promises. Furthermore, the sickness funds insiders who had direct control over the system all these years stood to lose the most if the plan were to be implemented. Therefore, while presenting themselves as supporters of the plan, they also intervened at the highest political level, as articles at the time charged,[35] and succeeded in postponing indefinitely the merger of the funds. Finally, whereas prior to 1983, the NHS occupied a top position on the governmental agenda, after the passage of Act 1397, none in government was really willing to invest time and political capital in a project that did not assure one of constant positive publicity. Being involved with the NHS placed people in the defensive position of having to explain the shortcomings of the system, and that is something that no politician is eager to do. The NHS never succeeded to earn the trust of the citizenry and has since then been faced with numerous attacks.

A reform attempt in 1985 (legislation 1579)[36] did little to correct the situation. Rather it was supplemental legislation, focusing on educational standards for medical and nursing personnel and for bringing marginal changes to the 1983 legislation. Soon everyone was attacking the system. The Communists were enraged that the private practice of medicine had not been eradicated outright. The coexistence of public and private practice gave reason for "public" physicians to practice illegally in private, neglecting their patients in the system, only to take care of them later on in their practice with higher fees. The underground economy, they charged, had violated the right of free medicine for all, and allowing private practice was at the core of the problem. Conservatives were also unhappy with the system. It consumed a great deal of money and, in the face of the poor picture of the Greek economy and of the first set of the austerity policies that PASOK implemented, they warned that public spending needed to be curtailed if the country was to emerge from its economic slump. Policy analysts and journalists, predominantly from the right but not exclusive of the left, were willing to play along the same themes, lamenting within their comfortable isolation that nothing had really changed and blaming the government for broken promises.

And even though the population's health was steadily improving, regional disparities and social inequalities remained as strong as ever. The political rhetoric about equality in access and benefits, which had created expectations, had failed to deliver. Reinforcing all this was the underlying economy triggered by the unprofessional behavior of physicians and the public's willingness to play along with it. It had been nine years since the passage of the NHS, economic scandals in 1989 had brought down the Socialist government and had returned the Conservatives to power for the first time since 1981, and it was becoming increasingly evident to all that changes were needed in the NHS.

Act II: Reforming the Reform. By 1992, however, the spirit of reform was not as powerful as it was in the glory days of "The Change."[37] The same ideological currents that characterized the pre-1983 era existed in this period as well. The NHS had failed to fully deliver on its promises, and that made the supporters for reform only that much more demanding. But, by and large, the population and the government for that matter were preoccupied with other issues, such as foreign relations, economic policies, and the treaty of Maastricht. The NHS was still criticized whenever it was discussed, but the window of opportunity that existed in 1983 was no longer open.

The political incentives of New Democracy were in line with small incremental reform for the NHS. Enjoying only a marginal majority in parliament, the governing party was already being wounded by some of its economic policies of privatization. Looking ahead to national elections in 1994 (they actually came in 1993 because of foreign relations issues), New Democracy did not want to consume any more political capital in the radical reformulation of the system. Overlaying all this was the Maastricht treaty whereby the economic and monetary union had been decided and the government was quick to decide that this was not the politically favorable timing for the significant changes that would no doubt be needed in the country's social policies.

It causes no surprise therefore that the changes that New Democracy introduced were rather small and cowardly and could not really correct the underlying inequalities of the system. There were three major points of differentiation, one ideological and two operational. The latter two were that legislation 2071/92 allowed once again the creation of private hospitals, and provided NHS physicians with a choice of full-time NHS employment or part-time employment in the system associated with the right to practice privately as well. The low reimbursement that was linked to the latter led only 400 physicians to take that route. The ideological difference was indicated implicitly in Article 1 of this legislation. It stated that

> Article 1 of legislation 1397/1983 is being replaced as follows: ...The state is responsible for the establishment, operation, organization and regulation of the necessary bodies to ensure health for all citizens. The state guarantees the right of the citizen to solve through prevention or cure his/her health problem, through procedures that would fully ensure free choice and respect for human dignity.[38]

It is a significant departure from the 1983 legislation that aimed at unifying all services under public auspices. Under the 1992 legislation, the conservative government was moving away from such a practice and indicated an erosion of the principle of social solidarity. The neoliberal current that had swept the Anglo-American world was being imported into Greece, demanding a smaller role for the government and a larger role for the private sector. Part of this ideological shift was that visitors to ambulatory clinics would be charged from that point on. Furthermore, since according to the legislation the sickness funds would become the main payer for hospital care (instead of government), hospital expenditures were expected to rise significantly. In any period, let alone in one of fiscal austerity, such measures were anything but welcome.

The loss of the 1993 elections by New Democracy, returned the Socialists to power, who had pledged to *make right the wrongdoings of the previous government*. The changes that were introduced in 1994 were a reversal of most of the New Democracy policies. The new government returned to the ideology of the original NHS legislation, based on health care as a public good. It appears, in retrospect, that the two main parties had used competitive reform proposals, not so much with their minds set on improving the system, but rather wanting to win the political battle. But Papandreou, an excellent political analyst, realized much as his predecessor had that fundamental changes in the NHS, based on the 1983 ideological currents, were not politically attractive. He must have realized, too, that if significant changes were to be made in the NHS, those changes would have to deal also with the painful issues of cost containment, managerial control and unification of the sickness funds, and these were issues that his political instinct was telling him to avoid.

The system was moving along in the midst of the criticism it received and the institutional problems it faced within. Another governmental change occurred in 1993. Papandreou's health was deteriorating quickly and this led to Kostas Simitis assuming the post of prime minister. Simitis took over with an ambitious modernizing plan for the country's economy.[39] "Modernization" was, in fact, the word that came to dominate political debates of the time and has continued since then. The new government's aim was to bring Greece successfully into EMU and provide in this fashion a solid economic basis for growth through which social protection systems could be sustained. Ten years after the original legislation, Greece had decided that it would join the Economic and Monetary Union, which, of course, required tight public budgets and generally a much stricter fiscal policy. In this sense, and much like the rest of Europe, the socialist spirit of the 1983 NHS would have to find new tools in order to be successfully expressed. The rationalization of the use of health care resources appeared as a one-way street, but political instincts dictated that it was not the right time to act. In an interview that Minister of Development Christodoulakis, given a week after the 2000 elections which had returned PASOK to government for an unprecedented third term, after the successful convergence to the Maastricht criteria, when asked about the future of social protection and that of the welfare state, pointed to this change in political discourse that had begun in 1993. He said,

> The traditional conceptualization of care systems is inadequate.... If one considers the great opportunities and the tremendous chances that exist today for each person to participate actively in the employment and social affairs, one realizes that social policy can no longer be moving within a framework of organized philanthropy.... It can no longer be perceived as a policy where the insiders...drop from the castle the remains to the outsiders.... In the new society that we aim to create, we will not give to the other what is left but we will create the framework of opportunities so that he himself can create with confidence...what has been kept from him, either because of wealth differentials, or because of other reasons..."[40]

In other words, the new political mentality was placing priority on economic growth and macroeconomic stability that EMU would guarantee. All other sectors of the economy, including health care, would have to follow this paradigm.

Thus, health care came to be viewed in a somewhat different light. Now, there was one added problem that made health reform imperative. The government had realized that increases in health care spending could put a stop to and even reverse the already shaky economic growth rate. To gain some valuable political time, the government resorted to a familiar tactic. It charged a commission of international experts to prepare a report about the NHS and the need for its reform. In June 1994, the Ministry of Health published the report by the special Commission, presided over by Brian Abel-Smith, which came to be known as the Wise Men Commission.[41] The Commission recognized many of the shortcomings of the system that others had also identified and collected them in one volume. They recommended a number of proposals. First, they proposed that a network of family doctors should be created and that these doctors should be reimbursed on a capitation basis. The Commission also suggested that these family doctors should manage a budget on behalf of their patients so that services could be purchased by hospitals, pharmacies, or specialists. The proposed system conspicuously resembled the British NHS after the reforms it had undergone at the time. But as analysts indicated,[42] importing a system of fund holding into the Greek system, where the organization of health services is distinctively different, would have been quite a gamble for a variety of reasons: the system is a rather weak command and control one; social health insurance is fragmented among a number of sickness funds; the private sector is large and growing each day; primary care has traditionally been offered by specialists because of the lack of general practitioners; and the uniquely Greek side economy has been the norm underlying the cultural differences between the two settings. It was for these reasons that the report was fought. Another reason was that a number of the interested parties were quite content to continue with the existing system since they all were able to exploit it.

The new PASOK government had pledged the modernization of the NHS before the 1996 elections. In June of that year, the government presented its reform proposals, which eventually made it through Parliament but certainly were not what most insiders wished for. The reforms aimed at the completion and simultaneous modernization of the NHS. More specifically, the legislation that passed (2519/1997) included among other provisions the following:[43] School Health Services Sites were to be created. Their main responsibilities would be the creation, implementation and evaluation of ways to provide preventive and primary care services. Public health physicians, specialized in family medicine or pediatrics, would be placed at these sites along with dentists, psychologists and social workers. In addition, the legislation introduced specific managerial responsibilities for the president or chief executive of the public hospitals, who would now be required to have specialized training in the field of health services management. Moreover, the legislation called for the evening operation of specific parts of a hospital, with the sole responsibility of providing post-operative or any other type of special care. Patients could also receive that type of care from private clinics, which would have specific contracts with the NHS. Furthermore, the legislation provided for the creation of a comprehensive primary care center network. The already existing primary care centers will be organized into this network, which will be connected with the NHS hospitals. The reform called for the introduction of the family physician, who would be freely chosen by patients and who would serve as the first point of contact within the system. Finally, the legislation introduced a more merit-based mechanism for the contracting of NHS physicians.

The legislation even at its proposal stage, however eloquent, came under vicious attack by practically everyone.[44] At the heart of this criticism was the objection that the legislation projected an image of a wish list again without practical guidance on how these measures would be implemented. There were five main points of disagreement that critiques brought up. First, the introduction of the family physician as well as that of the school-based physicians were terms that most likely would remain on paper. The government was hoping for a pilot program to have been in operation before the end of 1997. Critics were uncertain whether the implementation of this plan would actually be possible. They based their criticism on a lack of experience with the school health site part of the proposal and laughed off any possibilities of patients going to the family physician first, not to mention the high probability of unprofessional conduct (side payments, etc.) by these physicians even if the system were to operate.

Second, political opponents of the government charged that the measures were aimed at political control of the new organizations and the new operations. Characteristic is the statement by New Democracy spokesperson on health issues, George Surlas: "From the proposed measures, it turns out that the main goal is the party control of the selection process of the hospital executive board members, the hospital general managers, and of course of the public health physicians."

Physicians charged that the physicians hired by the NHS would not be guaranteed their permanence in the system. Ludicrous as this demand might sound to students of international health services management, it is nonetheless present in Greece. And even though there are merit-based criteria, which provide bases for the permanence of a physician in the NHS, physicians still argued against the measures. The physicians go on to charge that the introduction of health services management into the hospitals will cause a series of problems, mainly with the quality of services. The same story can be observed in all other countries that introduced hospital management techniques. The managers, at this point, are viewed as a foreign part of the hospital, not knowledgeable in the secrets of clinical practice, willing to curtail costs, and therefore disturb the practice patterns of physicians.

Finally, the bulk of hospital revenues would from now on come from the sickness funds and not from the state's budget. The arguments behind the legislation held that this, coupled with the introduction of trained management in the hospitals, would lower overall costs and actually provide enhanced quality of services for the population. Critics maintain the exact opposite, charging that such a measure will endanger the already low quality services that patients receive and endanger the financial viability of the sickness funds. Interestingly enough, this is also reminiscent of the 1992 battles with the roles this time reversed. But when all was said and done, all the criticism and well-intended legislation did not mean much. The lack of ways to implement any measure at the local level stands in the middle of any successful reform. Couple that with the always-present willingness by opposition parties to politically abuse any issue that is dear to the hearts of the public, and a very grim picture is painted.

Of course, such attitudes are common in Greece where non-working public systems dominate and "broken political promises" are the adored toy of critics from all political ideologies. In point of fact, the more melodramatic a situation is, the greater the gratification of blaming it on the opposing party, or on a personal and political rival. But in the case of health care in Greece, these melodramatic situations far outpace in the public mind's any well-intended and even well-planned reform. The wide open window of opportunity for effective reform in 1983 was not properly exploited. It closed and today the NHS is left wondering if, between the fulfillment of egalitarian promises and the need to contain health care costs, while improving the quality of the services offered, Greece is not to see further privatization of the health care sector. It is therefore safe to say that the reformers in the past fifteen years in many respects underestimated the magnitude of their reorganization attempt and the complexity of the issues involved.

A 1998 assessment of health reforms in Greece concludes that

> 10 years after full implementation of the reform shows that despite the expansion of the public sector, the public-private mix in financing and delivery has changed in favor of the private sector, making the Greek health system the most 'privatized' among the EU countries. The main reasons why the health reform failed to meet its objectives was the restrictive enforcement of full-time and exclusive hospital employment for doctors, the virtual ban on private hospital expansion, the much faster introduction and diffusion of new health technology by the private sector, and poor management, planning and control in the public sector.[45]

In fact, the expansion of the private sector after the 1992 legislation is largely explained by the poor services provided by the NHS. As the advertising pitch for one of the comprehensive private plans pointed out, "something had to change, someone had to be bold." Private companies played on the unsatisfying feeling that Greeks had in terms of health services, always emphasizing that their ventures into the arena were primarily motivated by social sensitivity. In one of their publications, they write,

> this is our answer to the fair and unfulfilled need of modern Greeks for a truly comprehensive system of health care services.... For the first time in Greece,...from the simplest and most daily health care to the hardest and most

complicated case, a complete network of health services with quality and care, embraces you constantly and turns your worries into safety and your weakness into hope. Hope for the better.[46]

Playing on the shortcomings of the public sector, the private health sector has found an opening and has expanded in the last few years with astonishing rates of growth.[47] In 1989, private health expenditure in Greece was only 1 percent of GDP. In 2000, it was 3 percent. More striking is that while private health expenditures tripled in this decade, total health expenditures increased only by 83 percent. This means that private health expenditures increased by 23 percent annually, indicative of the expanding market. It is estimated that within three years the private health care market will reach the 1.6 billion drachma (400 million dollars) mark, a very lucrative arena for a number of businessmen to get involved.[48] A number of different models exist as of today. Interamerican, an insurance company, has created a vertical system that offers both insurance and care. Its system is, however, the exception. Most companies in the field are private hospitals that are aggressively moving to buy out smaller units, improve their technological capacity and in general offer more services at better prices based on better management. The owners are either businessmen, who have not been traditionally involved in health care, or groups of doctors, who decided that they must move in this direction if they are to survive in the new era of health care. In short, the private sector is still in a formative stage without clear-cut guidelines. The one certainty is that the private sector in health care today is a reality. In this sense, the challenge for health policy at this juncture is whether or not the public sector will fold and whether it will compete or cooperate with the private sector and in what fashion. This consideration is what prompted participants in the second *Economist* conference[49] about the future of health care in Greece to urge policy makers to devise policies that would enable the two sectors, private and public, to cooperate. An idea that was proposed was the cooperation between private insurance companies and the public NHS hospitals, as occurs in other countries, based on agreed policies. If that were not to happen, as the participants saw it, the NHS would eventually lose out to private services since the better risks would choose to leave the public system. In the words of a special council to the prime minister, "If we do not proceed with the necessary changes, the danger of the incremental transformation of the NHS to a service provider only for the poor, immigrants and low income people is now visible."[50] One thing is certain and that is that if the public NHS does not improve, social solidarity will indeed be in grave danger.

This realization, which had occurred long before the conference, brought health care to the forefront in the last elections in April 2000. Newspaper articles and public speeches by political leaders and the positioning of interest groups prior to the elections formed the environment within which health policy battles played out in this election. The prime minister, in a speech a month before the elections, underlined the interest of the Socialist party in continuing plans for more equitable geographic distribution of hospital beds.[51] Furthermore, he pointed to the need that the health care sector remain primarily public with the private sector complementing it. This latter point is critical. De facto today in Greece, the private sector has assumed an active role. Forty-two percent of national health expenditures are private ones, either direct out-of-pocket payments or payments through private insurance. Either way, to the shortcomings of the NHS many people have found answers in the private sector. The question today in Greece, as in many countries, is how to formulate a framework so that these two sectors can best complement one another. Prime Minister Simitis, in the second part of his speech, stated the overarching theme of his party's ideology and attacked the main opposition party for its proposals. He said,

Our position is that health is a public good. This means for us that any criticism of the NHS, any analysis of possible shortcomings must declare its basis, its beginning and its goals. We recently heard many criticisms from New Democracy. But it did not explicitly state something fundamental: is health care part of its program for privatizing the public sector? What does New Democracy mean when it accuses the overspending by the NHS? Which funding will it cut? Which parts of the NHS will it eliminate? Which NHS services will it give to the private sector?

He went on to promise the modernization of the NHS so that equitable and universal access can remain the cornerstone of the health care sector. But how exactly was that to be achieved? Whereas eliminating services from the public sector appears to be unthinkable and properly so, the question still stands. In the days before the elections, administrators, academics and a number of other analysts presented sketches of reform ideas. Largely based on some of these, especially the ones coming from his close advisors, then Minister of Health Papadimas appeared to adopt five themes:[52]

1. The creation of a common financing body through the better coordination of sickness funds.
2. The development of a modern primary care network.
3. The change of the legal status of hospitals from public bodies to autonomous ones.
4. The change in the operation of certain small hospitals that should become specialized ones.
5. The employment relationship of physicians in the NHS, who according to most proposals ought to be fully and exclusively employed by the NHS.

With a reform based on these ideas, a better operating NHS and a more equitable health care sector would be created. The organized medical interests but also other unions were quick to criticize them. The president of the hospital workers' union (ΠΟΕΔΗΝ), Spyros Koutsioubelis, stated "that the change in the legal status of the public hospitals would be a cause for war."[53] This was to be expected since this would endanger the permanence of the positions of public hospital employees. A similar reaction came from the union of hospital physicians, who also stated that NHS reforms are welcome but they should not go through the changing of the legal status of the hospitals. The hospital unions tried to broaden the agenda by highlighting the shortcomings of the NHS. A number of sickness funds in the meantime were opposed to "the close coordination" (i.e., merger) of sickness funds assets. The president of the fund for bank employees (TYPET), D. Varelis, offered the model of that fund as an optimal solution. He argued that self-managed funds would be better placed to satisfy the needs of their employees.[54] On the other hand, of course, the specific fund is a relatively wealthy one with not too many enrollees and does not face the same issues that large ones like IKA or OGA face.

In the meantime, the three opposition parties offered their proposals for the upcoming reform.[55] The representative of the main opposition party, the conservatives stated that

New Democracy believed and believes still in the existence of an effective public health sector as well as in the existence of an effective private one, that would operate in a complementary way and in terms of quality, competitively. Both sectors will belong to a system open to all. The cooperation and the competition between these two sectors, under different conditions and different operational criteria are the key for the development of a real national health system. The priorities for New Democracy are: the increase of expenditures for health to the average level of expenditures for EU countries, the development of a health map for the land in terms of staffing needs, bed needs and generally all needs of each health district, the development of an educational health policy, of prevention and of primary care..., the emergency hospital medicine and the modernization of inpatient care in general, and the creation of modern care units. In terms of the latter, the hospitals should become private enterprises with the state being the sole shareholder.

One can discern a broad agreement of direction between the proposals of the two main parties albeit both of these were, due to the election, quite vague. It is one thing to offer that the two sectors would complement one another, it is a whole different matter to explain how. And all the parties including the governing one stayed away from this issue at least prior to the election.

The third and smallest party in Parliament, the Coalition of the Left, declared that a number of specific measures have been offered by health specialists...and from our party. Some of these are: financial support of the NHS with a rationalized effective use of resources, support of human resources in terms of medical but also nursing staff, radical shift towards primary care, establishment and operation of a complete primary care network in the entire country including urban centers, close linkages between primary care centers and hospitals...clear guidelines and terms for the private sector, initiatives for the sickness fund merger or their coordination, and effective use of the family physician.

The fourth minor opposition party also criticized the current situation and stated that a better more rationalized administration was in order. Moreover, it adamantly supported the public character of the NHS. Furthermore, the communist party (third in power) demanded an unrealistic eradication of the private sector. After a meeting in the party's offices the following statement was made public by the party's general secretary:

> We believe that even though time is short, it must be effectively used in order that physicians and nursing staff as well as all hospital workers and of course all workers, salaried personnel, farmers and small business owners understand that we are moving towards a complete Americanization of the social security system in Greece—as well as in Europe. This simply means that we will live in a super market where we could purchase luxury health care, but that we will not be able to afford it. Therefore a large portion of the Greek population will be forced to accept services from badly paid physicians...or to put its hand deep in its pockets to accept private health care services...[56]

Along similar lines was a statement by the member of parliament responsible for issues of health care who said that

> the communist party is fighting for a public and free for all health care system, that would cover the needs of the entire population, that would place priority in prevention and protection from occupational diseases...We would constrain, with the ultimate goal of eliminating, all the large private companies who are active in the health care arena...Our priorities would be an elevated public primary care system with urban and rural clinics and family physicians...We would take measures that would aim to the improvement...and modernization of the public sector, a political direction that demands in the first instance a doubling (at least) of today's public health care expenditures, the immediate filling of all empty positions in terms of both physicians but mainly in terms of nursing staff.[57]

Nevertheless, health care was mostly debated as part of the overall social protection reforms that would have to be made by the new government and there one could see broad agreement with the sole exception of the communist party. Economic growth was accepted by the other three parties as the number one concern in the EMU period, which meant the modernization of social protection systems including the health care system. These systems would have to adjust to the changing employment environment. Second, and equally important, social protection systems ought to be able to provide opportunities for all people to be actively engaged in society. Therefore, the NHS would have to improve its effectiveness and its efficiency in order to satisfy both goals. In the words of the current Minister of Health Papadopoulos, health reform "is a debt by the Greek state to the Greek citizen so that this public good can be guaranteed and there is no room to remain static."[58]

The election results of April 9 returned the socialists to power. The result indicated that the citizenry approved the government's policies in the previous four years and that it now demanded that convergence with Greece's European partners be paid off in terms of improvements in their daily lives. Joining the EMU appeared to be a small task in relation to the tasks of reforming social security, the national health system and labor relations. The prime minister knew it and he also realized that he had to move quickly on these fronts so that any political cost that his government would have to pay would be gone by the next elections since, as he expected, results from his reforms should have appeared by that time. He also knew that many groups would oppose his reform efforts, which is why he had adopted a political stand that viewed the role of government as one of making hard choices and not as one of satisfying interest group demands. He expected that the results of his policies would be rewarded by the public as they were following the first four years of his government.

To carry the task in the health care sector, Simitis offered the post of Minister of Health to one of his closest colleagues at the time and one of the most successful ministers in his previous governments. Minister Papadopoulos ventured on a four-month extensive study of the NHS. He charged a working group under the leadership of Professor Tundas to come up with a complete proposal package. With his traditional style, the minister avoided offering any details and when the working group delivered its report, and after necessary changes that the minister himself judged necessary, he revealed his reform plan to the council of ministers. As was expected, the reform proposal was extensive (some called it a big bang reform), but on closer inspection it takes quite an incremental approach to the radical solutions that the NHS requires.

It is quite interesting, however, that there were two kinds of criticisms during that meeting.[59] The first did not deal chiefly with the direction of the reforms but rather with the thorn that had blocked previous efforts, that of implementation. To that end, the minister replied that the measures would be implemented within a six-year period (by 2006), according to the general framework that was presented to them. In the words of the Prime Minister Simitis, "this time around we do not have any margin of error. Society is expecting us to act with care and decisiveness. The plan that the Minister of Health presented sets large goals and a general framework for meeting them in due time which extends to 2006. The implementation of the reform will proceed in stages and with careful steps, but it has to begin right away." Furthermore, the minister was quick to put any financing worries to rest by arguing that the current levels of financing of the Ministry, along with the customary increases in future budgets, will be enough to cover the cost of the reform, since he was able to ensure funds from the third financial support package from Brussels.[60]

The second criticism within governmental circles had to do with the degree of stateness of the reform. As a daily Athens newspaper commented, "one of the top ministers spoke of 'state perfume' in the reform plan."[61] Other ministers, like the Minister of Development Christodoulakis, argued that those who could afford it ought to participate in the cost of health care services while free care ought to be preserved for the poor and for those of the less wealthy social strata. The criticism here is indicative of a broader kind of struggle that exists in social democratic parties, not only in Greece but also throughout Europe. Much like the European Commission's struggle to strike a balance between social solidarity, rationalization of the use of limited resources and control of cost increases, the socialist government in Greece finds itself "divided" on the best way to approach health care reform. There was a basic common line of agreement in the meeting, however, and it was expressed by the prime minister who said, "more effective management of resources does not mean budget cuts, as is sometimes mistakenly argued, but rather has the meaning that the money goes where it is needed, and that is something that the citizen must see clearly since he pays taxes and expects satisfactory public services."

The published report, entitled "Health for the Citizen,"[62] indicated that there are two main objectives for the government: first, the strengthening of the public sector and, second, the transformation of the NHS from a physician-centered system to a patient-centered system.

The new proposal in many points resembles the original 1983 legislation, including the points that were not implemented, and also has a number of modernizing features that were not applicable in 1983, such as complete computer use in hospitals. According to the new proposal, the structure and the ways in which hospitals have operated is changing. The NHS becomes decentralized by the establishment of regional health systems, public bodies where all the regional hospitals, clinics, etc. will belong. These regional systems will be responsible for the more efficient and effective use of resources through plans that will be submitted to the central level. The sickness funds will stop being producers of health care services and limit their actions in terms of purchasing services through a newly established body (ODIPY), which will pool their financial assets and create a type of monopsony that has eluded the system so far. Furthermore, private insurance companies will be allowed to contract with the regional systems so that their enrollees can be cared for in public hospitals. This is indeed significant since the Ministry is attempting to create a framework of cooperation and continuity between the two sectors so that they do not compete against one another. The labor relations for both physicians and nursing staff with the NHS change with two basic goals: first, to eradicate any side economy effects that have plagued the system so far, and, second, to improve the human resources level of the system. At the same time, a number of issues that physicians have over the years asked for are being satisfied. For instance, hospital physicians will be allowed to operate private offices on hospital premises in the evenings, a system that has worked well in Germany. They will also be allowed to work with different hospitals under specific contractual arrangements if and when both parties judge such an arrangement to be worthwhile. And, whereas the cost of the reform has not been fully estimated the minister has already secured funds not only from the budget but also from the third EU support package, which is judged sufficient to cover the measures proposed. Finally, the Ministry invited all interested parties to come to a public dialogue about the proposal that went to the floor of the parliament at the beginning of 2001.

More specifically, the proposal that the Ministry published includes two hundred new measures and revolves around nine themes: five that deal with the daily operation of the NHS and four that deal with more meso- and macro-level policies, or with the implementation of the whole of the reform.[63] Here, I review the main ones.

Regional Development

In each administrative district of the country, a new regional health system will be established.[64] This will be a public body where all NHS units will belong and which will be responsible for the appropriate application of ministry policy guidelines in the region. It will also be responsible for the collective evaluation of the production and distribution of health resources in the region. It will advise the ministry on matters of health policy. It will be allowed by itself or in conjunction with other regional systems to establish companies for purchasing hospital and other medical supplies and in general it will be an autonomous entity and the highest level of authority for health care in each region. Recognizing that health care is by definition a local phenomenon, the new proposal tries to balance centralized decision making in terms of broad guidelines and local application.

Financing. A new organization (ODIPY) will be established. It will pool together and manage the financial assets of the largest sickness funds (IKA, OGA, OAEE, public) and, on a voluntary basis, the other sickness funds. It will also be operating regionally. It will allocate funds to the regional level based on a risk assessment mechanism. In the first instance, the different benefits provided by the sickness funds will not be tackled. However, in due time, a unified benefit package, at least at the level of the highest level of current benefits, will be established. As for the sickness funds that decide not to enter this new organization, they will be charged for NHS services according to prespecified charges. ODIPY will be purchasing services from the NHS and from the private sector as it sees fits in each region and according to the different prices and quality of the services offered. Hospital charges will be adjusted for current levels of expenditures that the sickness funds through ODIPY will have to honor.

Primary Care. A number of health centers, especially urban but also rural, will be created. Along with the already established ones, they will belong to the regional health system and will be connected to a hospital. They will, however, be administratively autonomous. This means that they can establish their own budget, their own labor relations, and the number of staff members, etc. Services can be offered to people who do not belong to ODIPY according to a fee for service payment mechanism. The legislation on family physicians will be implemented. They will be contracted by the regions, paid by ODIPY, and allowed to practice privately but not on ODIPY members. Each ODIPY enrollee has an annual choice between a family physician or enrolling at the closest health center for primary care needs. Family physicians will be paid on a capitation basis and will also receive additional payments for extra services provided.

Hospitals. They cease to be public bodies and become autonomous with independent management bodies that belong to the regional health system. They will from now on be divided into general and specialized hospitals, and hospitals with more than 400 beds will be recognized as academic medical centers. A manager who has the overall administrative responsibility along with four directors (for medical, nursing, financial, and technical-capital areas) will be appointed in each hospital. All appointments will be made through open procedures so that any political appointments can be avoided. Beds, staff and equipment from one hospital department can be moved to another if that is judged to improve the efficiency of production and the quality of services. The management of the regional health service to which the hospital belongs decides the annual hospital budget.

Human Resources. Responding to the overproduction of specialists, the proposal provides that in order to start a specialty program, a physician will have to undertake exams. Moreover, all the openings, especially in rural areas, are to be filled before 2003. Incentives are provided for continuing education for all scientific personnel of the NHS. One of the major proposals in terms of human resources that is expected to lead to a heated political debate is the reversal of the practice of academic physicians who would practice both privately and in the NHS. Under this proposal they will have to choose, something that is, of course, expected to constrain them from their point of view. On the other hand, they, along with other high seniority physicians of the NHS, are, as mentioned , allowed to practice privately on hospital premises so that both the hospital and the physician can have a financial benefit and at least try to counter the side economy that has developed. Furthermore, physicians are not allowed to agree to be sent abroad by pharmaceutical companies for conferences since this has been proven to be a cover up practice for kickbacks between the company and the physicians. Finally, a new NHS physician will not become tenured until he has been successfully judged three times and after an open competition.

Implementation of the Reform. Having studied the implementation problems of previous reforms, the Ministry proposed that a number of task forces (quasi-public consulting groups) would be formed that would assist the new management of hospitals and regional health systems to better implement the reform. Moreover, an open and continuous dialogue will begin with the aim of constantly responding to issues that may arise. Financial sources for the implementation of the reform have been guaranteed according to the Ministry from various sources and therefore that should not be an issue.

The other three themes deal with the new organization of the Ministry, which will become more of a supervisory body, measures for better organizing the study and development of a national health policy and prevention measures. Since they are not directly related to the main issue of my study, I will not go into great detail. Suffice it to say, they are consistent with a more disciplined and organized public administration of the health sector.

The responses to the proposal were various, ranging from warm support to cautious optimism to a wait and see attitude. Many sources referred to the plan as bold and brave, as it attempts to "surgically" remove many of the problems that the NHS faces. Minister Papadopoulus in his introduction to the proposal stated that "we maintain the public character of the NHS in a period in which one observes a rush to the private sector." Furthermore, trying to preempt any criticisms about the implementation potential of a radical reform, he argued: "The political leadership of the Ministry, with a sense of responsibility and with full understanding of the difficulties, but also with the protection of health for the Greek citizen in mind and the protection of the public interest, will move forward decisively with the implementation of the reform." The other political parties, as expected, were not as supportive of the reform. With the exception of the communist party, however, they were not adamantly opposed to the proposal, which indicates that the time might indeed be ripe for the reform.

The original reaction of the main opposition party was a cautious one. Its representative stated, "I hope through the dialogue that all the vague points of the proposal will become clear."[65] More specifically, New Democracy characterized the reform proposal as a text based on principles, many of which are in the right direction. This position alone is a change from previous political stand-offs in this area. If the main opposition and the government parties are willing to discuss the reform with an open mind and not revert back to their partisan cost-benefit analyses of the past, that alone can pave the way for an easier implementation time. Not everything was positive in the New Democracy assessment of the proposal, however. More specifically, New Democracy asked that the uncertainty that characterizes the proposal in their view be changed, with specific timelines and steps. Moreover, they asked for a policy around pharmaceuticals, for a common framework for both private and public health care services and for a clear explanation of how the creation of ODIPY will affect the pension system of the country.[66] And within a month of the publication of the Ministry report, New Democracy came out with its own proposal criticizing the Ministry plan more strongly this time around. In fact, the government proposal was characterized as "a monster, which because of its volume it will be extremely hard to implement."[67] The main opposition party focused on twelve mistakes in the proposal. The four most important ones deal with (a) the creation of ODIPY, which, according to the report, would lead to a monopoly on the demand side, (b) the overall generality of the proposal that has not even been studied from a financial perspective, (c) the enabling of physicians to establish private practices within the hospitals which would lead to a de facto acceptance of the side economy and lead to greater access inequalities, and (d) finally the inadequate numbers of trained personnel to see the Ministry proposal through at the local level.

The Coalition of the Left moved along more modest lines of criticism. The argument from that side was also based on the implementation potential of the proposal. They pointed out that the quality of the proposal can only be judged from its results. Therefore, they asked for specific timelines as well. But they also charged that changing the legal status of hospitals, health centers, and regional health systems is not consistent with strengthening the public face of health care.[68] Finally, the Communist party's criticism can be summarized in one phrase—everything to the private sector. It points out that the new system, if implemented, will operate based on market rules and ODIPY will very soon have to increase the premiums paid by workers and low-income people. Finally, it argued that the changes in the management of the system are, in a sense, making the private sector the ruler of the game, therefore moving the system away from any notion of social cohesion. The government is giving up the responsibility for the organization of the system as far as the communist party is concerned.[69] The reactions of the different parties could have been expected, based on their pre-election positions, especially when one considers that they are not under the same political pressures that a pre-election period adds. What is critical here, however, is that no party argued for the maintenance of the current system. Reform seems to be in demand. Along similar cautious lines were the original reactions by organized medicine.

The president of PIS stated that he hopes "that this last [plan] will be the best one." According to PIS, however, this requires many clarifications. The plan, says PIS, has many positive and many negative aspects. What they considered essential was that PIS was recognized as the institution that can assist in the design of policy based on studies and the interests of physicians.[70] The representatives of other medical societies focused on different aspects of the proposal. For instance, the secretary of EINAP, first stated that EINAP sees positive aspects in the proposal. It would also like to see a shortening in the time period needed for tenure for an NHS physician. At the same time, it points out to a number of positive aspects of the proposal.[71] The critical point here is that organized medicine did not appear to be fundamentally opposed to the reform plans at first. That was to change rather quickly. By the end of August, the managing board of EINAP had reconsidered its position and fundamentally opposed the reform.[72] According to EINAP, the reform plan attempts to overturn the public character of the health care system in Greece with the single goal of transforming it to a large business that will operate based on profit making and not on quality services universally and equitably offered to the citizenry. More specifically, they charged that the creation of ODIPY moves the financing burden from the public sector to the sickness funds. In light of past managerial experience by the sickness funds, the physicians expect that either qualitative or quantitative limits will be placed on care. As a result, out-of-pocket costs will increase. Furthermore, allowing private insurance companies to contract with the new regional health systems will erode solidarity since the better beds will automatically go to those who are privately insured, leaving the others either on waiting lists or in second-rate beds. The EINAP physicians are actually opposed to two aspects of the reform. First, the changes introduced to the legal status of the hospital, which, according to EINAP, mean two things. Physicians and other hospital workers become political hostages of a given government with respect to where, how and for how long they work in public hospitals. Moreover, they will no longer be in charge and therefore their opposition can be easily understood. Second, the reform proposal that a degree in medicine will no longer be sufficient for the practice of medicine, unless the young physician passes certain examinations, finds EINAP vehemently opposed. Instead it considers the degree sufficient proof of skills. EINAP is proposing instead that the problems of the NHS stem from the low levels of public financing. If the government were to increase funds, a number of the NHS problems, such as the building and technical capacity of hospitals or the lack of personnel in certain areas, would be solved. In light of the overall economic environment and of the poor performance of the NHS under complete physician control all these years, one has to wonder how viable, feasible or likely to work the EINAP proposals are.

Nevertheless, as one could have expected the political struggle behind the reform was only beginning. A number of factors converged to indicate that the reform would be implemented this time. First, was the governing style of Minister Papadopoulos, who had proven in other ministerial posts that he could see through the political and administrative traps of large scale reforms. Second, the original "neutral" reaction by opposition parties, despite their subsequent disagreements, looked to offer the government greater degrees of freedom to see the reform through. Third, the broadly prevalent belief among the citizenry that something had to be done with the health care sector, raised obstacles to opposing reform all together. The question was not whether reform was needed. Rather, the kind of reform was still up for grabs. Finally, the adaptation of the health care system along with all the other social protection systems to the EMU era, was and still is viewed as necessary if the country is to have the economic growth rates that it expects. Despite all these factors, however, the big bang approach that the government chose to follow did not work. At best, certain incremental steps were taken with the regionalization of the NHS, the change of the legal status of the hospitals, the improvements in existing hospitals and the creation of new ones. Still, most of the goals of the original reform plan as of mid-2002 remain illusive. One of the most fundamental ones, the reform of primary health care with the creation of ODIPY has not even been brought to Parliament as legislation. Moreover, a consistent struggle between the University professors on the one hand and Minister Papadopoulos on the other (over the issue of exclusive NHS employment) played a key role in the minister's decision to resign. Overall, one can say that the reform has stalled and if bold initiatives are not taken neither the financial nor the quality issues that the NHS faces will present much improvement.

In any case, as it becomes obvious from the historical overview of Greek health care politics, health care in Greece presents substantial differences and considerable similarities with the health care systems of other nations. Whereas the turn here, too, is towards a more efficient and effective distribution of resources, a more flexible political framework that can enable economic growth for the overall economy, internal politics, differences in understanding of various terms and the specific historical juncture ensure that health care in Greece will remain to a considerable degree different as it will in other member states as well.

Notes

1. www.odci.gov/cia/publications/nsolo/factbook/gr.htm.
2. Both the governing socialist party (PASOK) and the main opposition party, the conservative New Democracy, run on a pro-European Union membership agenda, advocating similar goals, albeit through different strategies. They were rewarded with close to 87 percent of the vote between them, underlying the choice that the country has firmly made to be in the core of Europe.
3. Interview of Finance Minister Papantoniou with *Eleytherotipia*, Sunday, August 6, 2000.
4. Minogiannis, P., "Greece and Health at the Dawn of the 21st Century: Trapped between Economics and Politics," Master's Thesis, Columbia University, 1997.
5. In 1974, the last military dictatorship that had lasted seven years (1967-1974) came to an end and democracy returned. In 1981, it was the first time that the government changed from the right to the left without incident. Since then, the quest for Greece has not been searching for democracy but searching for economic growth.
6. Kyriopoulos, J., and Tsalikis, G., "Public and Private Imperatives of Greek Health Policies," *Health Policy* 26(2):105-17, December 1993.
7. Wilsford, D., "Caught Between History and Economics: Reforming French Health Care Policy in the 1990s," in *Policymaking in France in the 1990s*, Martin Schain and John Keeler (eds.), St Martin's Press, New York, 1996.
8. Abel-Smith, B., Calltrop, J., Dixon, M., Dunning, Ad., Evans, R., Holland, W., Jarman, B., and Mossialos, E., "Report on the Greek Health Services," Ministry of Health, Welfare and Social Insurance, Athens, 1994. (in Greek)
9. Article in TO VIMA, July 30, 2000, A8-9.
10. OECD Health Data, 1999.
11. Figures from Ministry of Health, 1999.
12. Article in TO VIMA, July 30, 2000, A8-9.
13. National Statistical Service.
14. OECD Health Data, 1999.
15. Article in TO VIMA, July 30, 2000, A8-9.
16. OECD Health Data, 1999.
17. Yfantopoulos, G., "The Planning of the Health Care Sector in Greece," National Center for Social Research, Athens, 1985. (in Greek)
18. Colombotos, J., and Fakiolas, N. P., "The Power of Organized Medicine in Greece," in "The Changing Medical Profession: an International Perspective," F. W. Hafferty and J. B. McKinlay (eds.), Oxford University Press, New York, 1993.
19. Article in TA NEA on June 20, 2000, reported on their website at www.tanea.dolnet.gr.
20. Abel-Smith, B., Calltrop, J., Dixon, M., Dunning, Ad., Evans, R., Holland, W., Jarman, B., and Mossialos, E.," Report on the Greek Health Services."

21. In 1922, Turkish troops entered Smyrna (greater Minor Asia region) and slaughtered millions of Greek residents of the city. One and a half million Greeks were rescued and brought to Greece, where they became refugees.

22. Abel-Smith, B., Calltrop, J., Dixon, M., Dunning, Ad., Evans, R., Holland, W., Jarman, B., and Mossialos, E.," Report on the Greek Health Services."

23. Venieris, D., "Health Policy in Greece: The History of the Reform," in EniaioV ForeaV UgeiaV: Anagkaiothta kai Autapath, J. Kyripoulos and A. Sissouras (eds.), Themelio Publications, Athens, 1997.

24. Liakos, A., "Work and Politics in Greece between the two World Wars," Modern Greek History Studies, Institute for Research and Education by the Emporiki Bank of Greece, 1993.

25. Venieris, D. N., "The Development of Social Security in Greece, 1920-1990: Postponed Decisions," Ph.D. diss., University of London, LSE, 1994.

26. The Commission members were prominent scientists of the time such as Haven Emerson from Columbia University in New York City, Allen McLaughlin from the WHO, C. L. Park from the Australian Public Health Organization, Borislav Borcic, the director of the Zagreb Public Health School, and M. D. Mackenzie, a health expert from the League of Nations.

27. Op. cit. 13.

28. Stephanopoulos, S., "Pressures," *Asfalistikh EpiqewrhsiV*, October 1930.

29. Ministry of Labor Decision, Number 60556, February 1940.

30. Zilidis, C., "Evaluation of Primary Care Services for Rural Populations in Greece," Study performed for the Agricultural Bank, Athens, 1989.

31. Venieris, D. N., "The History of Health Insurance in Greece: The Nettle Governments Failed to Grasp," Working Paper, The European Institute, London School of Economics and Political Science, September 1996.

32. Sissouras, A., Yfantopoulos, I., et al., "Study for the Design and Organization of Health Services," Ministry of Health, Athens 1994.

33. Philalithis, A., "The Imperative for a National Health System in Greece in a Social and Historical Context," in *Socialism in Greece*, S. Tzannatos (ed.), Gower Press, Athens, Greece, 1986.

34. Newspaper of the Greek Government. Athen's Paper number 143, October 7, 1983.

35. Article in OikonomikoV TacudromoV, September 29, 1983, 28.

36. Newspaper of the Government, Issue Number 217, Athens, December 23, 1985.

37. "The Change" was the election motto of the socialists in 1981.

38. Newspaper of the Government, Issue Number 123, Athens, July 15, 1992.

39. In fact, the seeds of the economic policies that the Simitis governments have followed were designed by the last Papandreou government.

40. Interview of Minister of Development to newspaper TO VIMA, April 16, 2000.

41. Other members of the Commission were Professor Johan Calltorp, Dr. Maureen Dixon, Professor A. J. Dunning, Professor Robert Evans, Professor Walter Holland, Professor Brian Jarman, and Dr. Elias Mossialos.

42. Matsaganis, M., "From the North Sea to the Mediterranean? Constraints to Health Reform in Greece," *International Journal of Health Services* 28(2):333-48, 1998.

43. 1997 NHS Reform Proposal, Greek Ministry of Health, Welfare and Social Insurance, Athens, March 1997. (in Greek)

44. Komninou, N., "NHS: The Surgery Leaves Six Wounds Open," *Eleftheros Typos*, March 23, 1997, Athens. (in Greek)

45. Liaropoulos, L. L., and Kaitelidou, D., "Changing the Public-Private Mix: An Assessment of the Health Reforms in Greece," *Health Care Analysis* 6(4):277-285, 1998.
46. Advertising Pamphlet of Medisystem (1999).
47. Article in *Kathimerini*, June 4, 2000, 32.
48. Article in OikonomikoV TacudromoV, May 20, 2000, 20-25.
49. *The Economist* held a conference about the future of health care in June of 2000.
50. Report in TO VIMA, July 17, 2000, A18.
51. Prime Minister's Speech on PASOK's website at www.pasok.gr/gr/nea/06032000hospital.html.
52. Interview to newspaper TO VIMA, Mach 19, 2000, A4
53. Article in TO VIMA, March 19, 2000, A4.
54. Varelis, D., "The Third Way for the Sickness Funds," *H Nautemporikh*, April 2000, 22.
55. Article in TO VIMA, March 19, 2000, A5.
56. Report in *Rizospastis*, June 9, 2000, 15.
57. Report in TO VIMA, March 19, 2000, A5.
58. Article in TO VIMA, July 26, 2000, A16.
59. Article in *Ethnos* on July 29, 2000, 16.
60. Report in *Kyriakatikh Eleytherotipia*, July 30, 2000, 6.
61. Report in *Ethnos*, July 29, 2000, 16.
62. Report by the Ministry of Health: "Health for the Citizen," Athens, July 2000.
63. Report in TA NEA, July 29, 2000, 14-18.
64. The only exceptions to this rule will be the Athens and Salonika metropolitan areas due to the high population density where specific measures will be forthcoming.
65. Interview of Nikitas Kaklamanis, member of Parliament for New Democracy responsible for health care, with *Ethnos* on July 30, 2000, 24.
66. Many funds have been covering their pension responsibilities through funds from their health care sector. If these latter funds were to be pooled together in ODIPY, how would pensions be covered, is the criticism raised.
67. Report at www.in.gr, Tuesday, September 12, 2000.
68. Report in *Ethnos*, July 30, 2000, 24.
69. Ibid.
70. Report in Ethnos, July 30, 2000, 22.
71. Ibid.
72. Article in *Elytherotipia*, August 31, 2000, 47.

5

France and Health Care Policy Making:
Saying "*Non*" to Market Society

France, one of the largest European countries, has been over the years inconsistent in its attitudes. From being a founding member of the EU to impeding the integration process and back to galvanizing it in recent years; from a largely state-run economy to continuous privatization; from one of the strongest welfare states to issues of social exclusions for immigrants and French citizens born in former colonies; from exchanging the left and the right in its government seemingly as often as every election cycle to never-ending demonstrations about one policy or another, the only thing that appears to be consistent in France is the belief that there is one right way of doing things and that is the French way!

And it seems that it works for them, at least in health care. A recent WHO study ranked the French health care system as the best in the world.[1] And yet the French also find themselves under pressure to reform and modernize their health care system, much like they have found themselves having to reform their overall economy. Still, if there is one country that can serve as an example of vocal opposition to the Anglo-American version of neo-liberal welfare arrangements, this has to be France. It has from the beginning searched for an alternative proposition in the arrangements of its social affairs. And as one of the largest countries in the EU, it has been influential both in pushing forward economic reforms towards EMU and also in advocating a social aspect to the integration process. The French truly believe that an alternative version to the American style of governance can exist. And they seem determined to prove it.

In this chapter, I examine the policy path of French health care reforms over the past half century in order to understand the state of affairs today and the political and institutional constraints to reform that have been inherited. As in the other two cases, the Netherlands and Greece, a main theme that runs through the analysis is that the integration process has, among other factors, led to a quest for a more rationalized allocation of health care resources, but has fallen short of complete convergence. The

institutional heritage of the French health care system is yet another example of the distinct differences that exist among European systems and
part of the reason why integration or complete convergence is unlikely to
occur vis à vis the EU. I begin by a brief exploration of recent French
politics in order to understand the parameters within which recent health
policy reform efforts have been attempted. I go on to describe the main
elements of the system, focusing on the financing of the system, the delivery of services and the various policy-making styles in France. I then turn
the focus to my main theme through a historical exploration of French
health care policy making. I contend that French health politics have
revolved around the seemingly asymmetric goal of bridging social solidarity and laissez-faire medical practice, resulting in a heavy dose of
governmental planning. On the one hand, this has proven itself to be
politically effective, resulting in comprehensive coverage for the French
population and ,on the other hand, ironically, it has also resulted in raising political obstacles to reforming/modernizing the system as the surrounding parameters are changing. Whereas French health care policy
making has always found itself having to conform with the overall economic goals of the country (part of the EU effects on health care reform),
its internal politics have also allowed it to develop in its own distinctive
fashion. The French, perhaps more than any other people, as the title of
the chapter indicates, have decided to turn their backs on a market society.

Issues and Themes in French Politics

As in many other European nations in the last twenty years, the main
issue in the minds of voters and candidates alike has been the performance of the economy and the subsequent effect of the creation of new
jobs or the lack thereof. Despite recent advances in the fight against unemployment, the point still holds. The one issue that has dominated French
politics has been economic performance. It is within this framework that
any social policy must be viewed. France has consistently had one of the
highest unemployment rates in the OECD. The constitutionally strong
French government, independently of its political colors as we will see,
has not been able to produce notable results through its employment policies. This has created a perpetual state of malaise,[2] a never-ending crisis
whereby France seeks to identify its role in the world, and an alternative
way of arranging social affairs based on both solidarity and open markets.
Since the second oil shock of the late 1970s, this feeling of uneasiness
about where France is heading, how it is moving, and who is leading it has
deepened. And this has been evident in the turns of the electoral results. In
1981, the French elected François Mitterrand and his socialist party in a

dramatic fashion, primarily because it was believed at the time that Mitterrand's economic program of far-reaching nationalization of industries and social redistribution based on the principles of Keynes' economic theory would lead to the much needed economic development. Instead it led to the "Giscard-Barre crisis."[3] The polls taken right after the election in 1981 had indicated that more than 60 percent of French voters believed that Mitterrand's plan of nationalization was the one that would yield better results against unemployment. But such improvements never fully materialized and while the economic indicators (public debt, unemployment, inflation, etc.) were worsening, Mitterrand was forced to change gears in his economic policies. What is known as "The Socialist Experiment" of 1981-83 came to a halt and, from that point on, both left-oriented and right-oriented governments attempted to jumpstart the economy through a number of liberalization programs. After all, faith in Keynesianism had been eroded throughout the continent and almost all countries were experimenting with multifaceted programs of liberalization of the economy and privatization of industry. Still, French liberalization policies did not yield the expected results. Unemployment rates continued to grow under both the left and the right. The policy impasse was quite evident in the mid-1980s while unemployment was dropping elsewhere but not in France. When it finally began to decrease in the late 1980s, a European economic recession and the strict Maastricht criteria for EMU convergence did not allow for job creation and the French unemployment rate became once again one of the highest in the OECD.

This sense of government's inability to resolve the problem of unemployment led the always-precarious French voters to alternate the left and the right in their government.[4] Whereas the first twenty-three years of the French Fifth Republic had not seen a change in government, starting in 1981, this is the only pattern that one observes. It is indicative that in 1986, the socialists lost the elections for government, but the right coalition that found itself in government never got very far in addressing the issues for which its predecessor was ousted. Two years later, Mitterrand was able to win an easy reelection for the presidency and the socialists returned to government as well. Still, unemployment or the feeling of uncertainty was the big winner. Cited as the number one issue by voters, the exchange between Mitterrand and Chirac in the 1988 Presidential election debate is indicative of the state of the nation at the time. Mitterrand argued during the debate that in terms of unemployment there had been "a continuity of failure." Chirac, trying to win points in the debate, disagreed arguing that "No, we have not all failed in the same way." Unemployment seemed to have been accepted as a permanent characteristic of French political life.[5] Another change in government in 1993, when a coalition of the two major right parties handily beat the socialists, who were weakened by corruption scandals, did not lead to any better results in terms of unemployment than the earlier changes in government. Tiersky describes Prime Minister-Elect Edouard Balladur: "quickly told the French that unemployment would get worse before it got better and it did."[6] Partly because of this, Balladur was defeated by Chirac in the 1995 presidential election. Chirac emerged as the primary candidate of the right and even though in the first ballot he was trailing Socialist candidate Lionel Jospin by about 3 percent (23.3 percent vs. 20.8 percent), he was able to prevail in the second ballot with a 5 percent margin (52.6 percent vs. 47.4 percent). Unemployment was getting worse and it was yet again cited as the number one issue.[7] Clearly, more drastic measures were required, but was France ready for them?

Chirac continued the decline of traditional French dirigisme or, put differently, the traditional intervention of the state in the economy. This trend admittedly had begun with Mitterrand in 1983, as mentioned earlier, but Chirac became much more aggressive after 1995. Still, one can view this liberalization policy as the most recent stage of a trend that started in 1983, was accelerated by the Chirac government in 1986, and continued by Mitterrand and successive governments of both the left and the right (under Prime Ministers Rocard, Cresson, Beregovoy and Balladur[8]).

Unemployment was leading to uncertainty and to a feeling of protecting what was already gained. This, in turn, led to a deepening social division in France in the first instance and to a political cynicism that was not typical even for France in the second instance. By 1995, a quarter of the French population did not think it was well represented by any of the political parties. Moreover, a whopping 90 percent of voters in 1995 believed that France was increasingly being divided between the wealthy and the poor, the working and the unemployed, immigrants and native French citizens. And the sense that systems of social protection would be attacked in order to jumpstart the economy so that jobs could be created made social protection the number two issue behind unemployment.[9] Therein lies the French conundrum and in a sense the European one as well. How can jobs be created, the economy grow and social protection systems be maintained? As we saw in the Dutch and Greek cases, the issue was the same in those two countries. But in France, one aspect exists that has actually influenced thinking in other countries as well. Confidence in the unchecked liberalization of the economy and the business sector in particular has been on the decline for quite some time. Since 1995, French voters have indicated (67 percent) that the state ought to intervene in the economy, an increase of 38 percent from 1985. The French never really bought the argument that the market would bring solutions to their social problems and were horrified by the notion that their beloved system of social protection might end up like the American system.[10] Chirac's and his new Prime Minister Juppe's decision in the fall of 1995 to tackle the public deficit and the debt as well as to try to rein in inflationary pressures (in short to achieve economic convergence to the Maastricht criteria) by attacking, as it was perceived, the systems of social protection led to unprecedented demonstrations. In the following election Juppe was ousted. Jospin and his socialist party were brought in to succeed where everyone else had failed for the past twenty years. They are expected to beat the unemployment, maintain social protection and grow the economy.

And, in fact, the first signs are positive for France. The OECD, in its recent economic survey of France, writes that "France has not enjoyed such a favorable economic situation for ten years."[11] And as a recent article[12] on France's economic performance indicates: "Rising exports; revived consumer confidence; a falling unemployment rate; low inflation; the prospect that next year will be the fifth in a row of robust economic growth" must look pretty good. But all these occurred in the second half of the 1990s, a decade that has seen an unprecedented economic boom fueled by new technologies and increased globalization of markets. Could such results be sustained? The article goes on to argue that "if the celebrations are not to end with a hangover, some bad habits will have to stop." And, of course, that is where the issue and the politics lie. The article went on, "France's pension system...must be reformed sooner rather than later,... Spending on the health system...is too high and threatens sound government budgeting,... Poverty traps...are too prevalent: half of the eight basic income support schemes...discourage the search for a job." All these are indicative of the pressures that the French government finds itself facing and the threats that the French people perceive. The article forgot to mention that, whereas the unemployment rate is indeed falling, it remains high, and that the jobs that are being created are not the secure jobs of the past that the French are accustomed to. As far as the average French citizen is concerned, the economic prosperity that the OECD or other analysts may observe has not touched them yet. And to be asked for further sacrifices will be difficult. The French have never been willing to take such austerity (as they are perceived) policies lightly. As of 2001, a year before the next presidential election, the jury was still out for Jospin's government.

Whatever the verdict, however, one thing is certain. Economic turbulence, perceived broken promises of eminent prosperity because of European integration, and a fear of losing the most precious aspect of French life, its culture, has raised serious doubts about the EU. Whereas ever since Mitterrand, who had made a great commitment to the building of the Union (along with the then German chancellor Helmut Kohl), France was fully dedicated to the EU project, the aforementioned factors had begun in the 1990s to raise doubts. Since 1984, when France held the EC presidency, all through the drafting of the Maastricht Treaty, Mitterrand put his stamp on the process of integration and by many, this is what is considered to be his greatest legacy. Polls during the 1980s indicated strong support by the French public towards a united Europe and all major political parties had reached a consensus that closer integration was good for France. This support, however, weakened in the 1990s, largely because European integration had failed to deliver, at least immediately, the type of economic results that the French expected.[13]

Many, and interestingly enough from both the left and the right, actually perceive the EMU project as the source of economic problems. They argue that Maastricht was oversold as a solution to the country's problems and that the EU is posing more threats to French autonomy and French identity than the perceived benefits. Recent gains in the economy have helped alleviate the effects of such criticisms, but not to a degree of returning France to its 1980s relation to the EU. The integration process has altered dramatically the traditional patterns of state-business relations through both the creation of the common market and the establishment of the economic and monetary union. Business executives today view Brussels as equally a significant player as Paris. At the same time, the traditionally strong French labor movement is said to be in a state of crisis.[14] Since the socialist U-turn of 1983, all governments to varying degrees have moved down this path of a more conservative economic policy. The country has simultaneously moved closer to Europe, making it harder for Paris to regulate a number of sectors in order to please labor demands. Union membership has shrunk by almost 70 percent from 1980. And the average French citizen feels uneasy about his future, has second thoughts about the direction of the EU and wonders about the role of France in it.

It is this pause in French europhile sentiment that has led both Chirac and Jospin to call for a more social Europe. If the integration is going to move forward, according to the French, then social Europe has to become part of it. And in calling for a social Europe, the French have once again found their role in pushing for integration. The issue of employment was already placed on the agenda largely because of French pressures and with France presiding over the EU for the second half of 2000, social issues made considerable headway. The French perceive their role in the union now as that of the country that reminds the others that welfare policies and social responsibility cannot be abandoned but must be strengthened. The French have always had a different approach to capitalism, as a recent *Financial Times* article entitled "Capitalism Fails to Win French Hearts," indicates.[15] Therein, three cases of how public sentiment forced companies to withdraw business decisions that were socially unacceptable are described. The article concludes that "the moral of these tales is not simply one of more nimble public relations. Rather, companies have to make more effort to dispel the popular perception in France that they are big, rich and greedy."[16] And largely because of France's considerable influence in the EU, the Union has repeatedly called for a distinctly European approach to globalization and the arrangement of social protection quite different from the American version. Social solidarity seems to be well protected under such arrangements, since it is always one of the principles upon which policies are proposed. Of course, as we have seen, there are pressures that exist because of the integration process and because of internal system deficiencies, mainly in terms of modernizing social protection systems, and France is no exception to this. With these in mind, we shall explore the main elements of one such system, the French health care system.

The Design and Politics of the French Health Care System

Ranked number one in the world, the French health care system is characterized by the complexity that results from many compromises made in order to achieve incremental change in a system that is fundamentally based on three principles: the principle of social solidarity, the principle of health care as a public good and the principle of a liberal, pluralistic attitude towards health care. These three principles appear to be contradictory with one another and in many ways they are. Still, the French have based their entire medical infrastructure on these three principles, something that becomes quite evident when one observes both the financing and delivery aspects of health care as well as the different styles of policymaking in health care. I begin by briefly discussing these principles of the system as a background framework. I then focus on the financing and delivery of services and in the politics of the French system.

Principles and Ideas

Social solidarity, health care as a public good and liberal pluralism are as much principles upon which policy is based as they are ideas that transcend social policy making in France. Social solidarity in France has a somewhat different meaning than in other countries, encapsulating social cohesion, social inclusion and national strength. In an otherwise highly fragmented society, social policy in general is centered on the principle of *solidarite nationale* or national solidarity. As Wilsford observes, the term stands for the "agreement by all elements of an otherwise highly divided French society that social assistance is necessary to the strength and well being of France both to its 'internal cohesiveness and to its power in the international order. This unity of purpose is focused around the concepts of both mutual dependence and national obligation."[17] National solidarity is expressed through different types of solidarity. In France, besides the traditional cross subsidization from wealthy to poor and from healthy to sick, one observes both intergenerational solidarity, whereby the young subsidize the old and inter-group solidarity whereby one occupation group will subsidize another.

Moreover, in France, perhaps more than in any other country in the world, health care is accepted by virtually everyone to be a public good. It follows naturally for them that the state as the institutional personification of the nation will have to provide it, since public goods cannot be produced and allocated efficiently and equitably by the market. The combination of these two principles always made it difficult for ideas of managed competition to find fertile soil in France, whereas as we have seen in other countries like the Netherlands, the lack of these strong sentiments about the nature of health care allowed quasi-market notions to make a policy run.

The third principle upon which the French health care system is based is this principle of liberal pluralism in medicine.[18] The French *La Médecine liberale* or liberal medicine as it is translated, has become institutionalized in France since the 1930s. La Médecine liberale ensures the private practice of medicine, which, in the view of the French, protects the sanctity of the physician-patient relationship by safeguarding their independence. It does so through the application of four doctrines. First, there is the freedom of choice of physician for each patient. Second, physicians are free to prescribe as they see fit based on their medical judgment. Third, fee for service payment is guaranteed, and finally the payment is made directly by the patient to the physician for the services that were provided. Ironically enough, la médecine liberale has many of the elements of the practice of medicine in the country that the French consider to provide sub-optimal medicine to its population, the United States. As can be expected, of course, la médecine liberale applies to the ambulatory care sector where patients are free to choose and change their physicians as often as they like, and physicians are free to prescribe according to medical judgment without interference by third-party payers. Of course their fees are closely regulated.

The three principles just discussed have shaped the French health care system from its formation. Even today, they are exhibiting an unusual strength and endurance despite pressures that have faced the French health care system and policy responses that have been formulated over time as it becomes evident from the financing and delivery of services.

Financing of Services and Health Care Coverage

France is the fourth highest-ranking country in terms of national health expenditures. Health care costs today are estimated to have a rate of increase of 0.3 percent of GDP per year. They stand at almost 800 billion francs or 10.2 percent of GDP.[19] There are two main types of coverage in France. The first is the comprehensive and basic coverage, a general coverage scheme known as *Regime General* or *Assurance Maladie* and the second is the supplemental coverage. In terms of sources of financing, sickness funds, which administer the former coverage, pay for almost 74 percent of total health expenditures. Supplemental coverage covers another 6 percent of expenditures and out of pocket payments contribute another 19 percent, with direct government payments around the 1 percent mark.[20]

In terms of hospital care, the sickness funds are responsible for 89.5 percent of the total hospital expenditures, supplemental insurance covers an additional 2.1 percent and private expenditures reach the 7.5 percent mark.[21] This is quite indicative of the central role of the hospital in the provision of services in France. Moreover, the fact that almost 90 percent of hospital expenditures are covered by the national insurance is also indicative of the high degree of equitability that exists in the French system. With most services performed in the hospitals, either on an outpatient or an inpatient basis, it is significant to recall that the largest share of payment comes from social insurance schemes.

On the other hand, ambulatory care expenditures are split a bit more evenly with sickness funds covering about 57 percent of expenditures, private expenditures around 32 percent and supplemental insurance around 11 percent.[22] The high private expenditures through high copayments have been a persisting part of the French system and a point of dispute with patient's groups.

The essential coverage, which is quite comprehensive, is administered and financed through a scheme of sickness funds.[23] There are three major funds based on the occupational group of the enrollees, which is the way that contributions are made: the general sickness fund (*Caisses nationale d'Assurance Maladie des Travailleurs Salaries*), which is for employees in industry, government and commerce as well as their dependents; the agricultural fund, which is for workers in the agricultural sector and their dependents; and the fund for self-employed persons and professionals and their dependents. There are a number of other minor funds, which together cover about 1.5 percent of the population, but between the three major ones, almost 98 percent of the population is covered, which means that virtually the entire French population is covered by national health insurance. The general fund covers about 82 percent of the population, the agricultural fund about 9 percent and the fund for the professionals about 7 percent. Starting in 1978, workers who did not have obligatory coverage by their employer, had access to the funds through special individual contributions. Unemployed individuals are covered and the premium is paid for a given time period through social security. After that period ends, if the individual is still unemployed, he can still gain access to the sickness funds through special individual rates. At any moment there is an estimated 200,000 to 500,000 French people or permanent residents of France without coverage. This comes to between 0.4 and 1 percent of the population. The general fund, with over 80 percent of the population covered by it, operates as a quasi-public entity,[24] is self-supporting and is the prominent player among funds. All funds follow the model of operation of the general fund. A rather efficient administrative mechanism, the general fund is in charge of sixteen regional funds and a plethora of local ones.[25] Whereas the regional funds are primarily responsible for capital planning, the local funds oversee the collection of contributions and the reimbursement of claims. The general fund gives general policy guidelines, in cooperation with the government, in terms of levels of contributions and reimbursements. The other two funds as well as the smaller funds usually follow the same guidelines. The director of the general fund is appointed by the government and the governing board is representative of workers and employers. There are also representatives of the Ministry of Social Security and of the mutual insurance companies. It is the governing board that sets the levels of contributions, even though in practice it usually defers proposals to the Ministries of Finance and Social Security. The contributions are split between employers and employees with the former paying about two-thirds of the premium and the latter the remaining third. This comes to about 14 percent of the gross salary being paid by the employer and another 7 percent paid by the employee into the sickness fund.[26] A significant percentage of that money (around 5 percentage points), however, goes towards salary continuation benefits and therefore only the remaining goes to health care, and in the case of the general fund subsidization of the smaller funds.[27] Self-employed individuals pay the same premium that employers pay, but do not have to pay the additional employee contribution. For unemployed people, social security pays their premium for up to a certain time, as mentioned earlier.[28]

The second major type of insurance in France besides National Health Insurance is supplemental insurance, which insures against very serious and catastrophic illness, for some luxury benefits and for part of the copayments. It can be provided either by mutual insurance funds or by private insurance companies. Around 60 percent of those with supplemental coverage choose the former since private insurance has to pay a 9 percent tax on revenue, therefore making them a bit more expensive. Overall, almost 88 percent of the population carries supplemental coverage. Those who choose not to take it either cannot afford supplemental coverage, or consider themselves not to be at risk. Payments to the funds or to the insurance companies are a fixed flat rate based on salary. In this sense, many employers and the government have encouraged the French to take out supplemental insurance since the more people take out coverage the lower the rate can become.

In terms of provider payment, all public hospitals and most of the non-profits are paid with an annual global budget. These hospitals account for the largest percentage of inpatient days. The global budgets they receive cover all services provided in the hospitals except for the ones provided in the hospital-based private practice of physicians. Private hospitals receive per diem payments for their services. Auxiliary services like lab exams are paid on a fee for service basis and the principle of freedom of choice applies here as well. La Médecine liberale dictates the payment schemes for physicians as well. All physicians in the same specialty receive the same fee from the patient independent of which sickness fund the patient is enrolled. If the sickness fund of the payment does not cover the pre-negotiated fee completely, then the patient either has to cover the difference through out of pocket payments or through supplemental insurance. Payment is made directly by the patient to the physician after the services are rendered and therefore there is not a complicated administrative mechanism here. The fees are negotiated within a committee and the results become part of the national convention, a type of contract that all actors in the health arena pledge to adhere to.[29] The members of this committee represent the three major funds and the three physician unions. The results of the negotiation are subject to governmental approval. The fees agreed are mandatory for all physicians. However, before 1990, a physician could choose to opt out of this payment scheme, accept a lower fee but also negotiate with his/her patient for an additional charge. This had created a two-tier physician structure, with the first tier sticking to the higher pre-negotiated fees, and the second tier accepting the lower fees but charging the patient additionally according "to the code of medical ethics and with tact and restraint."[30] It is estimated that second-tier physicians charge their patients an additional 30 to 50 percent, an acceptable additional charge overall.[31] Allowing physicians to opt out was revoked in 1990, but it is estimated that by that time there were about 28.5 percent of the total physician workforce that had opted out, which included 39.5 percent of the specialists and 19 percent of the generalists. These physicians will for the foreseeable future continue to practice under *secteur 2* privileges because of "the strong French legal tenet of not revoking advantages previously granted."[32]

Finally, in France one observes relatively high out-of-pocket costs. They are not as high as the ones observed in Greece, for instance, but the interesting phenomenon here is that they are instituted here whereas in Greece they were due to the underground economy. Out-of-pocket payments, as we have seen, are the source of about 19 percent of total health care expenditures.[33] Copayments have been included in all health reforms in France as a way of avoiding moral hazard type of behavior. Copayments in France are called *le ticket moderateur* or moderating ticket. The rate of copayment varies depending on the sickness fund and on the service provided.[34] A number of other rules apply that seemingly complicate the administration and the calculation of the copayment. However, as one analysts puts it, "The rules are clearly defined, providing both specificity and predictability. Exactly how much an individual must pay and how much reimbursement will be obtained can be calculated with certainty in advance for those who seek care from physicians who accept nationally negotiated fee schedules."[35]

Overall, one observes that the French health care system has performed well in terms of covering the entire population with all the services needed. Still, high out-of-pocket payments and increased need for supplemental insurance jeopardize its status as an equitable system. On the other hand, rates of increase in health care expenditures can hardly be tolerated under the current technocratic thinking. Something has to give and the line that health policy is walking in France lies exactly between these two points. I will now turn my attention to the supply side of the system and focus on the providers of care.

System Structural design

The supply side of the French health care system is characterized by a mix of public and private providers. This mix highlights the tensions between the principles of La Médecine liberale on the one hand and social solidarity on the other and has developed through compromises made over the years.[36] Physicians are allowed to establish private practices anywhere they choose. Ambulatory care therefore is essentially private. Hospital inpatient care, on the other hand, is primarily public with most of the beds in the public sector. About two-fifths of the beds, however, are in the hands of either the private or the voluntary sector. Overall one observes a rather uncoordinated ambulatory care sector and a highly organized and planned hospital sector. Whereas La Médecine liberale dictates that ambulatory care has to be based on the four liberal principles mentioned earlier, in hospital care the state has appeared to be a heavy regulator.

The physician to population ratio stands at 2.8 physicians per 1,000 people and about three-fifths of French physicians are generalists.[37] Most of them are office based and practice medicine based on the four liberal principles mentioned earlier. A number of nurses, physical therapists, speech therapists and other non-physician clinician groups also offer ambulatory care services. There are also health centers, which are mostly urban where both generalists and specialists are occupied on a part-time basis. Primary care, therefore is provided by a mix of professionals, primarily in private offices, but also in health centers or at hospital outpatient consultations.[38]

This is part of the reason why, in France, generalists do not have a well-defined role like their Dutch counterparts, that seems to be confusing even to them. Whereas, on the one hand, they want to maintain the principles of La Médecine liberale in their practices, at the same time they have set up separate organizations and they lobby for the gate keeping roles. Therefore, one has to question the homogeneity of the private practitioners. As one observer put it, "the image and the identity of the medical profession are in crisis at a time when the call for spending regulation is growing."[39]

Office-based practitioners do not have admitting privileges for the hospitals so when a patient is admitted, his care passes from the generalist or specialist who treated him originally to the hospital based specialist. There is, however, an approximate 22 percent of office-based physicians who can still admit, but only for outpatient procedures. Hospital-based specialists in the public sector are salaried and are also allowed to have a private practice on the premises for a limited amount of time. The out-of-pocket cost for private consultations by the hospital-based specialists, however, is quite prohibitive and therefore one could argue that the choice that La Médecine liberale dictates in terms of outpatient care does not exist in the hospital sector. Public hospitals operate on fixed global and prospective budgets that are set by the Ministry of Health. In the private sector the remuneration of the hospital specialists takes many different forms, from full-time salaries like in the public sector to having private office-based specialists admit to the private clinics.

The clinics in the private sector deal mostly with maternity care, routine operations or specialize in a specific kind of treatment. Private hospitalization accounts for about a quarter of hospital expenditures. A typical clinic (*clinique*) is much smaller than a public hospital, averaging about eighty beds. During the 1990s, a number of changes occurred in the managerial structure of these hospitals. Whereas a complete assessment of the managerial logic behind these changes is beyond the scope of this essay, it appears that the old model of the clinic that was set up by private physicians was no longer viable, mainly because of the high cost of new technologies. A series of networks, mergers and affiliations has been observed, especially in the Paris area, with three main groups emerging as the key players and some private clinics now able to move aggressively into the markets for cardiac surgery and radiation therapy.[40] It is therefore a possibility that in the future, the private sector may compete with the public in terms of bringing the most sophisticated and latest technologies. Nevertheless, to the degree that public hospitalization remains of high quality, these developments should not affect the bulk of the French population.

Public hospitals are quite advanced in terms of technological sophistication and their personnel is also highly trained. There are both general hospitals and specialized ones. There is great variation in terms of size. At one end, one finds small general hospitals at the local level and mostly in rural areas and, at the other end, highly integrated regional medical centers (located mostly in cities) where research, education and care are all combined. These medical centers have traditionally had a monopoly in tertiary care since neither smaller public hospitals nor private ones could compete with them. The board of directors of each public hospital includes the mayor of the given locality where the hospital is located and other representatives of the local community. The government, however, is the one who appoints the director and has direct control over all appointments of medical staff and in terms of expansion of capacity. For example, any changes in the number of beds must be in order with the *Carte Sanitaire*, an instrument used since 1970 to define the regions and sub-sectors of the health care system and their needs in terms of beds.

Moreover, whereas La Médecine liberale has not traditionally allowed for much institutional cost control in the ambulatory care sector, there are cost control institutional mechanisms in place in the hospital sector. The system of global budgets that came into place in 1983, as we will see, has produced significant results in terms of hospital expenditures. Between 1983 and 1997, hospital expenditures as a percentage of total health care expenditures dropped from 51.8 percent to 48 percent, an average annual rate of decrease of 0.23 percent.[41] Still, however, problems persist mainly because the medical staff of the hospitals has perceived as expected global budgets and more recent attempts for data collection as efforts to micromanage the practice of medicine. An example would be the obligation since 1988 that a brief report called RSS is filed for each patient's discharge that would include the procedures performed and the reasoning behind them. RSS reports are rarely completed in detail. Ambulatory care expenditures increased from 24.7 percent in 1983 to 30 percent in 1992, but had dropped back to 27 percent by 1997. This was an average annual increase of only 0.37, but, as we will see, it came after significant policy developments and anticipatory behavior by French physicians. As mentioned earlier, French health care expenditures have continued to rise from 91 billion francs in 1975 to more than 700 billion francs by century's end, an increase from 6.2 percent of GDP where they stood in 1975 to 9.1 percent of GDP in 1999.[42] The large investment by the public sector into hospitals has brought the hospitals in the center of the system.

Actors in French Health Policymaking

Policy-making styles in France vary tremendously across issue areas and over time. As Baumgartner discusses,[43] when issues, even ones that are very important are low on the partisan agenda, they tend to be handled in a technocratic fashion by civil servants. When issues do not offer themselves for high politics, public exposure and winning political points, they tend to be devolved from the politicians to the civil servants. This creates a strong bureaucracy that is in and of itself an institution in the political process. On the other hand, there are also issues that at times occupy the front pages of newspapers and cause major public demonstrations. In France, over the years, one has observed this with issues such as social security reform, immigration and educational reform. These issues generate strong partisan conflict that characterizes French politics. Thus, public demonstrations place issues higher on the agenda, and along with the highly partisan policy-making style one, also observes a policy-making style that caters to social demands as to when reforms pass or do not pass based on such demonstrations.[44]

Health care politics in France are no exception to these two different styles of policy making. When health care reform is placed high on the agenda, then we see continuous partisanship, and when it is not, then the bureaucracy takes over. At any given historical juncture, one can discern both styles and it would be a difficult case to argue that one style excludes the other. French politics in health care have been characterized lately by this partisan conflict that caters to each party's constituency. And whereas the overall direction of policy efforts has been similar, the left and the right have not approached health reform with similar policy tools. The country has been governed in the last ten years by governments of both the right and the left. One observes marked differences both in the styles and in the reasoning behind the proposed reforms, as we will see later on. The Balladur and Juppe governments of the right shared a common conservative ideology based on regressive tax increases and cuts in public spending in terms of how to reform health care, whereas the Jospin government tried to give a progressive twist by targeting relief to lower-income people. More important, however, is the struggle and the rhetoric behind the reforms and the political advantages and disadvantages that the different positions had in store for the different players.

But as mentioned earlier, after the political storm passes, the institution that has most of the decision making power is the French bureaucracy through its highly skilled civil servants. The state here acts through the ministry of social affairs primarily, but also the ministries of finance and education have a say over the direction of health policy. The French system, from an administrative perspective, appears to be rather well organized with clear-cut lines of responsibility between the different levels of government and the different agents at any given governance level.

Paris has a number of responsibilities ranging from promoting healthy behaviors through educational programs, to protecting public health. Its most relevant responsibilities for our purposes are through the Ministry of Education for the supply of personnel, particularly specialists, and that it is also charged with safeguarding national social solidarity. Therefore, the central government closely watches and regulates, through the Ministry of Social Affairs and the Ministry of Finances, the rates of insurance premiums, the several financing schemes that exist in the system, ensures universal access to care. In so doing, its goals are, on the one hand, to maintain equitable access to services for all French citizens and also to ensure the financial viability of the system in the medium and long run.[45]

The hierarchical lines of responsibility continue at the local level with the Regional Bureaus of Health and Social Affairs and the Departmental Bureaus of Health and Social Affairs, which report to the departmental prefect. The former are responsible for capacity planning in the region and the latter are responsible for the efficient performance of all provider institutions. The regional bureaus utilize two planning methods. The first, as mentioned earlier, is the health map (la Carte sanitaire), which is used for planning bed capacity and technology investments. The second is the regional schema of health system organization (le Schema regional d'organisation sanitaire), which determines the regional distribution of health resources.

The French state in health care policy therefore enjoys much more autonomy and has much more capacity to act than the Dutch or the Greek ones. The autonomy is derived from the broad social consensus in terms of its authorization by society to ensure national solidarity and financial viability of the system, and its capacity from the technocratic skill of the regional and departmental bureaus. This is not to say, however, that pluralistic interests do not play a role in health politics. One cannot dismiss them as a factor but, from a comparative perspective, French interests groups do not enjoy the same access that the corporatist spirit of policy making in the Netherlands ensured for interests in that case. Be that as it may, organized interests do affect policy, especially when they are allowed enough access by the state.

As expected, the main interest group is the association of physicians, or better put, the many associations of physicians. This is, in fact ,the overriding characteristic of organized medicine in France, its divisiveness.[46] French physicians are divided between generalists and specialists, between different subspecialties, between older and younger physicians, between hospitalists and non-hospitalists, between men and women and so on. This divisiveness has not, of course, helped them much in the political process. In the words of David Wilsford, "Abetting the state's dominance making health care policy in France is the historical weakness of organized medicine. It has been weak since the earliest days of the nineteenth century because medicine, except for the occasional moment, has been deeply fragmented organizationally and poorly mobilized politically.... Therefore, in the French case, fragmentation and poor mobilization have weakened the influence of organized medicine, and by extension the profession as a whole, in the health policy universe. What is worse, organized medicine in France is riven by internal conflicts that manifest themselves in competing professional associations that are, in turn, plagued by very low membership levels."[47] This bleak picture for the profession has begun to change. Even though it remains highly divided, in recent years as we will see it has scored certain impressive political victories, even though the overall tide is against La Médecine liberale and less physician autonomy.

There are three major medical associations and a few more minor ones that supposedly are charged with representing the interests of private physicians, both generalists and specialists. There are a few more representing the hospital physicians. These unions oftentimes fight amongst themselves along political, ideological and even ethical lines and it has traditionally been difficult for physicians to present a unifying front. The largest association that represents private physicians is the CSMF (*Confederation des Syndicats Medicaux Français*) that was founded in 1928. The second main association is the FMF (*Federation des Médecins de France*). Up until 1980, FMF and CSMF had been able to somewhat coordinate themselves, but usually in favor of specialist interests. As a result, in 1980 a number of generalists from CSMF left and formed the third main physician group, the MG France (*Médecins Generalistes de France*). Within a decade, MG France had caught up with the other two unions in terms of membership and political influence and in some cases it has exceeded them. The rivalry between these three groups has allowed the French state to practice a divide and rule type of policy.

A second major interest group are the localities, which by their influence on the boards of the hospitals and in the regional offices for planning always try to sidestep the planning process and receive funds for the latest technologies in their hospitals and have more physicians appointed in their locality. Here again, however, the "competition" between the different localities leaves ample room for the central government to decide, and thus the planning process has not been derailed as it has been in other places. Finally, one of the most important interest groups is the public itself. Accustomed to the relative freedom of choice that they have had over the years and the high quality of services, they do not want to see major changes in the system. Furthermore, and as mentioned earlier, despite promises of economic growth that would lead to further prosperity, the French public remains rather suspicious of any reforms that may alter the structural dynamics of the system. And as they have proven time after time in the past and with issue after issue, the French are not afraid to take their demands to the streets if the issue is that important. Therefore, with any given reform proposal, one must be aware that at any point the public may make its presence dynamically felt.

In short, one could describe the French health care system as the result of fine balancing between maintaining social solidarity and treating health care as a public good, on the one hand, and the principles of La Médecine liberale and increasingly the search for efficiency on the other. The French system has evolved over time to provide comprehensive health coverage essentially to the entire population of the country. So whereas one must credit the efficacy of political institutions in achieving this balance, one must also explore their ineffectiveness in reforming parts of the system that are characterized by inefficient sub-optimality. National health expenditures in France have continued to rise throughout the second half of the twentieth century, and in light of changes in the macroeconomic thinking throughout Europe, public financing has to be controlled. Pressures for reform have forced the French like many other countries to debate the future of their system. But to understand these recent debates, we must trace the institutional evolution of the French health care system through history.

The Political Development of the French Health Care System

Despite the predominance of the state in policy making, health care reform in France has not moved in large big bang kind of steps, but rather in small increments. To understand the dynamics of policymaking in France and the current debates about its future, one has to understand how the current institutions came into place. We now turn our attention to the historical path development of the health care system.

1945-1970: Building National Solidarity and Expanding the System

The origins of the French health care system date back to the nineteenth century and even earlier with hospitals and poor houses being established as early as the French revolution. In the beginning of the twentieth century the system was primarily financed through philanthropic contributions and municipal budgets. As medicine began to progress, however, and the central government attempted to implement a third-party payer system, organized medicine opposed it vehemently. In 1928, the first French health care insurance bill was passed. It was by no means a comprehensive attempt to secure the population against the medical risks that they faced. Nevertheless, it was an attempt to introduce insurance and therefore alter the parameters within which medicine was practiced at the time. In a letter to the minister of labor, secretary general of CSMF (the medical union which at the time was still united) Paul Cibrie, raised the profession's opposition to the third-party payment system: "The medical profession is under no illusions about the consequences of the contractual liberty allowed for under the law. We understand administrative procedure well enough to know that the funds will want to impose allowable charges and third-party payment. And we have great difficulty identifying an impartial institution capable of arbitrating between the opposing positions of the medical profession and that of the health insurance funds."[48] It was to be the beginning of a struggle between the state and the profession, familiar from other countries. In the case of France, however, the interesting phenomenon is that the state ended up topping the profession.

An exogenous factor, the Second World War, may have had something to do with this. The French were defeated rather handily by Nazi Germany and that did not sit well with French national pride. One of the reasons for the defeat, identified by almost all observers at the time, was the lack of national solidarity in France prior to 1939. As mentioned earlier, national solidarity is translated in France as social assistance in order to ensure internal unity and external power. In 1945, social assistance focused on employment policies, health care, pensions and family allowances. This sentiment that, absent a major introduction of social protection measures, the future of France would be in jeopardy was the crucial factor that brought both the left and the right after the war to support social assistance reform.[49] Moreover, the post-world war period of economic reconstruction provided more financial degrees of freedom to the government to pass the legislation.

The Social Security system established in 1945 aimed at providing comprehensive health insurance to all workers and their dependents. This would mean that it would not only reimburse health care costs, but that it would also provide salary replacement up to a certain percentage due to illness. In this respect, choosing the Bismarck type of social insurance, rather than the British Beveridge system set the French upon a parallel trajectory with the systems of most continental nations. The system would henceforth mainly be financed through the contributions of employers and employees, making the connection between the labor market and health care policy stronger than it is in a nationalized system. Ups and downs in the labor market in this pay as you go system had the potential of bringing more immediate imbalance in the health care system since the government would not finance it out of general taxes and therefore could not shift funds around as easily. Moreover, it introduced two powerful interest groups in the health care system, the employer association and the labor union. From one perspective, it was politically easier to choose this kind of a system since it was a natural continuation of the preexisting system of health coverage whereby financing was the responsibility of collective mutual insurance based on occupational groups. Moreover, the French resistance during the war was successful largely because of the contributions of the various workers' unions and the incoming system was viewed as a reward for the workers for their struggles in the period of German occupation.

From the beginning, one of the goals of the French government was to institute a uniform and binding fee schedule for all physicians. This placed the government in direct opposition to the profession, a battle that according to most analysts was won by the government.[50] La Médecine liberale had already a stronghold on medical practice and the state was searching for a way to control excessive charges. The hunch that Paul Cibrie had in 1929 was correct and the quest for an equitable fee schedule began almost from the beginning of the new system in 1945. At first a suggested fee was introduced and the sickness funds would cover anywhere between 75 and 85 percent of that fee. Still, physicians were not bound to this fee and therefore charged more and as a result the reimbursement that patients received (the equivalent of 75 percent of the suggested fee) was sometimes as low as 40 percent of the actual charges. The large out-of-pocket costs angered the public, the sickness funds, the employers and the employees. A strong political coalition was formed against the profession, which was supporting the maintenance of the status quo. The government, however, sided with the larger coalition for a variety of reasons. First, the financial consequences of the overcharging practice by physicians threatened the long-term viability of the system. Unless certain controls were introduced, physicians would not only be able to practice medicine liberally under the principles of La Médecine liberale but also would be able to do so while profiting by taking advantage of the patients. In turn, the patients demanded that the sickness funds raise the suggested fees so that a higher percentage of their expenditures would be paid for or that their contributions to the funds would be lowered. In turn, this put the burden on employers who would have to cover the difference. There was no end in sight unless physicians agreed to the suggested fee. Another reason for governmental action was that during the postwar years, it was inconceivable that a certain professional group could practice in a manner that was opposed to the notion of national solidarity. The most important thing for France was to regain its stature in the world. To do so, it had to enjoy internal cohesiveness and if physicians stood in the way of this goal, they were certainly going to be fought.

Despite this dynamic, all through the 1950s, the CSMF was able to sustain the non-binding fee schedules. But in the latter half of the decade, a comprehensive reform attempt, what has been known as the project Gazier, after the minister of social affairs between 1956 and 1958, brought the two sides to a standstill.[51] And whereas organized medicine was able to win that round, a deep division among its ranks began to appear. One side, which included the official leadership, believed that cooperation with the government and ongoing negotiations would assure physicians of reasonable and customary fees. There was, however, another side in the internal CSMF politics that supported an all out war with the government to maintain the non-binding fees. It was the first time that such a division had occurred in organized medicine and it only spelled trouble for its future. And whereas political attention turned from social policy to other matters in 1958,[52] the issue never really went away.

On May 12, 1960, the new government came out with a decree that imposed the binding fees on physicians. What is more, it did so in a fashion that left little doubt about the governmental intentions. It not only asked organized medicine to respect the decree but it required all individual physicians to follow its guidelines. For those who did not, the consequences would be that their patient base would eventually shrink since their patients would not get reimbursed by the sickness fund, not even for a lower percentage.[53] This proved to work brilliantly since patients were not about to cover all the cost out of pocket. What is more, the internal divisions that CSMF had experienced resurfaced and led a number of physicians to leave and form their own association since as they saw it CSMF had let them down.

Whereas the ministerial decree of 1960 imposed certain limits on the practice of medicine, it was not truly a direct attack on the principle of La Médecine liberale. Physicians were still practicing on a fee for service basis and enjoyed freedom of prescription. What is more, patients enjoyed free choice of physicians. Strong supporters of La Médecine liberale argued that this was the beginning of a slippery slope and in protest left the ranks of the CSMF and formed the *Federation des Médecins de France*, the FMF. They thought that if enough physicians followed, the decree would be recalled. However, within four years 85 percent of all French physicians were participating in the new insurance scheme including most of FMF's membership.[54] From that point on and until the mid-1990s, the profession was not able to present itself unified, in the process making the governmental interventions easier to pass. The state had earned a political advantage that it was not going to give up easily even though by the end of the 1960s, additional measures were needed since health care expenditures continued to increase and the economy hit by the oil shocks seemed unable to recover.

A reason why the state found itself needing to take additional measures at the end of the 1960s was because, in the previous twenty years, it had fueled a tremendous expansion of the hospital sector and especially the public one. With the idea that national solidarity required strong social assistance dominating the politics after the war, and medicine making tremendous scientific gains, it was becoming quite evident that the hospital would be transformed from an institution on the perimeter and move to the center of the health care system. As early as 1958, the Hospital Reform Act provided for the merger between the largest and most technologically advanced public hospitals with the university medical schools, so that high tech medicine could be provided to regions with populations of over a million by the new institutional entities, the *Centres Hospitalier Universitaire*.[55]

But the major provisions of the 1958 reform act were the changes in the payment system for hospitalists.[56] Until that time, physicians who worked at hospitals were paid on a fee for service basis. The 1958 act began the shift from fee for service to salaries. As expected, this act was not welcomed by the profession. They argued that salaries would turn physicians into civil servants and indeed it would. The difference was that the government did not see anything wrong with that. And apparently a number of younger physicians at the time did not either. They split from the common physician position and accepted the legislation as a positive reform that would put an end to the feudal system of academic medicine that was dominated by the older highest ranking clinical professors, *les grands patrons*. The latter were, in fact, able to defend their right under the previous system to admit their private patients in "private" beds in the public hospitals. The act, however, was a large change and another victory for the government over the profession. Almost all French physicians today are either fully salaried at a hospital or part-time salaried in a public facility.

The impetus for the hospital reform act was, of course, deeper as mentioned earlier, and the act addressed this issue through a major reconstruction program in the period between 1958 and 1973. Besides all the institutional and managerial changes that the act introduced, a major goal of the act was the modernization of the hospital infrastructure.[57] It was thought that by improving the quality of stay at hospitals through measures like transforming old communal wards into private rooms, repainting, etc., patients would have a better experience in the public hospitals. It was known as *l' humanisation des hôpitaux*. The efforts, however, did not work. Even though by the late sixties, public hospitals were, in fact, superior to private clinics in terms of medical sophistication, they were still losing patients to them for routine operations largely because the clinics had better quality infrastructure and because the part-time physicians in the hospitals would bring the patients to the private clinics so as to avoid queuing.[58] Even the major public institutions in Paris, belonging to the *l'Assistance Publique* (AP) consortium, were not doing so well from an operational perspective despite attempts by the government to shore up support for the public institutions. According to Rodwin, "in 1973, the public image of l'Assistance Publique in Paris sank so low that the central administration ran spots on television, in movie theaters, and in the daily press to sensitize public opinion. On April 8, a publicity campaign was launched, bringing 70,000 to 80,000 Parisians to 28 of AP's 37 hospitals."[59]

But even such dramatic showings did not change the fundamental situation: for routine operations and maternity care, people preferred the private sector clinics. And physicians for their part also enjoyed practicing in the clinics since they were allowed to do so on a fee for service basis without much of the administrative hassle that the public sector was imposing on them. From the 1960s on, private sector capacity increased at higher rates than the public sector one. In 1963, 26.4 percent of all beds were private. By 1999, 36 percent of all beds were private.[60] This is one of the persistent problems in the French health care system. Nevertheless, as we will see, trust in public hospitals has somewhat been restored in subsequent decades.

Another attempt by the De Gaulle government was made in 1967 through the creation of CNAMTS, the main sickness fund. The idea behind it was that it would be able to administer and supervise closely the previously independent regional sickness funds and, in so doing, provide a financial balance for the entire system. The idea was not welcomed by certain funds that were operating with excess revenue and providing high quality medical services. It was, however, needed by funds that either because of worse risks or worse financing were unable to provide similar levels of care to their populations. By creating the main sickness fund, the government hoped to move towards closer national solidarity. And even though the plan was fought, it went through and was implemented providing essentially national health insurance to all French. The new fund was closely supervised by the government through the appointment by government of a significant number of members of its national board of directors. In this board employers and trade unions were also represented. By centralizing the sickness fund structure and placing them in a hierarchy, the government hoped, on the one hand, to be able to control rising costs and, on the other, to ensure access equitably to all medical services. But because of the strong decentralization and accountability tradition of the sickness funds prior to 1967[61] (leadership of the regional sickness funds was elected), CNAMTS has proven to be more effective in achieving the second goal rather than the first.

By the beginning of the 1970s, the same changes that had brought to a halt the expansion of the health care systems in Western Europe in general also operated in France. The system had reached a level of organizational maturity and the health care expenditures were increasingly being perceived as a macroeconomic destabilizing factor. And despite the introduction of the fixed fee schedule, the modernization of public hospitals and the centralization of the sickness fund structure, or maybe even because of these developments, rises in health care expenditures needed to be controlled. In 1970, the number one concern in the minds of policy makers in France was cost control.

1970-1992: Cost Control "Cures" for the French Health Care System

As can be expected, he first target area for cost control was the public hospital sector. After all, throughout the late sixties and the first half of the 1970s, an ideological war had developed between the private clinics and the public hospitals. Newspaper articles reported on the relative merits of the private and public sectors. The debate was further fueled by reports commissioned by the associations of private clinics that were trying to turn the tide in their favor in terms of state support. These reports indicated that private clinics were better managed than public hospitals, that the quality of care was of equal if not better level and that the hospital infrastructure was modern and comfortable. For these reasons, private clinics argued, the state ought to encourage the development of the private sector in the provision of services. Public hospital advocates came back reminding clinic administrators that they were not charged with the public services of research and education, that the private clinics almost never had to face conditions that required high cost surgery or use of other expensive technology, and that in the final analysis the differences in the cost structure of the two hospitals were not explained by better management in the private sector, but by more demands in the public one. At first the government did not respond to these debates one way or another, allowing the expansion of the private sector in the first instance and the further call for reforms in the public sector in the second instance. As a result, hospital expenditures in France between 1950 and 1983 had increased at an average annual rate of 15.1 percent.

There was obviously something wrong with the financial incentives in the system. Studies showed that in fact they favored private clinics.[62] Until 1968, the per diem rate for private clinics was calculated on the basis of the per diem rate for the closest public hospital. But since hospitals were spending more on research and education and were by law required to admit all emergencies and be open all day long, their costs were higher. Therefore, clinics were able to get a higher rate than what they needed. At the same time, public hospitals charged that they were receiving too little for their services. The sickness funds on the other hand countercharged that more than enough cross subsidies for the public services like research and education performed in these hospitals were included in the rates of reimbursement. In 1970, the government decided to take action and the hospital law was passed on December 31, 1970.[63]

On the one hand, the government hoped that through better management of public hospitals, public expenditures on health care could be controlled and, on the other hand, it expected that through the regulations placed on the private sector a more balanced distribution of beds between the two sectors would be achieved. A planning instrument, *Carte Sanitaire*, was introduced by the law. This instrument would be used by the regional and departmental bureaus for planning and regulation that were set up and therefore an era of managerial reorientation ensued for French hospitals, whereby the decisions by the regional bureaus for planning and the scrutiny by the Ministries of Health and Finance brought a different approach to the previous autonomous development of hospitals.

Three years after the law passed, private clinics were financially in trouble. Certain investment banks downgraded them in terms of being a good equity.[64] But that was to be expected. The shift towards focusing on cost control would first hit the private sector. Focusing resources on the public sector could not leave much room for the private clinics to flourish like they did in the 1960s. To survive they would have to come together, a process that did not occur until the 1990s. But even in the public sector, the 1970 hospital law was not very generous. It aimed to control hospital expenditures, but whereas it changed the managerial reorientation of the hospitals, it did not change their financial incentives. Hospitals would still make money if they maintained higher occupancy rates, longer average length of stay, and performed more procedures on an inpatient basis. And they did! Therefore, it is no surprise that hospital expenditures continued to rise as we saw by an average annual rate of 15.1 percent.

In the meantime a new convention, a new contract was signed between the government and the CSMF that determined the binding fee.[65] Once again, the physicians from the FMF denounced the convention and argued for a return to the pure principles of La Médecine liberale. But once again, they were unable to muster enough support to push their position through and they were forced to participate. From 1971 on, the FMF has reluctantly participated in the negotiations reverting back to the original CSMF position that preferred coordination and negotiation with the government and the sickness funds. The world was changing and medicine had to change with it and the FMF was only now realizing it. The effort worked. Physicians were able to get a guarantee that no competition to their private practices would be developed by the sickness funds and in that sense they still had the monopoly for ambulatory services under the principles of La Médecine liberale. Furthermore, the second sector of physicians was created whereby prestigious physicians could charge above the negotiated fee and the sickness fund would still cover a significant portion of the expenses.

In so doing, the physicians were able to preserve the principles of liberal medicine even while the government was pushing for cost controls and national solidarity. French physicians, by accepting lower reimbursement rates, had avoided at least for the time being a worse kind of restriction that would soon become prevalent especially in the United States but also in some other European countries and that is clinical micromanagement. They accepted that the government had to do something about cost control and therefore allowed it to manipulate the price of the service, but in so doing ensured that the volume and type of services ordered would still be decided only by the physician and the patient. Whether or not such an arrangement would work in the long run would depend on the way physicians practiced medicine. If cost increases were to stabilize the government would have no reason to step in and the physicians could go on practicing medicine with complete and autonomous clinical decision making. Whereas the physicians agreed to the collection of clinical data by the sickness funds, the process has not worked smoothly. The sickness funds on the one hand want to be able to create profiles of medical practice and eventually come up with medical guidelines, but the physicians have been able to draw the line and whereas data has been collected, it has been difficult to categorize it by physician or by patient since medical confidentiality has been used as a political weapon by the profession to fight off such demands.

Despite all these measures, health care expenditures and social expenditures in general continued to increase disproportionately to the GDP growth. The Ministry of Health in 1974 published a report indicating that the entire social security budget (both governmental and non-governmental payments for health care, pensions and family allowances) exceeded the entire state budget.[66] By the end of the decade, the Ministry argued that one-quarter of French GDP went to this social budget. It was becoming evident to the French that a liberal welfare state and extensive national solidarity were difficult to maintain. The Finance Ministry was particularly worried about the increases in social expenditures because of their implications in the overall economy. An article from 1981 summarizes quite well the economic thinking at the time:

> they [increases in social expenditures] lead to social security deficits, increase fiscal and parafiscal pressures (from income and payroll taxes) and affect both disposable income and the production costs of industry. Increasing costs of production get passed on to consumers either through real wage losses or price increases, and this runs counter to the Ministry of Finance's goal of promoting industrial development and international competitiveness."[67]

It is therefore small wonder that in its report in 1971, the National Planning Commission included a section entitled "The Limits of Solidarity."[68] Within this report the NPC argued that the rate of increase of the social budget could not be higher than the GDP rate of increase and that the marginal benefits obtained are not worth the rising costs. By 1976, the economic plan of the government, under Prime Minister Raymond Barre, concurred with this opinion.[69] As was the case in the Netherlands, where policy making that places macroeconomic stability has been the norm, so were the French looking at the end of the 1970s for a similar political response.

A number of measures were thought of so that the reforms would not be perceived as unpopular. Providing state subsidies to CNAMTS in combination with a premium raise vis à vis an increase in the payroll taxes seemed to be where the conservative government was leaning. But the Ministry of Finance opposed the state subsidies since in its view it would only further worsen an already bad financial situation. Labor was opposed to having its taxes increase whereas employer associations also opposed tax increases, which would increase their labor costs and, in turn, their production costs, therefore making them less competitive internationally. The economic logic of keeping health care deficits under control on the one side and the political demands on the other placed the government between a rock and a hard place. Cohen and Goldfinger phrased it nicely when they argued that "the lack of smooth fit between the imperatives of the economic system and the necessities of the political system is the key to understanding the contradictions of social security."[70]

As 1976 was drawing to a close, and France was facing an unemployment crisis amidst an international financial crisis, an internal memo was issued from within the Finance Ministry whereby four cost control measures had to be taken.[71] First, the supply of medical personnel had to be reduced. Second, the volume of procedures that physicians performed had to be limited. Connected to the second point was the third one, which called for improvements in the clinical data collection system. Finally, the number of hospital beds needed to be stabilized. No increases were to occur in the future unless absolutely necessary. In April 1977, the Council of Ministers endorsed this memorandum. Was it the beginning of the end of the French system? By the summer of 1979, a favorable time for French governments to pass unpopular measures since most people are on vacation and pay little attention to politics, the government introduced premium increases, established pilot programs with different hospital payment schemes, increased the copayments for nonessential drugs and suggested a copayment for hospital stays. Finally, it maintained the hospital and clinic per diem rates stable.[72] In October of that year and again in January 1980, the government refused to honor its 1976 agreement with the physicians for increases in the fixed fee. And in 1980, it even refused to negotiate a new contract unless both physicians and hospitals agreed to a prospective budget system. Both the hospitals and the providers were furious. The hospital federation, the *Federation Hospitaliere de France*, issued a statement condemning the proposed global budget system. The CSMF and the FMF joined forces charging that such measures would eliminate free choice and jeopardize the quality of care.[73] But the government pushed on with the reforms. It passed legislation limiting physician supply by reducing the number of open slots in medical schools and it introduced legislation that would lead to prospective global budgets for hospitals and to the closing of overcapacity beds. After all, the number of physicians had increased from 65,000 in 1971 or a ratio of 128 per 100,000 people to 110,000 in 1979 or a ratio of 201 per 100,000 people. At the same time, however, the government, through the 1980 contract between sickness funds, physicians and itself, introduced the second sector, or *secteur 2* physicians. This provision enabled physicians to exceed the national binding fee and charge their private patients more. In return, they ended up being eligible for lower pensions and lower sickness benefits. Moreover, they also had to make their patients pay the difference between the negotiated fee and the actual charge. For the government it appeared to be a good maneuver. The profession would be further divided between *secteur 2* and *secteur 1* physicians and therefore future negotiations would be relatively easy. And at the same time, whereas physicians were satisfied with the real income increases, the public accounts of the national health insurance would not be affected adversely since the patients would have to cover the difference. Criticisms of a two-tier health care system were raised throughout France, but the government argued that there was an excess supply of physicians and market mechanisms would force most physicians to stay within the traditional system. Furthermore, even those who chose to enter *secteur 2* would also be forced by the market to keep the prices relatively reasonable if they wanted to have a satisfactory patient flow.

The socialist opposition, however, had a different view. With an eye to the presidential election of 1981, socialist leader François Mitterrand opposed reform measures that would lead to a neoliberal version of the welfare state at a time that the country needed it the most. Unemployment was high and the sense of security that public programs provided to the French was a strong weapon in Mitterrand's campaign. And despite the measures taken, hospital expenditures where most of the attention was focused continued to leap upwards. Between 1978 and 1979 they increased by 20 percent, between 1979 and 1980 by 19 percent and between 1980 and 1981, the election year, by 19.4 percent.[74] The French people agreed with Mitterrand's assessment of the failures of the previous government and he was elected president in May 1981. What is more, the socialist party also won the majority in the National Assembly elections the following month and the first change of government in terms of ideology in the Fifth Republic was complete. The socialists and the communists formed a coalition government. But after the first two years (1981-1983) of Mitterrand's government, the results were not impressive in terms of the main enemy, unemployment. And Mitterrand decided to reverse course in his economic thinking. The U-turn of 1983 affected health care in many ways. But what is impressive is that the reforms that the conservatives had introduced in the late seventies were now being passed and implemented by the socialists. Things, however, had not started that way.

First, and because of the generous social policy making of 1981 and 1982, the first couple of years of the socialist and communist coalition government stood in direct contrast with the belt tightening austerity years of the Barre government between 1977 and 1981. France was attempting to spend its way out of the worldwide recession and the average citizen seemed to be content with this development since borrowing money that would eventually have to be paid off was not a concern at the time. The thinking was that increased consumption would lead to economic growth. Thus, previous budgetary restrictions were lifted for public hospitals. They were able to buy new technology more easily, create new positions for physicians and other personnel and if they were short of cash, Paris would bail them out at the end of the year. Two reforms were to mark this two-year period. The first was the attempt for decentralization and the second the attempt for departmentalization. The socialists presented the reforms in terms of bringing democratic values back into public affairs by making sickness fund leadership accountable to the fund's enrollees.[75] Returning social security to its original principles was the governmental angle of passing decentralization measures. As a result, the system was to become clearly hierarchical with distinct lines of responsibility for the Paris, the regional and local governments, the sickness fund and its subsidiary regional and local funds and so on. Eventually, integrated regional health systems to provide primary, secondary and tertiary care would be introduced. It was not to be. Even though decentralization was the rule in theory, in practice all decisions were controlled by Paris and the decentralization took place only in terms of administrative purposes.

Another reform attempt by the socialists based on the same theme of democracy in the work place had to do with setting up new departments within hospitals as is laid out in the *Projet Socialiste pour la France des Années 1980-1981*: "The internal activities of establishments must give up a rigid, hierarchical structure. In place of services, which are fiefs, there should be basic units grouped in departments under the direction of a person elected for a limited term. Instead of existing wage differentials and statutory differences, there should be team work."[76] What that meant was that in French hospitals, because of the hierarchical structure, a young physician has to wait for his chef de service (the older more prominent physician in charge) to either retire or pass away in order for the position to open. The only alternative would be for the young physician to sub-specialize, leading to a compartmentalization of services into expensive "estates" or "fiefs." In turn, this raises hospital costs and treats patients not in a holistic way, but rather as a subpart of an organ that the subspecialist happened to be an expert on. So the government proposed a single path of career development not based on seniority but based on personal and professional merit as well as on democratic principles, whereby any physician could pass exams to qualify for a higher position and could stand for election to head a department within a hospital.

As expected, the organized medical profession was not thrilled with the proposed reforms. Traditionally, a centrist or a conservative group, the physicians never welcomed state intervention in medical affairs. But it was tolerated when the conservatives were in government, but not when the socialists took over. In the words of de Pouvourville, "Doctors are wary of all public authorities but leery of leftists ideologies."[77] It was a series of moves by the government that led to the standstill. First, the Ministry of Health was given to Jack Ralite, a Communist, whom the medical profession viewed as a spokesperson for the union of hospital workers that had for over ten years denounced the current hierarchical structure in hospitals. Moreover, the first reform that was actually implemented took away the right that hospitalists had enjoyed to admit private patients in public hospitals. This reversal mostly affected the elite of the medical profession who saw a significant part of their income lost. Finally, the idea of departmentalization that had been discussed in French politics for ten years never found fertile ground in organized medicine except among a few young physicians. It is therefore not surprising that the profession viewed the government plans as attacks on the model of medical practice that they were accustomed to. In a period from 1981 until 1984, demonstrations against the proposed plans gradually increased, starting from an ad campaign in French newspapers in 1981 and culminating with strikes that included medical students, lower level doctors (*internes and chefs de cliniques*) and eventually the highest level physicians (*chefs de service*). The latter part of the demonstrations lasted for four months. In the meantime, the governmental coalition had broken up and the socialists were now governing by themselves. In 1983, however, the employment issue as well as the overall state of the economy led to the U-turn and, along with it, an end to the reform proposals of 1981-82. What remained from these years, however, was that the profession had the power, if it presented itself united, to reverse the course of reforms. Furthermore, another lesson drawn from the 1981-82 French experience has to be that policies need to be proposed at the appropriate time. The socialist reforms of the beginning of the 1980s were not addressing the fundamental issue of cost control and were, in fact, threatening further increases in health care expenditures. Unless the gamble of spending one's way out of recession paid off, the reforms had no chance of being implemented. And they were not.

By 1983, the government was searching for ways to control public expenditures without harming the quality of services offered. The plan Beregovoy was passed in that year and it froze physician fees and pharmaceutical prices, put into place the global budgeting method for hospital financing and introduced a small copayment for hospital care. With the leadership of Jean de Kervasdoue, the new director of hospitals, the first change in the financial incentives of French hospitals was implemented. Each hospital was given a lump sum of money in the beginning of the year and it had to cover both operational and capital expenses out of that pool of money.[78] The budget system was not perfect. It had frozen in the differential in hospital operations prior to its introduction and therefore in a sense penalized the well-run hospitals and rewarded the badly run ones. But its significance was that it instituted for the first time a serious cost control mechanism. The profession was outraged again, but this time the political cost did not frighten the socialists who had realized that their number one priority was to balance the national accounts in order to bring the country out of the recession. And as mentioned earlier, the global budgeting was the first control measure that actually produced measurable results in French health care.

After the introduction of hospital global budgeting, a number of other reform measures were introduced in the period between 1985 and 1993.[79] In 1985 under the Dufoix plan in June of that year, an increase of copayments for certain ambulatory services was introduced. The austerity policies of the socialists, however, along with the not-so-impressive record in terms of overall economic growth, led to a change in government in 1986. Chirac was elected prime minister and an odd cohabitation period of governance began for France for the next two years. It was odd since Chirac kept an eye on the presidency and the elections of 1988. The country therefore entered an extended pre-election period. Faced with fundamentally the same issues that its predecessor was, the Chirac government passed in 1986 a plan by the name of Plan Seguin. Plan Seguin aimed at reducing the levels of public financing. It did so by reexamining and limiting certain exemptions from copayment responsibility. It furthermore abolished reimbursement for vitamins and other nutritional supplements and it imposed an additional 0.5 percent on 1985 incomes. The 1986 plan was only an incremental step bringing marginal change along with it. The French government was once again stuck between economic discipline that would lead to economic growth and more jobs and social demands for more care in a political environment that is always volatile.[80] Amidst criticisms for its economic underperformance, the conservative government lost the 1988 election and the socialists, who had understood how much the Seguin plan had angered labor unions, made concessions three years later under the Evin plan by restricting the measures that the Seguin plan had introduced. Basically, the socialist government reestablished some of the copayment exemptions. Moreover, amidst criticisms of the two tiers of health care that the 1980 convention had created with the *secteur 2* physicians, in the 1990 convention, the socialists suspended the right of physicians to qualify freely for *secteur 2*. As an observer pointed out, "the strong French ethic of equality, including equal access for all, coupled with fear of institutionalizing uncontrollable physician expenditures with high out of pocket costs, pressured the government to suspend physician's election of tier two."[81]

By 1991, however, under the Bianco plan, as health expenditures continued to present the most alarming problem in social policy financing, the government, under Rocard this time, was once again forced to somehow find new revenue for the social security system.[82] It did so by the introduction of the *Contribution Sociale Généralisee* (CSG), which was a fixed 1.1 percent tax on all earnings including those of capital and property in December of that year and by increasing the payroll contribution towards health insurance by 0.9 percent. The introduction of the CSG was escorted by reductions in other social security contributions, thus neutralizing any effects on the size of the revenues. What had changed, however, was the source of these revenues. By taxing all sources of income and not only wages to finance social security, the government was in a sense creating a more equitable distribution of the financial burden. It was not to last for very long as we will see. The Rocard government also introduced a complement to the *Carte Sanitaire* planning instrument, the SROS (*schema regional d' organization sanitaire*) that regulated the geographical distribution of equipment.

All along, however, the financial problems of the national health insurance system persisted. And even though the early nineties had shown a few signs of economic recovery, France quickly returned to its poor economic performance. By 1993, Assurance Maladie was running a deficit that in that year stood at 26 billion francs and within a year it had reached 30 billion francs.[83] Something had to change and what the French changed was their government.

1993-   : Partisan Politics and Saying Non to Market Society

This most recent period of the historical developments of health reforms in France is the most interesting one in terms of political choices and directions that France has moved towards and therefore a closer examination is warranted. After 1993, the one characteristic that seems to characterize French health politics is the difference between the socialists and the conservatives in their attempts to curb health care expenditures. Whereas both parties had for over ten years attempted to bring the financial situation of the system under control and there was always confrontation, after 1993 this partisanship sentiment appears to be even higher than usual. The three governments that France has had in the post 1993 years have been the center right Gaullist ones under Premier Balladur between 1993 and 1995 and under Premier Alain Juppe between 1995 and 1997. Since then, the socialists have returned to power under the leadership of Premier Jospin. Although there are many similarities in the conservative approaches of the Balladur and Juppe governments, one also finds a deliberate attempt by the Jospin government to differentiate itself from its predecessors, not only in rhetoric but also in policy substance. The political fate of all these governments and their respective leaders indicates that the French have decided that they do not want a market society even while they accept that they need a market economy in the new global order.

In national elections in 1993, the left majority in the national assembly under Premier Beregovoy was replaced by a right majority under Premier Balladur. The economic recession of the early 1990s and the accumulation of large public deficits were even threatening France's meeting the strict Maastricht criteria. Coupled with the lack of results by the previous socialist government, the French turned once again to a center right government to resolve the persistent problem of economic underperformance. Balladur understood the role of his government to be one of fiscal responsibility. His aim was to balance the budget and if that meant cutting social expenditures, he argued he was prepared to do it. True to his conservative principles, he would rather not have to increase taxes. Again, however, if balancing the budget meant raising taxes, he was prepared to do it. Indeed, between 1993 and 1995 he would do both. What is more, the taxes he introduced were highly regressive, targeting middle-class and working-class people rather than capital, an anathema for the socialist opposition. Knowing that two years later, presidential elections would be held, Balladur aimed to position himself in such a way that he could win. To do so, he made a political calculation. On the one hand, he had to produce results in terms of economic development and, on the other hand, he had to do so in a manner of consultation so that he would not alienate potential voters.[84] As it turned out, his approach did not work because he was never really prepared to incorporate different views in his policy proposals.

But before the government even introduced any of its own policies, a new contract between the profession, the government and the sickness funds was signed in December 1993. It contain three new provisions.[85] The first was the introduction of clinical guidelines (*References Medicales Opposables* or RMOs). During the two years that followed a total of 212 RMOs were produced. According to the convention, physicians who fail to follow these guidelines are subject to financial penalties even though it has been extremely hard to impose such penalties because of the difficulty in providing credible evidence of continuous negligence by a physician for these RMOs. Whereas the RMOs were introduced finally, their practical use has to date remained in question. The first few months after the measure was introduced, a deceleration in the expenditures of the national health insurance was observed. A subsequent quickening in the rate of increase indicated, however, that the measures had only produced temporary effects. The second provision was the introduction of the *carnet de sante*,[86] a standardized set of medical records that each patient carried in the form of a computerized card that was the size of a credit card. This way, the duplication of tests would be avoided and continuity of care could be supported. The measure showed theoretical promise, but it also proved ineffective. Whereas plans were made for the *carnet de sante* to be given to four million elderly patients in the first phase of the implementation, as it turned out only 45,000 cards were issued before the measure was suspended by the Juppe government in 1995. Finally, an annual target of an increase by 3.4 percent for 1994 was introduced in prospective growth in total private doctors' fees and prescription expenditures. This latter measure also seemed to work at first, but after a few months it became evident that the target would not be met.

In the meantime, the Balladur government had introduced strict austerity policies throughout public financing. In health care it once again reduced the reimbursement rates that the sickness fund paid out, therefore cutting benefits or at least making it harder to access them.[87] The government also slashed the public hospital budgets, making their operation much harder than it had been. But probably the most indicative measure that the Balladur government took in this arena was an indirect one. The Balladur government increased the CSG that the previous socialist government had introduced from the original 1.1 percent to 2.4 percent. But it was not so much the increase that revealed the conservative approach of the government. The additional percentage was made tax deductible. As Levy explains, "deductibility meant that whereas a minimum wage worker had to pay the full 1.3 percent increase in the CSG, a wage-earner in the top bracket (with a 56 percent tax rate) would pay only 44 percent of the increase."[88] The regressive addition to the CSG was rescinded by 1994 under protests, but the next government under Alain Juppe reintroduced the increase. The only difference was that this time the increase was an additional 1 percent above the original 1.3 percent.

As presidential elections were nearing, Balladur, despite his unpopular regressive taxes and benefit cuts, had very little to show in terms of economic stabilization, let alone development. Public expenditures had increased and so had the budget deficit in both years. Moreover, as stated earlier, the social security deficit stood at 26 billion francs in 1993 and 30 billion francs in 1994. Balladur had not only failed in recovering the economy, but had also estranged a number of voters for the upcoming presidential election. The main reasons behind this were that in the first instance his policies were unpopular and in the second instance his lack of political courage in seeing his reforms through.

Whereas he truly believed that the neo-liberal model was the most appropriate model for state-society relations, he also believed that the transformation in France had to proceed slowly. In so doing, he would try to give the perception that he was consulting with all interested groups in a neocorporatist environment of policy making. But in the end, he never really paid attention to what these groups demanded and went on to propose the policies that he thought were proper. As a recent article describes,

> [Balladur] did not pursue a course of consultation with the representatives of the medical profession, but rather engaged in an enlarged consultation, whose objective was not to formalize agreement, but to find a way of avoiding outright conflict. The government did not seek the creation of an alliance with a professional group...but rather a minimal consensus that would allow the reform to be implemented.[89]

What was worse for him, however, was that the test for his policies was whether or not public protests occurred. If when the policy was introduced, there was not much protesting, he went through with the implementation. Upon the manifestation of large-scale opposition, he would quickly repeal those policies. As Levy states, "under the terms of the Balladur method, a kind of direct, post facto consultation with the streets substituted for prior negotiation and compromise with the concerned parties."[90] The French were quick to pick up the prime minister's weakness and interest groups were quick to mobilize against proposals that threatened them. An unbearable political stagnation ensued that destroyed Balladur's chances of winning the 1995 presidential election and indicated that the French were not willing to go down the path of regressive tax increases and benefit cuts. If the country were to follow such prescriptions, it would have to be dragged down such a path.

As mentioned in the beginning of the chapter, the 1995 presidential elections gave the presidency to Jacques Chirac in the election among the socialist Lionel Jospin, the two candidates from the right, Prime Minister Balladur and Chirac, the far right leader Jean Marie Le Pen and an array of candidates of smaller parties. Chirac was able to capitalize on Balladur's political failures in the social and economic policy fronts to edge him in the preferences of the voters of the left. A 1995 poll[91] indicates that 41 percent of the voters that identified themselves as progressive[92] voted for Jospin, but Chirac had a strong showing with an additional 22 percent, whereas Balladur only captured 8 percent of that vote. And by capturing 30 percent of the conservative vote, as opposed to 25 percent that Balladur got, he was in the words of an observer, "the only candidate to obtain—in the fashion of de Gaulle-solid support across the ideological spectrum."[93]

Chirac had campaigned by promising to heal the social divisions that the French observed in their country through an array of measures that would bring economic prosperity back to France. Right after his victory, he appointed Allain Juppe as prime minister and set out to achieve the aforementioned goal. But it was evident that things would not be as easy for President Chirac as they were for candidate Chirac. As an article from that time observed,

> [Chirac promised more jobs and spending, lower taxes and-*mirabile dictu*-a cut in France's public sector spending to meet the Maastricht convergence criterion [of a maximum budget deficit of 3 percent]. That was what Jacques Chirac promised. Something had to give, and it duly did.[94]

In October of 1995, a few months after the election, Chirac declared that the number one priority for him was to reduce the budget deficit so that France could in fact qualify in the first tier of countries for the monetary union. This meant only one thing; that public spending (essentially social spending) had to stabilize and even be reduced. Juppe found himself facing the same problem that many of his predecessors had faced. This time, however, he had the political catalyst of EMU membership that he could use to justify such reforms. Would it work?

Within the cabinet, a number of ministers and especially Minister of the Economy Alain Madelmi believed that strong austerity policies would be required in the short run to fix France's economy. But Juppe was not certain that such aggressive measures would work in France. Much like Balladur before him, Juppe believed that the liberal model had to be introduced in France, but the politics of it were quite tricky. The Juppe plan introduced a number of changes that were reminiscent of the previous government's policies, but fell short of what Mademli and other conservatives had hoped for. Mademli resigned in protest. Juppe was attempting to balance the pressures of conservatives like Mademli and the more than certain reactions he would receive from the public.

Juppe, however, had learned one thing from the Balladur era. Whereas the politics of implementation of austerity might be tricky, his government could not appear to be politically indecisive. This is what had brought down the Balladur government and Juppe was not about to make the same mistake. Moreover, knowing that he would have to stand for elections by 1998 at the latest, he figured that implementing the austerity measures sooner rather than later, joining the EMU and seeing the economy recover in time for that contest would work to his benefit. His reasoning was that the role of his government was not to cater to demands from different interest groups but rather to successfully bring the necessary reforms through hard and often unpopular choices. The technocratic approach to the solution of policy problems that the Juppe government brought to the table dictated that the proposals had to be based on pure economic reasoning, leaving politics aside. Juppe designed his entire reform plan in such a fashion that by his own admittance only very few close advisers knew the complete plan prior to its presentation. Juppe knew that things would have to change and if he were able to see the reforms through without caving to interest demands, he would have guaranteed both economic growth for France and a successful political future for himself.[95] He bet his political future on this gamble, on the *Plan Juppe*.

The cumulative French social security deficit was 90.7 billion francs by October 1995. One of the largest sources of that figure was the deficit in the health care expenditures accounts. Mainstream political thinking at the time believed that the problem lay in the out of order incentives of French health care consumers. As Claude Le Pen, a professor of health economics in Paris, put it at the time, "nobody in France realizes that health has a cost."[96] Chirac and Juppe realized it. In a speech at the Sorbonne in Paris to honor the fiftieth anniversary of the institution of the Assurance Maladie system, Chirac said "social security is part of the identity of France and of the French heritage. Facing unemployment, facing exclusion, it is the last rampart against a possible retreat of civilization... It would be irresponsible to postpone the choices that have to be made." He went on to state that medical costs among other things must be controlled. He urged health professionals to be rigorous and to accept necessary reforms because, as he put it, "this was probably a last chance for La Médecine liberale."[97] On November 15, 1995, Juppe presented his plan for comprehensive social security reform to the National Assembly.[98] He received overwhelming support in the voting for the bill with 463 deputies voting in favor and only 87 against. His plan was multifaceted, attempting to eliminate the 250 billion francs debt that the system had accumulated through an increase in the CSG, to streamline health care administration, to alter the public pension system and to empower government to impose expenditure ceilings for welfare spending. A few days after the Parliament supported Juppe's plan, the Senate also passed a vote of confidence for his government, leading the prime minister to announce that the most pressing measures would be implemented in the next few months.

More specifically, Juppe's plan had a two-step approach. In the first instance, he attacked the issue at the legislating process level.[99] He proposed and received an amendment to the French constitution that the government had to approve annual welfare spending. This prospect tremendously angered trade unions that saw it as a direct threat to their traditional participation in the management of welfare issues. He also passed a law that authorized government to pass welfare legislation through ministerial decrees rather than through bringing the whole bill to Parliament. The logic was that to implement the reform the government would have to be flexible and the time-consuming process of debating each measure in Parliament was grossly inefficient. Finally, his government adopted five decrees between January and April of 1996 and a few more after that to begin the implementation of his plan. In the second instance, he attacked runaway costs in all social security sectors. Public pensions were not cut, but the retirement age was raised by eliminating a number of provisions that allowed workers to retire as early as fifty years old. Furthermore, in order to qualify for a pension, one had to work according to plan for forty years instead of the 37.5 years that had been the requirement until then. Juppe also repeated Balladur's fiscal trick of increasing the CSG by an additional 1 percent from 2.4 percent to 3.4 percent. The additional 1 percent was also a tax-deductible increase, revealing the regressive nature of the new tax measure. Juppe also increased the value added tax (VAT) from 18.6 percent to 20.6, another tax of regressive character since the VAT is paid by all citizens independent of income. Finally, Juppe aimed to control health care expenditures by increasing controls on both hospitals and private physicians. Since health care is the focus of this chapter, it will be worth it to closely examine the health provisions of the Juppe plan.

The ideas in the Juppe plan were not new. They had been present in two reports from 1993 and 1994 on the conditions, issues and future of the French health care system.[100] It was, however, the first time since 1983 (when prospective budgeting for hospitals was introduced) that a government had dealt with the health care system in such a comprehensive fashion. There were two types of measures in the Juppe plan. The first were short-term fixes for the financial problems that the system faced. The second were long-term structural changes. As Juppe himself put it, "the government wants a reform that is made to last."[101] In the first instance, the plan provided for increases in the contributions by pensioners and unemployed people, reductions in the coverage rates for hospitalization with a copayment increase from 55 francs to 70 francs, a new one-time tax for the pharmaceutical industry of 2.5 billion francs and finally matching the growth of health care expenditures to general inflation (an estimated 2.1 percent at the time that decreased to 1.7 percent in 1997). The longer-term measures that the plan entailed were structural changes in the way the system operated. It aimed to introduce universal coverage by the sickness fund and a shift from payroll contributions to general taxes as the source of funds for the system. Moreover, it introduced new regulatory bodies. The *Agence Nationale d' Accreditation et d' Evaluation en Sante* (ANAES) was a body that regulate the overall finances of social security. The *Agences Regionales de l'hôpitalisation* were regional agencies supervising hospital operations. Finally, there were the *Unions Regionales des Caisses d' Assurance-Maladie*, which were also regional agencies supervising sickness fund operations. The state control did not end with these agencies. By having introduced the constitutional reform, Parliament was now empowered by law to decide on the revenues raised, the sources that they are raised from as well as the expenditure targets of the health care system. Furthermore, the Juppe plan tried to continue previous reforms like the introduction of the RMOs[102] and the continuation of the small electronic cards of medical records, the *carnet de sante*. More restrictions in terms of physician reimbursement were introduced. Physicians would now have to perform services that were included in a list of services. They would furthermore have to perform the services based on the clinical guidelines (RMOs) and they would have to meet government spending targets regionally if they were not to see their fees decrease for the region the following year. Physicians would also have to assist financially in the nationwide computerization aimed at reducing health care administrative costs. Juppe proposed that each physician contribute one franc per prescription to a nationwide fund. Finally, in terms of hospital care, the plan aimed to encourage hospitals to perform more services on an outpatient basis, create ambulatory sites, develop health care networks by affiliating themselves with a number of private physicians in their region and finally to introduce clinical data collection mechanisms. The planning of facilities and the allocation of resources was controlled by the ANAES as well as the regional agencies for hospitals. Both were controlled by the government.

As can be understood, the changes were not very welcome. Everybody found something to be unhappy about. And whereas Juppe's perception of government expected that, since his austerity policies were based on a principle of "equality of sacrifice," as one observer put it, he did not expect the public response to his plan, a response that was motivated by an odd coalition of groups like physicians, civil servants, labor and public advocates that usually did not find themselves on the same side of the negotiating table. But Juppe's belief that if he were to compromise with one group, he would have to compromise with all and his memory of the Balladur failings led him to disregard the objections of everybody. On November 24, 1995, within a week of the plan's introduction, the seven unions that represent the civil servants began a strike. Medical unions were quick to join, protesting the rationing of health care and the loss of income.[103] It was estimated that under the Juppe plan a GP with an annual income of 360,000 francs would see his income be reduced by 13,600 francs. Health care had, after many years, moved from the bureaucratic realm of social policy making to the top of the political agenda with large public demonstrations.

A six-week strike ensued and more significantly the public seemed to be in favor of the demonstrators.[104] They viewed the Juppe plan as eroding their social security system and in so doing eroding their idea of France. Juppe was forced to give into the demands, but not completely at first. In order to clear the streets of the demonstrators, he abandoned the public pension system reform, but he was adamant that the health care system had to be reformed. On December 17, 1995, doctors marched once again through Paris protesting the reforms. And in protesting the Juppe plan, the three major medical unions found that they could work together at least in terms of demonstrating. Their major goal was the repeal of the penalty on physicians if a given region exceeded governmental expenditure targets, but also a number of other issues like the mandatory contribution to the national computerization fund. As Richard Bouton, president of MG France, the general practitioners' union put it, "There are negotiable elements in the government's plan, but there are some elements not acceptable to doctors." The CSMF joined in with a statement that argued that "the freedom to prescribe remains an essential condition of the professional independence of the doctor."[105]

Juppe, much to his credit, did not give into the demands of the profession, but his reforms or at least the most significant structural changes he wanted to introduce never really took hold. There was not an easy way to enforce the penalty system when regions exceeded the expenditure targets and despite anticipatory behavior by the physicians, expenditures for physician services did not take long to start rising again. In 1998, a year after Juppe was ousted from the government, health care expenditures were increasing at a rate three times faster than inflation. Finally, in the middle of 1998, French courts gave a victory to the profession by eliminating the agreements that had been signed between the profession and the government up until that time. The Juppe plan reform was officially over. The political impasse that the Juppe plan had led France to was evident as 1997 was approaching. Chirac and Juppe decided that a new mandate was necessary if their modernizing plan was to be seen through. Elections were called for that following June. The French sent Juppe home and elected Socialist Lionel Jospin. He was to govern in a plural left coalition with the communists and the greens as the two minor partners in government.

The conservatives controlled the presidency, four-fifths of the National Assembly and two-thirds of the Senate prior to the June 1997 election. Moreover, they also controlled nineteen out of the twenty-two regions of mainland France. After the election, Chirac found himself once again in a cohabitation period caused by an election that he had called. Jospin knew that France could not risk staying out of the first tier of countries that would join in the common European currency. Therefore, he also practiced austerity policies. And he saw the economy beginning to perk up. The budget deficit declined from 4.2 percent of GDP in 1996 under Juppe to 2.9 percent in 1998.[106] France was able to meet the Maastricht criteria. The stabilization pact, however, dictated that similar economic policies had to be followed. And Jospin stuck to his earlier policies as well. The budget deficit declined further to 2.1 percent of GDP in 1999 and 1.8 percent of GDP in 2000.[107] Moreover, a surplus is projected for 2004 if the national debt is reduced as planned by 0.4 percent of GDP annually. Still, as mentioned in the beginning of the chapter, if economic success is to continue, there are pressures for social security reform. Jospin knew that if such reforms were to take place, this was the window of opportunity since economic times were better. He also knew that he had a chance of striking an appropriate balance between social solidarity and fiscal responsibility. With the European Left debating terms like the third way and the new center, Jospin aspired to find a way between what he essentially considered an adoption of Thatcherite methods of governance by so-called social democrats, and old style national control of the economy. To do so, he presented a completely different model of governance than the two previous governments. He negotiated policies during their formulation with all interested parties. In so doing, he moved France closer to a pluralistic neocorporatist style of governance. And, in turn, the policies that have been aiming at similar goals to the ones that Juppe, Balladur and many of his other predecessors have had, present a distinctly progressive line that is indicative of what Jospin envisioned as the new left and what he hoped European political discourse would become. Jospin tried to balance the social security accounts by imposing the additional costs on the wealthier groups in the population and by providing targeted relief to middle and lower income groups.[108] His policy proposals in health care are indicative.

After the Juppe plan debacle, national health care expenditures continued to increase at rates above inflation. With the courts having invalidated the agreements between the profession and the government, the

Jospin cabinet had to start from the beginning. Martine Aubry, the Minister of Labor and Social Security, appointed in June 1998 Gilles Johanet as new director of the national council of health insurance, the *Conseil National de l'Assurance Maladie* (CNAM). Johanet, who had published a book[109] presenting his views on the French health insurance that same year wasted little time. By the end of February 1999, he presented his four-year plan to the government. Within his proposals, there were promises for significant savings in prospective spending in the amount of 62 billion francs by 2002. He would try to alter the care-seeking habits of the French by turning the generalists into gatekeepers for the system. A patient could still choose to access a specialist without being referred by a general practitioner, but the reimbursement would then be lower. He also focused attention on limiting excess use of pharmaceuticals and of physician services, which would have to be justified based on clinical evidence and quality assessments. The final theme of his proposals was that public hospitals ought to be funded on a fee for service basis at comparable rates with the private clinics in order to foster competition among them. The Minister of Labor was willing to buy into the first couple of reform themes, but not into the third one. Aubry, and the entire cabinet for that matter, saw many benefits by adapting the first couple of measures. First, both physicians (a traditionally conservative group) and pharmaceutical companies (big businesses have always favored the RPR party) were good targets for savings in the view of the socialists. Furthermore, they anticipated that they would be able to fight off public demonstrations by the profession since their party basis was not aligned with the physicians' interests. By placing the cost of the reform essentially in these groups, the government was assuring itself of fiscal results in the first instance and a satisfied political base for their party. Such was not the case in terms of the public hospital reforms that Johanet had proposed. His proposals assumed that regional networks would emerge and unnecessary overcapacity beds would be closed. Such a policy, however, is not only politically risky but to a socialist it was also socially irresponsible. Public hospitals offered, besides care, employment to many people. Closing down and the subsequent firings of staff was not something that the government was willing to do. After all, public hospital workers are a group that has traditionally voted for the socialists, and attacking them through changes in the status quo in hospital funding could have led to a repetition of an odd coalition between physicians and hospital workers. The government was quick to state that public hospitals do not fall under the regulatory umbrella of the CNAM, but are the responsibility of the ministry of labor and social solidarity. As one observer put it, "Aubry declared that public hospitals fall within the jurisdiction of her ministry, rather than CNAM, and that in any case, these hospitals have been restructuring through a gradual, negotiated process that would only be disrupted by Johanet's provocative proposals."[110]

The government also looked to increase its revenues by increasing the CGG from 3.4 percent to 7.5 percent in 1998. But this time, it also reduced health insurance contributions for workers from 5.5 percent to a token 0.75 percent.[111] In so doing, the reform was fiscally neutral but politically brilliant. It had shifted the tax burden to higher income groups who made most of their income from property, stocks or other equities, thus protecting lower income people and thus offering increased social protection. It has been estimated that this change has provided an average worker in France with an increase of 1.1 percent in purchasing power. This policy fell under a pattern of tax relief policy that Jospin had enacted. Partially because of stronger than expected economic growth, he has seen the 2000 revenues increase by an extra 50 billion francs which he redistributed to lower income people through targeted tax cuts for the lowest income brackets, and a lowering of the regressive VAT from 20.6 percent after Juppe's increase to 19.6 percent. Finally, in early 2000, Jospin's government introduced the *Couverture Maladie Universelle* (CMU), a plan that will provide health care insurance to the uninsured in France. They are estimated anywhere between 200,000 (0.3 percent of the population) and 500,000(1 percent of the population). The CMU also aims to provide supplemental coverage based on means testing[112] for an additional 6 million low-income people who can not afford supplemental insurance through one of the mutual funds.

As the economy recovered, the French were determined to see austerity policies end. On the other hand, structural reforms were needed so that France could compete globally. Jospin attempted to pass such reforms by redistributing the costs and the benefits so that lower income groups, the traditional basis of his party, were not adversely affected by the reforms. In Jospin's mind, since higher income groups stand to earn more in the short term from the liberalization of the economy, the lower income groups ought to be protected until they can begin to take advantage of the opportunities that the new economy can offer them. The French people agreed with him in principle. But they apparently wanted results to come faster. In the 2002 presidential elections and against all polls, the far right candidate Jean-Marie Le Pen beat out Jospin and threw him out of the race. And despite Chirac's subsequent win the result shocked everyone including the French voters themselves. Explaining this result is not the aim of this chapter. For our purposes, it is sufficient to say that the center left suffered a bad defeat, which was followed by another one in the parliamentary elections a few months later. The fact, however, that the center right is in government by itself does not mean that the French are willing to go down a more liberal path. If past is prologue, reforms in both the social security and the health care systems can be expected, but they will have to be very carefully planned and balanced with the potential political cost. If the right is to be successful, it will have to learn the political lesson that the French have taught quite well. Time after time in the past, the French have thrown governments out of office because they tried to do too much too fast with too little consideration for social solidarity. The French realize that a market economy is necessary, but they have said "*non*" to a market society and that becomes clear from the historical review. To accept the former, the French were helped by their quest to join the Euro. Now they hope that they can change European views on political discourse in terms of the latter.

Notes

1. WHO Report, "2000 Health Systems: Improving Performance" at www.who.int.
2. For a good discussion of this identity crisis, see *Chirac's Challenge: Liberalization, Europeanization and Malaise in France*, J. T. S. Keeler and M. A. Schain (eds.), St. Martin's Press. New York, 1996.
3. Hall, P., "The Evolution of Economic Policy Under Mitterrand," in *The Mitterrand Experiment*, George Ross, Stanley Hoffmann, and Sylvia Malzacher (eds.), Oxford University Press, New York, 1987).
4. See Anderson, C., *Blaming the Government—Citizens and the Economy in Five European Democracies*, M. E. Sharpe, Armonk, NY, 1995.
5. Tiersky, R., *France in the New Europe*, Wadsworth, Belmont, CA 1994.
6. Ibid.
7. *Le Monde,* May 11, 1995, 9.
8. Michel Rocard's government was in power from May 10, 1988 to May 15, 1991; Edith Cressons's from May 15, 1991 to April 2, 1992; Pierre Beregovoy's from April 2, 1992 to March 29, 1993, and Eduard Balladur's from March 29, 1993 to May 18, 1995. They were all quasi-coalition governments. Respectively, the parties that constituted them were for Rocard's government, the socialist party (PS), the left radical movement (LRM) and the Union for French Democracy (UDF); for Cresson's government the PS, the MRG and the ecology generation (EG); for Beregovoy's government the PS and the MRG, and for Balladur's government the rally for the Republic (RPR) and the UDF.
9. Dupoirer, E., and Grunberg, G., "La Dechirure sociale,"*Pouvoirs* 73 (April 1995).
10. *LeMonde,* April 11, 1995.
11. OECD, "Economic Survey of France," Paris, July 2000.
12. *The Economist,* July 8, 2000, 50-51.
13. Cameron, D., "National Interest, the Dilemmas of European Integration and Malaise," in *Chirac's Challenge: Liberalization, Europeanization and Malaise in France*, J. T. S. Keeler and M. A. Schain (eds.), St. Martin's Press, New York, 1996, and *The Economist,* April 8,1995, 43.
14. Kesselmam, M., "Does the French Labor Movement Have a Future?" in J. T. S. Keeler and M. A. Schain (eds.), *Chirac's Challenge: Liberalization, Europeanization and Malaise in France*, St. Martin's Press, New York, 1996.
15. *The Financial Times,* Monday, March 6, 2000, 3.

16. The cases cited deal with Axa, the largest private insurer in France in a case about mental health coverage; Totalfina, the Franco-Belgian oil group which was forced to provide aid because of an oil spill even though it was not legally responsible for it and was not originally predisposed to offer aid; and Michelin, the international tire company that was castigated for placing profits above its employees' well-being when it announced a sharp increase in profits and a 10 percent cut in its international workforce.

17. Wislford, D., "Reforming French Health Care Policy," in *Chirac's Challenge: Liberalization, Europeanization and Malaise in France*, J. T. S. Keeler and M. A. Schain (eds.), St. Martin's Press, New York, 1996.

18. de Kervasdoue. J., Meyer. C., Weill. C., and Couffinhal. A., "French Health Care System: Inconsistent Regulation," in *Health Policy, National Schemes and Globalization*, J. W. Bjorkman and C. Altenstetter (eds.), MacMillan Press, London, 1998.

19. OECD Health Data, 1999.

20. Ibid.

21. Ibid.

22. Ibid.

23. Walliman I., "Social Insurance and the Delivery of Social Services in France," *Social Science and Medicine* 23(12): 1305-1,7, 1986.

24. All national health insurance funds are organized into regional and local funds, which are under French administrative law, private organizations charged with the provision of a public service. Since their total annual expenditures, however, often exceed that of the government's budget, all funds are closely supervised by the government and are thus quasi-public entities.

25. Fielding, J. E., and Lancry, P., "Lessons from France—'Vive la Difference,'" *JAMA* 270(6):748-756, August 11, 1993.

26. *Liaisons sociales*, Bareme Social Periodique, Paris, 1999.

27. Caisse Nationale de l'Assurance Maladie, La CNAMTS en quelques chiffres, CNAMTS, Paris, 1999.

28. Ibid.

29. The French fee schedule classifies all medical procedures according to their relative values. The charge for each procedure is calculated by multiplying that relative value by the negotiated rate (a conversion factor). Put differently, the charge for an appendectomy, which is coded as KC-50, is ten times the charge for the removal of an ingrown toenail, which is coded as KC-10. The relative values are decided according to the Nomencalutre Generale des Actes Professionels (NGAP), an instrument written in 1930 by the CSMF. The way it works is that procedures are classified around the so-called key letters. C, for instance, stands for a specialist consult, whereas V, a home visit by a generalist. The other categories are B (lab tests), Z (radiological procedures), K (diagnostic procedure), and KC (surgery). The system is flawed, however, in that many procedures can end up being coded with the same letter and the same coefficient making it hard to distinguish what procedure exactly took place. This has been a large part of the problem in the implementation of clinical guidelines.

30. In practice there are actually three groups of physicians who can charge more than the negotiated fees; those who have completely opted out of the system (0.3 percent) and who get no reimbursement from the sickness funds are the first category. The second group is those who, before 1980, had earned the right to bill extra due to their status and prestige in the medical community (3.4 percent). The third group is the one created from this secteur 2 provision. Although what it

means to bill extra with tact and restraint is debatable; estimates bring this charge anywhere between 30 and 50 percent of the negotiated fee.

31. French courts have ruled that physician charges in the second tier cannot be higher than 1.5 times the nationally negotiated rates. Physician rates are, however, almost never posted and thus the patient usually finds out the exact charge at the end of the visit.
32. Fielding, J. E., and Lancry, P., "Lessons from France—'Vive la Difference.'"
33. This figure also includes payments from private, non-mutual insurance companies that account for about 2 percent of total expenditures.
34. Under the General National Health Insurance Scheme rules, the copayment is 25 percent for physician services, 35 percent for private nursing services and lab tests, and 30 percent for prescription drugs. Essential drugs have no copayment. Patients in hospitals pay 20 percent of the per diem rate plus a small additional fee for meals.
35. Fielding, J. E. , and Lancry, P., "Lessons from France—'Vive la Difference.'"
36. Rodwin, V. G., "The Marriage of National Health Insurance and La Médecine Liberale in France: A Costly Union," *Milbank Memorial Fund Quarterly* 59(1):16-43, 1981.
37. OECD Health Date, 1999.
38. Rodwin, V. G., and Sandier, S., "Health Care Under French National Health Insurance," *Health Affairs* 52(3): 113-125, Fall 1993.
39. Ibid.
40. Ibid.
41. Lancry, P., and Sandier, S., "Twenty Years of Cures for the French Health Care System," in *Health Care and Cost Containment in the European Union*, E. Mossialos and J. Le Grand (eds.), Ashgate Publishing, Brookfield, VT, 1999.
42. Ibid.
43. Baumgartner, Fr., "The Many Styles of Policymaking in France," in *Chirac's Challenge: Liberalization, Europeanization and Malaise in France*, J. T. S. Keeler and M. A. Schain (eds.), St. Martin's Press, New York, 1996.
44. For more on the different styles of the policy process in France see Suleiman, E., *Politics, Power, and the Bureaucracy in France*, Princeton University Press, Princeton, NJ, 1974; Suleiman, E., *Elites in French Society*, Princeton University Press, Princeton, NJ, 1978; Suleiman, E., *Private Power and Centralization in France: The Notaires and the State*, Princeton University Press, Princeton, NJ, 1987; and Stevens, A., "The Higher Civil Service and Economic Policy-Making," in *French Politics and Public Policy*, Philip Cerny and Martin Schain (eds.), London, Frances printer, 1980.
45. Wilsford, D., "Reforming French Health Care Policy."
46. Wislford, D., *Doctors and the State*, Duke University Press, Durham, NC, 1991.
47. Wislford, D., "Reforming French Health Care Policy."
48. Cibrie, P., "Syndicalisme Medical," Confederation des Syndicats Medicaux Francais. Paris, 1954.
49. de Kervasdoue, J., Meyer, C., Weill, C., and Couffinhal, A., "French Health Care System: Inconsistent Regulation."
50. Rodwin, V. G., "The Marriage of National Health Insurance and La Médecine Liberale in France: A Costly Union."
51. Wislford, D., *Doctors and the State*.
52. In 1958, there was a political crisis in France that focused on the question of Algerian independence. The crisis led to the dissolution of the Fourth Repub-

lic, the return of De Gaulle to power, and the establishment of the French Fifth Republic.

53. Steudler, F., "L' Evolution de la Proffesion Medicale: Essai d' Analyse Sociologique," Cahiers de Sociologie et de Demographie Medicales, No 2.

54. Wilsford, D., *Doctors and the State.*

55. Jamous, H.,*Le Grand Tournant de la Médecine Liberale*, Edition Ouvrieres, Paris, 1963.

56. Rodwin, V. G., "The Marriage of National Health Insurance and La Médecine Liberale in France: A Costly Union."

57. Castaing, M., "L'Hôpital, Ce Malade Chronique," *Le Monde*, February 21, 1975.

58. It becomes obvious that the situation in France in the 1960s is very reminiscent of the situation in Greek hospitals in 2000. But for all my interviewing, I could not find any evidence of a side economy even while part-time hospital physicians would take patients from the public sector and admit them into private clinics.

59. Rodwin, V. G., "The Marriage of National Health Insurance and La Médecine Liberale in France: A Costly Union."

60. OECD Health Data, 1999.

61. Catrice-Lorrey, A., *Dynamique Interbe de la Sécurité Sociale et Service Publique*, Centre de Recherches en Science Sociales du Travail, Paris, 1979.

62. Brunet-Jailly, J., "Quelques Evidences sur l' Evolution du Systeme de Sante," *Revue Economique* No. 3, 1976. Also see Ministry of Health, "Les Conditions Actuelles du Financement," in *Pour Une Politique de la Sante*, Rapports Presentes à Robert Boulin, Vol 3, 1970.

63. Brumter, C., "La Planification Sanitaire," University of Legal, Political, Social and the Technological Sciences, Faculty of Political Science, Strassburg, February 1979.

64. *Le Monde*, January 10, 1979.

65. Glaser, W., *Health Insurance Bargaining*, Garner Press, New York, 1978.

66. Ministry of Health, "Sante et Sécurité Sociale," Tableaux, Paris, 1974.

67. Rodwin, V. G., "The Marriage of National Health Insurance and La Médecine Liberale in France: A Costly Union."

68. National Planning Commission, Sixth Plan: Economie Generale et Financement, Paris, 1971.

69. *Le Monde*, September 23, 1976.

70. Cohen, S., and Goldfinger, C., "From Real Crisis to Permacrisis in French Social Security," in *Stress and Contradiction in Modern Capitalism*, L. Lindberg, R. Alford, C. Crouch, and C. Offe (eds.), Lexington, MA, D. C. Health, 1975.

71. Ministry of Finance, Internal Memorandum No. B-6B-8157 from the Office of the Budget to the Minister, December 13, 1976.

72. *Le Monde*, July 26, 1979.

73. Look at Bles, G.,"Médecin de France," in Le Film des Evenements, No. 143, August 9, 1979. Also see Raynaud, P., Reflexions sur la Réforme Budgetaire et de la Tarification Hospitaliere: Réforme pour la Forme? Réforme de la Forme? Ou Réforme de Fond? In Revue Hospitaliere de France, 1979.

74. De Pouvourville, G., "Hospital Reforms in France under a Socialist Government," *The Milbank Quarterly* 64 (3): 392-413, 1986.

75. De Pouvourville, G., and Renaud, M., "Hospital System Management in France and Canada: National Pluralism and Provincial Centralism," *Social Science and Medicine* 20(2):153-67, 1985. For more information on the 1981-82 man-

agement of health reforms in France, see Rodwin, V. G., "Management without Objectives: The French Health Policy Gamble," in *The Public/Private Mix for Health*, G. McLachlan and A. Maynard (eds.), The Nuffield Provincial Hospitals Trust, London, 1982; US GAO: "Health Care Spending Control: The Experience of France, Germany and Japan," GAO/HRD 92-9, Washington, DC, November 1991; and Godt, P., "Health Care: The Political Economy of Social Policy," in *Policy Making in France*, P. Godt (ed.), Pinter Press, New York, 1989.

76. Club Socialiste du livre, "Projet Socialiste pour la France des annees 1980-1981," Paris, 1981.

77. De Pouvourville, G., and Renaud, M., "Hospital System Management in France and Canada: National Pluralism and Provincial Centralism."

78. Wislford, D., "Reforming French Health Care Policy."

79. Bach, S., "Managing a Pluralist Health System: The Case of Health Reform in France," *International Journal of Health Services* 24(4):593-606, 1994.

80. Stevens, J. B., "Health Services and Government. Some Lessons from France," *Health Services Management* 85(5):224-7, October 1989.

81. Fielding, J. E., and Lancry, P., "Lessons from France—'Vive la Difference."

82. Lancry, P., and Sandier, S., "Twenty Years of Cures for the French Health Care System."

83. Ibid.

84. Levy, J. D., "Partisan Politics and Welfare Adjustment: The Case of France," Paper presented to the 12th International Conference of Europeanists in Chicago, March 30-April 1, 2000.

85. Lancry, P., and Sandier, S., "Twenty Years of Cures for the French Health Care System."

86. Chambaud, L., "Health Care in Europe—France. A la Carte," *Health Services Journal* 103(5344):24-7, March 18, 1993.

87. Hassenteufel, P., "Les Médecins Face A l'Etat: Une Comparaison Internationale," Presses de la Fondation Nationale des Sciences Politiques, Paris, 1997.

88. Levy, J. D., "Partisan Politics and Welfare Adjustment: The Case of France."

89. Hassenteufel, P., "Les Médecins Face. A l'Etat: Une Comparaison Internationale."

90. Levy, J., *Tocqueville's Revenge: State, Society and Economy in Contemporary France*, Harvard University Press, Cambridge, MA, 1999.

91. *Le Monde*, April 11, 1995.

92. Progressive voters who viewed the state as obligated to maintain traditional welfare programs and alleviate social inequality.

93. J. T. S. Keeler and M. A. Schain (eds.), *Chirac's Challenge: Liberalization, Europeanization and Malaise in France*. St. Martin's Press, New York, 1996.

94. *The Economist*, July 15, 1995

95. Palier, B., "Réformer la Sécurité Sociale: Les Interventions Gouvernementales en Matiere de Protection Social Depuis 1945, la France en Perspective Comparative," Ph.D. diss., Institut d'Etudes Politiques de Paris, 1999.

96. Dorozynski, A., "France Gears Up to Fight Health Insurance Debts," *British Medical Journal* 311:967-68, October 14, 1995.

97. Ibid.

98. Dorozynski, A., "France Faces Radical Health Insurance Reforms," *British Medical Journal* 311:1386, November 25, 1995.

99. Le Plan Juppe, in Numero Special *Droit Social* 3, 1996/03.

100. Rochaix, L., Khelifa, A., Pouvourville, G. de, "Sante 2010: Equite et Efficacite du Systeme de Sante: Les Enjeux," CGP, Paris, 1993, and Soubie, R., Portos,

J. L., and Prieur, C., "Livre Blanc sur le Systeme de Sante et D'Assurance Maladie," La Documentation Francaise, Paris, 1994.

101. Dorozynski, A., "France Faces Radical Health Insurance Reforms," *British Medical Journal* 311:1386, November 25, 1995.

102. Durand-Zaleski, I., Colin, C., and Blum Boisgard, C., "An Attempt to Save Money by Using Mandatory Practice Guidelines in France," *British Medical Journal* 315(7113):943-6, October 11, 1997.

103. Dorozynski, A., "New Battle Looms for France over Health Reforms," *British Medical Journal* 312: 9, January 6, 1996.

104. Dorozynski, A., "French Protest at Health Budget Cuts," *British Medical Journal* 311(7015): 1247-8, November 11, 1995.

105. Ibid.

106. Levy, J. D., "Partisan Politics and Welfare Adjustment: The Case of France."

107. OFCE, L' Economie Francaise 2000. La Decouverte, Paris, France, 200.

108. Levy, J. D., "Partisan Politics and Welfare Adjustment: The Case of France"

109. Johanet, G., *Sécurité Sociale: L'echec et le defi*. Seuil, Paris, 1998.

110. Levy, J. D., "Partisan Politics and Welfare Adjustment: The Case of France."

111. *The Economist*, August 12, 1998.

112. The cut-off point will be those people living with less than 3500 francs per month for a single individual or 7700 francs for a family of four.

6

The German Flirt with
Managed Competition

We have reached the final case of this study, that of Germany. No book on the effects of European integration on member state health policy would be complete without exploring the German case. Germany is the largest member state, one of the wealthiest and, most importantly, is considered the economic locomotive of the Union. Therefore what is happening within German borders is no doubt influencing decisions in other parts of the union. Examining German health policy, two themes become quite evident. First, Germans, just as the Dutch, focus on a macroeconomic balance believing that this will indeed be the best way towards social solidarity. Second, Germany offers a prime example of how regional integration between wealthier and poorer states has led to a more rationalized allocation of health care resources. Having experienced its own reunification, Germany can be viewed arguably as a laboratory for future European developments. Throughout this chapter, the argument that convergence among the health policies of member states has occurred and is still occurring is presented. At the same time, just as in the other three case studies, historical influence, exhibited by today's institutions, has kept German political discourse in health care on its own path, falling short of complete convergence. The end result is a cautious German flirt with managed competition in the last decade or so that has tried to balance between these two goals, that of macroeconomic stability and that of social cohesion. And whereas Germany would have appeared an odd candidate for managed competition to the outside observer, in retrospect it is not difficult to identify the pressures that led the Germans down this path. Still, the results that managed competition has produced are not spectacular. But what is relevant for our purposes is the German willingness to experiment with it in the first instance and their persistence to stay with it in the second. As we saw in the Dutch case, it is difficult to claim that a system has not permanently moved down the path of including more market forces. It is not difficult, however, to underlie the contextual pressures that have led policy makers to a push for rationalization.

I begin by an admittedly cursory look at overall themes in recent German politics in order to understand the parameters within which recent health policy reform efforts have been designed. I then turn the discussion to the structure of the German health care system, focusing on the financing of the system and the delivery of services. Finally, through a historical exploration of German health care policy making, I contend that German political discourse exhibits one overarching element of stability: that of balancing its health policy goals with overall economic performance (an element that has influenced other European states), while at the same time internal dynamics have led German policy makers to flirt with both regulation and competition to suit that overarching theme.

Themes in German Politics

There are two overarching themes that have characterized German politics in recent years. The first is the reunification process,[1] which, on the one hand, has been elevated to a national goal of the highest priority and, on the other hand, has created a number of economic and policy issues in terms of its smooth implementation. At the end of the second world war, the defeated Germany was divided by the victorious allies into two parts, and the wall erected by the Soviets in Berlin separating the two parts of the city was the emblem of the Cold War. In 1989, a peaceful revolution that in fact began by the destruction of the wall led to the reunification of the two parts of Germany, the west Federal Republic (FDR) and the east People's Republic (GDR). The process had been cultivated over many years with Schmidt's Ostpolitik, but it was not until the end of the Cold War that the two parts of Germany could finally be reunified. An extensive analysis of this process is beyond the scope of this essay, but suffice it to say that bringing the two parts together had been elevated and remains to date a status of highest national priority. As many researchers have shown, Germans overwhelmingly favored the reunification process and were willing to pay for it with modifications in the preexisting policies to assist the poorer eastern states in this process. This, of course, meant in health care as in other areas of the social and economic life of the reunited Germany that funds had to be reallocated and pressures for reform were created if Germany were to maintain a strong economy. At the same time, the second theme that characterizes German politics has to do with economic performance and with German preoccupation with maintaining a strong overall economic performance. A strong economy has always been essential to Germany and all social programs have always had to adjust to this paramount goal. Germans believe that a successful future for their country depends on their competitiveness internationally. In fact, this is viewed as the only way of achieving social progress. Jeopardizing economic progress would automatically spell trouble for welfare programs.

Surrounding these two themes, one finds the institution of federalism, which, on the one hand according to the principle of subsidiarity, splits the responsibility of policy making between the federal government in Berlin, the sixteen Lands (states), and other related nongovernmental actors such as professional associations, and, on the other, institutionalizes a political framework whereby agreements must be achieved not only between professionals groups and the federal government but also between the federal government and the regional ones.[2] This principle predates the original unification of Germany in 1871 and Bismarck's public health insurance law in 1883. Subsidiarity provides the framework for the development of a public-private partnership, allowing a role in the implementation of national policies to all interested actors, public and voluntary.

Finally, the principle of solidarity[3] has always characterized German social policy and has over the years been adopted by parties across the ideological spectrum with little variation. Solidarity is so embedded in German social policy making that it is written in the Basic Law of 1949 and in subsequent related laws. Insurance-based rights and redistributive provisions are part of the national Bill of Rights that is part of the constitution. Both the social security code of 1988 and the Health Care Reform Act of the same year reinforce this principle providing specific measures to reinforce the overall social agreement that the healthy have to pay for the sick, the young for the old, and the wealthy for the poor. For an observer from the United States, legislation that ensures such rights might look odd at first sight but, nevertheless, solidarity here in Germany, as in all other cases we have examined is a pillar of social policy and, in fact, a pillar of the overall social structure. This is the reason that it has been a goal of all health care reform acts and it will most likely continue to be a paramount goal for policy makers.

It is within these four parameters that the German health care system has been designed and reformed over the years. These four themes—reunification, positive macroeconomic performance, subsidiarity and solidarity—shape and at the same time constraint health policy making. Before turning our attention to the historical development of the German health care system that has given origin to these constraints, we will first explore its structure.

The German Health Care System and Its Participants

The German system is a three-part system of statutory and social insurance which is able to cover almost 90 percent of the German population.[4] The three groups involved in this system are the federal government, the state governments and the corporate associations representing physicians, the sickness funds and other interested parties. The federal government sets the overall framework of operations for the other parties and is the one that brings forth proposals for cost containment. This overall structural framework is mainly contained in the Imperial Insurance Regulation (Reichs-Versicherungs-Ordnung, RVO) as well as in the Social Code Book V (Sozial Gesetz Buch, SGB V) which is mainly the revision of the RVO as far as health care is concerned, made in 1982. The federal ministry of health care became an independent ministry only in 1991. Until that point, health care affairs were under the jurisdiction of the Ministry of Labor and Social Affairs. Within the Ministry the less visible but highly influential as most observers admit, Abteilung II of the Ministry serves as the bureaucratic arm of this ministry. Furthermore, at the federal level, one finds the national advisory Council for the Concerted Action, which is a representative body of all the key players in the health care arena. It is composed of around sixty members, providing legitimacy to the ministerial decisions. The actual degree of influence of this council has varied, depending on the time as well as the person who is serving as Minister. In recent years, it has served more as an advisory council rather than a decision-making body.[5] Below this level, one finds a number of committees that negotiate the most minute details of health care operations. I will return to these committees later.

The state governments are responsible for investments in the hospital sector and as such play a fundamental role in the financial flows of the system. They are bound, however, by quite prescriptive rules set by the federal government in terms of public health insurance. They partly own and accredit teaching hospitals. They select teaching personnel. Furthermore, they are the ones responsible for social and nursing services, youth services. Moreover, they license other health facilities like nursing homes and set the necessary qualifications for the personnel working in such institutions. Finally, as mentioned earlier, they are responsible for hospital capacity planning. There is a joint conference of the state health ministers that allows the states to work together in dealing with these responsibilities. But as it becomes obvious, the states have little say over the public health insurance program and the statutes that govern this program.

The same does not hold true for the corporate bodies that represent the sickness funds, the physicians and others. They are by law given an elevated status allowing them to have a say in policy reform, thus bringing German health care policy making in the neocorporatist group. The hospitals also have their association, but it does not enjoy the same negotiating rights under law, even though in practice it actively participates in negotiations in terms of price setting, services offered, etc. One of the most influential groups is the Federal Committee of Physicians and Sickness Funds, which is comprised of representatives of both of these groups.

This group, as well as all other committees, both at the federal and at the regional level, is part of the elaborate network of non-state actors that have played an extremely strong role in health care policy making in Germany for over forty years. Instead of focusing on the larger picture, these committees negotiate the small details such as spending limits and the inclusion or exclusion of pharmaceuticals and medical procedures in the national health insurance program. Each party comes to the negotiating table well prepared with elaborate research preparation and with political allies that apply pressure in its favor. The end result has always been agreement, but the scholarly community is split whether these agreements are the result of political pressure by the state threatening intervention or a result of the corporatist attitude that characterizes these actors. In any case, at the end of the day, decisions are made that all actors have participated in taking and that allows the federal government more room for political maneuvering.

In short, one observes a collective bargaining arrangement that has developed over the years, which, on the one hand, allows each actor to bring issues of particular concern to the negotiating table and be satisfied from the outcome and ,on the other, allows the federal government to move political responsibility for developments to non-state actors. At the same time, maintaining the balance between political gridlock and political development is a delicate game that the Germans, just as the Dutch before them, have mastered.

As a result of this corporatist arrangement, Germany has performed extremely well by international standards both in terms of being able to insure its entire population and in terms of controlling health care expenditures. Germany has been able to control its health care expenditures as a percentage of the national GDP better than any other nation in the industrialized world. Or at least such was the case until the early 1990s. As of 2000, Germany spends around 11 percent of its GDP on health care, significantly less than nations like the United States but more than nations like France and England.[6] Moreover, this was one of the largest increases in the OECD during the last ten years. This amounts to $2,400 per capita spending, which is above the OECD median. From 1960 to 2000, the percentage of GDP allocated to health care has increased from 5 percent to 11 percent. This money has, however, allowed Germany to insure anywhere between 90 and 93 percent of its population under the statutory health insurance plan. When one considers that the remaining 8 percent of the population that is not obliged to carry health insurance does so anyway, universal coverage is achieved in Germany with health expenditures as part of GDP not exceeding 11.5 percent. From that, 12 percent of total health expenditures is spent by public budgets, 49 percent from the statutory health insurance and the numerous regional and occupational sickness funds, 7 percent from the retirement insurance, 3 percent from accident insurance, 7 percent from private health insurance, 7.5 percent is out of pocket spending and 16 percent is spent by employers.

Thirty-five percent of national health expenditures is spent on hospital care, which amounts to almost $800 per capita health spending on hospital care. The average length of stay in German hospitals stands at 14.3 days and has been declining, albeit slowly. Moreover, Germany has a rather remarkably stable number in terms of hospital beds. In 1965, the then West Germany had 107 hospital beds per 1,000 population. In 1975 it reached its peak (119 hospital beds per 1,000 population). And even though it has declined since and today it stands at 100, the overall decrease is only 6 percent from 1965. The occupancy rate stands at 84 percent, a small decline of 8 percent from the respective number in 1965. Furthermore, hospital expenditures per day in Germany stand at $228, just one dollar above the OECD median. For a country that has high technological level care, hospital expenditures can be judged as satisfactory from an outside observer. It is indicative that Germany has 6 MRI units per 1 million population and 17 CT scanners per million population. Still, Germans have always been worried about the amount of money spent on health care and a number of reforms that have passed, as we will see later on, tried to address these concerns.

Germany has an oversupply of physicians. It has four physicians per thousand population, with most of them being specialists. It has 6.5 physicians visits per capita, and the country spends 17 percent of total health spending on physician visits. This amounts to $375 per capita spending on physician services. Finally, Germany spends $289 per capita on pharmaceuticals or, put differently, 13 percent of total health expenditures goes to pharmaceutical spending.

Overlaying all these figures is an aging population that currently has 16 percent of its members above the age of 65, with projections that by 2010 this percentage will reach 20 percent. Furthermore, with a life expectancy of nineteen years for females and sixteen years for males at age 65, German policy makers realize that they will soon face a financing crisis for their system. Still, these figures indicate, when one compares them to international trends, that Germany has been quite successful in controlling health expenditures while insuring and caring for its entire population. Therefore, it is a major question why Germany has recently turned its focus from the corporatist arrangements that have shown success in achieving the goals of the system to managed competition. As we have seen in the case of the Netherlands, the jury on managed competition arrangements is still out. One has to wonder therefore why Germany would move towards such arrangements. The answer lies in its overall policy context as well as in outside pressures in terms of its macroeconomic policy, which one can understand through a historical overview of German health politics. I will now turn our attention to this overview, placing emphasis on the institutional and other constraints as well as the aforementioned pressures, the interactions of which have brought managed competition to Germany. We will focus on the last twenty years or so, to see the policy reforms and the political thinking behind them.

German Health Politics

Through the evolution of the German health care system one finds several themes that have developed that characterize the political side of the health care equation. As we have already examined, the corporatist arrangements in decision making are something that has been inherited from the past. The role of the state in Germany for a really long time had been to mediate among the different key parties. Moreover, one observes a shifting of power from the consumers to physicians and then to government. In other words, new players were introduced in the health care arena and they began to have a say in order to protect their interests. Furthermore, one sees one major constant in German health policy over the years, and that is that Germans have always embraced policy choices that are consistent with their overall macroeconomic policy. In fact, the explanation of the German flirt with managed competition may lie in these two characteristics, the power struggle between different key parties on the one hand and the macroeconomic policy goals of the country on the other. In the sections that follow, I trace the interactions between these themes.

1883-1945: The Origins of Corporatism

The German health care system was the first one established in the world under the then emperor Otto von Bismarck in 1883. Whether Bismarck chose to establish a social security system to protect his regime from public demonstrations or whether he truly believed in the development of the welfare state is an issue of discussion. What is pertinent for our purposes, however, is that he chose to base the new system on the preexisting occupational funds that had been established in Germany over the years. This decision placed Germany on a policy path quite distinctive from other states that chose to nationalize health services. As was the case in many states during the Middle Ages, different occupational groups had created collective arrangements to provide care. Churches and local charities were responsible for setting up care institutions. Not much could be done in those places, however, since medicine was not advanced. When industrialization reached Germany, Bismarck realized that a more organized system had to be set up and decided to base it on the preexisting sickness funds. By definition, however, the state was also introduced as a player in the arena. The beginning of the twentieth century meant for Germany as in many other industrialized countries the political struggle that the profession faced in order to establish its own parameters around its profession. As medicine progressed and physicians could actually do something for their patients, they gained political influence as well. The main issue in health care politics in the first decades of the last century was who would control the system. Because Bismarck had already set up a legal framework around health care and medicine still did not cost tremendous amounts of money, the issue was not a major political priority. Therefore, several calls to have physicians sit on the boards of sickness funds were heard. Physicians were allowed more than ever to have control over the system. In retrospect, one views a shift of power and control from the consumers who had set up the sickness funds to the physicians, with the state reserving a mediating role for itself.

The relationships established in this period were the base for the political future in health care. The state would soon institutionalize these different corporate groups and allow them to battle policy details out by themselves within predetermined parameters that it provided. The role that the state reserved for itself allowed it to choose at any time which group to treat preferentially by providing it more access to political institutions. By introducing a number of corporate bodies, which by law played a role in decision making, it would be able to gain legitimacy for the policy decisions and avoid unnecessary political battles. In this sense, it is easily understood why the policy making style of German health politics developed in a corporatist fashion.

1945-1975: Expanding Health Care

After Germany lost the war, the country found itself on the brink of financial collapse and divided in two parts. In the epicenter of the Cold War, the two parts of Germany diverged in their decisions about their health care systems. These decisions reflect more the overall differences in societal and political values of the two systems. So, whereas East Germany moved down the path of socializing its system and trying to move it as much away as possible from the capitalist model of social policy that existed in the West, West Germany moved in exactly the opposite direction. The years after the war are characterized by attempts by the government, with assistance from Germany's Western allies, to place a framework where private enterprise could produce economic growth in order for the overall standards of living in Germany to improve. This was the paramount policy goal and each policy, including health care, revolved around this goal. In this sense, governmental decisions dominated this time period. It is critical, however, that Germany chose to remain down the path of corporate politics and down the path of the social insurance model rather than choosing to nationalize its health care system. In choosing to maintain the social insurance system, the government also moved towards a greater regulatory role, realizing that the system would grow more complex.

A main measure that the government took was to try to minimize labor costs as much as possible so that employers could give a boost to the damaged economy. Whereas the government maintained this part of the financing as low as possible, it also realized that a major reconstruction effort was necessary and it made funds available for that. Just as in the rest of the world, here, too, major transformations in the postwar period included new technologies and new cures, and therefore the issue of access became a major one. One can summarize the logic in this period that one has to build more capacity to allow the German citizen access to these new cures. A public debate began that came to the conclusion that Germany needed more physicians, more hospitals and a better-equipped health care system. The Hospital Financing Act of 1972 and the establishment of new medical schools from 1955 on were results of this debate. In fact, the expansion of the system was in line with the overall policy goal of economic recovery. Expansion of the system created jobs and that affected GDP growth positively. With ample funds coming in from abroad, Germany increased its hospital capacity, reaching its maximum hospital bed figures in 1972, increasing the ratio of physicians per 1,000 population and investing money in research. These measures were in their own right successful. But while the system was expanding so were health care expenditures. Whereas, health expenditures stood at 5 percent of GDP in 1950, by 1970 this figure had increased to over 8 percent. The term cost explosion entered the German political debate about health care.[7] It was feared that these expenditures threatened overall economic growth by taking limited resources from other sectors. Financial planning was the answer that Germans had for he cost crisis. By returning to their familiar corporatist style of policy making, Germans tried once again to gain political legitimacy for cost control measures.

1975-1992: Planning Financial Controls

Between 1960 and 1975, Germany was governed by a coalition comprised of the social democratic party, SPD, and a smaller party, the FDP. As we saw, hospitals were modernized and both personnel and other resources (beds, for instance) were increased. Furthermore, new hospitals were built and new technologies were widely diffused. As Christa Altenstetter writes, "No one then challenged the fashionable equation that 'more' was indeed 'better' or that a qualitative improvement would automatically result from a quantitative expansion of resources."[8] And it worked well for a long time. But the early 1970s and the overall world economic recession made Germans realize that cost controls were necessary.

And there were a number of pressures placed on German institutions to respond to the cost explosion crisis. And overall, Germans were successful since they were able to stabilize health expenditures as percentage of GDP around 7.5 percent for about fifteen years. A number of measures that were passed starting in 1977 contributed to this. In 1977, the Krankenversicherungs-Kostendämpfungs-Gesetz (KVKG), the Health Insurance Cost Containment Act, passed. This act required both purchasers and providers to pursue a goal of contribution stability and is active to this date. Basically, all interested parties were required to hold increases in contributions level in order with rises in contributor income. A number of amendments passed in order to achieve compliance with this act. Two are the main ones. In 1981, the Cost Containment Amendment Act passed and this was followed in 1983 by the Budget Support Act. The 1981 act by the federal government in a sense urged hospitals to follow the non-binding recommendations of the federal Advisory Council. The politics behind this act gave birth to the application of the cartel of the states theory since state governments refused to give up control over the hospital sector. Therefore, any federal rules could only be applied to office-based medicine and to the pharmaceutical markets. But after the expansion of the system in the previous twenty years, it was the hospital sector where cost control was believed to be most effective. Failing to gain control over the hospitals, the feds had to settle for the act that urged hospitals to follow the Council's recommendations, but it also led to a switch in governmental policy to look for a different framework where office-based medicine was chosen as the tool for continuous health care. It was believed that office medicine could result in lower expenditures, higher quality medicine, allow more personal choice by the part of the consumers, not to mention that this part of the system was under federal control. A number of regional agreements between the physician associations and the respective sickness funds were an attempt through corporatist politics to reach the overall goal. And even though national health expenditures did not increase dramatically, German policy makers realized that office-based medicine was not in the long run the best candidate for sustained cost control.

If technology were allowed to diffuse to each and every office in the country, the cost would become unbearable and would jeopardize the financial stability of the entire system. And even though this was the understanding, no direct measures were taken to control this diffusion, which continued without explicitly set limits. Instead, the hospital sector was allowed to play the role of the fundamental provider of care. The

1988 Health Care Reform Act (Gesundheits-Reform-Gesetz) basically led to the reduction of hospital capacity in terms of beds, to the more effective management of these hospitals and to the more careful planning of technology diffusion.[9] Average length of stay was reduced and so were admissions. Even the hiring of physician assistants and nurses was cut back, which led to a personnel crisis. The 1988 act brought some temporary relief to the system's financing, but it was not able to bring fundamental reform. Health care expenditures slowed down as part of GDP and whereas health care used to consume 8.9 percent of GDP, two years after the act, only 8.2 percent of GDP went to health care. But no more reductions were possible since no structural change was accomplished. After 1990, health care expenditures started to rise again, partly because of the German reunification but also because hospital costs and subsequently sickness funds' costs had an almost uncontrolled rise.

In retrospect, even though the 1988 act was at the time viewed as extremely significant, it did not significantly alter the structure of the system. The corporatist politics were able to amend it so significantly that any benefits that the act brought were marginal. It is indicative that a provision that sickness funds would be able to break their contracts with hospitals judged as uneconomic or too expensive was scratched from the final act. It did, however, allow sickness funds significant freedom and negotiating power. They could refuse admission to sickness insurance services to physicians viewed as not being cost conscientious. Furthermore, they could require providers to take cost control measures. Through the same act, premiums were increased, and higher cost sharing was introduced. Some minor benefits were removed from the insurance package. Because of all these measures, the act was not very favorably viewed by both the public and the providers. At the same time, it was not able to deliver, as we saw, in terms of sustained cost control or fundamental structural change. While German reunification was proceeding and demanded more funds, health care expenditures had to adjust accordingly. And to top everything off, the 1992 Maastricht agreement required stricter fiscal discipline if Germany were to join the monetary union. It is thus easily understood why it was only a matter of time until a new reform would be brought to the table.

1993- : The German Flirt with Managed Competition

What is not so clear, however, is why Germany would move down the path of managed competition. By 1992, the German government had realized that structural reform was necessary if the longevity of the German health care system were to be assured. Two pieces of legislation resulted from this realization and both of these can be viewed together as a continuous package. In 1992, the federal government announced the Health Care Structural Reform Act (Gesundheits-Reform-Gesetz), which passed into law in January 1993. This act is indicative of the willingness of the federal government for fundamental change in the structure of the system. In a 1993 analysis, the National Economic Research Associates states that the act "introduced a mixture of radical organizational reforms and stringent cost containment measures, targeted at specific sectors of the health care sector." At the same time, Germans were and to a great degree still are to this date convinced that these reforms would not harm certain basic principles upon which their health care policy had been based throughout the second half of the twentieth century, namely solidarity, self governance, benefits in kind and plurality in the provision of services. In 1996, another act, the Health Insurance Contributions Reduction Act (Krankenversicherungs-Beltrage-Entlastungs-Gesetz) was introduced, basically to further assist in the implementation of the 1993 act. The political thinking behind both of these acts was similar.

What the 1993 act introduced was a framework for the development of competition among the different sickness funds. The 1993 act aimed at open enrollment for most funds by 1996. Therefore, the geographical and occupational restrictions that had limited individual choice were to be slowly removed. The thinking was that competition between the funds would lead to lower premiums, better management of limited resources, selective contracting and therefore increased pressure on providers for more efficient production of medical services. As Lieverdink and van der Made write,

> In the long run the government wants to create better conditions for competition along two lines. First, the position of the consumer in relation to the sickness funds will be strengthened by introducing open enrollment. People will get the freedom to choose their own insurer. Secondly, the competence of the sickness funds with regard to the providers will be improved.[10]

The 1993 act also included several other cost control measures. It introduced global budgets and expenditure ceilings for hospital treatment, office-based medicine and pharmaceuticals. Furthermore, copayments that had been introduced in 1988 were increased and new ones were introduced. The act also changed fee for service payment to physicians by service group payments (a variation of the American DRGs) and it also introduced prospective payment for hospitals.

In short, one observes a switch in the direction of German health care policy making. Whereas the German system had steadfastly been noncompetitive, Germans appear, starting in 1993, to be willing to experiment with managed competition. In retrospect, one can observe several factors why Germans opted to try managed competition. Partly, competition (even though absent from the policy agenda until 1993) is not foreign to the German line of thinking. At the same time, it can be argued that old policy tools no longer worked either for financial or political reasons. More analytically:

Germany has always considered itself a social market state, defined as a state that philosophically favors a creative mix of governmental and market forces in producing, regulating and delivering goods and services. And even though competition had remained out of the health care arena, developments in the Netherlands (as we saw), but also the British reforms in the 1980s under the Thatcher government, automatically put managed competition on the table. Without necessarily agreeing with the Dutch or the British approaches, German policy makers looked at managed competition as an attractive framework that, if implemented properly, could produce successful results. German health economist Klaus Dirk Henke,[11] the head of the expert commission that advised the federal Advisory Council on Concerted Action,[12] has been an adamant believer in managed competition and therefore it is small wonder why the expert advice to the German ministry of health care pushed for this policy development. Moreover, it was also quite attractive politically. The political left had criticized for quite some time that mandatory assignment to regional or occupational funds was outdated. Furthermore, the political right had been pushing for increased cost sharing. Managed competition appeared to be a political deal made in heaven.

Overlaying all these were the actual financial pressures that we have already seen, and managed competition was promising by most accounts financial benefits and more efficient management of the limited Marks going to health care. The financial framework that had sickness funds responsible for specific populations and for payment for increasingly complicated medical technology without allowing them to practice modern management techniques had come under attack. Sickness funds needed more funds than the extractions from employers and employees in order to keep up with costs, and the financing system at the time was viewed as an inadequate mechanism. Managed competition would allow sickness funds to increase their income through better management and lower expenses through increased competition. And managed competition appeared to be at the time the only politically appealing option by default. All other options presented tremendous political problems.[13] Increasing the contributions by either employers or employees or both in order to recapitalize the health care system would jeopardize loss of jobs and would also stir political turmoil. And as part of the overall thinking of not sacrificing macroeconomic development, this option was abandoned. They could also find new funds by increasing copayments, but this tool had been used extensively in the late 1980s and it was doubtful that Germans would have been happy and, more importantly, politically grateful to their government for increasing copayments. A third option would be to inject new funds into the system through general tax revenues as France had done.

But fiscal discipline, demanded both because of the reunification process and because of the Maastricht agreement, removed this option from the table. Finally, Germans could continue with their neocorporatist politics to try to reach solutions for the cost explosion problem that they faced. But German policy makers generally agreed at the time that such negotiations were useful only when they occurred within the appropriate structural framework. Put differently, if the structure of the system were not changed, not much could be expected from the discussions between physicians, sickness funds, hospitals and other interested parties. Finally, the promise that benefits would not be curtailed under managed competition enabled policy makers to argue that what the health care system lacked was proper management. Managed competition seemed to have the answer for each interested party and the window of opportunity for reform that had opened because of fiscal pressures and public complaints had not gone unnoticed by health minister Seehofer. He was able to build a political coalition behind managed care and passed the 1993 act and followed it through with the 1996 one. But managed competition also presented each interested party with the uncertainty of a competitive future and they rushed to lobby for their interests.

A number of observers have argued that both reforms were watered down enough to present numerous issues in terms of the implementation of the reforms that the two acts called for. Whereas, for instance, the left was in favor of the reform because of the increased choice it gave to the German citizen, it feared a certain loss of solidarity and it pushed for risk adjustment measures in order to ensure that higher risks (older people, for instance) would not end up paying more. And whereas the political right also favored the reform because of increased copayments and therefore increased cost awareness on the part of the consumer, it also wanted selective contracting. But in the political climate of the time where the CDU (the conservative Christian democratic union) was in charge at the federal level and the SPD (the social democrats) controlled the upper house of the legislative body (representing the states), the building of sustainable political coalition required political mastery and would, as it turned out, result in a weaker piece of legislation.

It was to be expected therefore that after eight years of the passage of the 1993 act, the results have not been spectacular. Even though the number of sickness funds has been reduced from about 1,000 in 1993 to fewer than 450 in 2000, health care continues to consume more than 10 percent of national GDP and even though the structure of the system has changed in writing, the daily operations have not. Political negotiations in the preparatory face of the legislation had made it quite difficult for competition to work effectively in the German system. In the words of Brown and Amelung, the general appeal of competition had sustained a coalition that had mixed and matched more particular appeals in ways that inhibited competition from performing as initially (and vaguely) envisioned. The political process had made a crude stab at Pareto Optimality and, by giving major contenders what they had sought while excising elements they had feared, had crafted a rather tame strategic contrivance."[14]

And both physicians and hospitals took advantage of this.

It is indicative what the head of a large German sickness fund stated in 1998 in an interview with an American researcher: "The function of the sickness fund is to pay the bills. How care is delivered is up to the doctors and hospitals....Who defines what is appropriate care—that's the big question in any system." The sickness fund had been charged with the rationalization of the use of resources, but they lacked the appropriate information to make these kinds of decisions. In the meantime, the self-governance tradition that physicians had built over the years makes it extremely hard to clinically micromanage care, to gather the necessary information to standardize medical practice. Funds still have to negotiate with physicians associations and therefore not much has changed in that sense. At the same time, the familiarity of these corporatist arrangements is at times welcomed by policy-making circles. Whereas passing managed competition made policy makers look as if they were doing something about the problems that the health care system faced, the dirty job of seeing managed competition implemented would mean also seeing and dealing with certain effects like job losses, closing of hospitals and pay differentials. No politician has much appetite for such unpopular developments and therefore the state has been content to allow the old type corporate negotiations to continue.

It is indicative of the unwillingness of the state to fully invest in managed competition that certain national rules that limit competition between funds have not been amended. Personnel still get paid according to national and regional fee schedules. Hospitals have to charge all sickness funds the same amount for the same procedure and therefore selective contracting is, in a sense, prohibited or at least made more difficult. Furthermore, the fact that each patient can choose his hospital further limits selective contracting with hospitals. And these are only but a few examples of national rules that have been inherited from earlier decades and that are deeply entrenched in the daily operations of the system that make it difficult to see managed competition fully implemented. In short, the lack of political will to push for further competitive measures, the unwillingness of physicians and hospitals to alter their long-term practices and the long tradition of corporate politics presented institutional constraints for the successful implementation of managed competition.

There are, however, those who argue that the mere fact that Germans have introduced managed competition in their legislation is in itself significant and that the cautious way that it is being implemented does not mean the experiment has failed. The debate is very much like the one in the Netherlands. Proponents of the competitive reforms argue that the German system has moved down this path and it is only a matter of time until competition will be fully implemented. Opponents of competition, on the other hand, argue that the reforms have not been successful and that, in fact, they have placed solidarity at a risk. Ironically, they claim it is because of the risk adjustment provisions that were put in the legislation exactly to avoid loss of solidarity. The technical difficulties of adjusting risk, coupled by the free choice of funds that each German has today, could theoretically lead to a situation whereby younger enrollees that are better risks could move to a private insurance fund because of the price differential and therefore erode the base where cross subsidies can occur. Older enrollees would find it more difficult to leave their plan exactly because of the price differences. If risk adjustment mechanisms are not perfected (an admittedly intimidating and arguably improbable task), this would lead to loss of solidarity. In short, just as in the Netherlands, here, too, the jury is still out on managed competition.

What is significant for our purposes, however, is the German willingness to flirt with these ideas. Contextual fiscal pressures of reunification, macroeconomic stability, and adherence to the Maastricht criteria and internal pressures of demographic changes and improvements in costly medical technology pushed Germans down this path. At the same time, historical pressures have kept a balance in the coming of competition. Germany through its influence in the European Union has affected many countries and its internal policy experiments provide evidence to all other member states. The convergence of technocratic thinking as presented in the Maastricht agreement and in subsequent amendments is commonly known as a result of German influence. The beginning of similar developments can be viewed in health care.

The institutional alignments and interactions between the different actors that set the German health care system upon its particular trajectory go a long way to explain this German flirt with managed competition. The corporatist character of German politics, the nature of the national health insurance system with the different funds, the need to have a health policy that is consistent with macroeconomic stability and development and the willingness of policy makers to experiment with unproven theories of public management, set the parameters of German health care policy making. One thing is certain, however, and that is that the Germans have, primarily through the EU, tremendously influenced technocratic thinking and macroeconomic planning approaches in many European countries. The approach to social policy that the economy must grow based on open markets and that social policy must accommodate this growth without leaving people behind, by finding fertile soil in Germany, has spread throughout the union and will for the considerable future affect social policy making in the continent.

Notes

1.   Andel, N., Henke, K. D., and Mackscheidt, K., "Finanzierungsprobleme der deutscen Einheit II" *Schriften des Vereins fur Socialpolitik, Gesselschaft fur Wirtschafts und Sozialwissenschaften* Neue Folge, 229:11-62, Duncker and Humboldt, Berlin, 1993.
2.   Scharpf, F., Reissert, B., Schnabel, F., *Politikverflechtung: Theorie und Empirie des Kooperativen Federalismus in der Bundesrepublik*, Scriptor, Kronber, 1976.
3.   Altenstetter, C., "From Solidarity to Competition? Values, Structure and Strategy in Health Policy in Germany, 1983-1997," in *Health Care Systems in Transition: An International Perspective*, C. F. Powell and A. F. Wessen (eds.), Sage, Newbury Park, CA, 1998.
4.   Iglehart, J. K., "Health Policy Report—Germany's Health Care System," *New England Journal of Medicine* 324, no. 24, 1991.
5.   Altenstetter, C., "Health Policymaking in Germany: Stability and Dynamics," in *Health Policy Reform: National Variations and Globalization*, C. Altenstetter and J. W. Bjorkman (eds.), MacMillan Press, London, 1997.
6.   OECD Health Data, 2001 (CD ROM).
7.   Satzinger, W., Leidl, R., and Lindenmuller, H., "Antihospital Bias," in West German Health Policy: A Return to Economic Trends or a New Trend in Medical Care?" in *Third International Conference on System Science in Health Care*, W. van Eimeren et al. (eds.), Springer Verlag, Berlin, 1984, 651-53.
8.   Altenstetter, C., "Health Policymaking in Germany: Stability and Dynamics."
9.   Schwefel, D., and Leidl, R., "Bedarfsplanung und Selbstregulierung der Beteiligten im Krankenhauswessen," in *Gafgen* 187-207, 1988.
10. Lieverdink, H., and van der Made, J. H., "The Reform of NHI Systems in the Netherlands and Germany," in *Health Policy Reform: National Variations and Globalization*, C. Altenstetter and J. W. Bjorkman (eds.), MacMillan Press, London, 1997.
11. Henke, K. D., "Quo Vadis, Health Care?" Discussion Paper, Technische Universitat Verlin, 1997.
12. Advisory Council for the Concerted Action in Health Care: "Health Care and Health Insurance 2000: Individual Responsibility, Subsidiarity and Solidarity in a Changing Environment," Expert Opinion Report, Bonn, 1994, abbreviated version, and Advisory Council for the Concerted Action in Health Care: "Health Care and Health Insurance in 2000: A Closer Orientation towards Results, Higher Quality Services and Greater Economic Efficiency," Summary and Recommendations of the Special Expert Report, Bonn, 1995.
13. Jost, T. S., "German Health Care Reform: The Next Steps," *Journal of Health Politics, Policy and Law*, August 1998:697-711.
14. Brown, L. D., and Amelung, V., "Manacled Competition: Market Reforms in German Health Care," *Health Affairs* 18(3):76-91, May/June 1999.

7

Conclusion: An Artful Dance
of Economics and History

This book has been concerned with the influences that the European integration process has had on health care reform attempts, and the underlying logic behind them in member states, examining four cases, those of the Netherlands, Germany, Greece, and France. The main interest in this study was the question of whether the European Union (EU) member states are still capable of ensuring equitable and universal access to health care, or whether the European integration process is a mechanism that leads to social exclusion. The way Europe answers this question is of critical importance for the future character of European society. From a normative perspective, this is actually the question that I took up. I asked what the effect of the integration process has been and is likely to be in the near future on health care protection, and on the enabling of all Europeans to have access to equitable and quality care. The research focused on two sets of interrelated questions: First, to what degree does European integration lead to convergence of the individual member states' health care systems, what is the character of such a convergence, and how is it being developed? Second, what is it about the decision mechanisms of European health care systems, that is the day-to-day decisions about the production and distribution of health care, that on the one hand sustains their differences and on the other hand presents us to a certain degree with assurances that social cohesion remains high on the agenda of policymakers?

In this final chapter, in trying to provide an answer to these questions, I assess the degree, the similarities and the differences of EU influence on different member states and their health care systems. I begin by briefly exploring the two opposite views on the fundamental role that European economic integration plays in terms of social affairs. Then, I turn the discussion to the main theme of this book: whereas health care financing and delivery is to date mostly absent from the European active integration agenda, it is not the whole story. Through spillover from other policy areas (caused by ECJ decisions and an ideological convergence around a financially disciplined logic of distributing finite resources), health policies are being influenced from the top and are bound to continue to be so. The three case studies, however, remind us of the differences in history, politics and culture of the different health systems, the different balances of influence among key players in the several health care systems and the different decision-making mechanisms, and explain why these systems will for the foreseeable future remain the responsibility of the member states. Notwithstanding these differences, however, the prominent place of the idea of social cohesion in decision-making mechanisms at both the central and the member state level all but assures us that social solidarity will remain a primary goal in any reform effort of European health care.

Diverging Views on Europeanization

It is unequivocally true that the integration process has progressed much further in the economic policy arena than in the social policy one. In fact, from the signing of the Treaty of Rome, a primary objective for the then-European Economic Community was the creation of a customs union to promote free trade. Because of difficulties inherent in the process and differences among the different participants, integration progressed, arguably, in the following manner. Member states moved only when they had to. By the late 1970s, with most internal tariffs abolished, the next step for Europeans, if they wanted to see their economies grow, was to focus on removing non-tariff barriers and introducing a common currency. With the signing of the Single European Act and the inclusion of the internal market program therein, the Union moved ever further down the path of economic integration, by transforming what was essentially international trade between the different member states to a competitive market within the Union. To support the internal market, a common currency was necessary and the Treaty on the European Union (the Maastricht Treaty) addressed the problems of exchange rate instabilities by introducing the criteria for EMU and the creation of the common currency, the euro.

As one observes the history of the Union, it becomes rather obvious that member states have gradually accepted, albeit reluctantly for some of them, and primarily within trade, competition, industry and monetary policy increased involvement from the EU center. Autonomous national policy making in these areas is to all intents and purposes a thing of the past. This pooling of economic power at the European level has demanded considerable policy changes. It is only a matter of time until more policy changes will be demanded (in fact, one could argue that as of 2001, changes in the social policy arena are already in order) to sustain what has been achieved through the economic integration process. Changes in the arenas of social policy (pensions, health care, family policy, etc.) are, however, certain to be contested and, in so doing, create a challenging climate for the EU and the integration process.

In fact, Europeanization has already been blamed or applauded, depending on one's perspective, for a number of apparent changes. In the words of one observer, Europeanisation has been blamed, or praised, for several transfers of power; from political authorities to expert and quasi-judicial agencies; the move from state to market; the shifts in industrial investment from loans to equity; the reduction of state industrial strategies; the reduction of taxes and public spending; and competitive deflation in monetary policy."[1]

Such changes, however, could have occurred in the absence of the Union as well. After all, concurrent with the European integration process is the process of globalization. In fact, many analysts believe that the effects previously mentioned have been caused primarily by globalization. The truth is that it is difficult to differentiate between the effects of European integration and globalization exactly because the two processes occur simultaneously and both seem to have embraced a similar model of economic affairs based on free trade. The question, however, that needs to be raised is whether European integration is a regional vehicle for a global drift towards completely unrestricted market economics that invariably leads to the dismantling of social safety nets, or a mitigating factor for those kind of effects that would have otherwise plagued European societies, and a facilitator for the materialization of a distinct and alternative European approach to welfare capitalism.

The first view on the European integration process is a gloomy scenario whereby EMU and the common market are turning Europe into a mere sub-section of the global economy unconcerned with social assistance. As one observer notes, as such, the global liberal market represents a victory of American philosophy and is nothing less than a Darwinian nightmare. It implies...for the entire EU, a significant transfer from the State to society, from the law-maker to free agents in the economy and from the principle of order to the principle of disorder."[2]

The opposing view holds, as implied earlier, that the EU, in fact, protects European societies from such a Darwinian nightmare, while it helps them adjust to the new global realities. This side views European integration and globalization as two sides of the same coin. So whereas certain features of traditional welfare capitalism are being changed as they would have even without integration, others (and especially the principle of social solidarity) are being maintained and aid in the emergence of a new model of capitalism. Through enabling European states to enjoy success in the globalized economy, the EU is allowing them to have more degrees of freedom in transforming and modernizing their welfare systems. Which view is right or whether both represent parts of a constantly changing and evolving process is anyone's argument. The one point, however, that both views seem to agree upon is that European integration has affected European welfare policies in general and health policy in particular. But the question remains: How has integration affected European health systems?

European Integration and Health Policy

The main theme of the book has been that European integration does indeed influence health policy and health care protection even though member states remain the primary decision makers in this policy arena. The EU has, from an administrative perspective, passed the point of a loose, even a strong international and intergovernmental organization. It exhibits clear signs of federal structures of federal systems of governance, albeit immature ones. Therefore, the Pierson and Leibfried view of the Union as an emerging multitier structure of governance, which according to them "is a system of shared political authority over social policy, though one that is far more decentralized than the arrangements of traditional federal states"[3] is quite consistent with what emerges from the book. By focusing on the constraints that the integration process places on the national sovereignty that member states have traditionally had in the health policy arena, this multitier formulation allows us to view the EU through a different prism that encapsulates the processes of welfare system modernization, state building and identity modification. Since very few, if any, policy areas are outside the reach of EU intervention today, even if it is through indirect paths, the multitier government formulation is needed to examine effects of European integration on different sectors of the economy.

This multitier structure of governance exhibits a number of characteristics that are helpful in understanding past developments and offer some insight on what the future may hold. By no means does it indicate that all policies will move to the center. In fact, as the earlier chapters indicated, in the case of health care policy, the primary focus as of 2001 remains at the national level. The strong representation of member states in the decision-making process is quite likely to continue, even if more active policy steps were to be taken by the center. Moreover, both state and non-state actors (employers association, trade unions, labor, etc.) are likely to increasingly raise issues of health care protection at the national level.

But if this were the entire story, then the simple answer would be that the EU has no effects on health policy. Every decision taken in Brussels by member states, no matter how difficult it may have been, has led to increased European influence in matters in which previously the state was the only decision maker. More importantly, it has progressed integration down a neofunctionalist pathway whereby, as a result of spillover from other areas, one policy brings another, since states find themselves locked in previous decisions that they have made. This process leads to new initiatives in policy areas previously thought of as exclusive areas of member states' competencies, mostly because states face the unpredictable and at times unintended consequences of their earlier joined policies. In so doing, the autonomy of the activities of EU institutions like the Commission and the Court increases and a stronger center appears.

This is, in fact, what seems to have been occurring in health policy developments. It is indicative of the growing degree of complexity in the relationships between the member states and the EU and the challenges that are both inherent to health care and caused directly by the integration process. Both sets of challenges raise questions for the future of European health care systems. On the one hand, one observes the issues that face all developed health care systems: demographic changes (especially the aging of the population) and their effects on both the demand for care as well as on the financing formulas, the issue of technological advances and the subsequent costs, the rising expectations about health care as the economies continue to grow, the macroeconomic context within which health care operates, and, of course, as always the double-edge sword issue of quality care at sustainable cost. On the other hand, one observes the issues that are raised because of the creation of the common market and the guarantees that accompany it in terms of free movement of capital, people, goods and services. In the framework of this study, the challenges that European integration raised are three: cross-border care, boundaries between Brussels and member state governments, and the understanding of the competition law as it relates to health care.

As it becomes evident, even though decisions may be the responsibility of the state government, the challenges that health care systems face lead the decision-making mechanisms to be shaped by the experience of both the center and the state levels of government. Brussels is indeed not pushing for harmonizing reforms in a coordinated fashion. Rather, through either market compatibility requirements or a convergence in technocratic thinking, the EU is more than ever affecting health policy decisions at the state level. More specifically, what this study has shown is that, whereas Brussels is quite willing to have member states deal with health care, it nevertheless represents a force for convergence through three mechanisms:

- First, through actions of active positive integration, directly targeting the issue of equitable health care access. Such actions are indeed limited.
- Second, through actions of negative integration (imposition of common market criteria through the European Court of Justice) that raise tensions between the principles of social cohesion, free movement of people, services, goods and capital and subsidiarity.

- Third, through a third type of integration that centers around an ideological convergence among European elites which calls for more efficient use of limited health care resources, more disciplined public financing and the maintenance of social solidarity.

The ECJ has through a number of rulings, most notably the Kohll and Decker cases, made health care goods and services subject to free movement. And even though these rulings will not automatically change everything in health care delivery in the Union, and there can be some advantages to them (through better prices for technology and pharmaceuticals, for instance), there are also potential problems. The rulings raise the administrative challenges that national systems or social sickness funds face by introducing a transnational aspect to health planning. Increased patient mobility can be expected. To the degree that the rulings simplify the bureaucratic process, to the degree that perceptions of differences in the quality of medical care in different states are real, and to the degree that waiting lists pose a problem for the individual patient, increased numbers of patients can be expected to seek care "abroad."

An immediate effect may be increased health care expenditures for the payers in countries with lower rated systems. Such pressures can be expected in the long run to lead to a convergence in prices of goods and services, and similar waiting periods. But it would be worth it for Europeans, if they were to institutionalize a collective set of rules that would produce results that are consistent with the principle of high health care protection for all, the principle of free movement of goods, services, capital and people and the principle of subsidiarity, instead of waiting and thinking that it will all sort itself out in the long run based on ECJ court decisions.

At the same time, economic integration has led both Brussels and, in turn, the member states to embrace a macroeconomic model of fiscal discipline, controlled public expenditures and a more efficient distribution of resources. The one goal that European leaders appear to be determined to achieve is sustainable economic growth and, in so doing, all other policy areas become secondary to economic policy. As is evident in the discussion on employment policy in chapter 2, modernizing labor relations became necessary to tackle unemployment and maintain macroeconomic growth. Similarly, the issue now has become the modernization of social protection systems, including health care systems. A similar path and a similar logic are followed in the cases of social security and education. One observes a progression of policy steps by Brussels, from placing the issue on the agenda, asking states and other social partners about it, coming up with broad ideas and then with more specific ones and, all along, creating a convergence around an ideological framework of the rationalization of available resources in health care. Throughout this progression, the Commission has gone out of its way to highlight that it is the member states that would remain in charge of social protections and that harmonization of policies or uniform policies across Europe directed by Brussels, is not the goal. Therefore, one sees only broad general themes coming from above that are nevertheless an important influence. Member states have found themselves walking or being pulled, depending on the state, the time or the issue down a convergence path of their social protection schemes in general and their health care systems in particular. If one were to take this to the theoretical extreme, it would lead to very similar health care arrangements.

The degree of influence of these general themes from Brussels differs from state to state. How much a state changes its system is a function of where its economy is, the beginning condition of its health care system and its internal politics. Whereas, for example, it has been Brussels that has led Greek policy makers down this path, through Greece's major economic transformation of the 1990s, the Netherlands was a state that had already, and for a considerable amount of time, embraced the overall framework that dictated that social protection systems had to evolve in order to promote overall economic growth. In this sense, ideas seem to travel from one member state to another through the Union's institutions. Similarly, the French case reminds us that the issue of social protection in general (including access to medical care) will not be sacrifices in the name of economic growth. Changes will occur and they will depend on the ideology of the governing parties and the direction of the overall economy. But to argue that social solidarity and social protection are under attack because of the EU is not valid. Moreover, and as all four cases of the Netherlands, France, Greece, and Germany indicated, the EU can be used as the political scapegoat for reforms that people may not favor. The "politics of avoidance"dictate that the political cost can be passed on to Brussels, whereas political credit for the things that are working well can be taken at the member-state level.

Since decision making still lies at the state level, to understand health care policy, one also has to look there. The history of the institutional developments, the constraints that these institutions place on decisions, and the ideas that affect state policy makers' decisions are all factors that have kept the several health care arrangements that the states have had distinct. As we saw, health policy developments are path dependent, and once a country has started down a policy path, the political costs of reversal, in order to converge with some other system, for example, are so high that absent a major critical juncture in the historical development of a health care system, a country will most likely continue down its original path. In that sense, absent a major common critical juncture for the development of all European health care systems, their distinct nature will remain the norm for the foreseeable future. Thus, the question that needs to be raised is whether, as of mid-2001, the integration process has caused such a critical juncture or is integration only part of the environmental context, which, along with political maneuvering, induces institutions to evolve but still on the same developmental pathway that they have found themselves throughout their history.

This study indicates that it is the latter. The EU has influenced health policy but not to the extent that an argument about reaching a critical juncture could be sustained. There is the technocratic thinking convergence around a different logic of allocating finite resources in health care, but not of harmonizing administrative mechanisms. Moreover, politics at the member state level has shown tremendous resilience and has exhibited great resistance and, in so doing, has not allowed systems to be completely transformed towards this new framework. Therefore, without that major critical juncture, crucial changes in the arrangements through which Europeans receive their health care cannot be expected. Furthermore, as long as current health care arrangements are not perceived as distorting the market, Brussels will not act, even though European directives will most likely increasingly have to deal with the issue of cross-border health more comprehensively.

In the end, one observes institutional changes so that current institutions can adapt to the contextual pressures that are not so much caused by the integration process but are inherent in the financing and delivery, in short in the nature of health care. For instance, one observes in all three of my case studies, dissatisfaction with the performance of parts of the health care system. These may differ depending on the case, but no country seems to be pleased with its system and therefore policy makers in all three cases have made continuous and ongoing reform efforts. Moreover, one discerns a preference for decentralization of administrative responsibility even as the central government supply and demand controls increase. In all three case studies, devolving decision-making power has been and continues to be a goal. At the same time, however, this has increased the responsibility of the state governments to regulate the system both at its supply and its demand sides. One also discerns a partial loss of autonomy by the profession. In light of their total control of the system until rather recently, the trend that has begun in the last twenty years is not difficult to comprehend. The physicians have been primarily responsible for health care outlays and their style of practice had led to a long separation between the services and their costs. In all fairness, governmental policies that insulated patients more or less completely from those costs did not help either. Either way, it was inevitable that physician control of the system would be wrested away. Primarily through the control of their fees, but increasingly with demands that physicians should adhere to practice guidelines, physicians have seen their independence diminish. One can in fact expect more arguments by physicians as they try to wrest control back. But even if successful, they will never return to their earlier decades of dominance. Finally, social cohesion is a principle that is still valued at both the central and the member-state levels. Therein lies the legitimization for the continuation of certain institutional arrangements in health care that, according to strict economic theory, may be less efficient than a perfectly utilitarian institutional arrangement and therefore arguments about Europe losing its strong social traditions are a bit alarmist.

The EU ought not be viewed as an entity whose goal is to dismantle the national welfare state or to eradicate the notion of solidarity. Rather, macroeconomic growth goals and micro-level efficiency considerations that are embraced by both Brussels and state capitals, but also inherent challenges to health care systems, have put pressure on the states to modernize these systems. The EU, by providing the framework for economic growth, is, on the one hand, pressuring for this modernization and, on the other, easing the transitional phase from the old systems to the new ones, whereby prized ideals like social cohesion are been carried through even as the management and allocation of resources is being changed to fit both the common market rules and to meet the cost control challenges. To use the metaphor that provides the subtitle for this book, European integration is affecting health policy through an artful dance between the historical development of the health care systems in the member states and the economics of the European integration process.

Notes

1. Guyomarch, A., Machin, H., and Ritchie, E., *France in the European Union*, St. Martin's Press, New York, 1998.
2. Minc, A., *La Grande Illusion*, Grasset, Paris, 1989.
3. Pierson, P., and Leibfried, S., "Multitiered Institutions and the Making of Social Policy," in S. Leibfried and P. Pierson (eds.), *European Social Policy: Between Fragmentation and Integration*, The Brookings Institute, Washington, D.C., 1995:1-41.

References

Aaron, H. J., and Schwarz, W. B. *The Painful Prescription: Rationing Hospital Care.* Washington, D.C. The Brookings Institute, 1984.

Abel-Smith, B., Calltrop, J., Dixon, M., Dunning, Ad., Evans, R., Holland, W., Jarman, B., and Mossialos, E. "Report on the Greek Health Services." Athens, Greece: Ministry of Health, Welfare and Social Insurance, 1994 (in Greek).

Advisory Council for the Concerted Action in Health Care. "Health Care and Health Insurance 2000: Individual Responsibility, Subsidiarity and Solidarity in a Changing Environment." Expert Opinion report, Bonn, 1994, abbreviated version.

_____. "Health Care and Health Insurance in 2000: A Closer Orientation towards Results, Higher Quality Services and Greater Economic Efficiency." Summary and Recommendations of the Special Expert Report, Bonn, 1995.

Altenstetter, C. "Health Policy Regimes and the Single European Market." *Journal of Health Politics, Policy and Law* 27 (4): 813-846, 1992.

_____. "From Solidarity to Competition? Values, Structure and Strategy in Health Policy in Germany, 1983-1997." In *Health Care Systems in Transition: An International Perspective,* edited by C. F. Powell and A. F. Wessen. Newbury Park, CA: Sage, 1998.

_____. "Health Policymaking in Germany: Stability and Dynamics." In *Health Policy Reform: National Variations and Globalization,* edited C. Altenstetter and J. W. Bjorkman. London: Macmillan Press, 1997.

Aminzade, R. "Historical Sociology and Time." *Sociological Methods and Research* 20:456-480, 1992.

Andel, N., Henke, K. D., and K. Mackscheidt. "Finanzierungsprobleme der deutscen Einheit II." *Schriften des Vereins fur Socialpolitik, Gesselschaft fur Wirtschafts und Sozialwissenschaften* Neue Folge, 229:11-62. Berlin: Duncker and Humboldt, 1993.

Anderson, C. *Blaming the Government. Citizens and the Economy in Five European Democracies* Armonk, NY: M. E. Sharpe, 1995.

Arthur, W. B. *Increasing Returns and Path Dependence in the Economy.* Ann Arbor: University of Michigan Press, 1994.

Bach, S. "Managing a Pluralist Health System: The Case of Health Reform in France." *International Journal of Health Services* 24 (4):593-606, 1994.

Baldwin, P. *The Politics of Social Solidarity.* Cambridge: Cambridge University Press, 1990.

Baumgartner, Fr. "The Many Styles of Policymaking in France." In *Chirac's Challenge: Liberalization, Europeanization and Malaise in France,* edited by T. S. Keeler and M. A. Schain. New York: St. Martin's Press, 1996.

Berman, S. "Path Dependency and Political Action: Reexamining Response to the Depression." *Comparative Politics* 30:379-400, 1998.

Bjorkman, J. W., and Okma, K. "The Institutional Heritage of Dutch Health Policy Reforms." In *Health Policy, National Schemes and Globalization,* edited by J. W. Bjorkman and C. Altenstetter. London: Macmillan Press, 1998.

Bles, G. "Medecine de France." In *Le Film des Evenements*, No. 143, August 9, 1979.

Brown, L. "Government and Market in Three Types of Health Care System: The Practical Dialectic of Accommodation." The Joseph L. Mailman School of Public Health, class notes, fall 1998.

_____. „Health Policy in the United States: Issues and Options." Ford Foundation Project on Social Welfare and the American Future Occasional Paper #4. New York, 1988.

Brown, L. D., and Amelung, V. "Manacled Competition: Market Reforms in German Health Care." *Health Affairs* 18 (3):76-91, May/June 1999.

Brown, M. K. "Remaking the Welfare State: A Comparative Perspective." In *Remaking the Welfare State: Retrenchment and Social Policy in America and Europe,* edited by M. K. Brown. Philadelphia: Temple University Press, 1988.

Brumter, C. "La Planification Sanitaire." University of Legal, Political, Social and the Technological Sciences, Strassburg, Faculty of Political Science, February 1979.

Brunet-Jailly, J. "Quelques Evidences sur l' Evolution dy Systeme de Sante." *Revue Economique* No3, 1976.

Buchele, R., and Christiansen, J. "Do Employment and Income Security Cause Unemployment? A Comparative Study of the US and the E-4." *Cambridge Journal of Economics* 22: 117-136, 1998.

Caisse Nationale de l'Assurance Maladi. "La CNAMTS en quelques chiffres." Paris: CNAMTS, 1999.

Cameron, D. "National Interest, the Dilemmas of European Integration and Malaise." In *Chirac's Challenge: Liberalization, Europeanization and Malaise in France*, edited by T. S. Keeler and M. A. Schain. New York: St. Martin's Press, 1996.

Caporaso J., and Keeler, J. "The EU and Regional Integration Theory." In *The State of the European Union, vol 3*, edited by. C. Rhodes and S. Mazey. Boulder, CO: Lynne, Reine and Golman Press, 1995.

Castaing, M. "L'Hôpital, Ce Malade Chronique." Article in *Le Monde*, February 21, 1975.

Catrice-Lorrey, A. *Dynamique Interbe de la Securite Sociale et Service Publique.* Paris: Centre de Recherches en Science Sociales du Travail, 1979.

CDA. "Betere zorg op basis van solidatiteit en eigen verantwoordelijkheid." Discussion of the CDA working group, The Hague, The Netherlands, 1992.

CEC. "Europe...Questions and Answers, How Does the European Union Work?" 2nd ed. DG for Information, Communication, Culture and Audiovisual Media, Brussels, 1997.

_____. *The Future of Social Protection: A Framework for a European Debate*, Communication from the Commission, Brussels: COM (95) 466 final, 31.10.1995.

_____. *Employment Rates Report 1998: Employment Performance in the Member States,* Luxembourg: Office for Official Publications of the EC (OOPEC), COM (98) 572 final, p 5.

_____. *The EU Economy at the Arrival of the Euro: Promoting Growth, Employment And Stability.* Luxembourg: OOPEC, COM (1999) 7 final, p 6., 1999.

_____. *The 1999 Annual Employment Report.* Luxembourg: OOPEC, Introduction, 1999.

_____. *Growth and Employment in the Stability-Oriented Framework of EMU: Economic Policy Reflections in View of the Forthcoming 1998 Broad Guidelines.* Luxembourg: OOPEC, II/33/98-EN, pp 5-6, 1998.

_____. *Growth, Competitiveness, Employment: The Challenges and Ways forward into the 21st Century.* Luxembourg: OOPEC, COM (93) 700 final, 1993.

_____. *Demographic Report, 1997.* Employment and Social Affairs, Social Protection and Social Affairs, DG for Employment and Industrial Relations and Social Affairs, Unit V/E.1, Brussels, Belgium.

_____. *Action for Employment in Europe: A Confidence Pact.* Luxembourg: OOPEC, CSE (96) 1 final, 1996.

_____. *The Amsterdam Treaty: A Comprehensive Guide.* Luxembourg: OOPEC, 1998.

_____. *An Employment Agenda for the Year 2000: Executive Summary.* Luxembourg: OOPEC, COM (97) 479 final, 1997.

_____. "Social Protection in Europe-1993," COM(93)531. Two further reports came out in 1995 and 1997, with an additional one in 2000, 1993.

_____. Communication: *Modernising and Improving Social Protection in the European Union* available at http://europa.eu.int/comm/dg05/soc-prot/social/commu/commuen.htm.

_____. Communication on the Development of Public Health Policy available at http://europa.eu.int/comm/dg05/phealth/general/phpolicy2.htm.

_____. Communication: *A Concerted Strategy for Modernising Social Protection.* (COM 99-347), July 14, 1999.

Chambaud, L. "Health Care in Europe—France. A la Carte." *Health Services Journal* 103 (5344):24-7, March 18, 1993.

Chavannes, M. Articles in *Handelsblad* of September 18, 21, 25, and 28, 1991.

Cibrie, P. "Syndicalisme Medical," Confederation des Syndicats Medicaux Francais, Paris, 1954.

Club Socialiste du livre: "Projet Socialiste pour la France des annees 1980-1981," Paris, 1981.

Cohen, S., and Goldfinger, C. "From Real Crisis to Permacrisis in French Social Security." In *Stress and Contradiction in Modern Capitalism,* edited by L. Lindberg, R. Alford, C. Crouch, and C. Offe. Lexington, MA: D.C. Health, 1975.

Colombotos, J., and Fakiolas, N. P. «The Power of Organized Medicine in Greece.» In *The Changing Medical Profession: An International Perspective,* edited by F. W. Hafferty and J. B. McKinlay. New York: Oxford University Press, 1993.

Commissie, Biesheuvel. *Gedeelde Zorg:betere zorg.* Rapport van de Commissie Modernisering Curatieve Zorg. Ministry of Health, Welfare and Sport, The Hague, The Netherlands, 1994.

Commissie, Dekker. *Bereidheid tot Verandering Rapport van de Commissie Structuur en Financiering Gezondheidszorg,* Ministerie van Wezign, Volksgezondheid en Cultuur, 1987.

Commissie, Van Rhijn. *Sociale Zekerheid.* Rapport van de Commissie ingesteld door de Minister voor Sociale Zaken op 26 Maart 1943. (3 delen), 1945.

Commissie, Willems. "Onderzoek Besluitvorming Volksgezondheid." Kamerstukken II, 1993-1994, 23666, nrs 1 en 2. The Hague, The Netherlands, 1994.

Committee, Dunning. *Choices in Health Care,* A Report by the Government Committee on Choices in Health Care, Ministry of Welfare, Health and Cultural Affairs, The Hague The Netherlands, 1992.

Council Recommendation 92/442/EEC of July 27, 1992 on the convergence of social protection objectives and policies, OJ L245 of August 26, 1992.

Council Recommendation 92/441/EEC of June 24, 1992 on common criteria concerning sufficient resources and social assistance in social protection systems, OJ l 245 of August 26, 1992.

Council Resolution, 15.12.1997; The 1998 Employment Guidelines, at *http://europa.eu.int/comm/dg05/-empl&esf/docs/guideen.htm.*

Daalder, H. "The Role of a Small State in the European Community: The Case of the Netherlands," Working Paper 1991/21. Centro de Estudios Avanzados en Ciencias Sociales, June 1991.

Dahrendorf, R. *Essays in the Theory of Society.* Stanford, CA: Stanford University Press, 1968.

Day, P., and Klein, R. "Britain's Health Care Experiment." *Health Affairs,* 10:35-59, 1991.

De Kervasdoue, J., Meyer, C., Weill, C., and Couffinhal, A. "French Health Care System: Inconsistent Regulation." In *Health Policy, National Schemes and Globalization,* edited by J. W. Bjorkman and C. Altenstetter. London: Macmillan Press, 1998.

De Pouvourville, G. "Hospital Reforms in France under a Socialist Government." *The Milbank Quarterly* 64 (3): 392-413, 1986.

De Pouvourville ,G., and Renaud ,M. "Hospital System Management in France and Canada: National Pluralism and Provincial Centralism." *Social Science and Medicine* 20 (2):153-67, 1985.

De Swaan, A. *Social Policy Beyond Borders: The Social Question in International Perspective.* Amsterdam: Amsterdam University Press, 1994.

_____. *In Care of the State. Health Care, Education and Welfare in Europe and the USA in the Modern Era.* Oxford: Polity Press, 1988.

Deutsch, K. et al. *Political Community and the North Atlantic Area.* Princeton, NJ: Princeton University Press, 1957.

De Volkskrant, J. Article entitled "Debat van scepticus met gelovige ongelijke strijd," October 4, 1991.

De Vree, J. K. *Political Integration: The Formation of Theory and its Problems.* The Hague: Mouton, 1972.

Dommers, J. "An Introduction to European Union health law." *European Journal of Health Law* 4:19-41, 1997.

Dorozynski, A. "New Battle Looms for France Over Health Reforms." *British Medical Journal* 312: p. 9, January 6, 1996.

_____. "French Protest at Health Budget Cuts." *British Medical Journal* 311(7015): 1247-48, November 11, 1995.

_____. "France Gears Up to Fight Health Insurance Debts." *British Medical Journal* 311: 967-68, October 14, 1995.

_____. "France Faces Radical Health Insurance Reforms." *British Medical Journal* 311: 1386, November 25, 1995.

Dougherty, J., and Pfaltzgraff, R. Jr. *Contending Theories of International relations: A Comprehensive Survey.* New York: Harper and Row, 1990.

Dupoirer, E., and Grunberg, G., „La Dechirure sociale." *Pouvoirs* 73 (April 1995).

Durand-Zaleski, I., Colin, C., and Blum Boisgard, C. "An Attempt to Save Money by Using Mandatory Practice Guidelines in France." *British Medical Journal* 315 (7113):943-6, October 11, 1997.

Editorial Comment (1998). "The US 'Employment Miracle': Employment Protection and Job Generation." *Comparative Labor Law and Policy Journal* 19, 278.

Edwards, G., and Pijpers, A. (eds.). *The Politics of European Treaty Reform: The 1996 Intergovernmental Conference and Beyond.* London: Pinter Publishers, 1997.

Eleytherotipia newspaper on Sunday, August 6, 2000.

Elsinga, E. "Political Decision-making in Health Care: The Dutch Case." *Health Policy* 11:243-55, 1989.

Enthoven A. "The History and Principles of Managed Competition." *Health Affairs* Supplement 1993:24-47.

_____. The 1987 Professor Dr. F. de Vries Lectures. *Theory and Practice of Managed Competition in Health Care Finance.* New York: North Holland Publishing Company, 1988.

_____. *Health Plan: The Only Practical Solution to the Soaring Cost of Medical Care.*, Reading, MA: Addison-Wesley, 1980.

_____. "Consumer Choice Health Plan." *New England Journal of Medicine* 298:650-58, 709-20, 1978.

Enthoven, A., and Kronick, R. "A Consumer-Choice Health Plan for the 1990s: Universal Health Insurance in a System Designed to Promote Quality and Economy." *New England Journal of Medicine,* 320:29-37 and 320:94-101, 1989.

Esping-Andersen, G. *The Three Worlds of Welfare Capitalism.* Princeton, NJ: Princeton University Press, 1990.

Ethnos, July 29, 2000.

_____, July 30, 2000.

Etzioni, A. *Political Unification.* New York: Holt, Rinehart and Winston Publishers, 1965.

European Council. Meeting of December 9-10, 1994, SN 300/64.

European Court Reports. Case 238/82, Duphar vs. The Netherlands, Jur. 1984; Royer case 48/75. 1976:497; Costa vs. Enel Case 6/64, CMLR 425, 1964:585; Administratione delle Finanze dello Stato v Simmental Case 196/77, CMLR263, 1978:629; Levin v. Staatssecretaris van Justitie Case 53/81, CMLR 1137, 1982:1035; Kempf v. Staatssecretaris van Justitie Case 139/85, CMLR 764, 1986:1741.

_____. Case C120/95- Nicolas Decker v. Caisse de Maladie des Employes Prives.

_____. Case C-158/96, Raymond Kohll v. Union des Caisses de Maladie.

"Europe's New Left." *The Economist,* February 12, 2000.

Eurostat. Statistical Office of the European Communities in Luxembourg (1999) *Press Release* No. 120/99, December 6, 1999.

Featherstone, K. "Jean Monnet and the 'Democratic Deficit' in the European Union." *Journal of Common Market Studies* 32 (2):149-170, 1994.

Fielding J. E., and Lancry, P. "Lessons from France—'Vive la Difference'." *JAMA* 270 (6):748-756, August 11, 1993.

Financiel Overzicht Zorg 1999. Kamerstukken II, 1998-1999, 230456, nrs1 en 2. The Hague, The Netherlands, 1998.

Flora, P. *Growth to Limits: The Western European Welfare State Since World War II.* New York and Berlin: Walter de Gruyter, 1988.

France, G., and Hermans, H. «Choices in Health Care in Italy and the Netherlands, I: Economic and Financial Dimensions.» In *Health Care and its Financing in the Single European Market,* edited by R. Leidl. Washington D.C.: IOS Press., 1998:254-264.

Friedman, S., and Weller, C. "One More Time: Labor Market Flexibility, Aggregate Demand, and Comparative Employment Growth in the US and Europe." *Comparative Labor Law and Policy Journal* 19: 307-319, 1998.

Gezondheidsraad Rapport. "Medisch handelen op een tweesprong." The Hague, The Netherlands, 1991.

Glazer, N. *The Limits of Social Policy.* Cambridge: Harvard University Press, 1988.

Glaser, W. *Health Insurance Bargaining.* New York: IOS Press, 1978.

Gobrecht, J. "National Reactions to Kohll and Decker." *Eurohealth* 5 (1):18-20, Spring 1999.

Godefroi, L. S. *Het ziekenjindswezen in Nederland: ontwikkeling en perspectieven* [Sickness Fund Insurance in the Netherlands: Development and Perspectives]. The Hague: Martinus Nijhoff, 1963.

Godt, P. "Health Care: The Political Economy of Social Policy." In *Policy Making in France*, edited by P. Godt. New York: Pinter Press, 1989.

_____. "Confrontation, Consent, and Corporatism: State Strategies and the Medical Profession in France, Great Britain, and West Germany." *Journal of Health Politics, Policy and Law* 12:459-480.

Goldmann, K.»Politikens Internationalisering och den Politiska Kulturen. En Pilotstudie.» Arbetsrapport, Stasvetenskapliga Institutionen, Stockholms Universitet, 1997.

Gough, I. *The Political Economy of the Welfare State.* London: Macmillan Press, 1979.

Gouvras, G. "Public Health Policy in the European Community." *Gesundheitswesen* 59 (12): 657-58, December 1997.

Greek Ministry of Labor Decision, Number 60556, February 1940.

Green, Cowles M. "Setting the Agenda for a new Europe: The ERT and EC 1992." *Journal of Common Market Studies* 33 (4):501-526, 1995.

Green Paper on European Social Policy: Options for the Union available at http://europa.eu.int/scadplus/leg/en/cha/c10111.htm.

Griffin, L. J. "Temporality, Events, and Explanation in Historical Sociology: An Introduction." *Sociological Methods and Research* 20:403-427, 1992.

Haas, B. E. *The Uniting of Europe.* Stanford, CA: Stanford University Press, 1968.

Hall, P. "The Evolution of Economic Policy Under Mitterrand." In *The Mitterrand Experiment,* edited by George Ross, Stanley Hoffmann, and Sylvia Malzacher. New York: Oxford University Press, 1987.

_____. "The Role of Interests, Institutions and Ideas in the Comparative Political Economy of Industrialized Nations." In *Comparative Politics: Rationality, Culture and Structure*, edited by M. I. Lichbach and A. S. Zuckerman. Princeton NJ: Princeton University Press, 1997.

Handelsblad. "Beschaafd welles-nietes over plan-Simons," October 4, 1991.

Hassenteufel, P. "Les Medecins Face A l'Etat: Une Comparaison Internationale." Paris: Presses de la Fondation Nationale des Sciences Politiques, 1997.

Henke, K. D. "Quo Vadis, Health Care?" Discussion Paper, Technische Universitat Verlin, 1997.

Hermans, H. E. G. M., Casparie, A. E, Paelinck, J. H. P. (eds.). *Health Care in Europe after 1992.* Dartmouth: Aldershot, 1992.

Hermans, H., and Berman, P. "Access to Health Care and Health Services in the European Union: Regulation 1408/71 and the E111 process." In *Health Care and its Financing in the Single European Market*, edited by R. Leidl. Amsterdam, ND: IOS Press, 1998.

Het Binnenhof. Article entitled "VNO-voorzitter: Kabinet moet verplicht eigen risico invoeren," October 4, 1991.

Het Financieele Dagblad. Article entitled "VNO cijfers Simons veroordeeld," October 4, 1991.

Hodges ,M. (ed.). *European Integration.* London: Penguin Press, 1972.

Hurst, J. W. "Reforming Health Care in Seven European Nations." *Health Affairs* 10:13-17, 1991.

Iglehart, J. K. "Health Policy Report-Germany's Health Care System." *New England Journal of Medicine* 324, no. 24 (1991).

Immergut, E. "The Theoretical Core of the New Institutionalism." *Politics and Society* 26 (1):5-34, 1998.

Isaac, L. W. "Transforming Localities: Reflections on Time, Causality, and Narrative in Contemporary Historical Sociology." *Historical Methods* 30:4-12, 1997.

Jacobs, L. "Politics of America's Supply State: Health Reform and Technology." *Health Affairs* 143-157, Fall 1995.

Jacob, P. and Teune, H. "The Integrative Process: Guidelines for Analysis of the Basis of Political Community." In *The Integration of Political Communities*, edited by P. Jacob and J. Toscano. Philadelphia: Lippincot Press, 1964.

Jamous, H. *Le Grand Tournant de la Medecine Liberale*. Paris: Edition Ouvrieres, 1963.

Johanet, G. *Securite Sociale: L'echec et le defi*. Seuil. Paris, 1998.

Johansen, L. N. "Welfare State Regression in Scandinavia? The Development of Scandinavian Welfare States from 1970 to 1980." In *Comparing Welfare States and Their Futures*, edited by E. Oyen. Hidershot, England, 1986:129-51.

Jost, T. S: "German Health Care Reform: The Next Steps." *Journal of Health Politics, Policy and Law* (August 1998):697-711.

"Kabinetsformatie 1998," brief van de informateurs, Tweede Kamer, 1997-1998m 26024, nr 9, 1998.

Kanavos, P. "Health as a Tradable Service: A Prospective View of the European Union." *Eurohealth* 5 (1):18-20, Spring 1999.

Kathimerini, June 4, 2000.

Katznelson, I. "The Doleful Dance of Politics and Policy: Can Historical Institutionalism Make a Difference?" *American Political Science Review* 92 (1);March 1998:191-97.

Keeler, J. T. S., and Schain, M. A. (eds.). *Chirac's Challenge: Liberalization, Europeanization and Malaise in France*. New York: St Martin's Press, 1996.

Keohane, R. *International Institutions and State Power*. Boulder, CO: Westview Press, 1989.

Keohane, R., and Nye, J. *Power and Interdependence: World Politics in Transition*. Boston: Little Brown, 1977.

Keohane, R., and Hoffman, S. (eds.). *The New European Community: Decisionmaking and Institutional Change*. Boulder, CO: Westview Press, 1991.

Kesselmam, M. "Does the French Labor Movement Have a Future? " In *Chirac's Challenge: Liberalization, Europeanization and Malaise in France*, edited by T. S. Keeler and M. A. Schain. New York: St. Martin's Press, 1996.

Komninou, N. „NHS: The Surgery Leaves Six Wounds Open." *Eleftheros Typos*, March 23, 1997, Athens, Greece.

Krasner, S. D. *International Regimes*. Ithaca, NY: Cornell University Press, 1983.

_____. "Sovereignty: An Institutional Perspective." *Comparative Political Studies* 21:66-94, 1988.

Kyriakatiki Eleytherotipia, July 30, 2000.

Kyriopoulos, J., and Tsalikis, G. "Public and Private Imperatives of Greek Health Policies." *Health Policy* 26 (2):105-17, December 1993.

Laetz, T. J., and Okma, K. G. "Rise and Demise of Health reforms in the Netherlands, 1988-1998." Ministry of Health, Welfare and Sport, The Hague, The Netherlands, 1998.

Lancry, P., and Sandier, S. "Twenty Years of Cures for the French Health Care System." In *Health Care and Cost Containment in the European Union*, edited by E. Mossialos and J. Le Grand. Brookfield, VT: Ashgate Publishing, 1999.

Lange, P. "The Politics of the Social Dimension." In *Euro-politics: Institutions and Policymaking in the "New" European Community*, edited by A. M. Sbragia. Washington, D.C. The Brookings Institute, 1992.

Lapre, R. M. 1988. A Change of Direction in the Dutch Health Care System? *Health Policy* 10:21-32.

L'Association Internationale de la Mutualite (AIM). *The Cross Border health Cares within the European Community*. Study for the Commission of the European Communities, Directorate V, Brussels, April 1991.

Leibfried, S., and Pierson, P. «Social Policy.» In *Policy Making in the European Union*, 3rd ed. edited by Wallace and Wallace. New York: Oxford University Press, 1996.

Leidl, R. "How Will the Single European Market Affect Health Care?" *British Medical Journal* 303:1081-82, 1991.

_____, (ed.). *Health Care and Its Financing in the Single European Market*. Washington D.C.: IOS Press, 1998.

Le Monde, April 11, 1995.

_____, July 26, 1979.

_____, September 23, 1976.

_____, January 10, 1979.

_____, May 11, 1995.

Le Plan Juppe. In Numero Special *Droit Social 3*, 1996/03.

Levi, M. "A Model, a Method, and a Map: Rational Choice in Comparative and Historical Analysis." In *Comparative Politics: Rationality, Culture and Structure*, edited by M. I. Lichbach and A. S. Zuckerman. Princeton NJ: Princeton University Press, 1997.

Levy, J. *Tocqueville's Revenge: State, Society and Economy in Contemporary France*. Cambridge, MA: Harvard University Press, 1999.

Levy, J. "Partisan Politics and Welfare Adjustment: The Case of France." Paper presented to the 12th International Conference of Europeanists in Chicago, March 30-April 1, 2000.

Liaisons socials. Paris, Bareme Social Periodique, 1999.

Liakos, A. "Work and Politics in Greece between the Two World Wars." Modern Greek History Studies, Institute for Research and Education by the Emporiki Bank of Greece, 1993.

Liaropoulos, L. L., and Kaitelidou, D. "Changing the Public-Private Mix: An Assessment of the Health Reforms in Greece." *Health Care Analysis* 6 (4):277-285, 1998.

Lichbach, M. I., and Zuckerman, A. S. (eds.). *Comparative Politics: Rationality, Culture and Structure*. Princeton NJ: Princeton University Press, 1997.

Liebowitz, S. J., and Margolis, S. E. "Path Dependence, Lock-In, and History." *Journal of Law, Economics and Organization* 11/1:205-226, 1995.

Lieverdink, H., and van der Made, J. H.: "The Reform of NHI Systems in the Netherlands and Germany." In *Health Policy Reform: National Variations and Globalization*, edited by C. Altenstetter and J. W. Bjorkman. London: Macmillan Press, 1997.

Lijphart, A. *The Politics of Accommodation: Pluralism and Democracy in the Netherlands*. Berkeley: University of California Press, 1975.

Lindberg, L. *The Political Dynamics of European Economic Integration*. Stanford, CA: Stanford University Press, 1963.

Lindberg, L., and Scheingold, S. (eds.). *Regional Integration: Theory and Research*. Cambridge: Harvard University Press, 1971.

Lipgens, W. *A History of European Integration, 1945-1947: The Formation of the European Unity Movement*. Oxford: Clarendon Press, 1982.

Maarse, H., and Paulus, A. «Health Insurance Reforms in the Netherlands, Belgium and Germany: A Comparative Analysis.» In *Health Care and its Financing in the Single European Market,* edited by R. Leid. Washington D.C.: IOS Press, 1998.

Mahoney, J. "Path Dependence in Comparative-Historical Research." Paper presented at the 1999 Annual Meeting of the APSA, Atlanta, September 1999.

Majone, G. "Regulatory Federalism in the European Community." *Government and Policy* 10:299-316, 1992.

March, J. G., and Olsen, P. *Rediscovering Institutions: The Organizational Basis of Politics.* New York: Free Press 1989.

Marshall, T. H. "Citizenship and Social Class." In *Class, Citizenship and Social Development.* Westport, CT: Greenwood Press, 1994.

Marx, K., and Engels, F. "Manifesto of the Communist Party." In *The Marx-Engels Reader,* 2nd ed., edited by R. C. Tucker. New York: W. W. Norton & Company, 1978.

Matsaganis, M. "Competition Types in Public Health Care Systems." In *The Competition Challenge in the Health Care Sector* (in Greek), edited by J. Kyriopoulos and D. Niakas. Athens: Center for Social Research in Health Care, 1993.

_____. "Quasi Market Reforms in Public Health Care Systems." Paper presented in fifth Conference, entitled Limits and Relations between Public and Private in Panteion University, in Athens, November 23-26, 1994.

_____. "From the North Sea to the Mediterranean? Constraints to Health Reform in Greece." *International Journal of Health Services,* 28 (2):333-48, 1998.

Maynard, A. *Health Care in the European Community.* Kent: Beckenham, 1975.

Mazey, S. "The Development of the European Idea: From Sectoral Integration to Political Union." In *European Union: Power and Policy-Making,* edited by J. Richardson. New York: . Routledge Press, 1996.

Mazey, S,. and Richardson, J. *Lobbying in the European Community.* Oxford: Oxford University Press, 1993.

McPherson, K. "International Differences in Medical Care Practices." In *Health Care Systems in Transition: The Search for Efficiency.* OECD Social Policy Studies No. 7, Paris, 1990.

Ministry of Finance: Internal Memorandum No. B-6B-8157 from the Office of the Budget to the Minister, December 13, 1976.

Ministry of Health. "Sante et Securite Sociale" Tableaux. Paris, 1974.

_____. "Les Conditions Actuelles du Financement." In *Pour Une Politique de la Sante.* Rapports Presentes a Robert Boulin, Vol 3, 1970.

Ministry of Health, Welfare and Sport. *Jaaroverzicht Zorg 1999.* Kamerstukken II 1998-1999, #1-3, The Hague, The Netherlands, 1998.

_____. *Health Insurance in the Netherlands* 4th ed. The Hague, The Netherlands, 1998.

Ministry of Public Health and Environment. *Memorandum on the Structure of Health Care.* Lcidschendam: Ministry of Public Health and Environment, The Hague, The Netherlands, 1974.

Ministry of Welfare, Health and Cultural Affairs. "Modernisering Zorgsector. Weloverwogen Verder" Kamerstukken II, 1991-1992, Tweede Kamer, 22393, nr 20, 1992.

_____. "Werken aan zorgvernieuwing (Working on health care innovation)." Tweede Kamer, 1989-1990, 21545 (2), The Hague, The Netherlands, May 1990.

_____. "Change Assured: Changing Health Care in the Netherlands." The Hague, The Netherlands, 1988.

_____. "Fact Sheet: Health Care Reform in the Netherlands." 1993.

_____. "Provincie en gezondheidszorg in beeld," The Hague, The Netherlands, 1992.

Minogiannis, P. "Greece and Health at the Dawn of the 21st Century: Trapped between Economics and Politics." Master's thesis, Columbia University, 1997.

Mitrany, D. *A Working Peace System.* Chicago: Illinois Quadrangle, 1966.

Monnet, J. *Memoirs.* New York: Doubleday Press, 1978.

Moran, M. „Death or Transfiguration? The Changing Government of the Health Care State." EUI Working Papers No 99/15, European University Institute, Florence, Italy, 1999.

_____. "Crises of the Welfare State." *British Journal of Political Science* 1988:397-414.

Moravcsik, A. "Negotiating the Single European Act: National Interests and Conventional Statecraft in the European Community." *International Organization* 45/1:651-688, 1991.

Mossialos, E., and Le Grand, J. (eds.). *Health Care and Cost Containment in the European Union.* Brookfield, VT: Ashgate Company, 1999.

Murray, C. *Losing Ground: American Social Policy, 1950-1960.* New York: Basic Books, 1984.

National Planning Commission: Sixth Plan:Economie Generale et Financement, Paris, 1971.

Netherlands Scientific Council for Government Policy. "Public Health Care" Report # 52, The Hague, The Netherlands, 1997.

Newspaper of the Greek Government. Athens Paper number 143, October 7, 1983.

_____. Issue Number 217, Athens, December 23, 1985.

_____. Issue Number 123, Athens, July 15, 1992.

Nivel/NZI. *Branche Rapport Curatieve Somatische Zorg (Branch Report Acute Care),* Utrecht, The Netherlands, 1998.

North, D. C. *Institutions, Institutional Change and Economic Performance.* Cambridge: Cambridge University Press, 1990.

NRV 1991 Annual Report. Zoeterme, The Hague, The Netherlands, 1992.

Nye, S. J. *Peace in Paris: Integration and Conflict in Regional Organization.* Boston: Little Brown Press, 1971.

OECD. *The Welfare State in Crisis.* Paris: OECD, 1981.

_____. *Social Expenditures 1960-1990: Problems of Growth and Control.* Paris: OECD, 1985.

_____. "Economic Survey of France," Paris, July 2000.

OECD Occasional Paper. «Health Care Systems in Transition: The Search for Efficiency» Paris: OECD, 1990.

_____. "Financing and Delivering Health Care: A Comparative Analysis of OECD Countries." OECD Social Policy Studies No. 4, Paris, 1987.

_____. "Measuring Health Care 1960-1983, Expenditure, Costs and Performance." OECD Social Policy Studies, Paris, 1985.

_____. "Measuring Health Care," Paris, 1988.

_____. "New Directions in Health Policy." OECD Social Policy Studies No 7, Paris, 1995.

Official Journal EC, No. C323, 1992.

OikonomikoV TacudromoV., September 29, 1983.

_____. May 20, 2000.

Okma, K. G. H. "Studies in Dutch Health Politics, Policies and Law." Ph.D. diss., University of Utrecht, The Netherlands, 1997.

_____. "Health Care, Health Policies and Health Care Reform in the Netherlands." Ministry of Health, The Hague, The Netherlands, March 2000.

Palier, B. "Reformer la Securite Sociale: Les Interventions Gouvernementales en Matiere de Protection Social Depuis 1945, la France en Perspective Comparative." Ph.D. diss., Institut d'Etudes Politiques de Paris, 1999.

Pentland, C. *International Theory and European Integration*. London: Faber and Faber, 1973.

Peters, G. "Agenda Setting in the European Community." *Journal of European Public Policy* 1(1):9-26, 1994.

Philalithis, A. "The Imperative for a National Health System in Greece in a Social and Historical Context." In *Socialism in Greece*, edited by S. Tzannatos. Gower Press, Athens, Greece, 1986.

Pierson, P. «Path Dependence, Increasing Returns and the Study of Politics.» Jean Monnet Chair Papers No. 44, European University Institute, Florence, Italy, 1997.

_____. *Dismantling the Welfare State? Reagan, Thatcher and the Politics of Retrenchment,* Cambridge: Cambridge University Press, 1994.

_____. "Irrestible Forces, Immovable Objects: Post-Industrial Welfare States Confront Permanent Austerity." *Journal of European Public Policy* 1998:539-60.

_____. «Social Policy and European Integration.» In *Centralization or Fragmentation? Europe Facing the Challenges of Deepening, Diversity and Democracy*, edited by A. Moravcsik. New York: A Council on Foreign Relations Book, 1998.

_____. "Not Just What, But When: Issues of Timing and Sequence in Comparative Politics." Paper presented at the APSA meeting, Boston, 1998.

Pierson, P., and Leibfried, S. "Multitiered Institutions and the Making of Social Policy." In *European Social Policy: Between Fragmentation and Integration*, edited by S. Leibfried and P. Pierson. Washington D.C.: The Brookings Institute, 1995.

Pierson, P., and Skocpol, T. "Why History Matters." Newsletter of the Comparative Politics Section, APSA.

Pinder, J. *European Community: The Building of a Union*. London: Oxford University Press, 1995.

Porter, D. H. *The Emergence of the Past: Theory of Historical Explanation*. Chicago: University of Chicago Press, 1981.

Prime Minister Simitis's Speech on PASOK's website at www.pasok.gr/gr/nea/06032000hospital.html.

PvdA: "Naar een nieuwe gezonheidszorg." Discussion of the PvdA working group, Amsterdam, The Netherlands, 1992.

Quadagno, J. "Theories of the Welfare State." *Annual Review of Sociology* (1987) 13:109-28.

Raynaud, P. "Réflexions sur la Réforme Budgetaire et de la Tarification Hospitalière: Réforme pour la Forme? Réforme de la Forme? Ou Réforme de Fond?" In *Revue Hospitalière de France*, 1979.

Reinhardt, U. *Accountable Health Care: Is It compatible with Social Solidarity?* London: Office of Health Economics, 1998.

Report by the Ministry of Health: "Health for the Citizen." Athens, July 2000.

Rhodes, M. "Subversive Liberalism: Market Integration, Globalization and the European Welfare State." *Journal of European Public Policy* (1995) :384-406.

Rizospastis on June 9, 2000.

Rochaix, L., Khelifa, A., Pouvourville, G. de. "Sante 2010: Equite et Efficacite du Systeme de Sante: Les Enjeux." Paris: CGP, 1993.

Rodwin, V. G: "Management without Objectives: The French Health Policy Gamble." In *The Public/Private Mix for Health*, edited by G. McLachlan and A. Maynard. The Nuffield Provincial Hospitals Trust, London, 1982.

_____. "The Marriage of National Health Insurance and La Médecine Liberale in France: A Costly Union." *Milbank Memorial Fund Quarterly* 59 (1):16-43, 1981.

Rodwin, V. G. , and Sandier, S. "Health Care Under French National Health Insurance." *Health Affairs* 52 (3): 113-125, Fall 1993.

Ross, G. "Assessing the Delors Era and Social Policy." In *European Social Policy: Between Fragmentation and Integration*, edited by S. Leibfried and P. Pierson. Washington D.C.: The Bookings Institution, 1995.

Ruggie, M. *Realignments in the Welfare State: Health Policy in the U.S., Britain and Canada*, New York: Columbia University Press, 1996.

Rutten, F. F. H. 1987. "Market Strategies for Publicly Financed Health Care Systems." *Health Policy* 7: 135-48.

Saltman, R., and von Otter, C. *Planned Markets and Public Competition: Strategic Reforms in Northern European Health Systems*. Buckingham, UK, Open University Press, 1997.

Sandholtz, W. "Choosing Union: Monetary Politics and Maastricht." *International Organization* 47 :1-39, 1993.

Satzinger, W., Leidl, R., and Lindenmuller, H. "Antihospital Bias." In West German Health Policy: A Return to Economic Trends or a New Trend in Medical Care?" In *Third International Conference on System Science in Health Care*, edited by W. van Eimeren, et al. Berlin: Springer Verlag, 1984.

Scharpf, F. *Governing in Europe: Effective and Democratic?* New York: Oxford University Press., 1999.

_____. "Economic Integration, Democracy and the Welfare State." *Journal of European Public Policy* (1997) :18-36.

Scharpf, F., Reissert, B., Schnabel, F. *Politikverflechtung: Theorie und Empirie des Kooperativen Federalismus in der Bundesrepublik*. Kronber: Scriptor, 1976.

Schwefel, D., and Leidl, R. "Bedarfsplanung und Selbstregulierung der Beteiligten im Krankenhauswessen." in *Gafgen* (1988):187-207.

Schmitter, P. C. "Interest Intermediation and Regime Governability in Contemporary Western Europe and North America." In *Organizing Interests in Western Europe*, edited by S. Berger. Cambridge: Cambridge University Press, 1981.

Schut, F. T. "Workable Competition in Health Care: Prospects for the Dutch Design." *Social Science and Medicine* 35(12):-55, 1992.

_____. *Competition in Dutch Health Care Sector*. Ph.D. diss., Erasmus University, Rotterdam, The Netherlands, 1995.

_____. "Health Care Reform in the Netherlands: Balancing Corporatism, Etatism, and Market Mechanisms." *Journal of Health Politics, Policy and Law* 20 (3): 615-646, Fall 1995.

Schwarz, W. B. "The Inevitable Failure of Current Cost Containment Strategies." *JAMA* (1987) : 257 (2):220-24.

Sewell, W. H. Jr. "Historical Events as Transformations of Structures: Inventing Revolution at the Bastille." *Theory and Society* 25/6 :841-881, 1996.

Siebert, H. "Labor Market Rigidities: At the Root of Unemployment in Europe." *Journal of Economic Perspectives* 11: 3, 37-54, 1997.

Simons, H. J., and Okma, K. *Mniselsel in de gezondheidszorg? De Toekomst van de Welvaarsstaat. Preadviezen voor de Koninklijke Vereniging voor de Staathuishoudkunde*. Leiden/Antwerpen: Stenfert Kroese Uitgevers, 1992.

Sissouras, A., et al. *Study for the Design and Organization of Health Services*. Athens: Ministry of Health, 1994.

Social and Economic Council. *Advies inzake de structuur van de verzekeringen tegen de kosten van geneeskundige verzorging* [Recommendation concerning the structure of insurances against the costs of medical treatment]. The Hague: Social and Economic Council, 1973.

Somers, M. R. "We're No Angels: Realism, Rational Choice, and Relationality in Social Science." *American Journal of Sociology* 104:722-784, 1998.

Soubie, R., Portos, J. L., and Prieur, C. *Livre Blanc sur le Systeme de Sante et D' Assurance Maladie.* Paris: La Documentation Francaise, 1994.

Stephanopoulos, S. "Pressures." *Asfalistikh EpiqewrhsiV*, October 1930.

Steudler, F. "L'Evolution de la Proffesion Medicale: Essai d' Analyse Sociologique." *Cahiers de Sociologie et de Demographie Medicales*, No 2.

Stevens, A. "The Higher Civil Service and Economic Policy-Making." In *French Politics and Public Policy*, edited by Philip Cerny and Martin Schain. London: Frances Printer, 1980.

Stevens, J. B: "Health Services and Government. Some Lessons from France." *Health Services Management* 85 (5):224-7, October 1989.

Stinchcombe, A. L. *Constructing Social Theories.* Chicago: University of Chicago Press, 1968.

Streeck, W. "From Market Making to State Building? Reflections on the Political Economy of European Social Policy." In *European Social Policy: Between Fragmentation and Integration*, edited by S. Leibfried and P. Pierson. Washington D.C.: The Bookings Institution, 1995.

Suleiman, E. *Politics, Power, and the Bureaucracy in France.* Princeton, NJ: Princeton University Press, 1974.

_____. *Elites in French Society.* Princeton, NJ: Princeton University Press, 1978.

_____. *Private Power and Centralization in France: The Notaires and the State.* Princeton, NJ: Princeton University Press, 1987.

Svensson, P. G., Stephenson, P. "Health Care Consequences of the European Economic Community in 1993 and Beyond." *Social Science and Medicine* 350: 525-29, 1992.

TA NEA on June 20, 2000, website at www.ta-nea.dolnet.gr.

TA NEA on July 29, 2000.

Teague, P. "Monetary Union and Social Europe." *Journal of European Social Policy* (1998) :117-37.

The Economist, July 8, 2000.

_____, April 8,1995.

_____, July 15, 1995.

The Financial Times, March 6, 2000.

Thelen, K. "Historical Institutionalism in Comparative Politics." In *The Annual Review of Political Science*, 1999.

Thelen, K., and Steinmo, S. "Historical Institutionalism in Comparative Politics." In *Structuring Politics: Historical Institutionalism in Comparative Politics*, edited by S. Steinmo, K. Thelen, and F. Longstreth. Cambridge: Cambridge University Press, 1994.

Theofilatou, M., and Maarse, H. «European Community Harmonization and Spillovers into Health Regulation.» In *Health Care and Its Financing in the Single European Market,* edited by R. Leidl. Washington D.C.: IOS Press, 1998.

Tiersky, R. *France in the New Europe.* Belmont, CA: Wadsworth, 1994.

Tilly, C. "Future History." *Theory and Society* 17 :703-712, 1988.

TO VIMA, July 17, 2000.

_____, March 19, 2000.

_____, July 26 2000.

_____, Mach 19, 2000.

_____, July 30, 2000.

_____, April 16, 2000.

Urwin, D. "*Western Europe since 1945: A Political History*," 4th ed. London: Longman Press, 1989.

US GAO: "Health Care Spending Control: The Experience of France, Germany and Japan." *GAO/HRD* 92-9, Washington D.C., November 1991.

Van Rossum articles in Elsevier numbers 32, 33, 34, and 35 of 1991.

Van Schendelen, R. (ed). *National, Public and Private Lobbying*. Dartmouth Publishing Corporation, Dartmouth, UK, 1992.

Van Schouwenburg, M. L. G. "Hevorming der sociale verzekering."*Sociaal Maanblad Arbeid* 12: 269-282, 1947.

Van den Broek, P. "Wie Met Wie 1995." *Zorgverzekeraars Magazine* 13 :17-39, 1995.

Van der Hoeven, H. C. *Voor Elkaar. De Ziekenfondsen te Midden van Sociale Veranderingen.* Utrecht: Centrale Bond van Onderling Beheerde Ziekenfondsen, 1963.

Van der Mei, A. P. "Cross Border Access to Medical Care within the European Union—Some Reflections on the Judgments in Decker and Kohll. *Maastricht Journal of European and Comparative Law* (1998) 5(3):277-97.

Van de Ven, W. P. M. M: "A Decade of Health Care Reforms in the Netherlands." Institute of Health Care Policy and Management, Erasmus University, Rotterdam, The Netherlands, October 1999.

_____. 1991. "Perestroika in the Dutch Health Care System." *European Economic Review* 35:430-40.

_____. "Choices in Health Care: A Contribution from the Netherlands." *British Medical Journal_51 : 781-790, 1995.

Varelis, D. "The Third Way for the Sickness Funds." *H Nautemporikh*, April 2000.

Vaughan, R. *Twentieth-Century Europe* London: Croom Helm Publishers, 1979.

Venieris, D. "Health Policy in Greece: The History of the Reform." In *EniaioV ForeaV UgeiaV: Anagkaiothta kai Autapath* , edited by J. Kyripoulos and A. Sissouras. Athens: Themelio Publications, 1997.

_____. "The History of Health Insurance in Greece: The Nettle Governments Failed to Grasp." Working Paper, The European Institute, London School of Economics and Political Science, September 1996.

_____. "The Development of Social Security in Greece, 1920-1990: Postponed Decisions." Ph.D. diss., University of London, LSE, 1994.

Vermeulen, H. J. J. M, et al. *Prognoses van knelpunten op de arbeidssmarkt van de zorgsector*. Tilburg: IVA, 1998.

Visser, J., and Hemereijk, A. *A Dutch Miracle—Job Growth, Welfare Reform and Corporatism in the Netherlands*. Amsterdam: Amsterdam University Press, 1997.

Von der Schulenburg, J. M. 1994. "Forming and Reforming the Market for Third-Party Purchasing of Health Care: A German Perspective." *Social Science and Medicine* 39 (10):1473-81.

Wallace, W. (ed.). *The Dynamics of European Integration*. London: Pinter Publishing, 1990.

Walliman, I. "Social Insurance and the Delivery of Social Services in France." *Social Science and Medicine* 23 (12): 1305-17, 1986.

Weaver, R. K. *Do Institutions Matter? Government Capabilities in the United States and Abroad*. Washington, D.C.: The Brookings Institute, 1993.

White Paper on European Social Policy: A way Forward for the Union available at *http://europa.eu.int/scadplus/leg/en/cha/c10112.htm*.

WHO Report: "2000 Health Systems: Improving Performance" at *www.who.int*.

Willis, F. R. *France, Germany and the New Europe 1945-1967*. Stanford, CA: Stanford University Press, 1968.

Wislford, D. "Reforming French Health Care Policy." In *Chirac's Challenge: Liberalization, Europeanization and Malaise in France*, edited by T. S. Keeler and M. A. Schain. New York: St. Martin's Press, 1996.

Wislford, D. *Doctors and the State.* Durham, NC: Duke University Press, 1991.

www.odci.gov/cia/publications/nsolo/factbook/gr.htm.

Yfantopoulos, G. *The Planning of the Health Care Sector in Greece.* Athens: National Center for Social Research, 1985 (in Greek).

Zeven, P. A. *De ziektekostenverzekering.* Amsterdam: De Bussy, 1963.

Zilidis, C. "Evaluation of Primary Care Services for Rural Populations in Greece." Study performed for the Agricultural Bank, Athens, Greece, 1989.

1997 NHS Reform Proposal. Athens: Greek Ministry of Health, Welfare and Social Insurance, March 1997.

Additional Bibliography

Books

Abel-Smith, B. et al. *Choices in Health Policy: An Agenda for the European Union.* Dartmouth, UK: Dartmouth Publishing Company, 1993.

Altenstetter, C., and Bjorkman, J. W. (eds.). *Health Policy Reform, National Variations and Globalization.* New York: St. Martin's Press, 1997.

Forget, M. J., White, J., and Weiner, J. M. *Health Care Reform Through Internal Markets.* Washington D.C.: The Brookings Institute, 1995.

Richardson, J. (ed.). *European Union: Power and Policy-Making.* New York: Routledge, 1996.

Roberts, G. K., and Hogwood, P. *European Politics Today.* Manchester, England: Manchester University Press, 1997.

Saltman, R. B., and Figueras, J. (ed.). *European Health Care Reform: Analysis of Current Strategies* Copenhagen: World Health Organization Report WHO Regional Office for Europe, 1997.

Saltman, R. B., Figueras, J., and Sakellarides, (eds.). *Critical Challenges for Health Care reform in Europe.* Philadelphia: Open University Press (forthcoming).

Saltman, R. B., and von Otte, C. (eds.). *Implementing Planned Markets in Health Care.* Philadelphia: Open University Press, 1992.

Schwartz, F. W., Glennerster, H., and Saltman, R. B. (eds.). *Fixing Health Budgets.* New York: Wiley and Sons Press, 1996.

Tsoukalis, L. *The New European Economy Revisited.* New York: Oxford University Press, 1997.

Vivekanandan, B. *International Concerns of European Social Democrats.* New York: St. Martin's Press, 1997.

Wilson, F. L. (ed.). *The European Center-Right at the End of the Twentieth Century.* New York: St. Martin's Press, 1998.

Articles

Anderson, G. F. „In Search of Value: An International Comparison of Cost, Access, and Outcomes." *Health Affairs* 16 (6) November/ December 1997:163-171.

Ashton, J. „Setting the Agenda for Health in Europe." *British Medical Journal* 304 (6843):1643-4, June 1992.

Belcher, P., and Mossialos, E. „Health Priorities for the European Intergovernmental Conference." *British Medical Journal* 314 (7095):1637-8, June 1997.

Birt, C. A. et al. „How Should Public Health Policy be Developed? A Case Study in European Public Health." *Journal of Public Health Medicine* 19 (3):262-7, September 1997.

Borst-Eilers, E. „Dutch Presidency Has Seen Quite a Revolution in Public Health." *British Medical Journal* 314 (7096):1713, June 1997.

Elsinga, E. „Political Decision Making in Health Care: The Dutch Case." *Health Policy* 11 (3):243-256, 1989.

Evans R. „Going for the Gold: The Redistributive Agenda behind Market Based Health Care Reform." *Journal of Health Politics, Policy and Law*. April 1997:427-465.

Figueras, J. et al. „Health Care Systems in Southern Europe: Is There a Mediterranean Paradigm?" *International Journal of Health Sciences* 5 (4) 1994:135-146.

Gervas, J. et. al. „Primary Care, Financing and Gatekeeping in Western Europe." *Family Practice* 11 (3):307-17, September 1994.

Gouvras, G. "Public Health Policy in the European Community." *Gesundheitswesen* 59 (12): 657-8, December 1997.

Ham, C., and Berman, P. „Health Policy in Europe." *British Medical Journal* 304 (6831): 855-6, April 1992.

Ham C., and Brommels, M. „Health Care Reform in the Netherlands, Sweden, and the United Kingdom." *Health Affairs* 13 (5): 106-119.

Hermans, H. E. „Europe 1992: Conflicts between European Law and National Health Law." *Medicine and Law* 11 (7-8): 591-5, 1992.

Hughes, C. „European Law, Medicine, and the Social Charter." *British Medical Journal* 304 (6828):700-3, March 1992.

Jacobs, A. „Seeing Difference: Market Health Reform in Europe." *Journal of Health Politics Policy and Law* 23 (1): 1-33, February 1998.

Kent, G. D. „Socializing Health Services in Greece." *Journal of Public Health Policy* 10: 222-45, 1989.

Leidl, R. „How Will the Single European Market Affect Health Care?" *British Medical Journal* 303 (6810): 1081-2, November 1991.

Liaropoulos, L., and Tragakes, E. „Public/Private Financing in the Greek Health Care System: Implications for Equity." *Health Policy* 43 (2): 153-69, February 1998.

Mossialos, E. „Citizens' Views on Health Care Systems in the 15 Member States of the European Union." *Health Economics* 6 (2): 109-116, 1997.

Niakas, D. G. et. al. „Private Consumption and Underground Economy in Health Sector in Greece"(Greek.) *Epitheorisi Ygeias*, September-October 1990.

Room, G. J. „European Social Policy: Competition, Conflict, and Integration." *Social Policy Review,* Number 6 Social Policy Association. Harlow, U.K. 1994.

Saltman, R. B., and Figueras, J. „Analyzing the Evidence on European Health Care Reforms." *Health Affairs* 17 (2): 85-108, March/April 1998.

Sendler, H. „The Development of European Public Health from the Viewpoint of One Country"(German). *Gesundheitswesen* 56 (2): 73-5, February 1994.

Svensson, P. G., and Stephenson, P. „Health Care Consequences of the European Economic Community in 1993 and Beyond." *Social Science and Medicine* 35 (4): 525-9, August 1992.

Watson. R. „How the Eurocrats Affect Our Health?" *British Medical Journal* 311(7000): 282, July 1995.

Index

For Product Safety Concerns and Information please contact our EU
representative GPSR@taylorandfrancis.com
Taylor & Francis Verlag GmbH, Kaufingerstraße 24, 80331 München, Germany